Kali Prasanna Sen Gupta

Speeches of the Marquis of Ripon Viceroy and Governor General of

India, 1880-1882

Published with the permission of His Excellency by Kali Prasanna Sen Gupta

Kali Prasanna Sen Gupta

Speeches of the Marquis of Ripon Viceroy and Governor General of India, 1880-1882
Published with the permission of His Excellency by Kali Prasanna Sen Gupta

ISBN/EAN: 9783337384562

Printed in Europe, USA, Canada, Australia, Japan

Cover: Foto ©ninafisch / pixelio.de

More available books at **www.hansebooks.com**

PEOPLE'S EDITION.

SPEECHES

OF

THE MARQUIS OF RIPON,

VICEROY AND GOVERNOR GENERAL OF INDIA

1880-1882.

VOL. I.

PUBLISHED

With the permission of His Excellency,

BY

KALI PRASANNA SEN GUPTA.

Calcutta:
PRINTED BY C. J. A. PRITCHARD, AND PUBLISHED
AT THE "STAR" PRESS,
19, LALL BAZAR STREET, CALCUTTA.

1883.

All right reserved.

INDEX.

SUBJECT.	PAGE.
A.	
ACT, KAZIS'	36,91
——VERNACULAR PRESS. Repeal of the—. . . . . [See also " Bill."]	211,351
ADDRESS from the Bombay Corporation	1
Umritsur Municipality	28
Native Christians of the Punjab . . .	31
Anjuman-i-Punjab	38
Senate, Punjab University College . .	42
Karachi Municipality	54
,, Chamber of Commerce . . .	57
Society of St. Vincent de Paul, Bombay .	67
Bombay Chamber of Commerce . . .	73
Poona Sarvajanik Sabha	82
,, Municipality . . .	84
Calcutta Corporation	85
British Indian Association . . .	87
Mahomedan Literary Society . . .	89
Delhi Municipality	110
Agra ,, ...	118
Ajmere ,, ...	134
Benares ,, ...	147

INDEX.

Subject.	Page.
Address from the Bengali Community of Benares	148
Rangoon Municipality	177
Burman Community	180
Mercantile Community, Rangoon	191
English-speaking inhabitants and other communities of Moulmein	200
Mercantile Community, Moulmein, on the Timber-duty	204
Lahore Municipality	304
Peshawur ,,	314
Lucknow ,, Fyzabad ,,	333
Canning College, Lucknow	340
Talukdars of Oudh	346
Rifah-i-Aâm Association, Lucknow	350
Afghan War, The—	2, 7, 30, 31, 38, 39, 46, 49, 51, 53, 89, 280, 114, 337
Patriotic Fund Meeting in connection with the —.	7
Agra. Address from the Municipality	118
St. Peter's College and Orphanage ; visit to—	124
Agricultural Loans Bill, The	294
Ajmere. Address from the Municipality of—	134
Distribution of prizes at the Mayo College	137
Alexandra Girls' School, Umritsur	31
Artillery, E. B. Royal Horse—Address to—at Jacobabad	53
Art, Native Industrial	19, 37, 104, 209
——Industrial Exhibition, Calcutta. Opening the—.	209
Assam Emigration Bill	161
Anjuman-i-Punjab. Address from the—	33

INDEX. iii

Subject.	Page.
B.	
BARRACKPORE PARK SCHOOL. Distribution of prizes at the—	242
BENARES. Address from the Municipality	147
Address from the Bengali Community	148
Dinner given by the Mahárájá	149
Opening of the Prince of Wales' Hospital	153
Visit to the Government College	155
BENGAL Land Laws	89
Light Infantry. Presentation of colors to the 2nd—	336
BILL. Vaccination—	4, 36
Appointment of Kazis –	36, 91
Exemption from Municipal Taxation—.	95
Factories—	76, 97
Assam Emigration—	161
Transfer of Property—	212
Easements—	219
Criminal Procedure—	233
Jhansi Encumbered Estates—	281
Petroleum—	284
Punjab University—	285
Agricultural Loans—	294
Central Provinces Local Self government—	295
Dekkhan Agriculturists' Relief Act Amendment—	352
BISHOP COTTON SCHOOL, SIMLA. Distribution of prizes at—	23
BOMBAY. Address from Corporation.	1
Dinner at the Byculla Club	61
Address from the Society of St. Vincent de Paul	67
Address from the Bombay Chamber of Commerce	73
Dinner to the 66th Regiment	77
Distribution of prizes at St. Xavier's College	78
Factories Bill	76, 97
BRITISH INDIAN ASSOCIATION. Address from the—	87
BUDGET, The, 1882-83	244

v   INDEX.

Subject.	Page.
Burma, British, The Viceroy's visit to—[See "Rangoon" and "Moulmein".]	
Byculla Club. Dinner at the—	61
C.	
Calcutta Corporation. Address from the—	85
British Indian Association. Address from the—	87
Mahomedan Literary Society. Address from the—	89
Volunteers. Distribution of prizes to the—	92, 230
Exemption from Municipal Taxation Bill.	95
Discussion of the Factories Bill.	76, 97
Distribution of prizes at St. Xavier's College	158
Discussion of the Assam Emigration Bill.	161
Distribution of prizes at La Martinière	173
Opening the Exhibition of Industrial Art.	209
Repeal of the Vernacular Press Act.	211
Discussion of the Transfer of Property Bill	212
Discussion of the Easements Bill. Codification	219
Discussion of the Criminal Procedure Bill.	233
Adjournment of the Legislative Council.	241
Distribution of prizes at the Barrackpore Park School.	242
Financial Statement, 1882-83.	244
University. Convocation of the—.	260
Laying the foundation-stone of the new Lecture Hall of the Indian Association for the Cultivation of Science.	274
Discussion of the Dekkhan Agriculturists' Bill.	352
Canal, Sirhind. Opening the—	328
Canning College, Lucknow. Visit to the—	340
Central Provinces Local Self-Government Bill	295
Chesney, Colonel. Lectures by—at Simla	278
Chittore. Dinner given by the Maharana of Oodeypore at—	143
Codification of Indian Law	219

INDEX.

SUBJECT.	PAGE.
COLORS. Presentation of—to the 2nd Bengal Light Infantry	336
COUNCIL, LEGISLATIVE. Adjournment of the—	241
CRIMINAL PROCEDURE BILL, The	233
CUSTOMS DUTIES	[245
D.	
DEKKHAN AGRICULTURISTS RELIEF ACT (1879) Amendment Bill	352
DELHI MUNICIPALITY. Address from the—	110
DURBAR at Lahore	47
Jacobodad	51
Rupar	328
Lucknow	346
E.	
EASEMENTS BILL, The	219
EDUCATION	23, 31, 34, 42, 48, 78, 82, 90, 117, 124, 130, 137, 156, 158, 173, 184, 199, 202, 242, 260, 274, 318, 340, 342, 350.
EGYPT. Address to Regiments returned from—	338
EMIGRATION BILL, Assam	161
F.	
FACTORIES BILL, The	76, 97
FAIZABAD MUNICIPALITY. Address from the—.	333
FAMINE	2, 120
FINANCIAL STATEMENT, 1882-83.	244
FINE ARTS EXHIBITION at Simla. Opening the—	15, 103
FREE TRADE	75

Subject.	Page.
H.	
HIGH COURT. [See " Rangoon" and " Moulmein".]	
HOSPITAL.] (OPENING the new Ripon—at Simla	287
I.	
INDIAN ASSOCIATION for the Cultivation of Science. Laying the Foundation-stone of the—	274
INDUSTRIAL ART EXHIBITION, Calcutta. Opening the—	209
INSPECTION of the 20th Punjab Native Infantry at Rupar	327
J.	
JACOBABAD. Durbar at—	51
Address to E. B., R. H. A., at—	53
JEYPORE. Dinner given by the Maharajah	127
Distribution of prizes at the Maharajah's College	130
JHANSI Encumbered Estates Bill, The	281
K.	
KARACHI Municipality. Address from the—	54
Chamber of Commerce. Address from the—	57
Laying the Foundation-stone of the Merewether Pier	59
KAZIS' ACT	36, 91
KHELAT, THE KHAN OF. Durbar to—	51
L.	
LAHORE. Address from the Anjuman-i-Punjab	33
Review of Troops at Mean Meer	38
Address from the Senate, Punjab University College	42
Durbar	47
Address from the Municipality	304
Inaugural convocation of the Punjab University	318
LEGISLATIVE COUNCIL. Adjournment of the—	241

INDEX. vii

SUBJECT.	PAGE.
LICENSE TAX	253
LOCAL SELF-GOVERNMENT	87, 115, 119, 135,178,295, 304, 333, 350
LUCKNOW. Address from the Municipality	333
,, ,, ,, Faizabad Municipality . .	
Presentation of colors to the 2nd (Queen's Own) Bengal Light Infantry	336
Address to Regiments returned from Egypt . .	338
Visit to the Canning College	340
Distribution of prizes at La Martinière . . .	342
Address from Talukdars of Oudh . . .	346
Address from the Rifah-i-Aám Association . .	350

M.

MAHOMEDAN LITERARY SOCIETY. Address rom the— . .	89
MAIWAND. Address to E. B., R. H. A.	53
Speech to the 66th Regiment	77
MANDALAY GOVERNMENT. Relations with the— . . .	191
MARTINIÈRE SCHOOLS, Calcutta. Distribution of prizes at the—	173
————————Lucknow. ,, ,, ,, . .	342
MAYO COLLEGE, AJMERE. Distribution of prizes at the—. .	187
MEAN MEER. Review of Troops at—	38
MEREWETHER PIER, Karachi. Laying the Foundation-stone of the—	59
MONUMENTS. Preservation of ancient—	123
MOULMEIN. Address of welcome by various Communities at—	200
Reception of Burmese Gentlemen at— . . .	202
Memorial concerning the Timber-duty.. ·. . .	204
Deputation on the establishment of a High Court .	207
MUNICIPAL SELF-GOVERNMENT. [See " Local Self-government",]	
————TAXATION EXEMPTION BILL	95

SUBJECT.	PAGE.

N.

NATIVE Industrial Art	19,37,104,209
Industries. Encouragement of—	114, 209
Infantry, Punjab. Inspection of the 20th—. . .	327

O.

OODEYPORE, MAHARANA OF. Dinner given by the— . .	143
OPIUM	256
OUDH. Address from the Talukdars of—	346

P.

PATRIOTIC FUND Meeting at Simla	7
PESHAWUR MUNICIPALITY. Address from the— . . .	314
PETROLEUM BILL, The	73, 284
POONA Sarvajanik Sabha. Address from the— . . .	82
———Municipality. Address from the— . . .	84
PRIVATE ENTERPRISE in Public Works	112, 201
PUBLIC WORKS. Extension of—	112
PUNJAB UNIVERSITY. The—	35, 42, 285
College. Address from the Senate . .	42
Bill. Discussion of the— . . .	285
Inaugural convocation of— . . .	318
———NATIVE INFANTRY. Inspection of the 20th . . [See also " Lahore"]	327

R.

RAILWAY Policy	74
RANGOON. Address from the Municipality . . .	177
Address from the Burman Community . . .	180
Dinner at Government House . . .	182
Reception of Burmese Gentlemen	188

SUBJECT.	PAGE.
RANGOON. Memorial from the Mercantile Community	191
Ball at—	198
Visit to St. John's College	199
Establishment of a High Court at—	191, 207
REVENUE & AGRICULTURAL DEPARTMENTS	121, 186
RIFAH-I-AAM ASSOCIATION of Lucknow. Address from the—	350
RIPON HOSPITAL at Simla. Opening the—	287
RUPAR. Inspection of the 20th Punjab Native Infantry at—	327
Opening the Sirhind Canal at—	328
S.	
SALT DUTIES	250
SARVAJANIK SABHA. Address from the—	82
SELF-GOVERNMENT. [See " Local Self-government".]	
SIMLA. Patriotic Fund Meeting at—	7
Fine Arts Exhibition. Opening the—	15, 103
Bishop Cotton School. Distribution of prizes at—	23
Volunteers. Distribution of prizes to the—	26, 301
Lecture by Colonel Chesney	278
Discussion of the Jhansi Bill	281
„ „ „ Vaccination Bill	4
„ „ „ Petroleum Bill	284
„ „ „ Punjab University Bill	285
Opening the new Ripon Hospital	287
Discussion of the Agricultural Loans Bill	294
„ „ „ Central Provinces Local Self-govt. Bill	295
SIRHIND CANAL. Opening the—	328
ST. JOHN'S COLLEGE, Rangoon. Visit to —	199
ST. PETER'S COLLEGE & ORPHANAGE, Agra. Visit to—	124
ST. VINCENT DE PAUL. Address from the Society	67
ST. XAVIER'S COLLEGE, Calcutta. Distribution of prizes at—	153
Bombay. „ „	78

Subject.	Page.
T.	
TALUKDARS OF OUDH. Address from the—	346
TELEPHONIC Communication	76
TIMBER-DUTY, Moulmein. Memorial regarding the—	204
TRANSFER OF PROPERTY BILL, The	212
TROOPS. [See "Colors", "Rupar", "Lahore", "Egypt".]	
U.	
UMRITSUR. Address from the Municipality of—	28
Pathancote Railway	30
Address at the Alexandra Girls' School	31
UNIVERSITY. [See "Calcutta", "Punjab".]	
V.	
VACCINATION BILL, The	4, 36
VERNACULAR PRESS ACT. Repeal of the —	211, 351
VOLUNTEERS, Simla. Distribution of prizes to the—	26, 301
Calcutta. Distribution of prizes to the—	92, 230
W.	
WALES, PRINCE OF—Opening hospital at Benares, named after the—	153

SPEECHES

BY

THE VICEROY AND GOVERNOR GENERAL OF INDIA.

ADDRESS FROM THE CORPORATION OF BOMBAY.

[ON Wednesday morning, the 2nd of June, a deputation from the Bombay Corporation waited on Lord Ripon at Government House, Malabar Point, to submit the address of welcome which had been drawn up by the Corporation for presentation to the Viceroy on the occasion of his landing in Bombay. The deputation, which was a large one, was headed by Rao Saheb Vishwanath N. Mandlik, who read the address. Lord Ripon, who was accompanied by Sir James Fergusson, Governor of Bombay, replied to it as follows :—] 2nd June 1880.

Mr. Chairman and Gentlemen of the Corporation of Bombay,—I am very grateful to you for the address which you have just been good enough to deliver. I have observed with great satisfaction the assurances which you give in that address of your loyalty and devotion to the Queen-Empress of India; but I can assure you that it is altogether unnecessary that you should give those assurances to me in words. I am very well aware of the feelings of loyalty and devotion to our Gracious Sovereign by which you are actuated—loyalty and devotion which is due, indeed, to the royal lady who has always taken, as you are all well

A

Address from the Corporation of Bombay.

aware, a very deep interest in all that concerns the welfare of her Indian subjects. (*Applause.*) For myself, gentlemen, I can assure you that I am deeply sensible of the great responsibility which devolves upon me in respect to the great office which Her Majesty has been pleased to entrust to me. We are told that it does not become him who putteth on his armour to boast himself as the man who takes it off; and therefore I am not at all inclined upon this occasion to make to you, and, through you, to the community of India, any large promises, or to lay before you any extensive programme. I should prefer that your judgment should be pronounced, as I am sure it will be, intelligently and fairly upon my conduct when you have been able to judge of me by my acts. (*Applause.*) I will only say this,—that it will be my constant endeavour to devote earnestly and assiduously any powers which I may possess, faithfully to discharge my duty to my Sovereign and to the people of India. (*Applause.*) You, gentlemen, have alluded to that grievous affliction of famine which during recent years has from time to time been productive of so great suffering and misery to many portions of the population of this great Empire. I trust that it may please God, in His providence, to grant us now a cycle of more prosperous years; but I hope also that the lessons of those periods of distress, hard though they may have seemed, will not be lost upon the Government of India, and that we shall profit by the experience which has been gained during those years of suffering, both in preparing such measures as may be calculated to guard against a recurrence of the evil, and also by alleviating in the most effectual manner the miseries entailed by famine, if it should again come upon us.

Gentlemen,—You have spoken also of the war which has been in progress almost without intermission for the last two years on our north-western frontier. No one can think

Address from the Corporation of Bombay.

of that contest without feeling his heart beat quicker with an honourable and just pride at the recollection of the gallant deeds which, in this war, as on so many previous occasions, have been performed for our Queen-Empress and our country by Her Majesty's troops, European and native alike; and we are proud to recollect that, in these later times, both these services have shown themselves fully able to maintain the great and glorious reputation which the soldiers of England have won for themselves in every quarter of the globe. (*Loud applause.*) But, gentlemen, it will be my most earnest endeavour to bring that war, so far as lies in my power, to an early and to an honourable conclusion, in the hope that, with returning peace, the Government of India may again be able to devote its attention to those works of internal improvement to which you have so rightly and wisely alluded. And I can assure you that if it should be my lot during my tenure of office to contribute in any degree to the development of the resources of this great country—agricultural and industrial—and to promote to any extent the happiness and the welfare of the people of India, of all races, and creeds, and classes, and especially the prosperity of the mass of the people, I shall esteem it the greatest honour of my political life. (*Applause.*)

Gentlemen, I thank you heartily for giving me this opportunity of meeting you—the representatives of the great and progressive community of Bombay. Through the kindness of Sir James Fergusson, I have already this morning had an opportunity of seeing something of this important city; and I need not tell you how greatly I have been struck by the beauty of the public buildings which have been recently erected here, and which certainly put to shame some of those which I have seen in great towns in England (*applause*); and yet more, I may say, by the proof that you are engaged in other works—not above

Vaccination Bill.

ground, but under ground—which are calculated to confer great benefits upon the community over which you rule, I am rejoiced to find that you are fully awake to the importance of sanitary improvements, which are of the greatest value to every country, and of the value of which men are becoming more and more convinced in the present day, and which, I venture to think, are as of great necessity in India as in any other part of the world. (*Applause.*)

Gentlemen,—I have mentioned the name of your Governor, Sir James Fergusson. (*Applause.*) I hope he will permit me to take the opportunity of expressing the great satisfaction I feel at finding that I shall have him, during my tenure of office as Governor General, as one of my colleagues in the administration of this country. (*Applause.*) Sir James Fergusson and myself sat for many years in that great school of public life, the House of Commons, and I know enough of him to be aware of the zeal and earnestness with which he will devote himself to the discharge of the great duties which will fall to his lot as Governor of Bombay; and I know also that I may rely with the most undoubted confidence on his support on all occasions, and on receiving every possible co-operation from him. (*Applause.*)

Gentlemen,—It only remains for me to say how heartily I wish you, as well as the community over which you rule, every possible prosperity. The kindness of your welcome to-day will be a great encouragement to me in the work which has been entrusted to me, which it will be my earnest endeavour, with God's assistance, faithfully to discharge. (*Loud applause.*)

VACCINATION BILL.

9th July 1880. [IN the Legislative Council, on Friday, the 9th July. the Hon. Sayyad Ahmad Khán moved that the Report of the Select Committee

Vaccination Bill.

on the Bill for giving powers to prohibit the practice of inoculation and to make the vaccination of children compulsory, in certain municipalities and cantonments, be taken into consideration. Mr. Grant and Sir Robert Egerton explained that, owing to the modifications made by the Select Committee in the Bill, they were now in a position to withdraw the opposition to it, expressed by them when the measure was introduced. The latter's opinion, however, was unchanged, that the time had not arrived for the introduction of compulsory vaccination into the Punjab; but as the application of the Act would rest with Local Governments, he thought it might be safely allowed to pass and introduced into places where its action was expected to be beneficial. Mr. Gibbs gave the Council a brief sketch of the circumstances under which vaccination measures were intoduced into Bombay and Karachi, and of the general success which had attended their working.]

His Excellency THE PRESIDENT remarked that what Mr. Gibbs had said afforded very satisfactory evidence that a similar measure to that now proposed had been introduced into a large city and into very small places with success, and with the approval of the people concerned. He was glad to see that the Bill had been amended and put into the shape in which it now stood. He thought that in legislation of this kind, particularly in India, it was very desirable to proceed in a cautious and tentative manner. In England we had had for a considerable time a Vaccination Act. There was a certain and rather increasing movement against it, and cases were cropping up from time to time, in which even persons in a respectable position in life absolutely refused to comply with its provisions. He might mention a case in point which occurred within his own knowledge—that of the organist of Ripon Cathedral, who had positively refused to allow his children to be vaccinated; had been fined from time to time, had regularly paid the fines, but continued to refuse compliance with the provisions of the Act, on the ground that one of his children had died, and he attributed its death to vaccination. Cases of this kind, where such feelings were evoked, required to be very carefully dealt with, and, of course, if in this

Vaccination Bill.

country any religious feelings were aroused, there again was a very delicate matter, which we should touch with a very light hand. It seemed, however, to His Excellency that the Bill as it now stood was so entirely of a permissive character, and gave such a complete opportunity to the inhabitants of each locality to state their objections, if they entertained any, that the measure itself, being extremely desirable, might be safely passed into law; and he thought that the Council was very much indebted to the Hon. Sayyad Ahmad for having taken up the question and brought to notice that, in generally extending vaccination, we would be conferring the greatest possible benefit upon the people of India. His Excellency was inclined to think that when the Bill was passed it might be advisable to consider, as an executive measure, whether a circular should not be issued to the Local Governments, impressing upon them the necessity of proceeding very cautiously and tentatively, of strictly conforming to the intentions of the Act, and seeing that not merely the views of the municipalities, but the feelings of the populations concerned, should be carefully considered.

There was one point to which he would wish to draw the attention of the Council, namely, the amount of penalty which it was proposed to inflict for continued non-compliance with the order for vaccination. Under section 22, sub section (*d*), of the Bill, it was provided that

"whoever neglects without just cause to obey an order made under section eighteen after having been previously convicted of so neglecting to obey a similar order made in respect of the same child shall be punished as follows (that is to say) :—

* * * * *

"in the case of the offence mentioned in clause (*d*), with imprisonment for a term which may extend to six months, or with fine which may extend to one thousand rupees, or with both."

HIS EXCELLENCY was not sufficiently acquainted with Indian legislation to know what was regarded as ordinary severity in this country; but he certainly thought a punishment of six months' imprisonment rather severe, and, if his memory served him right, there was no similar power taken in the English law. You could prosecute from time to time for continued disobedience, but there was no power that he was aware of for imprisonment.

[After some discussion, the Council agreed to the amendment of the last clause of section 22, so as to remove the Viceroy's objection on the ground of extreme severity. The motion was then put and agreed to; and the Bill was subsequently passed into law.]

PATRIOTIC FUND MEETING AT SIMLA.

[ON Tuesday afternoon, the 14th September, a meeting was held in the rooms of the United Service Institution, Simla, for the purpose of discussing proposals for extending the organisation of the Fund for the relief of sufferers by the Afghan war. The Viceroy presided, and took the chair at 5-30 P.M. The room was fairly well filled, and the audience was very enthusiastic.

In opening the proceedings, Lord Ripon, who was received with cheers, spoke as follows:—]

Your Honor, Your Excellency, Ladies and Gentlemen,— It becomes my duty, as occupying the chair on this occasion, to place briefly before you the objects of the meeting which is assembled here to-day; and I am confident that the purpose which has brought us together this evening is one which will fully command the sympathy of all who are present (*cheers*), because we are met here for the purpose of marking our sense of the great services rendered to their Sovereign and their country by the troops of the Queen during the Afghan war (*cheers*).

Now, ladies and gentlemen, it must be borne in mind that this is a public, and not an official, meeting. We are not met here to call for subscriptions by an order of the Government; but to submit an appeal which we think worthy of the attention of our fellow-subjects in this district, and, through them, to other parts of India: and I am bound

14th Sept. 1880.

Patriotic Fund Meeting at Simla.

to say, for myself, that I rejoice to find in India those free habits of public meeting to which I have been accustomed at home (*cheers*), and to be able to make my appeal to you not in the tone of command, but upon grounds which commend themselves alike to our hearts and to our intellects, and which prove how much of true and honest sympathy there may and ought to be among all the Indian subjects of our Queen-Empress (*cheers*). We stand here upon this occasion, ladies and gentlemen, upon common ground, and we appeal to feelings which are shared alike by all men: and I rejoice to think that the support which this movement is receiving on the present occasion, and has already received in other quarters from native gentlemen, as well as from Europeans is a happy omen of that ever-increasing co-operation which ought to exist, and which I trust will exist more and more, between men of all classes of the Indian community (*hear, hear, and cheers*).

Now, before I proceed to lay very briefly before you the grounds upon which I think this movement is entitled to your sympathy and support, I will recall to your recollection the steps which have hitherto been taken in this matter.

Some time ago, communications were received from various native princes and native gentlemen in different parts of the country, expressing their desire to contribute to the comfort of our troops in Afghanistan, and to the provision for the wives and families of those who fell in the war. Some very large subscriptions were offered upon that occasion, and the matter was brought under the consideration of my predecessor, Lord Lytton ; and he determined that it was desirable that this movement should not take an official form—a sentiment in which I cordially share—but that an independent Committee should be established to receive the subscriptions which might be offered, and to see to their proper application ; and a Committee was consequently formed by my predecessor, under the presidency of my honourable

Patriotic Fund Meeting at Simla.

and gallant friend Sir Edwin Johnson; and various subscriptions (some, as I have said, of large amount) have been received—entirely, I believe, from native gentlemen—by that Committee. Soon after the Committee was formed, there took place that unhappy and unprovoked renewal of hostilities in the southern part of Afghanistan which in its tragical, and also its glorious events, have excited so much of sympathy and of attention in the public mind (*cheers*); and the consequence was that, as a large portion of the troops serving in that country belonged to the Bombay Army, my right honourable friend Sir James Fergusson, the Governor of Bombay, yielded to a wish expressed to him on the part of the leading gentlemen of that city, European and native, and undertook to preside at a public meeting for the purpose of establishing what has been called a Patriotic Fund. That meeting, as my right honourable friend informs me, was of a most enthusiastic and loyal character, and it was, he tells me, a very great pleasure to him to preside on that occasion; and it was then determined that there should be opened a list of subscriptions for the Patriotic Fund in aid of the widows and families of our soldiers, European and native, who had fallen in the course of the Afgan war (*cheers*). The original Committee established by Lord Lytton—having to deal almost, if not quite, exclusively with the subscriptions of native princes and gentlemen—had intended, I believe, to devote any money they might receive to the native army alone; but when it became evident that the Bombay meeting had adopted a wider scheme, and had determined to include in the benefits of the Fund to be raised, all Her Majesty's soldiers, of whatever race, who were serving in the present war, it was clear, as it seemed to me, that it would be altogether impossible to confine the operations of the Central Committee within the limits originally intended. I am bound to say that I think the example set by Bombay was

Patriotic Fund Meeting at Simla.

a good one, and that I am very glad that we should now follow it (*cheers*); and I entertain no kind of fear that any of those distinguished native gentlemen who have already subscribed to the Fund will object to this extension of it to Europeans as well as to natives. I feel confident that it will commend itself to them as much as it does to us (*hear, hear*); and at all events, should any difficulty arise in the matter, it is one that can easily be arranged.

Such, ladies and gentlemen, is the history of what has passed in respect to the Fund in whose interests we are assembled this afternoon. And now let me ask you to consider for a few moments what is the nature of the claims which our soldiers of the armies engaged in the Afghan war have upon the sympathy of their fellow-countrymen, and I may also say, of their fellow-countrywomen. We are not here, ladies and gentlemen, to discuss any questions of policy; we are here to consider the claims of those who have performed, bravely and loyally, the duties which were imposed upon them, and have responded unhesitatingly to every call (*cheers*).

The late Afghan war has been distinguished by many acts of bravery, and by many deeds which show that British soldiers, European or native, have not degenerated from their former reputation (*cheers*). Ali Musjid, the Peiwar Kotal, Charasiab, Kabul, Ahmed Kheyl, and Kandahar are there to prove the truth of my assertion (*loud cheers*). But it seems to me that no less honour has been won by the patient endurance of the weary march, of the wearing escort duty, of the climate so trying, especially to native troops, and of the long waiting when no active duty was going on, and when thoughts of home naturally rushed into the soldier's heart *(loud cheers)*, than was secured by the desperate charge, the gallant onslaught, or the firm resistance to the attack (*continued cheers*). I admire, ladies and gentlemen, with a just pride, the deeds of the

Patriotic Fund Meeting at Simla.

victors of Ahmed Kheyl and Kandahar; I admire those splendid soldiers who, under their gallant chief, Sir Frederick Roberts (*loud cheers*), have lately performed a march which will long be famous in Indian military history, and who won a battle which has displayed alike the skill of the general and the admirable qualities of his troops (*cheers*). But I no less admire those who for long weary months have guarded the Khyber Line, and who, in a pestilential climate and ever-recurring round of monotonous duty, have fulfilled the task entrusted to them with unalterable steadiness and devotion; and I admire yet more the conduct, scarcely sullied by a single crime, which our troops have manifested towards the people of the country which they have been lately occupying (*cheers*). We have here, it seems to me, ladies and gentlemen, a display of all the best military qualities—courage, endurance, patience, self-restraint; and it is to honour such qualities that we are assembled this evening (*cheers*). In those armies, European and Native, so gallant, so loyal, so enduring, many have fallen—some in battle, some by disease, some by the ambush of a desperate foe; and they have left behind them wives and children, dear to them, dependent on their exertions, and in their dying moments they have entrusted them to the care of their fellow-countrymen (*cheers*). Shall we not, then, answer to that call? Have they no claim upon us, who have not had to endure any of those trials, but who on this, as on so many former occasions, will profit by the valour and the firmness of our troops *(cheers)*. Surely, ladies and gentlemen, we may hold it an honour to be permitted to minister to the wants of those who have been left behind by the men who have suffered and died for their country *(cheers)*. The Government of India is not ungenerous toward the families of its soldiers, and upon this, as upon other occasions, it is most ready to do its duty; but the powers of the Government of India in

Patriotic Fund Meeting at Simla.

this matter are necessarily limited by the consideration that the money at its disposal comes from public taxation, and that we cannot be generous at the expense of others, when our taxes come, as they do to so large an extent in this country, from the pockets of the poorest classes of the community. There is, therefore, as it seemed to me, a large field for public exertion and a just and ample necessity for an appeal to public support. Everything which tends to promote independent public action in India seems to me to be in itself a great benefit, and I rejoice that we should upon this occasion be able to afford to the public of all classes and of all races an opportunity of taking part in this noble work *(hear, hear).*

Ladies and Gentlemen,—This is not a large meeting such as might have been assembled in Calcutta or Bombay; but we have present here to-day some who are well entitled to be heard on an occasion like this. In the first place, we have His Excellency the Commander-in-Chief, the head of the Army in India, European and native, with whom I rejoice to think that ever since I came out here I have co-operated with the most entire and unclouded cordiality *(cheers).* From him I have received the most hearty assistance, and to him it has been my pleasure as well as my duty to render the utmost support in my power *(continued cheers).* We have here also one, not to speak of others, who has won for himself the acknowledgments of his Sovereign and of his countrymen *(loud cheers)* by his eminent services, both military and political, in Afghanistan. . . . . I see, ladies and gentlemen, that you know I am alluding to my gallant friend Sir Donald Stewart *(loud cheers).* They are ready to address you, and I will not, therefore, detain you longer, except once more to exhort you, and, through you, the people of India, to mark, by your free and ready answer to the call which is now made upon you, your deep sense of the claims which our soldiers of every

Patriotic Fund Meeting at Simla.

race and every clime have upon the generosity of those who have witnessed their courage, their patience, and their endurance, and who, without sharing their trials, will still partake of their glory (*loud cheers*).

*Ladies and Gentlemen,—*I wish to state that it is my intention to contribute Rs. 3,000 to the Fund it is intended to raise (*cheers*). I will now call on his Excellency the Commander-in-Chief to move the first resolution.

[His Excellency was warmly cheered on resuming his seat.

The following resolutions were then proposed to the Meeting, and carried,—the proposers and seconders in turn addressing the audience at some length :—

Proposed by the Commander-in-Chief, and seconded by Archdeacon Mathew :—That, in order to mark the high appreciation in which their countrymen hold the gallantry displayed by the troops in Afganistan, and the courage and endurance with which they have borne the hardships of the campaigns, a fund be raised for the relief of those who have been disabled, and of the families of those who have died, during the war.

Proposed by Sir Donald Stewart, and seconded by Mr. A. C. Lyall :— That the fund be called " The Patriotic Fund " ; that the subscriptions already received from the Princes of India and others be incorporated with the Fund, subject to the consent of the donors ; and that further subscriptions be invited from all classes of the community.

Proposed by Mr. Gibbs, and seconded by Mr. James Walker :—That the following gentlemen be invited to act as a central working Committee :—Lieutenant-General Sir Donald Stewart, Mr. A. C. Lyall, the Hon. C. Grant, Colonel Allen B. Johnson, Colonel T. E. Gordon, Colonel S. Black : with Lieutenent W. J. Bird as Secretary ;—and that on the arrival of the Government in Calcutta there be added to the Committee, on the invitation of His Excellency the Viceroy, representatives of the non-official sections of the community.

Proposed by Sir Robert Egerton, and seconded by Lieutenant-Colonel Peterson (Simla Volunteers) :—That the Committee be instructed to take such steps as may be found desirable for organising local Committees to receive subscriptions in the various provinces, and to put itself into communication with the Committees which have already been formed in Bombay and in London, with a view to arranging a concerted plan of action.

Patriotic Fund Meeting at Simla.

At the close of the proceedings, the Commander-in-Chief proposed a vote of thanks to Lord Ripon for the manner in which His Excellency had presided. The proposal was warmly received, and was seconded by Major Nisbet. The Viceroy, in returning thanks, said :—

Your Honour, Your Excellency, Ladies and Gentlemen,—I am much obliged to you for the very kind manner in which you have received this resolution, and which I think, from the manner in which you have acknowledged it, I may take as having been passed cordially on your part *(cheers)*. I can assure you that it has been a very great pleasure to me to be able to be present on this occasion. Naturally, from the position which I have been called to fill, I must feel the strongest possible interest in all that interests those brave men who have been fighting now for two years the battles of their country beyond the frontiers of India *(cheers)*. Besides this, I may perhaps be permitted to say that I have all my life had a very deep interest in the welfare of our soldiers. Indeed, in my early youth it was the great object of my ambition, if I had been permitted to follow it, to have had the honour of serving in Her Majesty's army myself *(cheers)*, and, having served for a few years under that distinguished man who, as Secretary of State for War, did perhaps more than any one else to promote the welfare of the British soldier—I mean Mr. Sidney Herbert—I have, from the lessons learnt at his feet, always felt an earnest desire to promote in every way in my power everything which could tend to increase the happiness or the welfare of the British soldier; and I heartily recognise that the same sentiments which prompt us at home to look after the interests of the European soldier, should prompt us equally and to the full share in India in regard to all that concerns that gallant native army which has, in late campaigns, so highly distinguished itself *(loud cheers)*.

[The Meeting then dissolved. A sum of nearly Rs. 10,000 was subscribed in the room, in addition to Rs. 6,000 recorded by Dr. Leitner

Opening of the Fine Arts Exhibition at Simla.

on behalf of the Anjuman-i-Punjab, for the education and maintenance of ten sons of native soldiers killed in action, till they are able to gain their own livelihood.]

OPENING OF THE FINE ARTS EXHIBITION AT SIMLA.

[On Saturday afternoon, the 18th September, the Viceroy opened 18th Sept. 1880. the annual Exhibition of Fine Arts at Kennedy House, Simla. His Excellency, accompanied by his Staff, arrived at the Exhibition-rooms at half-past four o'clock, and was received at the entrance by Sir Robert Egerton, Vice-Patron and President of the Society, and the members of the Committee. A large number of visitors were present, though the evening was gloomy and unfavourable for viewing the pictures. In opening the proceedings, Sir Robert Egerton made the usual statement regarding the progress of the Society during the year. He thanked the Viceroy for consenting to become Patron of the society and presiding on the present occasion; he explained the causes which had tended to diminish the number of contributions; conveyed his acknowledgments to those who had assisted in the work of arranging the pictures, and concluded by requesting His Excellency to declare the Exhibition open.

The Viceroy (who, on rising, was received with cheers) then delivered the following address:—]

Your Honor, Ladies and Gentlemen,—In rising to comply with the request just made to me by the Lieutenant Governor, I feel myself in one respect at some disadvantage, because, although this is (as you have just told us, Sir Robert) the thirteenth Exhibition of the Simla Fine Arts Society, it is the first occasion upon which I have had an opportunity of seeing the collections made for the Exhibition, and, under these circumstances, I have no means of instituting any comparison between this Exhibition and those which have preceded it, and knowing, so far as my own judgment might go, the progress which I doubt not has been made by this Society from year to year (*applause*). I must therefore content myself—in the remarks which, according to custom, I am about, with your permission, to address to you before formally opening the Exhibition—

Opening of the Fine Arts Exhibition at Simla.

with asking you to consider with me, for a short time, what are the objects of the institution on whose behalf we are assembled here to-day? It must be borne in mind that the Exhibition collected within this compound has a twofold object. Here in the house itself we have a collection of drawings and paintings, and in the building outside we have another collection of Native works of industrial art; and it is in these two separate aspects—first as a Fine Arts Society, and then as an Exhibition of Native Industrial Art—that the exhibition ought to be considered. Now, ladies and gentlemen, with respect to the object of the Fine Arts Society, I think it may briefly be defined to be to promote to the utmost the cultivation of the fine arts by persons in private life, and to establish, by means of prizes, a relative standard of excellence. Now, let us consider for a moment under what difficulties amateur artists in India have to do their work in connexion with artistic matters. It seems to me that those who devote themselves to the cultivation of the fine arts in this country generally labour under some disadvantages to which persons at home are not so much exposed, because I think it may be said with truth that almost everybody in India has plenty to do. There seems to be much less of that leisure which is so largely enjoyed by persons in England, and which those who are very fortunate devote to the cultivation of the fine arts; for the military man in India has a hundred calls on him daily, and the civilian is hard at work from early morning till the shades of evening, and has but little time to devote to the worship of the Muses. But yet, if I mistake not, this Exhibition shows what soldier and civilian can alike accomplish, even under the difficulties which I have described, when they devote their leisure (perhaps the more keenly enjoyed because it is so short) to the cultivation and pursuit of the fine arts *(applause)*; and we see on these walls ample proof that the amateur artist in India does not fall behind the same description of persons in England, and that, in spite

Opening of the Fine Arts Exhibition at Simla.

of such difficulties as hot sun, and scorching wind, and sandy desert, he is still able to give us records of places famous in history, of the grand scenes of oriental nature, and of the customs and features of the many races which dwell in this land (*applause*). We have, for instance, here an interesting spot on the coast of Bombay, represented alike in storm and in calm; the Himalayas, on whose ridges Simla has so strangely perched itself, are depicted under various and striking aspects; the sports of the field have supplied their characteristic subjects; and, in the midst of all their arduous and successful labours, those gallant officers whose absence Sir Robert Egerton has so justly lamented, and who, I trust, will soon return and next year fill these rooms with their works, have found time to give us spirited sketches of those scenes in Afghanistan which have been rendered memorable by the deeds of the British army (*applause*). Take it all in all, as it appears to me, India is a rich field for the artist, abounding, as it does, in places of interest and buildings of great architectural beauty, and in scenes upon which Nature has lavished all her grandeur and her charm; and I think that the truth of this estimate may be proved by even a cursory examination of the works which now adorn these walls. I feel, ladies and gentlemen, no little diffidence in venturing even upon the faintest criticism of works such as those which we see before us to-day, because, unfortunately, I am nothing of an artist myself, and I particularly dislike to hear people talking about that which they do not understand (*laughter*). I am bound to say that I never felt greater regret that, if I have any artistic talent, it was unfortunately so ill-cultivated that it was never developed (*laughter*), as I have done since I came to India, because it would have been most interesting and agreeable to me to have taken back with me on my return home some sketches which would have served to recall the beautiful and interesting scenes which I have already passed, and

c

Opening of the Fine Arts Exhibition at Simla.

yet hope to pass through during my connection with this country *(applause)*. But if you look at the pictures on these walls, representing Indian scenes, I think you will find ample proof that India is, as I have said, a rich field for the artist. There is that drawing of Major Pullan's of "Dwarka in storm," which is a remarkable work of art, and Captain Strahan's most successful representation of mountain scenery "On the Chini Road;" while Lieutenant Radford and others give us very interesting reminiscences of the scenes through which our army has passed in Afghanistan, and Colonel Sankey contributes some charming landscape pieces. We have, too, a flower subject by Mrs. Graham, which, I confess, gave me quite a start, from the feeling of freshness, and the odour of flowers that seemed to come from it as one stood before it *(applause and laughter)*. But it is not India alone that we find depicted here. We have also most pleasant reminders of England and the English life to which we hope some day to return; we have those shady beeches so characteristic of many parts of our country, the representation of which by Dr. Willcocks has been so highly appreciated that the Committee have awarded to him the prize which I have the pleasure of giving upon this occasion *(applause)*. And then we have a charming pair of "Blue Bells" by Captain Pierson, which I am certain all of you have seen with very great pleasure *(applause.)* But I have heard it remarked that there is some dissatisfaction in Simla Society because there are so few works from Captain Pierson's pencil in this Exhibition. Well, ladies and gentlemen, I feel bound to take this opportunity of defending my gallant friend from any criticisms of that kind, by pointing out to you that the person who is addressing you is the real culprit in the matter, because I have been guilty of throwing upon him an amount of work, which he has done to my great advantage in a very able manner, however much it

Opening of the Fine Arts Exhibition at Simla.

may have been to your detriment (*applause*). There is yet one other picture to which, even in this cursory examination of the contents of this Exhibition, I must invite your attention. To my mind it is a very striking picture, a picture in the other room by a native artist, Mr. Pestonjee Bomanjee, representing a Parsi priest at prayers; and, I am bound to say, it seems to me that in its highly effective light and shade and warmth of colouring it is well worthy of the prize awarded to it, and an admirable example of what native artists are capable of doing (*applause*).

And now, ladies and gentlemen, I will pass on, that I may not detain you long, to the consideration of the claims which the other portion of this Exhibition has upon our attention—I mean that part of it which contains specimens of Native Industrial Art, and which owes so much to the zeal, taste, and ability of my friend Captain Cole (*applause*). To me, ladies and gentlemen, that Exhibition has an especial interest. It is only in its infancy, for this I understand, is the second year of its existence; but I hope and believe it may ultimately accomplish a valuable work, and that it will help to cultivate and encourage Native Art; that is to say, Art really native, instinct with the style of the country, and based upon its ancient and historical artistic traditions (*applause*). I will venture to say that all the best Art which the world has ever seen has been truly national, the outcome of the religion, the history, and the civilization of each race. I confess, for myself, that I have no faith in eclecticism in Art. Art is not a dead thing, to be merely copied from the models of the past; it is in its full power and perfection, the result and, as it were, the flower of a nation's whole life (*applause*); and therefore, if Art is to flourish among the Natives of India, it must be Indian Art, not a cold and barren imitation, however clever, of the Art of Europe, but the real product of the life and traditions of this land (*applause*). I rejoice to hope that, from the small and

Opening of the Fine Arts Exhibition at Simla.

humble beginnings of this Exhibition which we see here to-day—those small beginnings from which almost all great and useful things have their commencement,—may come forth the cultivation by the natives of this country of their own Art, which will restore their claim to be counted among the artists of the world (*applause*). In this, as in all things in India, it is our duty, not to stifle or overpower the national life of the country, but to develope and uphold it (*applause*). If we were here only for a day, holding our position solely by our power, and retaining our grasp on India merely from the lust of empire, then we might perhaps desire that all national feelings, all recollection of their early history, all love of their characteristic art, should die out of the hearts of the Indian people. But if we believe, as I believe, that we occupy our present place in India in the course of God's providence, not merely as passing conquerors, but with a great work to do for the people of the country, which will be interwoven with their history, and which has its due part to fulfil in their progress, then it should be our aim to keep alive all that is high and beautiful and noble in their past traditions and their past national life, and to encourage them to reverence and to admire it (*applause*). Nothing is easier than to destroy, and of all things Art can perhaps be destroyed most easily; and one form of destruction is sometimes known in Europe under the name of restoration. I hope the day is not far distant when the ancient monuments of India may be placed under such control as will tend to preserve them intact and unmutilated to future ages (*applause*),—for it should be our endeavour more and more in this country, not to destroy, but to improve; not to overthrow the traditions and native civilization of some of the most ancient races of the earth, but to elevate and purify and develope them; to retain and strengthen what is good, to remove what is false and evil, and thus to wed together in indissoluble and prolific union the earliest and

Opening of the Fine Arts Exhibition at Simla.

latest developments of the Aryan races (*applause*). I am the last man in the world to shrink from changes which the advance of time renders necessary, or cling to obsolete usages merely because they are old. I have no sympathy with the dry and barren spirit of conservation which struggles to preserve institutions and habits from which all life has departed ; but, at the same time, I am strongly convinced that reform, to be real and effective, must be tempered by reverence, and must be a growth, and not a mere construction ; and, while I would give the people of India the fullest benefit of modern science and modern knowledge of Western progress and Western civilization, I should desire to blend them with their own historical traditions so as to supplant no portion of them, except by something better, and to retain the harmony and continuity of their national life (*applause*).

Now, if I am not mistaken, it is in something of this spirit that the Committee who have got together this Exhibition—and who, I trust, will continue their labours in future years—are conducting their work. There are there, in that outer building, many works which are modern in date, but what all those who have most judgment in this matter value in those works is the skilful reproduction of ancient patterns, or, what is better than the most skilful copying of such patterns, the working on ancient lines. It can be seen, from an examination of this Exhibition, how successfully this has been done in many cases ; and I am very glad to find that many Schools of Art (and I think I may specially mention the School of Jaipur) are working thoroughly in the true spirit, and have already done much to resuscitate the beauties and attractions of Ancient Indian Art. Therefore it is, ladies and gentlemen, that I rejoice to see such an Exhibition as this, and that I trust, as I have said, that it is only the beginning of a large and valuable work (*applause*).

There is one circumstance which has been mentioned to me to-day, which, I think, is interesting, and that is, that

Opening of the Fine Arts Exhibition at Simla.

this exhibition contains, in much larger proportion than the Exhibition of last year, works which have been contributed by the artists or manufacturers themselves,—the proportion of loan articles being much larger last year than this year. Now if an Exhibition of this kind is to have any practical effect upon Art, that is exactly what we want. Up here at Simla, the exhibition of the best models of Ancient Art would have very little influence on artist workmen; but the bringing together the works of the present day and submitting them to the criticism of competent judges, and sending down the best of them with prizes and commendations—that is the most effective mode of cultivating good taste and encouraging the advance of Art (*applause*).

Ladies and Gentlemen,—I feel a great interest in this undertaking, not only for the reasons which I have mentioned, but also for another. There is, I fear, much in the conditions of modern life which tends to separate and keep apart the European and Native in this country somewhat more than was the case in former days. The rapidity of communication, the weekly mails, the frequent furloughs, in spite of their numerous advantages, all tend to a certain extent in that direction; and therefore it is a great satisfaction to feel that there are other circumstances connected with our time which may counteract the evil; and among them we may count that greater acquaintance which we possess in the present day with the history, the art, and the jurisprudence of the past, which ought to help us to know better, to appreciate more highly, the native civilization of India,—to feel how ignorant is the inclination to disparage it, and that it is upon the ancient foundations of that civilization alone that we can hope to erect firm and enduring the superstructure of that wider and higher life which it should be the great aim of our Government to foster and advance.

Ladies and Gentlemen,—I now declare this Exhibition open (*loud and prolonged applause*).

BISHOP COTTON SCHOOL, SIMLA.

[The annual Distribution of Prizes took place at Bishop Cotton School, Simla, on Saturday, the 25th September, the Viceroy presiding. His Excellency arrived at the School shortly after 5 P.M., and was accompanied by the Lieutenant Governor of the Punjab, Mr. Primrose, Private Secretary and Major White, Military Secretary. He was received by the Head Master and the Governors, and was conducted to the School Hall, a guard of honour of the School Volunteers being drawn up on the ground. The proceedings were opened with a statement by the Head Master, the Rev. S. Slater, in which he reviewed the progress of the School, remarked upon its success in recent competitive examinations (more particularly in the Vernacular languages), explained some of the causes which tended to apparent inefficiency in the students, and concluded by bringing the pressing want of a cricket-ground to notice. After distributing the prizes, the Viceroy spoke as follows :—]

25th Sept. 1880.

Ladies and Gentlemen, and Boys of Bishop Cotton School,—It gives me great pleasure to be present on such an occasion, and at such an interesting institution as this; but it would have been far more pleasant if it had not fallen to my lot to be called upon by the Head Master to say a few words. For many years I have bored my countrymen with speeches on education, and now I am going, as it seems, to bore an Indian audience with the same subject. I have felt all my life a very deep interest in education, and therefore it is most agreeable, so early in my period of Indian affairs, to be present at an institution which, notwithstanding Mr. Slater's modest assertions, is, I am sure, well worthy of the support of the public. This school was, I believe, originally established as a thank-offering for the ultimate suppression of that fearful event—which, fortunately, none of you boys remember—the Mutiny, by one who did good service to this country, and who in the midst of labour met his death by an untimely end. And it seems to me that no more appropriate offering to God for that deliverance could have been made than an establishment for the education of European boys, for I feel con-

Bishop Cotton School, Simla.

fident that there is no better means of strengthening British rule in India than by taking every opportunity of training English youths in this country to show themselves worthy the position they hold by the uprightness of their lives, and that there is nothing so dangerous to our position as that the lives of Europeans should be disgracefully and dishonourably spent. I listened with great interest to the speech of the Head Master, and wish to make a few observations on it. Now, one reason why I feel a deep interest in this institution is that it combines religious and secular training. We all know that Government made a solemn promise that it would observe a strict and impartial neutrality in all matters relating to religion, and it is quite right that it should be so; but this does not imply that individual responsibility is thereby set aside. I feel convinced that we cannot have a true education unless religious and secular training are combined, as both are in the teaching of this school, so that you may have a complete education. It gave me great pleasure to hear from Mr. Slater of your success in the native languages; and I consider it a great satisfaction to have disturbed the authorities in the Adjutant-General's Office in the manner described: and I hope you will continue so to astonish them. Mr. Slater has mentioned some of the difficulties that beset such an institution as this, but I am not altogether ignorant of them, as it has been my duty to read Archdeacon Baly's excellent report. One difficulty is very trying, namely, that boys should so frequently come up later than the fixed time for returning to school. If such a thing happened in England, the boys would be sent home again, and not allowed to return. So if my voice can reach your parents through you, I would earnestly entreat them to remember how hard it is to you boys, how injurious to your prospects in the future, if by any weak indulgence on their part you are kept at home; and I would urge upon them not to deprive you of the

Bishop Cotton School, Simla.

advantages you might gain, and to allow you to come up in time, for, if they do not, it is impossible to give you the education you would otherwise receive. Mr. Slater also alluded to the few openings for European boys, and the increasing competition. I hold that that competition should exist, and boys of English birth must look for a keen competition with the intelligent native races, which competition will become yet keener; and the only way to meet it successfully is by the cultivation of your intellects. I can scarcely count the difficulty of finding employment a ground for listlessness in your studies; for, granting the difficulty, you have not a ghost of a chance unless you avail yourselves of the opportunities here afforded you. Education now becomes more and more a matter of necessity. In former days there were many ways in which men could get a living without it; but this is not the case now, and those who do not develope the intellect which God has given them will be beaten in the race,—and there are few things more unsatisfactory than a listless, idle European in India. Let me say, however, then, that I hope you will set before you a higher standard of education than that of merely getting employment. You must recollect that God has given to all certain faculties, for the right employment of which he holds them responsible. They are no inheritance of class or station—talents are not possessions: they are entrusted to you to be employed in the service of God and of your fellow-men, and for your own advantage—and mark, I put this in the last place. The curriculum here appears to me wide and extensive, and I hope that the returning arts of peace will open a larger field for employment. I see here (referring to a motto on the wall) *Arma cedant togæ*, and I hope that the great battle which has been won by Sir Frederick Roberts. and which I am sure will be thoroughly appreciated by you boys who are volunteers, will restore peace to India and that once more we may say *Arma cedant togæ*. And there I see (referring to another motto). *In veritate victoria.* Yes; the real source of our power is not so much the victories won by the gallantry of our noble soldiers, as that the natives feel that they can rely on the truth and honour of England. And one word with regard to the volunteer movement. I had the honour, not actually of being its father, but of being entrusted with the care of nursing the infant, and had the responsibility attendant on its teething. For I was at that time Under-Secretary at the War Office. I have therefore a great interest in it, and rejoice that the movement has spread to India, and congratulate you and your commanding officer on the appearance you presented to-day. I could tell, by simply looking at you, that you had a good officer, for regiments, as well as schools, depend for their proficiency on their leaders. What I have seen to-day will make me watch your progress with increasing interest, and I hope you will all endeavour to profit to the utmost by the education you receive here, and that when you go forth from hence to fight the battle of life, you will remember that you have to maintain the good name of Englishmen and the honour of Bishop Cotton School.

[His Excellency concluded his speech (which was frequently interrupted by bursts of applause) by offering a donation of Rs. 100 to the cricket field, and took his seat amidst the cheers of the boys.

The Lieutenant Governor moved a vote of thanks, saying:

" I ask you to join me in thanking the Viceroy for coming here, and for delivering the soul-stirring address which he has given, and which I am sure will go to the hearts of all here. The advantage to the schools of his presence and what he has said, cannot be over-estimated."

Archdeacon Mathew seconded the resolution, which was passed enthusiastically—the boys loudly cheering; and the proceedings were brought to a close by the choir singing "God save the Queen."]

DISTRIBUTION OF PRIZES TO THE SIMLA VOLUNTEERS.

9th Oct. 1880. [ON Saturday afternoon, the 9th October, the Viceroy presided at the annual Distribution of Prizes to the Simla Volunteers at Annan-

Speeches by His Excellency the Marquis of Ripon. 27

Distribution of Prizes to the Simla Volunteers.

dale. A large number of people were assembled on the parade-ground ; and with the Viceroy, within a small *shamianah* pitched on the hill side, where the distribution took place, were Sir Donald Stewart; the Hon. C. U. Aitchison; Mr. Primrose, Private Secretary ; Major White, Military Secretary ; Lieutenant-General Olpherts, and a number of others, including many ladies. After going through some "extended order movements," the corps advanced in review order and formed up three sides of a square in front of the *shamianah*, when His Excellency the Viceroy addressed the regiment as follows :—]

Officers, Non-commissioned Officers and Members of the Simla Rifle Volunteers,—I can assure you that it is a great pleasure to me to meet you upon this occasion. I believe that this Volunteer Corps now numbers some twenty years of its life; and that reminds me that twenty years ago, in England, I was engaged under the orders of my distinguished chief, the late Lord Herbert, in taking a part, as Under-Secretary of State for War, in the organisation of the Volunteer movement at home. It is therefore natural that I should feel a deep interest in this, the first occasion on which I have had an opportunity of seeing before me an Indian Volunteer Corps ; and it was with unfeigned pleasure that I heard the remarks which have been made by Colonel Williams upon the result of his inspection of the corps to-day, and that I was able to conclude, from the language of that experienced and distinguished officer, that you, the Simla Volunteers, are in a condition of high efficiency, and would be ready at any moment faithfully, valiantly, and effectively to discharge your duties, if called upon to do so. (*Cheers.*) In England, it was a great object in the Volunteer movement that the Volunteer force should be as numerous as possible. I have never been one of those who have thought for a moment that any force of Rifle Volunteers would enable us to dispense with the services of any portion of the regular army. (*Hear, hear.*) In India, however, we cannot look to raise such a large force of Volunteers as has now, happily, for twenty years existed at home ; but if

Address from the Municipality of Umritsur.

you are less numerous, that is an additional reason why you should endeavour to make yourselves as efficient as possible. (*Cheers.*) You must recollect that the existence of such a force—the existence of corps like this—leads the Government to expect that they may rely upon you in the hour of danger, if ever it should arise, and that you must use your best endeavours not to disappoint the hopes and expectations which are raised by such efficient manœuvres as have been witnessed upon this occasion. These are days in which all opinion points to the concentration of military force at great centres, and therefore it becomes more and more necessary that we should be able to rely upon a force like this, of Volunteers, to do such duty as might be required in a station such as Simla. I am convinced that if you should ever be called upon—as I trust, please God, and as I hope and believe, you never may—to discharge active duties in the defence of your Sovereign and your countrymen, that you will answer gallantly to the demand—(*cheers*)—and therefore it is that I offer you my congratulations to-day on the efficiency to which you have attained, and that I ask you to remember that the confidence of the Government rests upon you, and that it is your bounden duty and highest honour fully to justify that confidence. *Loud and continued cheers.*)

[The distribution of prizes was then proceeded with.]

ADDRESS FROM THE MUNICIPALITY OF UMRITSUR.

10th Nov. 1880. [ON Thursday morning, the 28th October, the Viceroy left Simla for his autumn tour. His Excellency was accompanied by the members of his personal staff, and, after a pleasant trip through the hills by Nahan and Dehra Doon to Saharunpore, during which some good shooting was found, arrived by special train at Umritsur on the evening of the 9th November. At 11 o'clock next morning, the Vice-

Address from the Municipality of Umritsur

roy, accompanied by Mr. Burney, Commissioner of Umritsur, and his staff, and escorted by a troop of the 14th Bengal Lancers, drove to the Town Hall, where the Municipal Committee and a large number of the native gentlemen of the district, and native officials, were assembled to meet him. His Excellency was received at the entrance by the Committee, headed by Khan Mahomed Shah, Khan Bahadoor, and conducted to the top of the Hall, where a canopy was erected, within which he took his seat. Khan Mahomed Shah then read an address of welcome on behalf of the Municipality in which they gave some facts regarding the origin and history of Umritsur and its progress under British rule; expressed satisfaction at the prospects of peace with Afghanistan and the renewal of commercial intercourse between Umritsur and Kabul and the countries beyond; and pointed out the advantages of connecting Umritsur with Pathancote by railway—a scheme which they hoped would receive His Excellency's favourable consideration and appoval.

Lord Ripon replied as follows:—]

Gentlemen,—I beg to think you most sincerely for the address which you have just presented to me. I have listened with especial satisfaction to the expressions of loyalty to our Queen-Empress which are contained in it, and it will be my duty to make them known to Her Majesty. I rejoice to be able to assure you that Her Majesty ever feels the deepest interest in the welfare of her Indian subjects, of all classes and creeds.

I am very glad to have had this opportunity of visiting this interesting city, connected, as you remind me, with so many historical recollections, and to be able to-day to return you my hearty thanks for the very kind and cordial reception which you have accorded to me on my first visit to your district, and for the many beautiful scenes with which, by night and by day, your streets have been adorned, and which I have witnessed with the utmost gratification.

But, gentlemen, it is especially gratifying to me to learn, as the representative in this country of the Queen-Empress of India, that you date the commencement of the commercial prosperity of Umritsur from the period when this city

Address from the Municipality of Umritsur.

passed under British rule. The description which you give of that rule in the address which you have presented to me shows me how justly you appreciate the principles by which I trust the Government of the Queen-Empress in India will ever be guided; and I can assure you that it will be my constant endeavour, so long as I hold the office of Governor General of India, to apply those principles impartially and fully.

I rejoice with you, gentlemen, at the prospect of restored peace, and at the return to India of so many gallant soldiers who have been serving their Queen and their country beyond the frontiers of this land. I congratulate you heartily upon the part—of which you, gentlemen of the Punjab, may be justly proud—which has been taken by the regiments from these districts in the warlike operations of the last two years. It will be my especial duty and my most earnest desire, under the blessed auspices of returning peace, to labour to the utmost to promote the well-being of the people of India, and to develope the resources of this great country; and you may rest assured that among the measures of that kind which will engage the attention of myself and my colleagues in the Government of India, the scheme for connecting Umirtsur with Pathankote by railway will receive full and ample consideration. You will, of course, gentlemen, not expect me upon this occasion to make any promise as to the period at which it may be possible to undertake that work, the importance of which I fully recognise.

Gentlemen,—I am very glad indeed to have had this opportunity of meeting you, and to find that, while on the one hand you recall with a wise interest the past history of your country and your city, you look forward on the other to a prosperous and progressive future under the just sway of our Gracious Sovereign.

[Mr. Johnstone, the Assistant Commissioner of Umritsur, translated the Viceroy's reply into the vernacular, after which the Committee's address, which was enclosed in a handsome casket, was formally presented to His Excellency.]

ADDRESS AT THE ALEXANDRA GIRLS' SCHOOL.

[AFTER leaving the Municipal Hall, Lord Ripon drove to the Alexandra Girls' School, where an address was presented to him by the Native Christians of the Punjab, who had assembled at Umritsur (the head station of the Church Missionary Society in the Province) for the purpose of meeting and welcoming His Excellency. The address referred to the conclusion of the Afghan war as an especial cause for thankfulness and rejoicing, conveyed the thanks of the Native Christian Community to his Excellency for his kindness in visiting the School, and concluded with expressions of loyalty and good wishes for the success of His Excellency's administration.
Lord Ripon replied as follows :—]

Gentlemen,—I have to thank you most sincerely for the address you have been kind enough to present to me on this occasion ; and I assure you that it has given me great pleasure to accept your invitation to visit this Institution to-day, and to receive this address at your hands.

You speak of the fair prospects which are once more opened to the Indian Empire by the termination of the Afghan war. I, like you, heartily rejoice that it has pleased God,' in His good providence, to bring to an end those military operations which have continued for so lengthened a period ; and I earnestly trust that we may now be blessed with a continuance of peace and prosperity, during which it may be possible for me and my colleagues in the Government of India to devote ourselves to promoting to the utmost the welfare of the people of this land *(applause)*.

I am peculiarly glad to have met you in this Alexandra School, because the name of the Institution recalls to me the fact that, on the last day spent by me in England before I left my own country to come here amongst you in this distant land, I was honoured by an interview with that

Address at the Alexandra Girls' School.

illustrious Princess whose name this school bears—the Princess of Wales—at which both she and the Prince of Wales expressed their deep interest in India, and at which His Royal Highness assured me of the agreeable recollections he brought back with him from this country, and how heartily he desired to hear, from time to time, of the welfare and happiness of its people (*applause*).

Gentlemen,—I have been connected now, for more years than it is altogether in some respects agreeable to recollect, with the subject of education in my own land, and therefore, I naturally feel a very deep interest in all that concerns the progress of education in India. You are aware that it is the bounden duty of the Government of India to preserve the strictest neutrality in all that relates to religious matters in the country. That is a duty imperative upon us in fulfilment of distinct pledges definitely given, and to which we are bound to adhere. I have never thought, gentlemen that the strict performance of that duty, both as regards the natives of this country and the various Christian denominations in India, involves in the least degree, on the part of individual members of the Government, any indifference to religious education. (*Hear, hear, and applause.*) And, for myself, I have always held and maintained at home—and my views upon that subject have undergone no change though I have come many miles across the sea—that no education can be complete and thorough if it does not combine religious and secular education. (*Loud and continued applause.*)

I am therefore very glad to have the pleasure of coming amongst you to-day and of visiting this school—one of the first, though not quite the first, among those which I have seen in India—and I can truly say that I wish this Institution, and those connected with it, all possible prosperity. (*Applause.*) I trust you may accomplish the work which you have set before you, and that, in the words of the motto

Address from the Anjuman-i-Punjab.

which I see in front of me, "your daughters will be as polished corner-stones." *(Applause.)* If it should please God to aid you in advancing the great work of education in India, you will by your efforts be doing a great service to the people of this country, and you will be carrying out an object which I know Her Majesty the Queen-Empress has closely at heart. *(Applause.)*

[Mr. Lewis, the Officiating Judge of the Small Cause Court, a native gentleman who read the address, translated the Viceroy's speech into the vernacular, after which the Viceroy inspected the Institution.]

ADDRESS FROM THE ANJUMAN-I-PUNJAB.

[THE Viceroy reached Lahore at a quarter to 5 on the afternoon of the 10th of November—the Municipality presenting him with an address of welcome at the Railway Station on his arrival. To this address a reply was subsequently sent in writing. At the Railway Station Lord Ripon was received by the Lieutenant Governor of the Punjab, the Commander-in-Chief in India, the Maharajahs of Khasmir and Puttiala, the Rajas of Kapurthala, Mundi, Furreedcote, and Chumba, and other native noblemen of the Punjab, and by a large number of Civil and Military Officers. A procession of elephants was formed, in which the Viceroy, the principal officials and native chiefs, took part, and which proceeded, by the Delhi and Lohari gates of the city, and the Sudder Bazar, to the Viceroy's Camp, which was pitched near the Racecourse. The whole of the forenoon of the 11th of November was occupied by Lord Ripon in receiving the visits of the native chiefs. At half-past 6 in the evening, a large and influential deputation from the Anjuman-i-Punjab and its various branch associations waited upon His Excellency with an address of welcome. Dr. Leitner, the Registrar of the Punjab University College, read the address. It urged upon the Viceroy the redemption of the pledge given by his predecessor to raise the Punjab University College to the status of a University—a pledge whose fulfilment had been delayed by the complications in Afghanistan ; it expressed the thanks of the Society to His Excellency for his sanction to the Kazi Bill recently passed by the Legislative Council, and for the precautions

11th Nov. 1880.

E

Address from the Anjuman-i-Punjab.

[taken to ensure the careful working of the Vaccination Act; it described the arrangements which had been made by the Society for the supervision, training, support, and eventual employment of ten sons of soldiers killed in the late Afghan war; it referred with satisfaction to the Viceroy's recent remarks at the Simla Fine Arts Exhibition on the cultivation of native art; and it concluded by drawing Lord Ripon's attention to the aim of the Guru Singh Sabha Association (a branch of the Anjuman) to spread knowledge among the Sikh Community by means of the Punjabi language, to extend female education, and to open out the cultivation of the agricultural and industrial resources of the country. At the conclusion of the address, the members of the various associations forming the deputation were introduced to the Viceroy, after which His Excellency replied to the address as follows:—]

Gentlemen,—I can assure that I have had very great satisfaction in receiving this large and important Deputation, and in meeting you upon this occasion. The reputation of the Anjuman-i-Punjab had already reached me before I came to Lahore, and I am extremely glad to find, from the evidence contained in this address, and that which is afforded by the fact of gentlemen from so many parts of the country being now gathered here together, that the institution is gradually gaining in influence. I particularly rejoice to meet the members of the Anjuman, because it is, if I mistake not, a society which has sprung up altogether from the exertions of the intelligent population of the Punjab. It has, I believe, no direct connexion with the Government, but is the spontaneous product of the desire of the educated classes of this great community to spread knowledge and science around them, and to give to others the advantages which they have themselves obtained from various branches of study. Now, it is no doubt true that in all countries of the world at the present time, and, in some respects, especially in India, it is necessary that the State should take a large part in the support and advancement of education; but I for one always very greatly rejoice when I see wealthy and educated persons coming forward themselves

Address from the Anjuman-i-Punjab.

to advance the cause of education, because I am convinced that by such free and voluntary efforts more is really done for the cause of solid education than can be done by the operations of any central government; and I am very glad indeed, therefore, to have a proof that here in the Punjab you feel with me, that this is a matter of very great importance, and that you desire, by your liberal subscriptions, and by your zealous labours, to show the earnestness of your conviction in that respect. As you are very well aware, it would be impossible to provide, out of the taxation of the country, such sums as are really required if the people of India are to be thoroughly educated; and it is only by the spontaneous and liberal assistance of educated native gentlemen, and by their coming forward themselves to take their fair share in the work more and more, that education can be placed upon a sound basis, and can attain to that position to which I hope and trust it may ultimately attain in this country.

You have alluded, gentlemen, in your address, to the question of the proposed University for the Punjab. I am about, a few days later, to receive an address from the Senate of the University College which at present exists, and I think that it would probably be better that I should reserve any observations I have to make on that point until I receive that address. The subject is one to which I have not yet been able to give as much attention as I should most earnestly desire to do; but I trust that when, to a considerable extent, those pressing anxieties which have been of late cast upon the Government of India have passed away, I shall be able to give my careful consideration to the question, the importance of which I fully recognise, and regarding which I trust, with the assistance of my colleagues in the Government of India, to be able to come to a satisfactory decision.

I have been much gratified, gentlemen, by the allusion which you have made to two measures of legislation which

Address from the Anjuman-i-Punjab.

have been passed by the Legislative Council of India since I came out to this country. I am very glad indeed to find, from the remarks contained in this address, that the Bill relating to the appointment of Kazis is one generally acceptable to the Mahomedan community. I felt it my duty to give that measure an unhesitating support, because I found that it was one calculated to supply a want felt in many parts of the country by persons of the Mahomedan creed; and I need not assure you that it is always my desire to meet the views of all classes of the community, whether Mahomedan or Hindu. I am also much pleased to find that those who represent the Hindu community in this part of the country recognise the spirit in which the Government of India has acted with respect to the Vaccination Act. That was a question, no doubt, involving very delicate considerations. I can say, for myself, that I am strongly and deeply convinced of the value and importance of vaccination, and of the great benefits it is calculated to confer upon the community at large in the prevention of a terrible disease; but at the same time I was well aware that it was perfectly possible that errors might arise in respect to the intentions of the Government in the matter; that it was calculated to touch upon the religious feelings of a large portion of the community, and therefore that it was essentially necessary to apply its provisions with the utmost possible consideration and caution. The principle upon which the Government of India acted was, in the first place, to leave it to the Local Governments to decide whether the Bill should be applied at all, or not, under their jurisdiction. But we went further than that, and we said that we desired that it should be applied in no case in which there was a decided feeling on the part of the population against the adoption of the measure. I am perfectly confident that the Local Governments will fully understand the object which the Government of India had in view, namely, that the feeling of the populations should be

Address from Anjuman-i-Punjab.

ascertained and considered to the utmost; that the fullest opportunity should be given to them of expressing their opinions freely; and that no attempt should be made to force the measure upon them, or even persuade them to adopt it, until they were convinced, by seeing the advantages resulting from its working in other places, that it was really for their good.

You are kind enough to allude to some remarks made by me a short time ago, at Simla, on the subject of the cultivation of Native Art. I can assure you that those remarks were the result of strong convictions on my part, and of a very earnest desire to see the Arts of India cultivated in a manner consistent with their past traditions. I am firmly convinced that no art except that which is spontaneous and grows naturally upon the soil of any country, is ever likely to be carried to real success; but I can assure you that, while I feel a great interest in the development of Native Art upon the lines of the ancient and indigenous Art of the country, I feel also an equal interest in those other important objects to which you have alluded, namely, the commercial development of the country and the spread of Western science. What you want in your education, as it seems to me, is that it should have its roots in the past, and that you should avail yourselves of all that is good and valuable in the result of times which are gone by; but that you should at the same time combine with those ancient historical recollections, the advantages of modern Western civilisation. Doubtless, gentlemen, the task is a difficult one. It is not easy to blend together even the knowledge and science of communities separated so very widely in many respects as are the peoples of the East and of the West; but, on the other hand, I see in the assembly of gentlemen now around me the best augury that could possibly be afforded that some such union of Western science with Eastern knowledge is before us in the future, and will be advanced by your efforts.

Review of Troops at Meean Meer.

I have learned, gentlemen, with peculiar pleasure that you have already done your part in marking your sense of the services rendered to the country by our gallant soldiers engaged in warlike operations beyond the frontier for the last two years. You may well, here, gentlemen, in the Punjab, have done this, because you have every reason to be proud of the distinction won by the Punjab regiments upon every field upon which they have been engaged.

And now, gentlemen, I will detain you no longer, except to say that if it should be given to me, through God's will, to realise in any degree the character which your address has been good enough to attribute to me, and if, when my term of office comes to an end, whenever that may be, there should be any in this country who are willing to accord to me the honourable and distinguished title of a friend of India, I shall, I can assure you, regard it as one of the proudest distinctions of my life; and I am further sure that it will be by acting in a spirit of warm and friendly feeling for the populations of this country, and with an earnest and deep desire to promote by every means in my power their happiness and their welfare, that I shall be most perfectly obeying the orders which our Queen-Empress entrusted to me on my departure from England.

REVIEW OF TROOPS AT MEEAN MEER.

13th Nov. 1880. [On Saturday morning, the 13th of November, the Viceroy held a review of all the troops assembled at Lahore, numbering nearly 10,000. The review took place at Meean Meer. His Excellency the Viceroy accompanied by the Commander-in-Chief, the Lieutenant Governor of the Punjab, and their respective Staffs, arrived on the ground about half-past 7 o'clock,—the troops being drawn up on parade in line of quarter columns,—and was received with a royal salute. A large body of spectators was gathered near the saluting flag. After the salute the Viceroy rode down the line accompanied by the

Review of Troops at Meean Meer.

Body-guard and Staffs. The Native Chiefs joined him near the saluting flag. The troops then marched past, and at the close of the parade advanced in review order. His Excellency the Viceroy then rode forward and met the Commander-in-Chief and the Commanding Officers and delivered the following address :—]

Your Excellency and Gentlemen,—It has been a very great pleasure indeed to me to have the honour of meeting, upon this, occasion, the worthy representatives of the British Army, both European and Native, who are at present before me, and especially to have been, as it were, thus introduced to our army in India, under your auspices. It would be impertinent in me, as a civilian to express any opinion upon the bearing and appearance of the troops, and yet I cannot resist the impulse which prompts me to say how greatly I have been impressed today by the sight, which has been presented to me by them, of the discipline and power of the troops of our Queen-Empress upon this Indian soil, whether they be those who have been sent from England, or raised in this country. But, Your Excellency, if I am bound to abstain from criticism, which you might regard as out of place, I may be permitted to refer to acts which have entered into the domain of history, and for a few moments briefly to recall the actions of the force which we have seen to-day in the most trying periods of the war which has just been, and I trust happily, brought to a conclusion. We may well be proud of that which history will have to tell to future generations of the deeds of the British Army during that war—whether we look to that earlier and shorter campaign which was marked by the actions of Ali Musjid and the Peiwar Kotal or whether we look to those events which followed upon that dark and melancholy occurrence at Kabul, when the representative of Her Majesty's Government fell the victim of a treacherous attack. When the soldiers of England, to vindicate the honour of their country, marched upon Kabul, nobly did they do their work ; and the great deeds which they did at that time will stand

Review of Troops at Meean Meer.

recorded in the pages of the military history of India. And then there came a later period of the campaign, when the Goverument of India called upon the force under the command of my gallant friend Sir Donald Stewart, to accomplish a march from Kandahar to Kabul, in the midst of which he again encountered the foe, and he encountered them at odds at which British troops are wont to meet their enemies in this country; for I believe in the lines of Ahmed Kheyl he had not more than twelve hundred men to meet some fifteen thousand. And then we hoped that we saw before us the dawn of peace, and a speedy return to thier homes of the native troops of India ; but again, another circumstance arose, which called for great exertion at the hands of the British Army and the hopes of the return of the force, and satisfactory peace, were for the time dashed aside ; and we had to call upon the army in Afghanistan to retrace their steps from Kabul to Kandahar. Of the history of that great march, I need not remind you. I wrote to Sir Frederick Roberts when he started from Kabul, and told him I had no doubt his march would be famous in military history. Was I wrong, gentlemen ? The trade of a prophet is generally dangerous ; but at least on this occasion my prophecy has been amply fulfilled. That great march was nobly accomplished ; its speed and skill have attracted the admiration, not only of Englishmen, but of Continental military critics, and it was wound up by a battle which may be hoped to have a lasting effect.

Gentlemen,—These are great deeds of which Englishmen may be justly proud ; and I have more than once had the pleasing duty of assuring the troops of the great sympathy which Her Most Gracious Majesty has felt for them in the dark hours which have from time to time overshadowed us, and of the gratitude and joy with which she had heard of the successes by which this war has been brought to a termination. But, Sir, if we recall with pride these gallant and stirring deeds of war and victory, there have been

Review of Troops at Meean Meer.

other incidents in these operations which we cannot in justice overlook. We cannot forget the services which have been rendered by those officers and regiments who were set to guard the lines of communications ; and I hold, as I have already had occasion in this country to state, that our gratitude is equally due to those who performed that duty with such unvarying patience, and such firmness in difficulties and trials—quite as great as those which were undergone by their comrades who had the better fortune to be engaged in the front.

Sir Frederick Haines,—There is one other circumstance to which I should desire to advert upon this occasion, and it is one of which I, at all events, am deeply proud. I have heard on all hands, and especially from Sir Donald Stewart, of the admirable discipline which has been maintained by the British army when occupying a foreign country. They have given, during the term of occupation, the greatest proof that they can give of the true character of Englishmen ; and I believe that by that discipline and moderation and justice towards the people in those countries in which they were stationed, they have done as much for the fame, reputation, and honour of England, in a political point of view, as they have in a military point of view by the victories they have gained. It would be too long on this occasion to recount the acts of individual regiments ; but I will venture to say this,—that a finer force of Her Majesty's troops has seldom, if ever, been brought together upon the plains of India. That Artillery whose fame is known in all lands, and whose motto shows that they are ready to do their duty in every part of the world, those magnificent Cavalry Regiments which we have seen upon this occasion, and that splendid line of unbroken infantry, I venture to think, Sir, you would not fear to lead against any army in the world.

Sir Frederick Haines,—I have on this occasion a duty of a singularly pleasant nature to perform. It was known to

Deputation from the Senate of the Punjab University College.

Her Majesty that this review was about to take place to-day; and last night I received a telegram from the Secretary of State, desiring me to inform the troops assembled here that it was Her Majesty's pleasure, in addition to the medal which has been already granted for the Afghan campaign, to attach to that decoration clasps for six different actions—Ali Musjid, Peiwar Kotal, Charasiab, Kabul, Ahmed Kheyl, and Kandahar; and yet more, Sir, in accordance with your recommendation, the grant of a special decoration to those who took part in the march of Sir Frederick Roberts' force to Kandahar, in the form of a bronze star. I am confident that you and the troops under your command will recognize this concession on the part of the Queen-Empress as another proof of Her Majesty's regard and affection for the army, which forms the foundation of her country's greatness and power, and as an incentive to deeds such as you and your troops have performed so loyally and well, and for which, in the name of Her Majesty, I now thank you from the bottom of my heart.

DEPUTATION FROM THE SENATE OF THE PUNJAB UNIVERSITY COLLEGE.

13th Nov. 1880. [On Saturday evening, at half-past nine o'clock, Lord Ripon received a large and influential deputation from the Senate of the Punjab University College who presented him with an address of welcome. The deputation was headed by Sir Robert Egerton, the President of the Institution, and there were also present the Maharajah of Kashmir, the Rajahs of Jhind and Mundi, and the Pattiala Council of Regency, besides a large number of European and Native officials and Native noblemen. The Lieutenant Governor (Sir Robert Egerton) opened the proceedings by introducing Dr. Leitner, who, he said, would read the address of the Senate. A copy of the address in the vernacular, enclosed in a handsome gold case, was then presented by the Maharajah of Kashmir to Lord Ripon; after which, Dr. Leitner read the address, the main object of which was to enlist the Viceroy's

Deputation from the Senate of the Punjab University College.
aid in raising the college to the status of a university. The numbers of students were stated, previous promises were recapitulated, the liberality of the Punjab Chiefs was dwelt upon, and, finally, the services of the Punjab troops in the Afghan campaign, were urged as an additional ground for the special favour sought. The Viceroy replied as follows:—]

Maharajah and Gentlemen,—I am very grateful to you for the address which you have presented to me upon this occasion, and especially for the manner in which you have spoken of those efforts which I have made in my past life to promote the cause of education in England; and I can assure you that that interest in education which prompted me to advocate its extension at home has kept with me here in India, and that I am equally convinced that all that concerns the advancement of education is of the highest importance in this country, as I was convinced that it was of vital interest in England. I am sorry to say that, in consequence of the many and anxious duties which have pressed upon the Government of India since I came out to this country, I have not been able to give that full and complete consideration to the questions connected with the establishment of a complete university in the Punjab, which I naturally should have desired, and that I have not had sufficient opportunity for consultation upon the subject with my colleagues in the Government of India, with whom it is my pleasure, as it is also my duty, always to act in the most cordial co-operation. I am therefore not in a position at the present moment to express any positive opinion as to the steps which may be taken for the promotion of an object which I earnestly desire to see advanced so far as may be consistent with the general interests of the country; and I am the more anxious to abstain from promises upon this occasion because I learn from your address that you have been waiting for some years for the fulfilment of hopes that have not yet been realised; and I should greatly prefer to have the opportunity of fulfilling my promises, if I may use the expression—even before I make them. At the same

Deputation from the Senate of the Punjab University College.

time, gentlemen, I am very glad to seize this occasion of explaining to you my general views upon some of the questions in which you are so greatly interested, and I rejoice to find from your address that those views are likely to meet with your approval. In the first place, gentlemen, I desire to express my high appreciation of the great liberality which has distinguished the Princes and Chiefs of the Punjab in coming forward, as they have done, to promote the establishment of the University College, as I understand, in the firm expectation that it will ultimately grow and flower into a perfect University. I beg, on behalf of the Government of India, to tender to those distinguished persons our best thanks for that generous liberality; and then I would state the conviction which I feel, that it is undoubtedly desirable to promote the cultivation and the extension of Oriental languages and Oriental literature. I entirely agree with the opinions of those who think that that is an object in itself desirable; and, so far as my limited acquaintance at present with India carries me, I am inclined to agree with the sentiments, which I believe you entertain, that it is through the medium of the vernacular languages of this country that science and literature can most easily be advanced and cultivated. We live in times, gentlemen—at least, we in the West live in times—of great and rapid change; and I am inclined to believe that those changes have not been without their operation in India. I sometimes hear it said that there is not in the present day the same intimate communication and relation between Europeans and Natives that existed in former times. I do not know how far that statement may be true, but I am quite sure of this,—that if there be any truth in it, it is matter for very serious consideration. It is a state of things which we ought to desire to remove; and I can quite perceive that there are circumstances in these times which tend of themselves to lead to that result. Now, gentlemen, I believe that it is vain to contend against the natural tendencies

Deputation from the Senate of the Punjab University College.

of the age in which our lot is cast. We shall not be able to return to those somewhat patriarchal conditions which may have existed in the past; but I believe that we shall find in the future the means of a sounder and yet closer union between European and Oriental races if we endeavour to cultivate a mutual understanding of the traditions of the West and the traditions of the East, of the Oriental and of the Occidental literature : and that we shall discover, in the spread of a general education, a new mode of supplying that bond of union which may have, to a certain extent, been wanting in recent years. I am rejoiced also to find, from the address which you have presented to me, that, although you mainly desire to promote the cultivation of Oriental languages and Oriental studies, you by no means are inclined to overlook the importance of a solid European education ; and that you are not desirous to put aside the cultivation of English language, English literature, and English science. I am confident that it is only by advancing both Oriental and English studies that we can hope to bind together more closely the various races which meet upon the common soil of India ; and I am very glad indeed to learn, from the evidence which your address presents, that you have by no means overlooked that consideration. Again, gentlemen, I think I am in sympathy with you when I say that I have always been a friend to a certain amount of variety in education. We have it in England, where, in the two great Universities of that country, there is a marked distinction in the branches of study to which pre-eminence is given. Oxford is mainly classical, Cambridge is mainly mathematical ; and I confess I do not see why Oriental languages and studies should not have a pre-eminence in Lahore, just as a special English education has a pre-eminence elsewhere. There are two theories of education : there is one theory which I may call the despotic theory—the theory that it is the business of the State to lay down an iron rule

Deputation from the Senate of the Punjab University College.

of education, and to try to force everybody into one groove, and to make submissive and obedient subjects of the State, without variety and without individual character. There is another theory of education, which I call the free theory, which adapts its methods to the necessities of the different portions of the population, to the tastes of individuals, to the varieties of religious opinion, and to the qualities of races; and I believe that you will find in such educational variety, as you find in the natural variety of the forests of this country, the true and free development which you desire to give to the human intellect. I say frankly, gentlemen, that I am an advocate of the latter theory. You have, in the conclusion of your address, put forward a claim to the consideration of the Government of India which I, for one, most readily recognise. You have alluded to the great and eminent service which has been rendered to our Queen-Empress and to the State by the regiments which have been raised within the limits of the Punjab. Gentlemen, you could not have addressed to me this evening an appeal which went more straight to my heart; because I had the pleasure this morning to see one of the most remarkable and one of the most beautiful sights which it has ever been my good fortune to witness. I saw that combination of Native and European troops which has ever been, and ever will be, the strength and security of India: I saw those Punjabis who fought so gallantly for their Queen-Empress and their country —those men who have endured conditions the most trying to the native soldier, and have endured them with courage, with patience, and with firmness. I can therefore truly say that, when you make that appeal to me, you make an appeal to which no man can be more ready to listen than I.

Gentlemen,—I do not know that I can say more to you at the present moment, or give you a more positive assurance with respect to your immediate request, because I believe that I shall best consult alike your interests

Durbar at Lahore.

and the interests of the Government of India if I content myself with telling you that, animated with the sentiments which I have expressed, I intend to approach this question in the leisure which I hope returning peace will give me, with the most earnest desire of meeting to the utmost of my power the wish of this distinguished community. *(Applause.)*

DURBAR AT LAHORE.

[THE public Durbar for the reception, by the Viceroy, of the Chiefs, Sirdars, and Native Gentlemen of the Punjab assembled at Lahore, took place at 11 o'clock on Monday morning, the 15th November in His Excellency's Camp. The Durbar was preceded at 10 o'clock by an investiture of the Order of the Bath, when the Viceroy formally invested Sir Donald Stewart with the insignia of a Knight Grand Cross, and General Maude with that of Knight Commander. At the conclusion of the ceremony, the Viceroy proceeded in procession to the Durbar Tent, where a large number of spectators, besides the native Chiefs was assembled. The Maharajah of Kashmir and the other Chiefs occupied the seats on the right of the Viceroy—the Lieutenant Governor, the Commander-in-Chief, the Viceroy's personal staff, and the principal officials of Government those on the left. The ceremony of presentation commenced as soon as His Excellency was seated; the chiefs and sirdars were presented in the order of their rank, and, as the number of ruling chiefs was fourteen, and that of the sirdars and native gentlemen probably over four hundred, this part of the ceremony occupied a considerable time. It was followed by the presentation of the Viceroy's *khillats* (presents) to the chiefs, at the conclusion of which, Lord Ripon rose and addressed the assembly as follows :—]

Maharajahs, Rajahs, Chiefs and Gentlemen of the Punjab,—It is to me a source of sincere gratification to have an opportunity of meeting in the capital of this province, so soon after my assumption of the office of Viceroy, the leading chiefs, and so large and influential a representation of the people of the country. With some of you I was

Durbar at Lahore.

already acquainted; others I meet now for the first time; but to all I offer a hearty welcome.

I have been very glad to observe, during my passage through the province, many signs of progress and prosperity, and I have derived much pleasure from the friendly and cordial reception which has been accorded to me. The well-being of India very largely depends upon the state of agriculture, and upon the condition of those whose interests are connected with the land; and it is therefore very satisfactory to me to be informed that in this part of the country questions affecting those interests have been placed, so far as the administration can place them, upon a sound footing.

I believe that throughout the Punjab, the land tenures of every district have been carefully examined, defined, and recorded, and that the assessment of the whole revenue has been settled upon a fair basis for a term of years calculated to afford free scope to the development of the resources of the province and to the enterprise of its people. Special attention has been paid by the Punjab Government to the adjustment of the tenure of land along the north-west frontier, so that the duties of watch and ward, which have been so long (and, on the whole, so well) performed by the chiefs and landholders on that exposed border, may be duly acknowledged and recompensed.

The extension of the Punjab Railways must have a marked effect both on agriculture and on trade. We have now two lines traversing the province—one already completed and connecting the Punjab with the sea, and the other to Peshawar, nearly finished, and forming the great high-road from Central Asia to the heart of India. These railways open out remote districts, promote internal communication, and strengthen the defences of the Empire.

I have learnt with great pleasure that education is spreading among all classes, and that the people of the Punjab are giving strong proofs of their capacity for mental training and their appreciation of its advantages. I trust that the

Durbar at Lahore.

real aim of higher education will be kept steadily in view and that it will be directed, not to separate classes by difference of culture, or by an undue desire to introduce foreign ideas and habits of thought, but to throw open to all a common ground for intellectual development, and to preserve and improve whatever is good in the indigenous literature of the country.

All that I have seen appears to me to indicate the steady growth of reciprocal relations of friendship and confidence between the Chiefs and the Supreme Government, and to show forth the attachment and devotion of the Chiefs to our Queen-Empress, and the complete trust which the Government can place in them for all the services which they are so well qualified to render. No better proof of this can be found than their readiness to aid in the late war, and the excellent spirit shown by their sirdars and officers, as well as by their troops. The loyal co-operation of the Chiefs, and the conduct of their contingents have, by the gracious permission of her Majesty, been recognised in various ways by decorations and titular distinctions; and the Government of India are also fully prepared to mark, by substanial and public tokens of approval, the services of others, sirdars and native gentlemen, who have accompanied our troops and our officers or have in other ways given signal mark of their ability and their devotion in the performance of the several duties assigned to them.

Her Majesty the Queen-Empress has commanded me to convey to the Chiefs of India her warm interest in their welfare—and not in their personal welfare alone, but in the success of their administration and in the well-being of the people of their States. For it is well known, and should be everywhere understood, that the British Government always entertains not only a desire for the honour and advantage of the Chiefs, but also a deep solicitude for their subjects; and that we measure the greatness of a State

G

Durbar at Lahore.

and the degree of its prosperity not so much by the brilliancy of its Court, or even by the power and perfection of its Army, as by the happiness and contentment of the peoble of every class. It is my earnest hope that the Chiefs now assembled around me will remember this, and that they will continue to administer their hereditary dominions, the possession of which is secured to them under Her Majesty's Empire, with justice and moderation—being careful to retain the affection of their people, and even to introduce necessary reforms with moderation; for when disorders arise, the British Government will judge that evils have crept in, which require remedy.

The population generally of the Punjab may be justly congratulated upon the manner in which they have utilised the advantages of a generation of peace under our rule without losing their tradition of hardihood, or their aptitude for military service. The general spirit of a people is reflected in its army, and, whatever benefits the British Government may have been enabled, through God's assisttance, to bestow on the Punjab, it could not have realised a better return than it has received in the untiring endurance and devoted courage displayed under circumstances especially trying to Native troops by the Punjab regiments who have served during the last two years in Afghanistan.

Maharajahs, Rajahs, Chiefs, and Gentlemen,—It has given me great pleasure to have this opportunity of addressing you in public Durbar. I believe that no such Durbar has been held in Lahore by the Viceroy since 1864, when Lord Lawrence spoke to the Chiefs, assembled around him in their own language. Unhappily, I am not able to follow his example in that respect; neither can I present myself to you, as he did, as an old friend and trusted guide; but, having enjoyed the friendship of that great man for many years, and being animated by sentiments of the heartiest admiration for him, it will be my constant endeavour during my administration of Indian affairs to walk in

Durbar to the Khan of Khelat.

his footsteps and to apply his principles; and I know well that I could not give you, here in the Punjab, a better assurance than by this declaration of my earnest desire to promote your prosperity and to advance your welfare to the utmost.

[The Foreign Secretary then translated His Excellency's speech into the vernacular, after which *attar* and *pan* were distributed, and His Excellency left the tent in procession, as he had entered it; and the Durbar was closed, having lasted nearly four hours. In the evening Lord Ripon was present at a ball given at the Montgomery Hall to the officers who had returned from Afghanistan, and on the following morning (the 16th) His Excellency left Lahore, by special train, at 11 o'clock, for Mooltan, where he arrrived on Wednesday morning, the 17th, having stopped *en route* at Changa Manga for a few hours' shooting.]

DURBAR TO THE KHAN OF KHELAT.

[THE Viceroy arrived at Jacobabad on Thursday evening, the 18th 19th Nov. 1880. of November, after having visited Bhawulpore (where he met with a very hospitable reception from the Nawab) and Sukkur. At the Railway Station, Jacobabad, His Excellency was met by the Khan of Khelat, his two sons, Major Sandeman, Agent to the Governor General for Biluchistan, and his political officers. On Friday morning, the 19th November, the Viceroy received the Khan of Khelat and his two sons in private Durbar, when His Excellency formally invested the Khan with the insignia of a Grand Commander of the Star of India. This was followed two hours later by a public Durbar for the reception of the Khan, his Sirdars, and the principal Chiefs of Pishin, Sibi, Thul Chotiala, &c. Many of the Chiefs present had not attended a British Durbar before, and formed (with the Khan's Sirdars, who were all seated in rows on the ground) a curious and picturesque assembly. The introductions to the Viceroy, of the principal Chiefs, were made by Sir Robert Sandeman, and, at the termination of the proceedings, Lord Ripon rose and addressed the Khan as follows :—]

Your Highness, —I am much gratified by this opportunity of receiving, in public Durbar, Your Highness and

Durbar to the Khan of Khelat.

your principal Sirdars, and of expressing to you personally the high sense which the Government of India entertain of the consistent loyalty and friendship displayed by your Highness in the assistance rendered to the Political and Military Officers of the British Government during the recent military operations in Afghanistan. I am aware that Your Highness' co-operation was effective and unreserved, and that whenever the British officers desired to be aided, your authority and influence were always promptly employed in their behalf.

I recognise in Your Highness a valuable and trustworthy ally of Her Majesty the Queen-Empress, faithful to his engagements, and cordially desirous of strengthening and confirming the friendly relations which exist between the British Government and your State.

It has afforded me great satisfaction to have been entrusted by my Sovereign with the honourable duty of investing Your Highness this morning with the Insignia of the Most Exalted Order of the Star of India, and I offer to Your Highness my most sincere congratulations upon having received this signal proof of Her Majesty's consideration and esteem.

I desire also to acknowledge the services which Your Highness' principal Sirdars (whom I am glad to see here on this occasion) have rendered during the past two years in preserving, under Your Highness, the tranquillity of the country, in protecting convoys and merchandise, and in their greatly aiding the uninterrupted maintenance of our military communications. I rejoice that the whole of Biluchistan is at peace, and that nothing has occurred to disturb the harmony which should prevail between a Prince and his people.

ADDRESS TO E.-B., ROYAL HORSE ARTILLERY BATTERY.

[AT the conclusion of the Durbar to the Khan of Khelat, the 19th Nov. 1880. Viceroy held a Levee, and in the afternoon paid a return visit to the Khan. As His Excellency was coming away, the salute was fired by E.-B., Royal Horse Artillery Battery, which distinguished itself so much at Maiwand. His Excellency stopped his carriage, and when the salute was over, addressed them as follows:—]

Major Tillard,—As I pass this Battery, I cannot resist the impulse which prompts me to address a few words to you and to your officers and men, in order to express my deep sense of the gallant services of the Battery at the battle of Maiwand, when, in the hour of difficulty and danger, they firmly upheld the reputation of the distinguished corps to which they belong, and when, as I may say without exaggeration, they even wreathed fresh laurels round the guns of the Royal Artillery. It is not alone in the hour of success and in the triumph of victory that the qualities of true soldiers are displayed—they are called forth no less when the tide of battle turns against them, in the stubborn resistance and the perilous retreat. Such occasions afford special opportunities for the display, not only of that valour and discipline which are common to all British troops, but also of the noble qualities of pity and self-sacrifice; and you, officers and men, may be proud to recollect in after days how many of the survivors of the 27th July owe their lives to your exertions. Sir, I rejoice to feel that the honour of Her Majesty's arms will ever be safe, in weal and in woe, in the hands of this Battery, and I esteem myself very fortunate to have had this opportunity of seeing them.

54 *Speeches by His Excellency the Marquis of Ripon.*

ADDRESS FROM THE KARACHI MUNICIPALITY.

22nd Nov. 1880. [THE Viceroy arrived at Karachi on Monday, the 22nd November, at 5-30 P.M., having visited Sibi, Pir Chowkey, and the Bolan Pass before leaving Jacobabad. At the Karachi Railway Station His Excellency was received by Mr. Erskine, the Commissioner of Sind (whose guest His Lordship was during his stay in Karachi), the principal Civil and Military officials and a deputation of the Municipality, who presented him with an address of welcome. The address congratulated Lord Ripon on being the first Viceroy who had travelled the whole length of the Indus Valley Railway; it pointed out the necessity for bridging the Indus between Rori and Sukkur; solicited the Viceroy's support to the works for the improvement of the harbour; it congratulated His Excellency on the close of the Afghan war and the successful evacuation of Afghanistan; it represented the hardship and inconvenience to the mercantile community of the abolition of the daily postal service between Bombay and Karachi by the overland route, in favour of the present bi-weekly service by steamer, and it concluded by drawing His Excellency's attention to the works under construction for giving Karachi a plentiful supply of pure drinking-water. To this address Lord Ripon replied as follows:—]

Gentlemen,—I thank you very sincerely for the address which you have been good enough to present to me, and I am extremely glad to have this opportunity of meeting you and visiting the city and port of Karachi.

A glance at the map of India is sufficient to show to any one the importance of the situation of Karachi, lying as it does at the mouth of one of the great rivers of India, and opening direct communication between the sea and the whole of the vast districts which form the watershed of the Indus; and, therefore, when I found that the other arrangements of my autumn tour were likely to bring me to the western frontier of India, I was extremely anxious to avail myself of the opportunity (the earliest afforded me since I assumed the office of Viceroy of India) to visit your town; and I can assure you, gentlemen, that the various important questions connected with your local

Address from the Karachi Municipality.

prosperity and your commercial advantage, which you have brought under my notice in the address which you have just presented to me, shall receive my most careful consideration.

I am very well aware that not much, perhaps, can be learnt from so short a visit as that which it will be possible for me to pay to your town on this occasion; but at the same time, it will always be an advantage to me, in considering the various questions connected with Karachi, that I should have had this early opportunity of making myself personally acquainted with the situation of your town and with your local requirements on the spot, and of entering into personal communication with the representatives of this large and important community.

Gentlemen,—You will, I am confident, not expect me upon this occasion to enter into any detail with respect to the various questions you have raised in your address, as you are well aware that some of them involve the expenditure of very large sums of money, and you must know that it is not altogether dependent upon the Government of India to what extent money may be available at any particular period for such large undertakings. But I can assure you that, in regard to the interests of Karachi, as well as in regard to the interests of India generally, it will always be my endeavour, while I have the honour of holding the great office which I now fill, to do everything in my power, consistently with the financial interests of the country, to promote intercommunication, and to develope the resources of the country at large; and nothing, of course, can tend more directly to those great and desirable objects than anything which helps to improve and extend a port of so great importance as that which you possess in this place.

It is, gentlemen, on account of considerations of that kind that I accept with great pleasure the congratulations which you have been good enough to offer me upon the conclusion of the war in Afghanistan. The conclusion of

Address from the Karachi Municipality.

peace is, at any time, one of the greatest of earthly blessings, and it is of special advantage when it affords, as I trust it may afford in this case, enlarged facilities to the Government of a country for turning its attention to all that tends to develope the internal resources of the country and to promote the prosperity of the people, whether agricultural or commercial.

Gentlemen,—I have observed with much satisfaction in several of the addresses which have been presented to me of late by bodies like your own, how much appears to be being done in India at the present time for the improvement of the water-supply and for various other objects connected with the improvement of the sanitary condition of our large cities. I hold this to be a matter of very great importance. I rejoice to see that attention to such questions, which is so general now in England, is extending itself to India; and I feel that British rule in India can scarcely be marked by any more honourable monuments than those which tend, so much as sanitary improvements do tend, to promote the general welfare of the people at large.

Gentlemen,—I will not detain you longer, except to thank you very heartily for the kind expressions used towards myself in this address, and to say that my earnest endeavour during my administration of Indian affairs, in obedience to the commands which I have received from the Queen-Empress, will be to promote, so far as may be in my power, by God's assistance, the happiness and the welfare of the people of India (*applause*).

[The Viceroy, accompanied by the Commissioner and His Excellency's Staff, then drove to the residence of the Commissioner of Sind. The roads and the principal buildings *en route* were decorated with flags, and several handsome triumphal arches were erected.]

ADDRESS FROM THE KARACHI CHAMBER OF COMMERCE.

[AT one o'clock on the 23rd November, the Viceroy received a deputation from the Karachi Chamber of Commerce, who presented him with an address of welcome. The address pointed out the great improvement effected in the harbour by Government expenditure, as shown by the extent to which it had lately been utilised for the importation of troops and stores for service in Afghanistan, and for railway material to the frontier. It recorded the deep sense of the Chamber's gratitude for the commercial advantages also derived, and urged the speedy construction of a bridge across the Indus at Sukkur,—representing that the saving effected would repay the outlay in a few years. It drew attention to the commercial advantages to be derived from the extension of the railway system towards Southern Afghanistan, the development of other systems in the Punjab, and to the desirability of a direct mail service between Karachi and Aden. The inadequacy of the postal service with Bombay, and the restoration of the overland service with that city, as also the abolition of the municipal duty on oils and seeds, were subjects on which His Excellency's favourable consideration was solicited, should they come before him. The address also drew attention to the inequitable incidence of the license tax, its distastefulness to the commercial classes, and urged the extension of the exemption from duty of all classes of grey goods when financial considerations would admit.

His Excellency replied as follows :—] 23rd Nov. 1880.

Gentlemen,—I have great pleasure in meeting you upon this occasion, as the representatives of the mercantile community of Karachi; and I am glad to find that you have rightly interpreted the motive which induced me to make an effort to include a visit to Karachi in the arrangements for my autumn tour during this, the first year of my Viceroyalty. I did so because I was much impressed with the importance of this rising community, and because I was desirous of seeing the progress made, especially with the Harbour Works of this port ; and, having visited those works very carefully this morning, and having had them very fully and ably explained to me by Mr. Price, I was glad to learn and to observe that considerable progress has

Address from the Karachi Chamber of Commerce.

already been made in the improvement of the port, and that measures are still being taken, or are in contemplation, which, it is hoped, will produce yet further improvement. I have examined the plans which have been adopted and those which are in contemplation, with care, and I can assure you that any questions connected with this interesting subject will always receive the most careful consideration from me and my colleagues in the Government of India.

Gentlemen,—I am very glad to find that you have adopted what seems to me to be an excellent course in your address, and that, instead of simply presenting a few words of compliment to the Viceroy, you have taken this opportunity of bringing under my notice the various questions in which your important community is interested. That is a most judicious course for a body like a Chamber of Commerce to pursue, because it is really calculated to bear practical fruit and to bring before the notice of the Governor General and of his colleagues the wishes of a community like yours; and it is by such a course that you can best show the utility of such institutions as the Karachi Chamber of Commerce.

You will hardly expect me, gentlemen, I am sure, upon this occasion, to reply in detail upon the various matters you have touched on in your address. They cover a very large field, and they open questions of very great importance, many of which, I need not tell you, have already engaged my attention; but I can assure you that I esteem it a great advantage to have learnt, as I have from your address, the views which the Chamber of Commerce and the Mercantile Community of Karachi entertain upon the various subjects to which you have alluded.

In conclusion, I can only say that I have derived great pleasure from my visit to Karachi, and that I shall carry away with me an agreeable recollection of all that I have seen this morning, and that any matters in which the

Laying the Foundation-stone of the Merewether Pier.

mercantile community of this town and port are interested will always have a claim upon my earnest and careful attention.

LAYING THE FOUNDATION-STONE OF THE MEREWETHER PIER.

[ON Wednesday afternoon, the 24th November, the Viceroy laid 24th Nov. 1880. the founadtion-stone of the Merewether Pier, at Keamari, in the presence of large numbers of the English and Native residents of Karachi who were conveyed to the Harbour by special train provided by the Harbour Board. Raised seats accommodated the spectators, and the place was tastefully decorated. His Excellency, accompanied by Mr. Erskine, Sir R. Sandeman, and his personal Staff, drove to the Customs pier at 4 o'clock, and proceeded thence by trolly to Keamari, where he was received by the members of the Harbour Board and Colonel Wallace, the President, who presented the address of the Board. After describing the services which the late Sir W. Merewether, Sir B. Frere, Sir R. Temple, Sir Andrew Clarke, Mr. Erskine, and Mr. Price had rendered to the Harbour, the address stated that the present work was carried out by local funds on the model of similar works at Calcutta and Bombay, and would accommodate the largest steamers ; but that several minor works, costing three or four lakhs more, were required for present equipment, for which local funds were inadequate. Statistics were given, showing a large increase in the trade of Karachi since 1844, and it was represented that the usefulness of the Harbour was cramped by the absence of the Sukkur bridge.

Lord Ripon replied as follows :—]

Colonel Wallace, Ladies and Gentlemen, and Gentlemen of the Harbour Board,—I beg to thank you very much for the address which you have just presented to me ; and I assure you that I was very glad to find myself in a position to accept your invitation to lay the first stone of the Merewether Pier, both on account of the character and importance of the work itself, and also because I learnt that it was your desire to connect with it the name of that distinguished officer, whose untimely death I am confident that

Laying the Foundation-stone of the Merewether Pier.

every one in Karachi and in Sind deeply mourns. I am glad, gentlemen, to have had this opportunity of thus marking my respect for the memory of Sir William Merewether and my high appreciation of his public services. You, gentlemen, have explained the various difficulties which the erection of this pier has hitherto had to encounter. It is often the fortune of excellent works that they should commence under the auspices of difficulties; but I trust that the time has now arrived when this important work will speedily be brought to a satisfactory conclusion. No one can doubt that if it had been in existence during the last two years the Government of India would have derived much advantage from the facilities which it would have afforded for the landing of troops and stores in this port. I have learnt, gentlemen, from your address, with much satisfaction, that this work will be undertaken out of the resources of the port itself; because it seems to me of great importance that, so far as possible, local works should be undertaken out of local funds, and under local management. No doubt, in a country like India, it is necessary that appeals should be made to the Supreme Government for assistance in regard to large and important works of general utility; but I always rejoice when operations of this kind can be undertaken from the funds of the localities themselves, and under the control of the representatives of the local population—not only because by this means relief is afforded to the burdened finances of India, but also (and yet more) because it is thus that self-reliance is fostered, and opportunity afforded for the practical extension of self-government. I had, yesterday morning, the satisfaction of visiting, under the able guidance of Mr. Price, the port of this place, and of having explained to me the various works which have been already undertaken for the improvement of your harbour, and those which are still in contemplation and which are held to be required for its completion. My visit will thus enable me to bring to the consideration of

Dinner at the Byculla Club.

those questions, whenever they come before the Government of India, a certain amount of acquaintance with the localities concerned, and the great advantage of having conferred upon them with those who are best acquainted with your local requirements. The figures, gentlemen, which you have laid before me in your address afford a very gratifying proof of the progress of your trade; and although, no doubt, the great increase which took place last year was due, to a considerable extent, to exceptional circumstances which, so far as they relate to war, will not, I trust, be repeated—nevertheless, I hope that no material check will be placed upon the progress of your town and harbour; and I can heartily say that if this pier, of which I most readily consent now to lay the first stone, shall tend—as I have little doubt it will—to promote your prosperity, it will be to me a matter of the greatest satisfaction. (*Cheers.*)

[Lord Ripon then descended the steps to the place where the foundation-stone was held in position by pulleys, and with a silver trowel performed the ceremony of laying it. At the conclusion of the ceremony, a royal salute was fired, and, shortly after, the Viceroy with his Staff embarked on board the *Tenasserim*, for Bombay.

DINNER AT THE BYCULLA CLUB.

[THE *Tenasserim* arrived in Bombay Harbour on Saturday morning, the 27th November. As the vessel dropped anchor, the Government ships manned yards and the Flag Ship *Euryalus* fired a salute of thirty-one guns. The *Tenasserim* was boarded by a deputation consisting of the Chief Secretary to Government, the Superintendent of Marine, and the Military Secretary to the Governor; and shortly afterwards, the Viceroy accompanied by Admiral Gore-Jones, was rowed to the steps of Apollo Bunder, where he was received by His Excellency the Commander-in-Chief of Bombay, upon whom had devolved the duty of welcoming His Lordship, in company with the Hon. L. R. Ashburner, the Hon. E. W. Ravenscroft, Sir Michael Westropp, and the Bishop of Bombay. A large number of civil and military officials were also in attendance at the landing-place.

27th Nov. 1880.

Dinner at the Byculla Club.

As the Viceroy stepped on shore, a second royal salute was fired by the Apollo Bunder Saluting Battery. The landing-place was crowded with spectators, who cheered the Viceroy as he started for Parell. All the available troops in garrison, including the Volunteers, were employed in lining the roads to Government House, where His Excellency was received by Sir James Fergusson. In the evening, the Viceroy was entertained at dinner by the members of the Byculla Club. The chair was occupied by Sir Michael Westropp, who was supported right and left by the Viceroy, the Governor, the Commander-in-Chief, the Naval Commander-in-Chief, the Hon. J. Gibbs, the Hon. L. R. Ashburner, the Hon. E. W. Ravenscroft, the Bishop of Bombay, the Roman Catholic Bishop of Bombay, and most of the prominent military and civil officials in the city and district. In replying to the toast of his health, proposed by the Chairman, Lord Ripon, who, on rising, was received with loud and continued cheering, spoke as follows :—]

Mr. Chairman, Your Excellency, and Gentlemen,—I assure you that I am deeply grateful for the manner in which you have received the toast which has been proposed in such friendly terms by the Chief Justice of Bombay. You, sir, have truly said that I have somewhat of an hereditary interest in India. My grandfather was Governor of Madras, and my first recollections of life are connected with those stirring scenes which marked the Governor-Generalships of Lord Ellenborough and Sir Henry Hardinge, when my father was President of the Board of Control; but I have been frequently reminded, on the short tour which I have lately made through the northern and north-western parts of India, of the many distinguished men who have proceeded from the presidency of Bombay. (*Cheers.*) Even before I came under the shadow of your administration, I was reminded, at Mooltan, that, of those two distinguished officers who are commemorated in that monument in the fort in Mooltan, in stirring and inspiriting language by Sir Herbert Edwardes, one—Lieutenant Anderson—was a member of the Bombay Army. (*Cheers.*) And then when I entered Sind, you will easily believe how the recollection of Bombay officers, civil and military, filled my mind. At Jacobabad,

Dinner at the Byculla Club.

the modest tomb of General Jacob recalled to my memory the eminent services of one who was a great master and ruler of men, who knew how to control wild tribes, and to spread cultivation and agriculture in the districts with which he had to deal. (*Cheers.*) And as I came down the Indus, I passed, if not in actual sight with my eyes, at least in full view with my recollection, that residency of Hydrabad where Sir James Outram won not the least of those marked distinctions which characterised the famous life of one who carried high the reputation of the Bombay Army, not only in India, but throughout the entire East. (*Cheers.*) At length I came to Karachi, where I was called upon to lay the first stone of a pier which is to be known by the name of one whose untimely death and sudden removal from amongst us was a cause of regret to every one who knew the services which Sir William Merewether has rendered to his country. (*Cheers.*) Gentlemen, I cannot forget that the first occasion upon which I had the honour to make the acquaintance of Sir Bartle Frere was when he retired from the position of Commissioner of Sind, to be honoured by all people in England who knew his career, up to that time (*loud cheers*);—that career, which has since been rendered more distinguished by his services as Governor of Bombay —(*cheers*)—services which are not unworthy to be recorded upon that roll upon which are inscribed the honoured names of Mountstuart Elphinstone and George Clerk, and which recalls the calm firmness of Lord Elphinstone in the hour of danger (*cheers*); the administrative ability of Sir Philip Wodehouse, and the indomitable energy of Sir Richard Temple. (*Loud and prolonged cheering.*)

Gentlemen,—These memories refer to the past, although some of them recall a past which is still recent; but I believe that those high qualities which have marked the civil and military services of Bombay in days gone by, mark them still in the present, and will mark them yet in the future. (*Cheers.*)

Dinner at the Byculla Club.

I am confident that, in the hour of danger and in the time of need, Her Majesty's Government may never fear to call upon the able and zealous services of the Government of Bombay. (*Cheers.*) Gentlemen, I would say to you (especially to the younger members of your distinguished services), set before you the example of the men to whom I have alluded; act in their spirit—in no slavish imitation of their individual opinions, but in that noble spirit which has won for them in the past the admiration and the gratitude of their country. I am sure, if you act in that spirit, and apply it to the changed circumstances of altered times, the military and civil services of Bombay will receive, and will deserve from their country, the same acknowledgment in the future that they have obtained in the past. (*Cheers.*) I cannot forget that I owe to the Presidency of Bombay, and especially, if I mistake not, to the Byculla Club, a peculiar debt of gratitude, because you have given me, in one of your ex-presidents, a colleague whose assistance I greatly value (*cheers*); and I can most heartily thank you for the great and marked advantages which I have derived from the wide experience, the judicial temper, and the administrative knowledge of my friend Mr. Gibbs. (*Loud cheers.*)

Gentlemen,—This review of the past services of Bombay to India and to England, and the confidence which I entertain that Bombay will render yet more important services in the future, makes it natural that I should rejoice to find myself, within six months of my first advent to India, once more amongst you. But, gentlemen, I like to be frank, and I am bound to say that, great as is my respect and regard for this presidency, it is not simply for the purpose of visiting Bombay that I have come here now. (*Laughter.*) I frankly admit that I have been led here by gentler influences—(*laughter and cheers*)—and it is in the hope that, please God, I may next week welcome my wife to India that I came here. (*Cheers and laughter.*) I don't

Dinner at the Byculla Club.

think you will think the worse of me for that frank remark. (*Cheers.*) Those of you who have got good wives well know their value and comfort, and those who have not got them had better get them as soon as they can—(*laughter and cheers*)—through the medium of the ample opportunities afforded them by the charming society of Bombay. (*Cheers.*) Gentlemen, no man who knows what are the blessings of a good wife will doubt that it is a great advantage to a Governor-General of India to have his wife by his side. (*Laughter and Cheers.*) My experience of the last six months has shown me—what no man could doubt, and what certainly I did not doubt when I felt it my duty to accept the heavy task which was entrusted to me by Her Majesty's Government—that the magnitude and the extent of the work and of the responsibilities which are cast upon a Viceroy of India, in days like these, cannot be underrated. Gentlemen, since I came to India I think I have had my fair share of those anxieties and those responsibilities. (*Cheers.*) They have been very great, and I can only submit my conduct under them to the fair and impartial consideration of my countrymen in India and in England (*cheers*); and say that, so far as I am conscious, I have endeavoured to do my duty. (*Cheers.*) And, further, I can say without any hesitation that I have received that which I fully expected to receive when I came out here,—the able, the earnest, and the loyal support of the civil and military services throughout India. (*Cheers.*) Gentlemen, the Governor-General of India is the ruler of the whole of India; he is not the ruler of any part of it alone. It is his duty to take into consideration the interests of every portion of those vast dominions which fall under the rule of our Queen-Empress; to endeavour to understand the nature and the interests of all of them; and he is entitled, I think, to look to the support and assistance of all. (*Cheers.*) Gentlemen, I fully believe that I may count to the utmost on the support and assistance of the

I

Dinner at the Byculla Club.

presidency of Bombay, and may rest assured that the confidence which I feel in the loyalty of the inhabitants—European and Native—of every part of this presidency, and in the zealous and public-spirited assistance of the civil and military services in Bombay, will never be falsified. (*Cheers.*) Therefore, gentlemen, it is with great satisfaction that I have met you upon this occasion, and that I return to you my hearty thanks for the reception which you have given me; and assure you that all which concerns your interests, of whatever kind or description, will always receive from me, and, I am confident, from my colleagues in the Government of India, the most careful and impartial consideration.

[His Excellency resumed his seat amid loud and prolonged cheering. The health of the Governor of Bombay was then proposed and responded to, and was followed by the toasts of "The Army, Navy and Volunteers," and "The Bench and the Bar." His Excellency the Commander-in-Chief replied on behalf of the Army, and in doing so referred to the Maiwand disaster as an event which, though it cost a great many valuable lives, yet attained the end which was desired, namely, that of stopping Ayub Khan's advance. The event had been subjected to many adverse remarks; but he could assure his hearers that, speaking simply as Commander-in Chief of the Bombay Army, he had not in any way lost confidence in the Bombay Sepoys, and he trusted he might yet have the opportunity, which hitherto had been denied him, of leading them against an enemy. Lord Ripon, in proposing the toast of the Byculla Club, spoke as follows:—]

Gentlemen,—I am the last man in the world who would desire for a moment to depart from official routine; but I find there is one omission from this toast list, which the natural modesty of the Byculla Club failed to supply, and that is the toast of the club itself. In recognition of its splendid hospitality on this occasion—(*cheers*)—permit me to go beyond that list, and add at least one toast. I am sure that, while we all desire that the Byculla Club should prosper and flourish, we do so the more because we have

Address from the Society of St. Vincent de Paul.

had an opportunity of learning something of the hospitality of the Club, of which all who are acquainted with India have long heard, and because we find that it is not the mere self-love of the inhabitants of Bombay, or the mere conceit of the members of the Byculla Club—(*laughter*)—that has occasioned its wide-spread fame. For this opportunity which we have had of tasting the hospitality of the Club, I heartly thank its members, and in doing so, I am sure I am only speaking the sentiments of all the other visitors. (*Cheers.*) There is nothing which is more undesirable than, upon occasions of this kind, for any one to allude to previous speeches, for the inevitable result of such a procedure would be to prolong to an inconvenient period the oratorical efforts of the evening. Nevertheless, I desire to say with reference to what has fallen from my friend the Commander-in-Chief, that the Government of India, and myself individually, highly appreciate those great and undoubted efforts which were made, under difficulties which it is difficult to over-estimate by General Phayre and the troops under his command. (*Loud cheers.*) Gentlemen, those are not sentiments which I express on this occasion because I am the guest of the Byculla Club in Bombay; they are sentiments which have been expressed in official despatches by the Government of India, to the Secretary of State. (*Loud cheers.*)

[The Chairman returned thanks on behalf of the Club, and the proceedings came to a close.]

ADDRESS FROM THE SOCIETY OF ST. VINCENT DE PAUL.

[On Sunday evening the 28th of November 1880, Lord Ripon 28th Nov. 1880. received an address from a numerous Deputation of the Society of St. Vincent de Paul who waited on him at the Parell Convent His

Address from the Society of St. Vincent de Paul.

Excellency, accompanied by the Rev. Father Kerr, walked from Parell to the Convent where he was received by the Right Rev. Bishop Meurin, the Rev. Fathers of the convent, the Deputation, and a large number of the Roman Catholic community, and conducted up-stairs to the principal school-room, which was prettily decorated and hung with suitable mottoes, and where the young ladies and children of the convent were assembled. After a selection on the piano, and a glee, one of the young ladies advanced to the centre of the room, and, addressing His Excellency, read in a clear, unfaltering voice, the following address :—

"May it please Your Excellency,—We, the happy children of the Convent, Parell, cannot express in fitting terms the gratitude with which we receive this unexpected proof of the kind interest Your Excellency deigns to take in our welfare. The intense satisfaction we feel in being honoured by a visit from our gracious Ruler is, however, damped by the consciousness of our inability—with so short a notice, too—to make known, by a becoming display, our deep sense of so great an act of condescension. Yet we rejoice in the presence among us, in these circumstances, of one whose benevolence of disposition and rare merit have gained for him so wide a celebrity. We cannot but hope that Your Excellency will be pleased to accept our protestations of loyal homage, as well as hearty appreciation of the precious favour which has made this auspicious occasion an epoch in or childhood's days upon which we will ever look back with happiness and delight. We would also add the assurance of our continued daily and earnest supplications that the best blessings of heaven may ever remain with one so honoured and esteemed, while we beg leave to present once again the sincere and heartfelt expression of the sentiments of respect and gratitude and loyalty entertained towards Your Excellency by us,

THE BOARDERS OF THE CONVENT CHILDREN OF PARELL."

Lord Ripon replied as follows :—]

I am very much obliged to you for your address, and I can assure you that there could be to me no pleasanter sight than that of seeing your smiling faces, and no greater pleasure than that of listening to your merry, happy voices. It is to me far more agreeable than any other entertainment you could have offered to me ; and I can only say that I hope this institution may continue to flourish, and that you, my dear children, who are here now, will use to the utmost the great advantages you possess in an institution of this kind

Address from the Society of St. Vincent de Paul.

not only by cultivating the intellectual gifts which God has given to you, but by remembering that you must use them for His service, and for the benefit of those around you, and that you can only hope to do so by God's grace and by carefully following the precepts of His religion.

[The Viceroy, accompanied by the Bishop and the assembly, then proceeded to the Chapel, where a holy benediction was performed, after which His Excellency rceived the Deputation. Their address referred with pride and satisfaction to His Excellency's presence amongst them, reviewed in some detail the work of the Society since its foundation in India by Bishop Meurin, explained the various good works with which it is associated, and concluded by warmly thanking His Excellency for sanctioning by his presence the labours and objects of the institution. His Excellency, in reply, spoke as follows:—]

My Lord, and Brethren of the Society of St. Vincent de Paul,—It gives me, I assure you, great pleasure to meet you on this occasion. It has been one cause of regret to me, which has resulted from the office with which I have recently been entrusted, that the circumstances of my position as Viceroy of India render it impossible for me any longer to continue an active member of the Society of St. Vincent de Paul. I do not mean, when I say that, for a moment to imply that there is any position, however high, or any office, however laborious, which is inconsistent with the position of a member of the Society of St. Vincent de Paul. (*Cheers.*) The history of the Society shows us that some of its most active and earnest members in various countries of the world have been very busy men and yet that they have found opportunities to steal, from their very scanty leisure, the means of devoting many an hour to the service of God and the assistance of His poor. But there are circumstances connected with the position of Governor General of India which would render the duties of an active member of the Society, as you will understand, impossible.

Brethren,—I was first led to join the Society of St. Vincent de Paul from a perusal of your rules, which seemed to me

Address from the Society of St. Vincent de Paul.

to present a singular combination of sincere piety, of wise charity, and of most loving consideration for the poor. It was that spirit of true piety, combined with a knowledge of the world, and especially of the poor as they really are, which led me to see the great importance of the Society of St. Vincent de Paul to the suffering populations among which it may be established in any part of the world. But Brethren, as you know very well, this Society is not to be regarded as a mere philanthropical institution. If we were to look at it in that respect, we should lose what is most valuable of the spirit of those devoted men who founded the Society, and yet more of the spirit of that great Saint whose name we have taken, and under whose protection we range ourselves. It is not only a Society for the purpose of giving a certain number of rupees, or of sovereigns, or of francs, to the poor of any country: it is a Society for the purpose of binding men together, and of bringing to the homes of the poor that which is more valuable than money—a deep, earnest, loving Christian sympathy. (*Loud cheers.*) But, Brethren, we are bound to say that it is not only for the sake of the poor that we do this; it is for our own sakes also. We have many a lesson to learn from those poor who are the dear children of our Lord; we can derive, from the assistance rendered to them in a true spirit of Christian love, many spiritual advantages for ourselves; and it is in that spirit, and with those objects, that this Society was founded.

Brethren,—I have listened with very great interest to the statement which you have been kind enough to make to me this evening, of the nature of the work in which you are engaged here in Bombay; and I am very glad indeed to find how large and extended is the sphere of your usefulness, and how strong you are in numbers; and, my Lord, perhaps you will permit me to say that I cannot but think that it will be remembered among one of the foremost of the many benefits which you have conferred, not on the

Address from the Society of St. Vincent de Paul.

Catholic community of Bombay alone, but on the general public of this great Presidency, that you have founded here, on the soil of India, the Society of St. Vincent de Paul. (*Cheers.*) I am happy to say that I have the pleasure of the acquaintance of Mr. Dallas, who, I am glad to hear, was your first President, and that I know well—having often met him at meetings of the Society—how zealously he is still working, in spite of indifferent health (*loud cheers*), in the cause of the faith and of the poor. (*Continued cheers.*)

Brethren,—It seems almost superfluous to suggest even any additional work for you to undertake, when you have put before me so long and honourable a roll of labours in which you are already engaged; but, nevertheless, I cannot let this opportunity slip—the first which I have had since I came to India of addressing my Brethren of this Society —without drawing your attention to one other work which has been recently developing itself in England, and which has been long established in France, and is called the work of Patronage. There is nothing about it, Brethren, I need not tell you, of patronage in the offensive sense of the word. It is used, not in the sense ordinarily implied by the word in English, but in the sense of the word *patronage* in French; and the object of that work is to take care of young boys who are just leaving school and entering upon life— mostly young boys who have just made their First Communion, and who are going forth to meet all the trials and temptations—the fiery trials and terrible temptations—which beset them in these days. The object is that boys of this description should be brought under the notice of the various Conferences, and that some of the members of each of the Conferences should undertake to look after them for a certain time. The Patronage Committee in London endeavours to find situations for them with respectable employers or respectable firms; not content with doing that, it delegates some of its members to visit them from time to time;

Address from the Society of St. Vincent de Paul.

while in France, where funds are more easily procurable for the Society, they have in many parts (especially in Paris) erected very large and beautiful establishments in which these youths are gathered together on Sundays and on holidays, and in which they have their innocent amusements, and are able to partake of the consolations of religion. I do not know how far a work of that kind might be possible under the conditions of the Society in India; you, of course, can judge of that far better than I can; but I have felt in England a very deep interest in work of this kind. It is progressing slowly, as most important things do; it is growing up from small beginnings, in the same manner as your Society (as mentioned in your address) grew up from eight young men in Paris to its present large dimensions in France; it is, I say, progressing slowly but satisfactorily in England, and I shall be very glad if the few words I have said this evening induce you to consider the possibility of making an attempt in the same direction in India. Of course, you must exercise your judgment and discretion in determining whether the circumstances of this country afford an opening for anything of the kind. (*Cheers.*)

Brethren,—I will say no more on this occasion, except to assure you how deeply grateful I am for the kindness with which you have addressed me this evening; how heartily I thank you for assembling in such numbers on this occasion—I am afraid, at some inconvenience to yourselves, at such a distance from the city;—that I shall always feel the deepest interest in this Society; and that it will be to me a source of great pleasure, as also of great advantage, when I am able once more to resume my position in the honourable and noble work of an active member of the Society of St. Vincent de Paul. (*Loud and continued cheers.*)

[Bishop Meurin then addressed the assembly, thanking His Excellency heartily for his suggestion regarding the work of Patronage, and appointing a special committee from among the assembly to put His Excellency's suggestion at once into action. After some further

Address from the Bombay Chamber of Commerce.

remarks by His Lordship, on the excellence of the work being done by the Society in Bombay, the proceedings which lasted till after dark, were brought to a close with prayer. In the Convent grounds below, the children had prepared some excellent tableaux, which were illuminated by limelights as the Viceroy and assembly passed through.]

ADDRESS FROM THE BOMBAY CHAMBER OF COMMERCE.

[ON Monday afternoon, the 29th November, the Viceroy held a *levée* which was very numerously attended, at the new Secretariat. At the close of the *levée*, His Excellency received a large and influential deputation from the Bombay Chamber of Commerce, who waited on his Lordship to present an address. The address, which was a very long one and touched upon most of the questions in which the Chamber is interested, was chiefly devoted to the subject of railway communication; it pointed out in forcible language the grievous error committed, in the opinion of the Chamber, in constructing any portion of the Great Trunk Line between Bombay and Delhi on the narrow gauge; it urged the resumption of useful public works, and the construction of certain lines of railway which the Chamber believed would be of immense value in developing the resources of the Presidency, and strongly objected on grounds which were explained, to any State subsidy or aid being given to the Marmagoa railway; it directed the Viceroy's attention to the Bill in respect of Petroleum and other inflammable oils, and to the Factories Bill regarding which it was urged that certain recommendations which had been made by the Chamber with a view to modifying the powers proposed to be conferred by those Bills, should be considered before they were passed into law. A reduction was also asked for in the present rates for inland telegrams, and a recommendation was made that the Government should encourage the introduction of telephonic communication into the city of Bombay, by private enterprise.

To this address His Excellency replied as follows :—]

Gentlemen,—I am much obliged to you for the address which you have presented to me, and for the kind and flattering terms of your reference to myself; and can assure you

29th Nov. 1880.

K

Address from the Bombay Chamber of Commerce.

that I am very glad indeed to have this opportunity of meeting the representatives of the mercantile community of Bombay. I appreciate very highly the enterprise of that community, and beg to assure you that I set a very high value on the maintenance and extension of all that concerns your interests. I am very glad, gentlemen, that you have, in this address, entered so fully into your views and opinions on the various important questions so closely affecting the interests of your community. It is a great advantage to the Government of India that they should have, from time to time, an opportunity of learning the views of the mercantile community of the great cities of this Empire; and I rejoice, therefore, that you have set forth, in the manner you have done, the views and the opinions which you entertain on many points of great importance and interest at the present moment.

Gentlemen,—You will not, I am sure, now expect me to enter into any detailed answer to the questions which are raised in your address. You are well aware that many of them are questions of great magnitude, and, just because they are so large and so important, they require the most careful consideration at the hands of the Government of India, and not of the Viceroy alone. The individual opinion of the Viceroy is not in itself sufficient to dispose of them. The very large questions of railway policy which are raised in your address require to be considered, and ultimately decided by the Government at home. For myself, I do not think that I shall be going beyond that discretion which every one in my position is bound carefully to maintain, if I say that, in the case of trunk lines, I approve of the principle that a break of gauge should be avoided; for I think it very desirable in the interests of trade that through communication should not be interrupted by the necessity of transhipping goods in transit. But at the same time you will, of course, clearly understand that it is a very

Address from the Bombay Chamber of Commerce.

different thing to decide a question in the first instance and to be called upon to reverse a policy already determined upon, and to a great extent carried into execution. All I can say is, that the question shall receive my consideration and that of my colleagues, and the member of my Council who has been specially deputed to investigate it. When I remind you that the member of Council so deputed is our friend Mr. Gibbs, I am sure you will agree with me in thinking that the interests of Bombay are not in dangerous hands. I am not an enemy of the narrow-guage system, nor do I believe are you, under proper conditions; and I should be sorry if any expression of mine led persons to entertain the idea that that was my view; but I do feel strongly that uniformity of guage on main lines is a matter of great importance. As regards the particular lines to which you have alluded, I can only add that some of them have already—indeed, all of them have more or less—received the consideration of the Government of India; and that it will be a great advantage, in dealing with the questions connected with them, to know your views; and, from the friendly assurances contained in your address, I am sure you will be very glad to afford the Government any assistance in your power with a view to their elucidation.

With respect to the question which relates to the Bill for the purpose of restricting the trade in petroleum, and which you have raised in your address, I wish to say that I have been all my life a free-trader. I have a very lively belief in free-trade; but, at the same time, you are well aware that in England, where free-trade principles are so firmly established, a Bill has been passed (and a very stringent Bill) regulating the trade in petroleum, on account of its explosive and dangerous character; and it seems only natural we should endeavour to work somewhat on the lines of English legislation. But I can only say for myself—and I am quite sure I speak the sentiments of my colleagues—

Address from the Bombay Chamber of Commerce.

that we shall be glad to receive and consider such observations as a body so well qualified to deal with this subject as the Bombay Chamber of Commerce may desire to offer.

As regards the Factory Act, that again is a question of great importance, and, I do not deny, of considerable difficulty. But I have lived in England for many years in the immediate neighbourhood of manufacturing towns, and although I know the objections which were raised to factory legislation when first introduced in that country, I have also seen the many advantages which have followed from it. It will be my desire that any legislation which may ultimately be adopted by the Government of India should be calculated to reconcile, to the utmost, the interests of the employers and the employed.

You have spoken, gentlemen, of the question of telephonic communication. With regard to that, I may say that the subject is still, to a certain extent, under the consideration of the Government of India, who will give every possible weight to the suggestions which you have made. I myself, in accordance with the principles to which you have just alluded, am generally in favour of entrusting matters which can be carried out by private enterprise to that enterprise: but when you do set up a monopoly, as the telegraphic communication is in India and at home now, it is necessary for you to carefully guard that monopoly, and not to allow the rights of the State to be at all infringed. The Government here and the Government at home have not found it altogether easy to deal with this matter. It is one of the utmost importance, and I will only say this,—and I say it without any hesitation,—that, whatever may be the ultimate decision of the Government of India, I feel entirely that the public have a right to say that if the Government take the duty upon themselves, they are bound to see that the wants and requirements of the public are amply supplied. But the matter has not yet finally been determined in all its details, and we have at this moment a proposition before us which we have only just received, and have not yet had time fully to consider.

Gentlemen,—I need not detain you longer, except to assure you that, so long as I have the honour to hold the great office which has been entrusted to me, it will always be my duty and my pleasure to encourage and advance, by any means in my power, the interests of commerce and industry in India. I am perfectly convinced that it is by encouraging the industrial and commercial enterprise of this country you can best secure for India that progressive development which I myself heartily wish for it.

DINNER TO THE 66TH REGIMENT.

[AFTER the Viceroy had received the Deputation from the Bombay Chamber of Commerce, His Excellency proceeded to the parade-ground close by, where he reviewed the troops in garrison and the volunteers, numbering in all about 1,500 men. Subsequently, the non-commissioned officers and men of the 66th Regiment, which suffered so severely at Maiwand, were entertained at dinner by the members of the Bombay Government. About 400 men sat down; and during dinner, Lord Ripon, accompanied by Sir James Fergusson and General Warre, entered the dining-tent. Lord Ripon having expressed a wish to address a few words to the men, a deep silence ensued, when His Excellency spoke as follows :—] 29th Nov. 1880.

Non-commissioned officers and men of the 66th Regiment,—I am very glad to have this opportunity of associating myself with the welcome which is given to you upon this occasion by the members of the Government of Bombay. That great feat of arms which was performed by your gallant comrades, who died to the last man in defence of the standard of their Queen-Empress, has been already acknowledged, as you are probably aware, in glowing terms by the Commander-in-Chief for India, Sir Frederick Haines, whose words have been cordially endorsed by the Government of India. (*Hear, hear.*) That feat will live in the memory of Englishmen—aye, and in the memory of the world—so long as great deeds and noble self-sacrifice have their value among men. But, 66th, you must remember that to have been the comrades of those who died so gallantly throws a great responsibility upon this regiment, because you have to maintain, each and all of you, in your future history, the fame which has been won for you by those who have died for their country. (*Loud cheers.*) I will not detain you longer, except to say how heartily I wish you God-speed, and how firm is my confidence that throughout the world, if you are called upon you will know how to defend those colours which will soon be afresh entrusted to you by your Queen.

[Three cheers were then called for the Viceroy, and heartily responded to, and three cheers were called for the Queen. Colonel Hogge, Commanding the Regiment, thanked the Viceroy for the kind words he had uttered, remarking that if upon any future occasion the 66th should be called upon, they would fight equally as well, but, he hoped, with a better result. Colonel Hogge then called for three cheers for the Commander-in-Chief, which were heartily given, and one of the men called for three cheers for General Burrows, which were also enthusiastically given.]

DISTRIBUTION OF PRIZES AT St. XAVIER'S COLLEGE, BOMBAY.

30th Nov. 1880. [THE Viceroy having consented to preside at the distribution of prizes to the students of St. Xavier's College, Bombay, drove, with Lady Fergusson, to the college building at half-past four on Tuesday afternoon, the 30th November. His Excellency was received at the college door by the Right Rev. Father Meurin, Vicar Apostolic, the Rector, and other gentlemen of the college management, and conducted to the hall upstairs, which was tastefully decorated with flags and mottoes. The hall was filled to overflowing, every available seat being occupied, principally by the parents of the boys and the friends of the institution. After an overture by the band, a prologue was recited by one of the boys, containing complimentary references to His

Distribution of Prizes at St. Xavier's College, Bombay.

Excellency. A tableau from the "Merchant of Venice" followed, after which the annual report was read, and showed the institution to be in a flourishing condition. The distribution of prizes was then proceeded with, and at its conclusion Lord Ripon addressed the assembly as follows :—]

Your Lordship, Ladies and Gentlemen,—I had very great pleasure in accepting the invitation which was sent to me a few weeks ago, to be present upon this occasion and to take part in the distribution of these prizes, because I was already aware that this college was, by common consent, numbered among the best educational institutions of the city of Bombay *(applause)*; and I expected, therefore, to derive no little gratification from being here upon this occasion and becoming personally acquainted with the managers and students of this institution. And certainly the report which was read to us just now, couched in such modest and unassuming terms, has proved—not by large words, but by the hard facts of educational statistics—the success of the education which is given here. (*Applause.*) I am quite sure that all the friends of this college will have heard with great satisfaction the proof which that report contained of how well able the students of St. Francis Xavier's College are to hold their own in the race of life. But, ladies and gentlemen, I confess that the scene which we have witnessed this evening has had for me a larger share of attraction than I anticipated, and has raised thoughts in my mind more far-reaching than those which I expected to meet here. For surely there is something very remarkable in the fact that we should—in this hall, in the midst of this great Oriental city, and before such a company as this, containing the most distinguished inhabitants of Bombay, of all races and all creeds—have had a *tableau* presented on that little stage with such marked ability from one of the great plays of Shakespeare. I wonder what would have been the feelings of Queen Elizabeth and her courtiers, in Shakespeare's days, had they known that in less than three short centuries his play would become famous

Distribution of Prizes at St. Xavier's College, Bombay.

in India. But what are three centuries in the life of a country like India, one of the most ancient countries in the world ? And surely we may see, in the honour thus accorded to the first of English poets, a happy augury of that union which, year by year, is becoming closer and stronger between the civilization of the West and of the East. I myself look upon it as a circumstance of happy augury for the future of India when I see so many of our Indian population assembled on this occasion to listen, I doubt not, with much appreciation, to the words of the greatest English poet.

Ladies and gentlemen,—It is not for me to occupy your time with any eulogy of St. Francis Xavier's College. Of course, I can only judge of it first by what I have heard on all sides and from many lips, and then from all that I have seen to-night with so much pleasure. You know—you who have assembled here in such large numbers, who place confidence in those who manage it, and send your children to it—you know far better than I do the benefits which it is calculated to confer. More I cannot do than to offer to you, my Lord, and to the managers and students of this college, my hearty congratulations upon the flourishing condition in which you find yourselves now. (*Applause.*) But before I sit down I should like to say one or two words to those who are students in this college, that I may exhort them to avail themselves to the utmost of the great advantages here presented to them. My young friends, we live in days in which education has become almost a necessary of life in all ranks and all classes, and those who have not mental development will inevitably fall behind in the race of that keen competition to which all must be subjected in these days. But if I exhort you to use the advantages you now possess to the utmost, I do not desire to put before you any low or sordid motive. It will be greatly to your interest in after life that you should use them well;

Distribution of Prizes at St. Xavier's College, Bombay.

but I can tell you that, should you endeavour to acquire knowledge for any reason other than her own true worth, she will not reveal her secrets to you. Knowledge is a fair and noble dame, but she is proud, and cannot be won by those who do not woo her for herself. (*Cheers.*) Let me, then, earnestly exhort you to seek for knowledge for her own sake, and to go on step by step and stage by stage, through the classes and forms of this institution, advancing day by day, in order that in after-life you may use the advantages offered here to a good and praiseworthy end. The poet tells us that

"A little knowledge is a dangerous thing;
Drink deep or taste not the Pierian spring."

There is much truth in these lines, but they always seem to me to contain a half truth. A little knowledge is no dangerous thing provided you know that it *is* little. It is a dangerous thing if it makes you proud and conceited, if you use it to flourish in the face of those more ignorant than yourselves, and if you seek to make use of what you know in order that you may obtain a little temporary praise. The true student is ever modest, and of a reverent spirit. Let such a spirit be yours, and let me beg you now—you who have so many advantages—to use them for the development and cultivation of those intellectual faculties which are the inheritance and possession of all races alike. Let me ask you to use them well for your intellectual development: and not for that alone. Let me entreat you to lay firm and deep the foundation of that character by which you are to be hereafter distinguished, and which will form a solid basis to those moral qualifications which alone conduce to true happiness and will win for you the respect and affection of your fellow-men. (*Loud applause.*)

ADDRESS FROM THE POONA SARVAJANIK SABHA.

3rd Dec. 1880. [THE Viceroy, accompanied by his Staff and the Governor of Bombay, left Bombay by special train at 1 P. M. on the 2nd December, for a brief visit to Poona. His Excellency was received on his arrival at the Kirkee Railway Station by the Civil and Military authorities at Poona, and drove at once to Gunesh Khind, the occasional summer residence of the Governor of Bombay. The platform at the railway station was crowded with spectators, and large numbers of natives were assembled in the neighbourhood of it. At half-past 10 in the morning of the 3rd, the Viceroy received an address of welcome at Gunesh Khind from a deputation of the Poona Sarvajanik Sabha, consisting of sirdars, landholders and other representatives of the people of the Deccan. The address referred with satisfaction to the views expressed in recent speeches by the Viceroy on education, and to his declaration of policy, at the Lahore Durbar—especially to his assurance that, in his administration of Indian affairs, he would apply the principles which had guided Lord Lawrence's government. His Excellency's remarks on municipal institutions and municipal self-government were also reviewed and heartily concurred in, as indicating an effectual means of advancing the welfare and prosperity of the people. The address concluded by thanking his Excellency for restricting the too rigorous operation of the Arms Act, which it was hoped would, in course of time, be altogether repealed.

Lord Ripon replied as follows:—]

I beg to thank you for the address you have presented to me. I can assure you it has been a great satisfaction to me to have been able, under the auspices of the Governor of this presidency, to visit Poona, and make myself acquainted —slight as the acquaintance must necessarily be—with the interests of this city and district. I am glad to find, gentlemen, from your address, that various remarks which I have made since I came to India have commended themselves to your approval. The time at my disposal is too short to allow of my entering into any lengthened reply to the several matters touched upon in your address; but there are one or two points upon which I should like to say a few words. I was very glad indeed to observe that, in speaking

Address from the Poona Sarvajanik Sabha.

of higher education, you are, in the first place, entirely alive to the great importance of the spread of education throughout the country; and I would say that I trust that it may not be higher education alone which will be spread more and more in India, but that we may in future have more done than has been done in the past for the education of the masses of the people. It gave me great pleasure to hear the terms in which you referred to the despatch of 1854 in your address. I have always looked upon that despatch as the charter of Indian education; and, gentlemen, it is upon the lines of that despatch that I should desire to found my educational policy in this country, at the same time having regard to the changed circumstances of the advancing times in which we live.

Gentlemen,—You have also alluded to some remarks which I made at the durbar at Lahore, in addressing the native princes who were present on that occasion. It is hardly necessary for me to tell you that the policy of the Queen-Empress and her Government is founded firmly and unchangeably upon the principles laid down in the proclamation of Lord Canning, and which were embodied in the *sanads* that he granted. We fully recognise that it is a great advantage, not only to the Chiefs themselves, but to the British Government, that there should be Native States in India; but at the same time, gentlemen, that era of peace which English rule has established throughout this country, under the government of the Paramount Power, of itself renders it necessary that we should, from time to time, remind those who dwell under its shadow that they are bound to show that the administration of their States is good.

Gentlemen,—I will not enter into the further points which you have raised. I do not think that the Viceroy of India ought to be given to much speaking, and, certainly, I for one would much prefer that when my term of office comes to an end, the people of India should be able to say, " Well,

Address from the Poona Municipality.

he has on the whole been better than his word," than that they should say, " He has used large-sounding and big phrases, but has done nothing to give them a tangible shape." (*Hear, hear.*) It seems to me, what India wants at the present moment is peace and rest, that she may devote herself to the advancement and progress of agriculture and commerce. Of course, in such a country as India, it is necessary that the Government should take a considerable part in the development of its resources; but I hope and trust that the people of India will more and more show that they can help themselves in these matters, and then, with the co-operation and help of Government, you may hope thoroughly to develope the resources of this great Empire.

ADDRESS FROM THE POONA MUNICIPALITY.

3rd Dec. 1880. [AFTER receiving the deputation from the Sarvajanik Sabha, His Excellency, accompanied by Sir James Fergusson, drove in procession through the Native city, the streets of which were decorated with triumphal arches, flags, festoons of flowers and evergreens, and thronged with people. At the Boodhwar Palace, where a large number of natives were assembled, who cheered heartily as the procession approached, a deputation of the Poona Municipality presented Lord Ripon with an address of welcome, to which His Excellency replied as follows :—]

Members of the Municipal Committee of Poona,—It is a great pleasure to me to have been able on this occasion to visit this ancient city, around which cluster so many historical associations well known to the student of Indian history ; and to have had this opportunity afforded me, by your address, of tendering to you my warm thanks for the reception which you have accorded to me. I am well aware that that reception is due to the fact that I occupy the great position of the representative of your Queen-Empress

Address from the Corporation of Calcutta.

in India. I doubt not you are well aware how deep is the interest which Her Majesty takes in all that concerns the welfare and advancement of her Indian subjects. Her Majesty, from time to time, does me the honour of addressing to me a few words, and I can truly say that there is scarcely an occasion which, in those letters, there is not contained some message to her people in India,—messages always expressive of the deep personal interest with which she ever regards the inhabitants of this great jewel of the English crown. I am very glad to have been able to come here to-day, because, although my visit is necessarily brief, yet it is probable that I shall not have another opportunity, while I am in India, of visiting the Deccan, and I am greatly obliged to your Governor, Sir James Fergusson, for having afforded me the means of meeting you upon this occasion. Gentlemen, I have passed of late through many parts of India, and I have received at the hands of various races, creeds, and populations, much kindness, and always a cordial welcome. For the welcome you have given to me I beg to tender my heartfelt thanks, and to assure you that I shall ever retain a lively recollection of your kindness, and a deep interest in your prosperity.

[The Viceroy's speech was received with loud cheering, which was followed by three more cheers for His Excellency, called for by Sir James Fergusson. Cheers were then given for the Governor, after which the Viceroy drove to the railway station and left for Bombay, which was reached in the evening.]

ADDRESS FROM THE CORPORATION OF CALCUTTA.

[AT 3 P.M. on the 8th of February, a large and influential deputation consisting of the Chairman, the Vice-Chairman, and the members of the Corporation of Calcutta, waited on the Viceroy at Government House, to present him with an address. The address, which was read by Mr. Souttar, the Chairman, was one of welcome to Lord and Lady

8th Feb. 1881.

Address from the Corporation of Calcutta.

Ripon, and of congratulation on His Excellency's restoration to health, and did not touch on political questions.

In replying to it, Lord Ripon spoke as follows :—]

Gentlemen,—I am very glad indeed to have this opportunity of meeting you, the Corporation of Calcutta ; and I thank you most sincerely for the address which you have just presented to me, and for the kind welcome which you accord to me in that address, for which I thank you all the more because you have been good enough to include in it my wife, Lady Ripon. I am also deeply touched by the sympathy which you express towards me in connexion with the recent illness with which I have been visited. I am glad to say that it has pleased God to raise me from that illness, and to restore me once more to health and strength ; and I can assure you that the kind sympathy which has been expressed towards me under that trial—not by you only, gentlemen, but I may say, I think, throughout India and by men of all classes, opinions, and creeds—will tend greatly to stimulate me to discharge to the utmost of my ability, and to the full extent of my energies, the great responsibilities which have been entrusted to me by my Sovereign.

Gentlemen.—I rejoice to observe, though I was not surprised to hear, the heartfelt sentiments of loyalty to Her Majesty, contained in the address which has just been read. I say I am not surprised to have observed those expressions, because, naturally, you are well aware of the deep interest which the Queen-Empress takes in everything which concerns the welfare of Her Indian subjects ; and I can assure you that Her Majesty has always inculcated upon Her Ministers the duty of treating Her subjects in India with the same equal justice, the same consideration, and the same regard for their interests, with which they treat the Englishmen who dwell most near to Her throne: and it is in that spirit, gentlemen, I shall endeavour to administer, with the co-operation of my colleagues, the

Address from the British Indian Association.

affairs of this great country, so long as they may be entrusted to my hands.

I am, gentlemen, much gratified by the expression of confidence in myself which you have been pleased to include in your address. I value it very much as coming from such a body as yours, and, although throughout my Viceroyalty I shall feel bound to follow the dictates of duty without regard to any desire to obtain the favour of this, or that, class of the community, yet I can truly say that shall I regard it as a fortunate circumstance if, when my administration of Indian affairs closes, you are able to inform me that I still possess your confidence.

Gentlemen,—I watch with the greatest interest the progress of municipal institutions in this country, and especially in the case of a Corporation like this, which is possessed in part of a representative character.

I do not think that I need detain you longer now, except once more to tell you that I am deeply grateful for the kind and graceful words which you have been good enough to address to me, and to assure you in all sincerity that I shall ever have deeply at heart the interest of your famous City.

ADDRESS FROM THE BRITISH INDIAN ASSOCIATION.

[A numerous deputation of the British Indian Association waited 15th Feb. 1881, upon the Viceroy at 3 P.M. on Tuesday afternoon, the 15th February, at Government House, to present him with an address of welcome. Lord Ripon received the deputation in the Throne Room, and was attended by Mr. H. W. Primrose, Private Secretary, Major White, Military Secretary, Lord William Beresford, and other members of his Staff. The address—which was read by Maharajah Narendra Krishna, President of the Association, who prefaced it with a few congratulatory remarks on the Viceroy's recovery—referred to Lord Ripon's assumption of the Viceroyalty at Simla, expressed satisfaction at the assurance that England would bear a portion of the expenses of

Address from the British Indian Association.

the Afghan War, and that due consideration would be given by Lord Ripon to the Vernacular Press and Arms Acts, and to questions relating to taxation, and concluded by drawing His Excellency's attention to the question of land Law reform in Bengal.

His Excellency replied as follows :—]

Gentlemen,—I am very glad to see you upon this occasion, and to receive you as the representatives of a body so well entitled as the British Indian Association is, to receive every consideration at my hands, and composed of gentlemen who, by their position and talents, have a just claim to be listened to in any representations which they may make.

I can assure you that it was a source of great and sincere regret to me not to be able to enter upon the post of Governor General of India in the city of Calcutta, in accordance with, I believe, the unbroken precedents of those who have preceded me in that great office; but I rejoice to find that you frankly recognise that that change of proceeding was the result of circumstances beyond my own control. I should have been very proud to have taken up my office in the Council Chamber of this house, full as it is of the memories of such men as Lord William Bentinck, Lord Metcalfe, Lord Canning, and Lord Lawrence.

Gentlemen,—I thank you very heartily for the kind and friendly expressions contained in your address, which have been heightened by the remarks made in introducing the deputation to me just now ; and I can assure you that those expressions will strengthen and encourage me in the discharge of the arduous duties of my present office. I rejoice with you at the prospects of returning peace which lie before us, and which will make it the duty of the Government of India to endeavour fully to realise those economies which are only possible in peaceful times; and I can assure you that it will be my earnest endeavour to carry out every just and reasonable retrenchment which it may be in the power of the Government to effect.

Address from the Mahomedan Literary Society.

Gentlemen, the principles by which I hope to be guided in my administration of Indian affairs have been stated by me upon more than one public occasion, and they are already, I imagine, known to you; indeed, you have mentioned the circumstance in your address, and it is therefore not necessary that I should, upon this occasion, repeat them. It is sufficient that I should say that to those declarations it is my intention steadily to adhere.

I am confident, gentlemen, that you will not look for any expression of opinion on my part at the present moment upon the important subject of the Bengal Land Laws. That subject embraces some of the most difficult of political questions, and all that I can say now is that, when the occasion arises, I will give to its consideration my most earnest attention, and that I shall examine it with a sincere desire to promote to the utmost the just and fair rights and claims of land-owners and their tenants.

Gentlemen,—You have been good enough in your address to express your confidence that "in my hands the stability of the beneficent rule of our Sovereign Mistress, and the well-being of her subjects, are safe." I thank you for these words. You have rightly interpreted the objects which I have set before me, and I can assure you that if I shall be able, with God's help, in any degree to accomplish those objects, I shall feel, when I lay down the office of Viceroy of India, that my public life has not been barren.

Gentlemen,—I heartily thank you for your address.

ADDRESS FROM THE MAHOMEDAN LITERARY SOCIETY.

[ON Friday, the 16th February, the Viceroy received a large and influential deputation from the Mahomedan Literary Society, who

16th Feb. 1881.

Address from the Mahomedan Literary Society.

presented him with an address of welcome. His Excellency, who was accompanied by his Staff, received the deputation in the Throne Room, at Government House, at 3 P.M. Nawab Abdul Luteef, Khan Bahadur, Honorary Secretary of the Society, read the address, which referred with satisfaction to the Viceroy's recent public utterances on education; it explained the difficulties which have hitherto beset education among Mahomedans, and gratefully recognised the efforts of Government to encourage and foster it; it expressed a hearty approval of the Bill for the appointment of Kazis; and concluded by a hope that the Viceroy would continue to the Society the encouragement and support accorded to it by his predecessors.

His Excellency replied as follows :—]

Gentlemen,—I beg to thank you very much for the address which you have just presented; for the welcome which is contained in it to this city of Calcutta, and, still more, for the kind expressions with which it concludes with respect to my recent illness.

It is most agreeable to my feelings to believe that you are right in saying that all classes in this country were good enough to show much sympathy with me upon that occasion; and I can assure you that to you, and to all those who have entertained those sentiments, I shall always feel that I owe a deep debt of gratitude.

You are quite right, gentlemen, in saying that I feel a very deep interest in the question of education in this country. For many years before I came out to India, that question had largely engaged my attention; and, certainly, when I came to this country it was with a feeling that education was a matter not less important in India than it was in England—indeed, in many respects I think I may truly say it is of greater importance here than there, and I rejoice extremely to find that the efforts of your Society (representative, as I take it to be, of the Mahomedan community in this country) are steadily devoted to the encouragement of education, and to the removal of any apathy or any prejudices which may in former times, as you have informed me, have existed among some of the members of your body; and I cannot doubt, gentlemen,

Address from the Mahomedan Literary Society.

that those efforts will be crowned with complete and peedy success, when I recollect how many men, distinguished in science and in literature, have belonged in past ages to the Mahomedan community in Europe and in the East.

I am very glad to find that the Act which has recently been passed by the Legislature of this country for the appointment of Kazis is, in your opinion, calculated to supply a want which has been felt by the Mahomedans of this country. It was upon that ground, and in the hope that we were meeting a reasonable requirement on their part, that that Act was passed; and I rejoice that the judgment of the Government in that respect is confirmed by what you have stated in your address.

Gentlemen,—You could do nothing more calculated to promote the good, whether of the Mahomedan community in India, or of the country at large, than by endeavouring, as you tell me it is your desire on all occasions to do, to interpret the acts and the measures of the Government of India in a fair and loyal spirit. I can assure you that it is my firm determination, during the period for which the administration of Indian affairs may be entrusted to my hands, to act strictly upon the Queen's proclamation issued when Her Majesty took over the direct administration of India, in which she laid down the great principle that it was the duty of Her Majesty's representatives in this country to act with the strictest and most absolute impartiality between the various religions professed by the inhabitants of India. To that principle I am firmly determined strictly to adhere.

Gentlemen,—I can assure you that I shall have very great pleasure in extending to your Society the same encouragement which has been given to it by so many of my predecessors. The work in which you are engaged—your educational work—is one upon which, as I have said, I set a very high value, and therefore it will afford me much satisfaction to assist you in that work in any way in my power; and I can assure you that I have had very great pleasure in meeting you upon this occasion.

DISTRIBUTION OF PRIZES TO THE CALCUTTA VOLUNTEERS.

23rd Feb. 1881. [ON Wednesday, the 23rd February, the Viceroy inspected the Calcutta Volunteers, and Her Excellency Lady Ripon distributed the prizes to them for shooting. The ceremony took place on the Cricket-ground at half-past 5 in the evening, in the presence of a large number of spectators. On his arrival, the Viceroy, accompanied by Sir Frederick Haines and their respective Staffs, inspected the corps, after which the regiment was drawn up facing the assembly, and His Excellency addressed them as follows:—]

Colonel Graham, Officers, Non-commissioned Officers, and Members of the Calcutta Volunteers,—I can assure you that it is a great pleasure to me to meet you upon this occasion,—the first opportunity I have had of seeing this corps since I accepted, with much satisfaction to myself, the post of your Honorary Colonel. I could not hesitate to accept that post when it was proposed to me to do so, because I believe, from all I have heard of the Calcutta Volunteers, that this corps are well worthy to represent the Metropolis of India at the head of the volunteer force of this portion of the Empire; and all that I have heard since then, and that which I have seen this afternoon, confirm me in the belief that the report of your efficiency and of your bearing was well deserved.

I rejoice to understand that during the past year you have made considerable progress both in military efficiency and in the numbers enrolled in your ranks; and I am not at all surprised to find that that should be the case when I recollect the patriotic and loyal spirit by which the inhabitants of Calcutta have always been animated, and when

Distribution of prizes to the Calcutta Volunteers.

I remember that this corps is under the command of so able and energetic an officer as my friend Colonel Graham. I think his Excellency the Commander-in-Chief will permit me to say, even in his presence, that the efficiency of any military body depends very greatly upon its Commanding Officer ; and you of the Calcutta Volunteers are fortunate indeed in possessing such a Commanding Officer as Colonel Graham, the successor of one not less able than himself, my friend Colonel Walton.

The Volunteer force, whether at home or in India, has never been supposed by those who have been its best friends and its most ardent supporters to be in any degree calculated to supersede or to take the place of the regular army. It is, on the contrary, intended to set free that army from the occupation of many minor posts, in order that in time of difficulty it may be at liberty to execute those great movements of concentration which form the necessary preliminaries to war. In England it has been felt that it was of the highest importance that the volunteer force should be very numerous. We cannot, in the circumstances of India, look to approach to the large numbers which have been enrolled in the ranks of the Volunteers at home ; and if that be the case, it seems to me that it only behoves you—Indian Volunteers—to labour the more to make up by your efficiency for the comparative paucity of your numbers. But I have never held that you ought to estimate the importance of the Volunteer force by the number of men who are actually enrolled in its ranks at any given moment ; I believe that it is a very great advantage that you should have passed through your ranks a large number of men, and should have given to them a certain amount of military training which they would, I am confident, be ever ready in the hour of necessity once more to render available for their country.

I find, from the statement made to me, that your strength upon the books at the present time is between 600 and

Distribution of prizes to the Calcutta Volunteers.

700 members; but I also find that you have passed through your ranks no less than something short of 3,000 men. Well now, of course a certain proportion of these persons have left the country, or have passed the age of military service, or in one way or another would not be available if they should be at any time called upon; but I cannot doubt that there still remain here in Calcutta many men who at one time or another have been enrolled in your ranks; and I can doubt still less that if a call should be made upon them at any time by the Government of India, they would be prepared to return to those ranks once more, with all the advantage that they would bring of the energy and training which they had previously acquired; and I would venture to suggest that, from this point of view, it is exceedingly desirable that you should endeavour to maintain the interest of persons who seek to be admitted members of the corps, in your proceedings and your welfare; and that you should give them to understand that you have a certain claim upon them which you will not forget to put forward if the necessity should arise.

I rejoice to perceive that you have a goodly array of handsome prizes upon that table, and to understand that your shooting, both for those prizes and in the ordinary course of your practice, has been of a very satisfactory character. And I am particularly glad to observe, from an inspection of the prize-lists, how readily gentlemen in this city, European and Native, have come forward to give prizes for the encouragement of this gallant corps; and to see the names of many distinguished native gentlemen connected with Calcutta and its neighbourhood figuring upon those lists.

I should be the last man in the world to say a word that would seem to disparage the importance of good shooting to any military body. In these days of arms of precision, it is of signal importance that every military body should be well trained in that science; but I always feel that there is a certain danger that when handsome prizes are ditributed by fair hands as the reward of triumphs in the matter of shooting, there is another essential point in the efficincy of every military body which may possibly be somewhat thrown into the shade —I mean the matter of drill. Now, permit me to say that it is drill which distinguishes the organised from the unorganised body—it is drill which gives that cohesion, and unity, and steadiness which mark the true soldier; and let me earnestly exhort you, while not neglecting your shooting, not to be less zealous than you have been in attaining to perfection in that important point; and let me exhort you also if you desire to be worthy of the position you hold and the confidence which the Government of this country places in you, to devote yourselves earnestly and zealously to learn your drill; let me give you, in three words, the short advice—stick above all things to your drill.

And now I will no longer delay you from that moment which is the most interesting of the day upon this occasion. I will no longer stand in the way of her who is about to distribute these prizes to you, and for whom, and on whose behalf, I desire to say that her interest in the Volunteer movement is not a thing of to-day, and that it is a great pleasure to her, so soon after her arrival in India, to have this opportunity of marking her interest in a corps the uniform of which her husband is proud to wear.

[Her Excellency Lady Ripon then distributed the prizes.]

EXEMPTION FROM MUNICIPAL TAXATION BILL.

[IN the Legislative Council, on the 25th February, the Hon. Mr. Colvin 25th Feb. 1881. moved that the Report of the Select Committee on the Bill to exempt

Exemption from Municipal Taxation Bill.

certain persons and property from Municipal taxation be taken into consideration.]

His Excellency the PRESIDENT said that he had looked at the Report of the Committee, and was very glad to see the alterations which they had introduced into the Bill as originally introduced. He confessed that it appeared to him that the Bill as first proposed, gave too extensive powers to the Government of India, and that the amount of uneasiness that was felt on the subject by a considerable number of municipal bodies in the country was justified by the very sweeping character of the clauses of the Bill as at first drawn; and he was very glad that the Select Committee had taken into consideration the representations made by them, and had modified the Bill and had removed all reasonable objection to it. His Excellency thought that it was worthy of consideration by Government in the Executive Council, whether it would not be desirable to issue a circular to Local Governments after the Bill had been passed, drawing their attention to the provision, and suggesting that they should appoint a person to communicate with the municipalities, with a view to settling what Government should pay towards the municipal rates. This was the course followed in England. The right of the Crown on behalf of Crown property to exemption from rates had been maintained; but a sum had been settled in each case which was paid to the municipality in the place of Crown rates; and he could only say that he hoped the Local Governments, in dealing with the question, would deal with it in a considerate spirit, and that, under the particular circumstances of each case, the Government of India would be made to contribute, in regard to their own property, whatever would be fair and reasonable towards municipal rates.

[The motion was put and agreed to, and the Bill subsequently passed into law.]

THE FACTORIES BILL.

[THE reconsideration of the Factories Bill was proceeded with in the Legislative Council on the 11th of March, when Mr. Colvin moved that the Report of the Select Committee on the Bill, which had been before the Council for nearly two years, be taken into consideration. Mr. Colvin explained briefly the changes made by the Committee in the Bill and the manner in which it was intended that the law should be worked. Maharaja Jotindro Mohun Tagore expressed himself not altogether favorable to the Bill. He would have retained its permissive character and allowed discretion to the several Local Governments to extend it to their respective provinces. He thought, however, that Mr. Thompson's proposed amendments would modify the effect of the Bill. Mr. Rivers Thompson then proceeded to move several amendments to the Bill, all of which were carried after some discussion. One of these amendments occurred in Section 3, which related to the appointment of Inspectors; and it was proposed, in deference to the representations of the Lieutenant Governor of Bengal, to eliminate the obligatory provisions contained in the section regarding such appointments, and to leave it to the discretion of the Local Governments either to appoint a special Inspector or to invest the Magistrate of the District with power to supervise the working of the law. Sir Ashley Eden explained why he was desirous for the alteration of the section: he thought that Mr. Thompson's proposed amendment of it would answer all the purposes of the Government, and afford quite sufficient security to the manufacturing interests of the community, to the employer and the labourer.]

His Excellency the President remarked that, in his judgment, he thought that it would be perfectly open to the Local Government, even if the section had not been altered, to have appointed a District Magistrate to act as an Inspector. He did not wish to put any interpretation of a legal nature upon the point, because he should thereby be going beyond his proper sphere in the presence of legal gentlemen much more competent to speak than he was; but he thought it was perfectly clear that the first paragraph of the section left it entirely free to the Local Government to appoint any person whom it thought fit; and consequently, as it appeared to him, the Local Government, if it wished, might in every case appoint a

The Factories Bill.

District Magistrate to discharge the duties of Inspector. However, as he found that there was a doubt upon that subject in the mind of his honourable friend the Lieutenant Governor, he was quite willing to agree to such an amendment as would clear up any possibility of doubt upon the point, especially as his honourable friend had pointed out the difficulty which would arise in this country in obtaining really competent men, except at great cost, to fill the individual and special office of Inspector under the proposed Act.

His Excellency, therefore, had no difficulty in acceding to the amendment suggested by his honourable friend, and which he believed only made more clear what would have been in the power of any Local Government under the Bill as sent up by the Select Committee.

He had only one more remark to make, and that was that, while he was perfectly willing to agree to that amendment, he was certainly not prepared to give up inspection altogether, because to do so would be to give up that without which all experience showed that any measure of this kind would be a perfectly dead letter. As to the persons who exercised the inspection, His Excellency was most anxious to leave that to the discretion of Local Governments, being quite confident that, when the Bill was passed, they would put its provisions into fair and proper execution.

[The amendment was agreed to. Mr. Pitt-Kennedy then proposed in Section 2 an amendment which was directed to confining the application of the Bill to cotton factories. Messrs. Grant and Thompson opposed the amendment.]

His Excellency the President said that he felt himself entirely in accord with the view taken by his honourable friend Mr. Thompson. He did not think that it would be possible to accept the proposed amendment. He had no doubt that it was brought forward in the most perfect good faith by Mr. Kennedy, but he could not help thinking

The Factories Bill.

that it would be regarded at Bombay as another mode of practically exempting, at all events, Bengal from the operation of the Bill. We had decided not to do that; we had made considerable concessions with the view of meeting the feelings and opposition of the manufacturing industry in Bengal, and he did not think that, under those circumstances, it would be desirable to go back from what had been thus practically determined; for that, in His Excellency's opinion, would be the result if the proposed amendment were adopted.

He had only one word more to say. His honourable friend Mr. Kennedy had alluded to the desire expressed by the manufacturers in England for the adoption of legislation of this kind in India. He was quite aware that Mr. Kennedy did not for a moment attribute the course taken by the Government of India to any undue pressure from that quarter; and His Excellency could only say for himself that, having come out here not very long ago from England, no motive of that kind had anything whatever to do with the support he gave to the Bill; and that he felt it his duty, in the office which he had the honour and the great responsibility of filling, to look at such questions mainly from an Indian point of view, and to regard all subjects in the interests of this great country with whose Government he was connected. He could truly say, therefore, that that was the motive which guided him in the support which he had given to the Bill. The subject was not a new one to him : it was one with which he had been occupied in England for a long time since the commencement of his public life,—certainly not in the interests of the manufacturers, but in those of the working classes. He himself believed that the practical result of legislation on the subject had been beneficial to the manufacturers, as well as to the labourers;—at all events, the fears entertained in the beginning by the manufacturers in England, and which were very similar to those now entertained in India, had completely died away, as he knew

The Factories Bill.

from long and intimate intercourse with manufacturers in his own part of the country; and he could not help thinking that, if the Bill was worked as he trusted it would be worked, it would be found to place no injurious restrictions on manufacturers in this country, while it would afford a reasonably fair protection to the children of the working classes, and, as regards the fencing of machinery, to all persons employed in mills of any description. That was the sole reason why he gave his support to the Bill, and he should be exceedingly grieved if any notion got abroad that the Government of India, in this respect, were in the least degree influenced by a mere desire to meet any wish, if such wish did exist, on the part of manufacturers in England to place restrictions upon their competitors in this country. That was not the view he took, at all events, and he was quite sure that none of his colleagues were influenced by it in their support of the Bill. He regarded the measure entirely upon its merits, and he believed it would be found to confer great benefits upon both classes—the employers and the employed.

[Mr. Kennedy explained that His Excellency was not responsible for the original introduction of the Bill, and that, though he could not doubt His Lordship's statement that he and his colleagues were acting quite in accordance with their conscientious convictions as to the necessity for the present legislation, he remained under the impression that the original inception of the measure had been much influenced by Parliamentary pressure.

The amendment was put and negatived. A discussion then followed on an amendment proposed by Mr. Kennedy, the object of which was to exclude from the operation of the Bill, children who accompanied their parents to the factory but received no wages for any slight or unimportant work they might do while there. Sir Ashley Eden supported, and Sir Donald Stewart and Messrs. Colvin and Thompson opposed it,—the latter holding that it would vitiate the working of the Act, and result in a great number of children being employed on no wages, while they would be subject to all the overwork and hardship which it was the object of the Act to suppress.]

His Excellency the President observed that he had certainly taken the same view of the case as his honourable

The Factories Bill.

colleague Mr. Thompson. It appeared to him that the amendment, if carried, would practically render the Bill nugatory altogether, especially as it seemed to be the habit of persons in this country to take their children to the factory with them. Under those circumstances, it would be almost impossible, as it appeared to him, ever to get a conviction under the Act, if the proposed amendment were adopted. Of course, it was impossible to be certain that there would not be found, from time to time, official persons who would act in a very foolish manner; but His Excellency thought that no legislation could provide against such a case of exceeding folly as that quoted by his honourable friend Mr. Kennedy, and which could not seriously be used as an argument against legislating in the sense which the Legislature of the country might on the whole think right. It must be borne in mind that no prosecution under this Act could be instituted except under the authority of the Inspector, and that the Inspector was either appointed by the Local Government or else he was, as it was desired should be the case in Bengal, a District Magistrate. It was also provided, in section 3, that the Inspector "shall be officially subordinate to such authority as the Local Government may, from time to time, indicate in this behalf ;" and it was thus distinctly pointed out that the Inspector should take his orders from the Local Government. His Excellency was sure that Mr. Kennedy did not think that any Governor or Lieutenant Governor in India would be likely to act in the manner in which the Magistrate to whom he alluded acted, and certainly he (Mr. Kennedy) could not think that anything of that kind would be permitted under the firm rule of his honourable friend the Lieutenant Governor of Bengal. It seemed to His Excellency, therefore, that to adopt the proposed amendment would be to render the Bill altogether a sham. It was said of the late Mr. O'Connell that he used to boast of being able to drive a coach and four through any Act of Parliament; but His Excellency was of opinion that

The Factories Bill.

it would not require all the knowledge and legal acumen of Mr. O'Connell to drive a coach and six through this Act if the amendment of his honourable and learned friend were adopted.

[The amendment was put and negatived. Mr. Kennedy next moved that the first clause of Section 16 of the Bill be omitted. The section ran thus:— "Where an act or omission would, if a person were under seven or twelve years of age, be an offence punishable under this Act, and such person is, in the opinion of the Court, apparently under such age, it shall lie on the accused to prove that such person is not under such age." A discussion ensued,—Messrs. Thompson and Colvin speaking against the amendment, Mr. Stokes and Maharaja Jotendro Mohan Tagore in favour of it.]

His Excellency the President said that, so far as he understood it, this was a question in which the physical mode of judging of the age of children was much the same in India as it was in England, and that the difficulties were of the same kind. His honourable friend Mr. Kennedy had quoted the answers given by certain medical men to questions put to them. Members of Council would observe that the question put to those gentlemen was this—whether, in the absence of proof of date of birth, there was any rule or law of nature by which the age of a child could conclusively be certified to be within the age of seven and a half, eight, or nine years? And to this question more than one replied—" If you produce me the child, I will give you an opinion. I cannot tell you the age of the child conclusively, but I can do so approximately." Of course, it would be impossible to say that that child would be seven years old on the 11th of March 1881, but it was quite possible to say that the child, for all practical purposes, might be considered to be either seven, or eight, or twelve. His honourable friend Mr. Kennedy referred to the English system of registration. His Excellency thought, if his memory served him correctly, that when the English Factory Act was first enacted, in 1841,—and this clause would be found in the original Act,—the registration system was not in perfect operation at the time, and that was the reason why originally the system of certificate by surgeons was adopted. Of course, as the system of registration had grown in England, the use of the surgeon's certificate had died out; but originally the English manufacturers were subject under their Act to precisely the same liability as it was proposed now to extend to this country; and, as his honourable friend Mr. Stokes had pointed out, there were a great number of cases, both in English and Indian legislation, where the same principle of throwing the burden of proof on the defendant had been adopted. Among others, if he was not mistaken, one was the English Passengers Act, which was an Act of somewhat the same description as the Factories Act; and it would also be found that in many other Acts of a similar description, regulating the relations between employers and employed, —certainly in the Customs Act, regulating the relations between the Government and the importers of goods,—the same principle had been adopted. Under those circumstances, His Excellency thought that the Bill should stand as it was now sent up by the Select Committee.

[Ultimately the amendment was put and negatived; and after some further discussion, the Bill was passed into Law.

OPENING THE INDUSTRIAL AND FINE ARTS EXHIBITION AT SIMLA.

[On Saturday afternoon, the 24th September, the Viceroy opened the Fourteenth Annual Exhibition of Industrial and Fine Arts at Simla. The Exhibition was held at Ravenswood, which was lent by the Raja of Faridkot for the purpose. His Excellency, accompanied by the Marchioness of Ripon, Mr. H. W. Primrose, Colonel White, and other members of his Staff, arrived at Ravenswood at 4. P.M., and was received by Sir Robert Egerton, the Vice-President, and the Committee, Sir Robert Egerton made the usual annual

Opening the Industrial and Fine Arts Exhibition at Simla.

statement of the affairs of the Society, and concluded by acknowledging the services of the Committee and of the Ladies and gentlemen who had assisted in arranging the pictures, and by asking the Viceroy to declare the Exhibition open. His Excellency then spoke as follows:—]

Sir Robert Egerton, Ladies and Gentlemen,—Before I proceed to comply with the request which has been made to me by the Lieutenant Governor, to declare this Exhibition open, I am anxious, in accordance with the usual custom, to address a few words to you in connection with the Exhibition on behalf of which we are assembled here to-day; and I must say that I am particularly glad that my honourable friend the Lieutenant Governor has entered so fully into an account of the progress of this Exhibition, and of the pictures and works of art which are here displayed; because, ladies and gentlemen, it would be impossible for me to address you at any length to-day, as, unfortunately, I am suffering from that very uninteresting malady, a very bad cold, which, as you are aware, does not tend to promote either power of voice or flow of ideas; and therefore I hope you will excuse me if I do not enter at any great length into the many interesting topics suggested by an occasion like this. I am the less sorry that this should be the case, because I took the opportunity last year to submit to the Simla Society my views generally on the subject of art in India, and I should probably find it extremely difficult now to avoid going over again the ground which I then traversed, unless, in the words of a distinguished statesman of the last generation, I was to proceed to turn my back upon myself.

I congratulate you heartily, ladies and gentlemen, upon the progress which this Exhibition—or, I should say, which these Exhibitions have made—both the Exhibition connected with Fine Art and that connected with Industrial Art—during the past year.

It seems that in all respects the present collection, both of paintings and of works of Industrial art, is more

Opening the Industrial and Fine Arts Exhibition at Simla.

numerous; and I think we shall all agree that, at all events, it is fully equal in talent and interest to that which we saw last year at Kennedy House. It is true that my honourable friend the Lieutenant Governor has pointed to one feature of this Exhibition which seems to cause him some little pain, for he has informed us that there is a smaller proportion of unmarried ladies contributing to the Exhibition on this occasion than was the case last year. It would not become me, ladies and gentlemen, to compare the artistic talents of married and unmarried ladies; but I must say that, as a member of society and holding a public situation, I very much rejoice to hear that the number of unmarried ladies has decreased (*laughter*), and that those charming persons who were not provided with husbands last year have most wisely procured for themselves that necessary appendage during the twelve months that have elapsed since then. (*Applause and laughter.*)

Sir Robert Egerton,—You have reminded us that there are necessarily absent from these walls the works of several of those whose names figurred in the catalogue of last year; and, although you have mentioned in terms of deserved praise the name of one whose pictures are not here on this occasion, I must be permitted, even at the risk of repeating what you have said so well, to express the deep regret with which I recall to mind that we have not upon these walls to-day any work from Major Pierson. He was a gallant and scientific soldier; he was a distinguished artist and a most attractive friend; he fell as much in the service of his country when he died from the effects of a trying illness as if he had been slain by the bullet of a determined foe; and I am quite sure you will all share the feelings which I entertain for the great loss of one whom I shall always recollect with sincere respect and regard. (*Hear hear.*)

I look upon it, ladies and gentlemen, as a very fortunate feature of this Exhibition—and I believe that it is a feature

Opening the Industrial and Fine Arts Exhibition at Simla.

which distinguishes the Exhibition of this year more than the previous ones—that it has met in various ways with a considerable amount of support from the native chiefs and gentlemen of India; and I was particularly glad to hear from Sir Robert Egerton that the Society had received a contribution from His Highness the Gaekwar of Baroda. I trust we may see in that, proof of the interest which His Highness takes in art and in the cultivation of intellect as connected with art, and also of the sentiments by which he will be guided when, very shortly, he will take over the administration of his State; and that he is determined to devote himself to the higher branches of knowledge and to the cultivation of those abilities which, I am happy to believe, he possesses in a large degree. (*Hear, hear.*)

We are also greatly indebted to the Raja of Faridkot for the use of this house on this occasion. It is one of the great drawbacks under which the Simla Fine Arts Society labours, that it should have been—now for a long time, I believe—necessarily a migratory bird. Birds, indeed, are accustomed to build new nests every year; but it is rather hard for a Society of this description that it should have to go about in the spring of the year searching for some place where it may settle itself, at the risk of not being able to find such a situation, and with almost the certainty that the building it does find is not altogether suited for the purposes of an Exhibition of this kind. We are deeply indebted as I have said, to the Raja of Faridkot for the use of this commodious mansion; but nevertheless it must be obvious to all that the whole of it is not altogether suited for the purposes of an Exhibition. You see how greatly crowded the walls are with the works of art sent in, and you will observe that it has been necessary to resort to dark corners to provide places for pictures, where I fear they cannot be favourably seen: and that unfortunate circumstance makes it necessary that the Society should appeal to the

Opening the Industrial and Fine Arts Exhibition at Simla.

considerate indulgence of contributors to this exhibition if any of them should not find their works in the positions which they think they ought to occupy. It is, of course, impossible in a building of this kind—or, indeed, in any building—to give a good light or a good situation to all the pictures that may be exhibited; and I am quite certain that, should any of the contributors think that their works are not in so fovourable a position as they might be, they will not attribute it to ingratitude on the part of the Committee, or to want of appreciation on the part of the Simla public, but to the unfortunate position in which the Society is placed by being obliged to seek for a new place to hold its exhibition every year—a position from which I trust before long that the Society may be relieved. (*Hear, hear, and applause.*)

Ladies and Gentlemen,— I will not trouble you by any lengthened reference to the various pictures which adorn these walls: the Lieutenant Governor has mentioned those to which prizes have been awarded, and it would not become me, who have no right to put myself forward as an art critic, to pass any judgment upon those works. I can only say that I rejoice to find that my prize has gone to a work so beautiful as that by Major Strahan, to which it has been most deservedly awarded; and it is also to me a source of great pleasure that the next prize upon the list (that presented by His Honor the Lieutenant Governor) should have fallen to the son of one to whom India owes so much—of one who is so distinguished an ornament of the Indian service as Sir Richard Temple (*hear, hear*); and I only trust—indeed, I may say I have every reason to believe—that Mr. Temple, in his future career, will be no less distinguished in the service of his country than he is as an artist. (*Hear, hear.*)

I observe that the Commander-in-Chief's prize has fallen to Dr. Willcocks. This proves to me that, besides his great artistic merit, Dr. Willcocks is a discriminating man, because last year my prize went to Dr. Willcocks (*laughter*),

Opening the Industrial and Fine Arts Exhibition at Simla.

and it is obvious from his having taken the Commander-in-Chief's prize this year, that he desires to stand well with both the Civil and Military Authorities of this country. *(Hear, hear, and laughter.)* I am also glad to observe that the principal native prize has gone again to Mr. Pestonjee Bomanjee—not that I desire that any one artist should monopolise the prizes from year to year, but that, having been much struck with Mr. Bomanjee's talents as an artist last year, and having had the good fortune to possess myself of the picture which secured for him the prize on that occasion, I am very glad to observe that he still holds the place which he occupied twelve months ago. *(Hear, hear.)*

I would also draw your attention to some other productions by a native artist,—namely, the four drawings which hang on either side of this room, by a student, I believe, of the Calcutta School of Art, which strike me as affording a great and interesting proof of the progress Art is making among the natives of this country, and of which also, I am glad to say, I have become the happy possessor. *(Hear, hear.)*

And now, ladies and gentlemen, I must say a few words with respect to the other branch of this exhibition,—that which is connected with the industrial art of the country, and which has been brought together and arranged with so much zeal, skill, and industry by Captain Cole, to whose exertions we are so deeply indebted. *(Applause.)* I made some observations last year upon the subject of industrial art in this country, and upon the importance of upholding native art and of endeavouring to revive native models. I will not repeat those observations now. I hold entirely to the views I then expressed, and I am glad to see proof in this Exhibition that the lines which I ventured to suggest were the true ones for industrial art in this country have been followed succesfully to a great extent in the various branches of that art which have been collected together on this occasion. But I am anxious just to remark

Opening the Industrial and Fine Arts Exhibition at Simla

that a Society, the object of which is to bring together a collection of native industrial art from year to year, has not only an important use in developing good taste in the workmen who produce the works exhibited here and on other similar occasions; but also that it has a very useful work to do in cultivating the taste of the purchasers of works of art of that description. (*Applause.*) It is, of course, absolutely necesary in regard to industrial art, if you wish that art to be good and truly artistic, and based upon sound principles, that you should not only have good inclinations and good training in the workmen or persons who construct the works of art, but that they should be encouraged by good taste on the part of the public. Industrial art is art which is meant to be sold; and persons who live by their arts (as workmen and persons engaged in any branch of industry necessarily do) cannot afford to give good things to the public—I mean things really good in themselves—true developments of the national and native art of the country—unless they can find a body of intelligent and educated persons ready to buy works of art of that description. Therefore I regard it as a very important feature of an Industrial Exhibition such as this, that it may do a great deal to educate the taste of the public, so that that taste being developed by the contemplation of so many beautiful and suitable things, the demand for those things may produce an adequate supply. (*Applause.*) I remember, ladies and gentlemen, that a good many years ago, if I mistake not, there was an Exhibition in London in connection with the Department of Science and Art, which, if I am not wrong, was called by a curious title, you will think, —' An exhibition of false principles '—that is to say, it was an exhibition of all the most fearful examples (*laughter*) that could be got together, of the ugliest things that could be found, and in the worst taste; and these objects were exhibited to the public, that the public might see how ugly they were, and get utterly sick of them, so that their ideas and

Address from the Delhi Municipality.

taste might be reformed, and their attention directed to the purchase of what was interesting and beautiful in art.

That experiment could only have been carried out by a great public department and under the shadow of a Government; but nevertheless, a young Society like this—though perhaps it can scarcely venture to offend the public by showing some of their favourite specimens in a collection of false principles—may do something in this direction by exhibiting, not indeed these fearful examples, but good examples of what is really true work, and specimens of the real national art of the country, as it can be produced in these modern days *(applause)*, so that the purchasing public may turn their attention, not to buying bad and vulgar imitations of European articles, but to the purchase of real specimens of a renewed national and native art. *(Applause.)*

Ladies and Gentlemen,—I do not think I need detain you any longer on this occasion. I cannot, however, sit down without once more congratulating the members of this Society, and the inhabitants of Simla also, upon the progress which both these Exhibitions have made during the past year, upon the good work they are doing, and without making an earnest appeal to all here present to afford to this Society that support, countenance, and encouragement which seem to me to be so justly its due. *(Applause.)* I now declare this Exhibition open, and I wish it every success. *(Continued applause.)*

ADDRESS FROM THE DELHI MUNICIPALITY.

5th Nov. 1881. [On Tuesday, the 1st of November, their Excellencies the Viceroy and Lady Ripon left Simla for a tour in Rajpootana, visiting Delhi and Agra *en route.* The party accompanying their Excellencies consisted of the Hon. C. Grant, C.S.I., Officiating Secretary to

Address from the Delhi Municipality.

Government in the Foreign Department ; Colonel G. T. Chesney Secretary to Government, Military Department ; H. W. Primrose. Esq., Private Secretary ; Captain the Lord William Beresford, V. C., Officiating Military Secretary ; the Rev. H. S. Kerr ; Surgeon-Major, J. Anderson, C. I. E ; Captains E. L. Brett, C. W. Muir, A. W. Perry and A. Durand, Aides-de-Camp. Mr. H. M. Durand, C. S. I., Under Secretary, Foreign Department, joined the Viceroy's Camp at Agra. Their Excellencies arrived at Delhi on the morning of the 3rd, and remained for four days, visiting the various objects of interest in the city and neighbourhood. The Viceroy held a levée on the evening of the 3rd, at Ludlow Castle (where their Excellencies resided during their stay) and on Saturday night, the 5th, an address of welcome was presented by the members of the Delhi Municipality at a crowded assembly in the Durbar Hall of the Queen's Institute, which was illuminated and decorated for the occasion. The address was read by Lieutenant-Colonel Young, the president of the Municipal Committee ; the subject of it will be apparent from His Excellency's reply, which was as follows :—]

Lieutenant Colonel Young, and Gentlemen of the Municipal Commitee,—I beg to thank you very sincerely for the address which you have been good enough to present to me, and which is in itself a very interesting proof, from the illuminations which adorn it, of the state of art in this ancient city of Delhi, and which is contained in a box itself also a mark of the progress of those arts amongst you. I thank you very heartily for the cordial welcome which you have given me to this city ; and I rejoice extremely to observe the expressions of devotion and loyalty to our gracious Sovereign the Queen-Empress, contained in your address. I accept those expressions in the firm confidence that they truly represent the sentiments of your hearts ; and I can assure you that Her Majesty very highly appreciates such expressions when they are laid at the foot of her throne by her Indian subjects ; because, gentlemen, as I have no doubt you are well aware, our gracious Sovereign feels the deepest interest in all that concerns the prosperity and happiness of the Indian people. She is always anxious to hear of the well-being of the Princes, of the Chiefs, and of the people of

Address from the Delhi Municipality.

India. She knows all these Chiefs and Princes by name; she is intimately acquainted with the character of different parts of your country; with the history of your famous cities; and it is to Her Majesty, I know well, a source of deep satisfaction that you are truly animated by such sentiments as I find in this address.

Gentlemen,—I quite agree with you in feeling the great importance to India of the progress and extension of public works. I am happy to think that much has been done in that direction now for many years; but I feel also that much remains to be accomplished, and that there are few subjects to which the Government of India can direct its attention, of greater importance than the advancement and the extension of public works. But, gentlemen, as you are aware, there are limits to the powers of the Government of India in that respect—strict limits, of a financial nature, conected with our financial interests. We are bound to recollect that we must preserve the credit of India and must take care cautiously to limit her indebtedness; and we have therefore turned our attention to inquire whether we might not be able to call in the aid of others in this great undertaking of public works, and whether the time has not come when, in India, we might hope to apply to this great object the resources of that private enterprise which has worked such marvels in England. The present moment is one in which, as it appears to me, such an appeal to private enterprise may be most appropriately and most hopefully made; and I can assure you that, in the declarations which have emanted lately from the Government of India upon that subject, we have been animated by the most sincere and honest desire to afford to private enterprise every possible opportunity of aiding the Government and the people of this country in the spread of public works of a remunerative and advantageous character. I see no reason gentlemen, why capitalists should not be found ready to come forward to invest their money in undertakings for the development of

Address from the Delhi Municipality.

the magnificent resources which are to be found within the bounds of Her Majesty's dominions. I cannot help thinking that if gentlemen possessed of capital, both at home and in this country, only made themselves better acquainted with the resources and opportunities of India, they would find that they might safely invest their money in undertakings which would develope its resources and aid its wealth and prosperity. But, gentlemen, while we have made our appeal to capitalists in England, we are also especially desirous to encourage to the utmost of our power the application of local capital to works of this description; and it will be an especial object with us, in any concessions which we may hereafter make, to see that the fairest and fullest opportunity is given to local capital to come forward and aid in undertakings of this description; and I trust that while the Government, on the one hand, within the limits which financial necessities impose, steadily does its work for the development of these undertakings of public utility, we shall by an honest and frank appeal to public aid, find ourselves assisted, on the other hand, by the energy of private enterprise. And, gentlemen, it is not only because we desire to supplement the resources in the possession of the Government that we make this appeal to private enterprise; it is also because we believe that there are many works of this kind which can be much better and more effectually undertaken by private enterprise than by the Government. The task of the Government of India is an immense and most difficult task: we have to do many things in this country, which, in England, are done by the people themselves. The task of administration here is one to tax the faculties and the energies of the ablest public servants; and for my part I believe that it is a very great advantage to limit that task as much as may be possible, and to leave to others—to private individuals, and to the people themselves—as much of the work of developing and advancing their own prosperity as the circumstances of the country admit.

P

Address from the Delhi Municipality.

Gentlemen,—You have alluded to that happy restoration of peace which has terminated a war which lately taxed the resources and energies of this country. I rejoice to think that in the war British and Native troops fought side by side with equal gallantry, and won for themselves equal distinction. I am as proud as any man of the triumphs which attended the famous engagements by which that war will ever be remembered, and of the steadiness, patience, and endurance with which its trials were borne; but for myself, I rejoice indeed at the return of peace, and I am sure you will agree with me that the first necessary of India is the maintenance of peace; and while I should never hesitate for one moment to sacrifice even that great blessing to maintain the honour of the country or the welfare and the true interests of the people, it will be, so long as I am called to rule in this country, my constant endeavour to promote to the utmost the maintenance of peaceful relations, both within and without the boundaries of the Queen's dominions. And, gentlemen, that fortunate restoration of peace both enables the Government of India, and makes it their first duty, to turn their attention to the consideration of measures calculated to improve the internal condition of the country and develope its resources. You have alluded in your address to one or two steps which have recently been taken by the Government with that object; and you have spoken of our desire to encourage native industries. Yes, gentlemen, we *do* desire to avail ourselves of the assistance of native industry, to the utmost possible extent wherever articles can be produced in this country of which the Government stand in need, at a rate which would financially justify us in procuring them here in preference to elsewhere. It is a part of our policy that we should by that means endeavour to encourage industry and develope it to the utmost of our power; and although I am not one who believes that it is in the power of any Government to do very much in the direction of encouraging industry—though I believe that it is the people themselves who ought to be

Address from the Delhi Municipality.

relied upon for that purpose—nevertheless we shall avail ourselves of all the resources which are at the command of the Government of India (and doubtless there are many) for the purpose of aiding in that great work of industrial advance, which I trust has already commenced in this conntry, and for which I venture to prophesy a great future extension.

Then, gentlemen, you have alluded to a recent Resolution of the Government, intended to promote sound and reasonable decentralization, to develope local self-government in this country. Now that is a subject in which I feel the very deepest interest. I trust that the Resolution which we have recently issued may be the commencement of a steady advance in the direction of the development of self-government in India; and I am glad to take this opportunity of expressing my acknowledgments to my honourable colleague, Major Baring, and to Mr. Hope, the Secretary of the Financial Department of the Government of India, for the zeal, earnestness, and ability with which they have laboured to prepare that Resolution, and with which they are devoting themselves to the work of practically carrying it out. Gentlemen, I am very well aware that such a work as that of developing self-government in a country like this must necessarily be a gradual work; that it must be carried out in one way in one part of this great peninsula, and in another way in another—that one portion of the country may be more fit for the wide application of the principles of self-government than another; but the object of that Resolution was to call public and official attention to the great importance of the principle itself, and to mark emphatically the desire of the Government that every effort should be made to afford it all that development and extension which the special circumstances of each locality might render possible. I look upon the extension of self-government as the best means at the disposal of the Government of India at the present time of promoting and extending the political education of the people of this country. I have no doubt that there are in India,

Address from the Delhi Municipality.

just as there are in England, Municipal bodies that are not always wise; who are sometimes found to obstruct measures of importance, and possibly even seriously to neglect their duties. I very well recollect, a good many years ago, the late Lord Palmerston (who, as you know, was a great English Minister) telling the House of Commons, when he was advocating sanitary reform, that there was always in every town in England a clean party and a dirty party—a party that was in favour of a good water-supply and good drainage, and a party opposed to measures of that kind. I have not the least doubt that there is a clean party and a dirty party in the towns and cities of India, and I can quite understand that, to men zealous for improvement, it may often be trying to see important schemes, calculated to confer great benefit on a large community, postponed, or marred, or laid aside from ignorance, or apathy, or indifference. But I may venture to say to those who may be not unnaturally impatient at such untoward occurrences, that they should not let their impatience run away with them to the extent of allowing them to obstruct or abandon the principle of self-government. Patience is necessary in the beginning of all things; it is necessary in the conduct of all public affairs, especially where a more or less numerous body of men have been brought together; and I would ask those whose favourite schemes may be thwarted, or opposed, to remember that the establishment, development, and practical working of self-government is in itself a great benefit to the country; that it is not only an end to be pursued, but a great object of political education to be attained, and therefore that we may well put up with disappointment and annoyance rather than sweep away those institutions which are calculated in the end—as they become better understood, and as the people become more accustomed to work them—to confer large benefits upon the community in general. Gentlemen, I therefore desire, and my colleagues desire with me, to see the powers and independence of local bodies increased and

Address from the Delhi Municipality.

extended as opportunity may offer. We desire to see the principle of election extended where it may be possible, although we are well aware that we can only proceed gradually and tentatively in that direction. I have ventured to detain you on this topic, because it is one to which I personally attach very great importance, and because, if I should be able to feel at the close of my career in this country that I had done something to develope local government in India, I should esteem it a great honour and distinction.

Gentlemen,—There is one matter with which bodies, local or municipal, have to deal, and in which I personally also feel a very deep interest, and that is the question of primary education. A good deal has been done in this country, I rejoice to think, for higher and middle education, and I trust that all the results that have been attained will be maintained and extended. I am the last man in the world who would grudge the advance that has been made in that direction —an advance of which I most cordially and heartily approve ; but I think the time has come when we ought to look to the education of the general mass of the people. We cannot hope, among the vast millions of India, to do much in that direction except by the labour of years— I may say, of generations—but the time has come when public attention and the attention of Government, and of local bodies, like that which you represent here, should in my judgment be turned to the question of developing primary education, so far as financial and other circumstances may permit.

Gentlemen,—You have mentioned at the conclusion of your address the labours in which you have been now for a long time—pardon me for saying, for too long a time—engaged in connection with the water-supply and drainage of this city. Heartily do I wish that those labours may at length be crowned with success. I am convinced that a wholesome supply of water and good drainage in a city like this are among the greatest blessings you can confer on your

Address from the Agra Municipality.

fellow-citizens. I am rejoiced to hear that you are now taking measures which I hope may prove successful, and I trust that it will not be long before Delhi is as well supplied in this respect as are many of the principal cities of India.

Gentlemen,—You are kind enough to regret the shortness of my stay among you. I can assure you that I share sincerely that regret, for I have already seen enough of your city and its neighbourhood to appreciate very highly those treasures of art with which you are so richly provided. You have among the buildings of this city and its suburbs— you have in the Dewan-i-Khas, the Jama Musjid, the Moti Musjid, and the Kutub, from which I have just come, monuments that might be placed, without fear of comparison, by the most famous and proudest monuments of the world. I have seen them with the greatest gratification; I expected much, from what I had heard, but I have found that they surpass in beauty, in taste, in elegance of design, all that I had anticipated. They are a proof of what can be accomplished by the people of India, working upon their own national art. I have seen them with the deepest interest, and I trust that they may be not only monuments of the past, but models for the future; and, gentlemen, I can assure you that, while I have derived great pleasure from the inspection of those delightful works of art, and from witnessing scenes to which are attached historic memories so great and so famous, I have derived still more satisfaction from the friendly and cordial reception which you have been kind enough to accord to me. (*Applause.*)

ADDRESS FROM THE AGRA MUNICIPALITY.

10th Nov. 1881. [THEIR Excellencies left Delhi on the night of the 6th November and arrived early next morning at Agra. Here a week's stay was made in camp, during which the principal buildings and places of interest in Agra and its neighbourhood were visited. On the evening of the 9th the Viceroy held a Levée in camp, and on the following

Address from the Agra Municipality.

[evening His Excellency received a deputation from the Municipality, who presented an address of welcome. The address expressed gratification at His Excellency's visit so soon after the announcement by the Government of its intention still further to develope and extend the principles of local self-government, and at a time when agricultural prospects were so favourable ; and concluded by thanking the Viceroy for the generous aid which had been given towards the restoration of ancient monuments. His Excellency, in replying, spoke as follows :—]

Gentlemen,—I am very much obliged to you for the address which you have been good enough to present to me, and for the welcome which you have offered to me on my visit to this beautiful and interesting city ; and I can assure you that I have derived very great satisfaction from that visit, and from all the many interesting monuments of ancient times which I have been already able to examine.

In your address you have alluded to a recent Resolution put forth by the Government of India upon the subject of the extension of the principles of decentralization and the development of local self-government in this country. I had occasion, only a few day ago, to make some public remarks upon this subject in the city of Delhi; and in these days, when the newspapers report to us all that passes in the various cities and districts of India, I have no doubt that some of you, at all events, may have seen what I said upon that occasion, so that it is unnecessary for me to go over again, after so short an interval, the ground which I then traversed. But I cannot help expressing my satisfaction at the fact that in this city of Agra the principle of election has been so largely applied in the choice of the members of the Municipal Committee. I am perfectly aware that that principle is one which cannot be applied in all the towns and cities and districts of India, and that it must be extended gradually and cautiously. It may, perhaps, be to some extent an importation from the West, not altogether consonant with the habits of this country ; and I am the last man who would think it wise to proceed hastily with the adoption of a principle of that description in districts to which it may not

Address from the Agra Municipality.

be applicable; but at the same time, fully believing that it is a principle of the greatest value, and which I trust may ultimately be widely and universally extended in this country, I rejoice to meet gentlemen who have been themselves chosen by the election of their fellow-citizens, and who are a proof that—in some cities, at all events—that system can be established with advantage.

You have, gentlemen, expressed your congratulations to me upon the most gratifying circumstance that the present season has been one calculated to bring prosperity to those who are devoted to the cultivation of the soil in this part of the country. For that great blessing we must, all of us be deeply thankful to God. It depends upon no Government to regulate the seasons, and it is indeed a source of the deepest gratification to me that—as I have watched with interest and anxiety the progress of the weather during the past few months—I have been able to hope that, at all events as regards the present crop, the weather has been calculated to bring prosperity to the great mass of the people of this country, who live by agriculture. And, gentlemen, your allusion to that subject reminds me that there is no question which can engage the attention of the Government of India, of greater importance at the present time than that of the best means of providing against, and preventing the recurrence of those terrible famines by which various parts of this country have been visited from time to time, and of taking measures by which, if unfortunately so great an evil should again befal us, we might be able to meet it more readily and effectually than has been the case occasionally in the past. I can assure you, gentlemen, that that subject has already occupied the deep attention of the Government of India. Holding, as I do, and as I have just said, that it is one of the most urgent which can engage our attention, I have, from the first moment when I took up my present office, devoted myself to an endeavour to solve the many problems which it involves; and in order to enable

Address from the Agra Municipality.

the Government to deal more effectually with the question of famine and with the development of the agricultural resources of the country, we have determined, as you are aware, to re-establish, and have re-established, the Revenue and Agricultural Secretariat of the Government of India, believing that these questions required to be specially dealt with by a department of that Government devoted mainly to the consideration of their various branches. And, gentlemen, when we came to consider how we should deal with questions of this kind, where was it that we turned? To whom was it that we found that we could best go for instruction and guidance? Why, gentlemen, it was to my honourable friend, the Lieutenant Governor of the North-Western Provinces. You are aware that you have had the great advantage in these provinces of having had an Agricultural Department now for several years. The credit of initiating that department belongs not to Sir George Couper but to Sir John Strachey. But Sir George Couper has developed that department; he has devoted himself with characteristic zeal and energy to carrying out the scheme of his predecessor, and to advancing gradually and carefully the various measures which are calculated to render it most efficient; and therefore we had the great advantage, when we came to look at this question from a general point of view—from the point of view of the Supreme Government of India—of being able to avail ourselves of the experience gained for us by my honourable friend, and of turning to him for counsel and advice in this most important matter. And, gentlemen, it was to these provinces I turned when I wanted to find a Secretary for the new department; and I found in Mr. Buck who had served for many years under my honourable friend, a Secretary who combined the utmost zeal, energy, and devotion for the work, and who has entered on its duties with all the vigour and determination which may be expected from one to whom his labour is in truth a labour of love. I mention these things

Q

Address from the Agra Municipality.

because I feel that the Government of India in this respect owe a great debt to Sir George Couper and the authorities of the North-Western Provinces; and that it is only just that the credit due to them should be given to them on an occasion like this—the first public occasion on which I have had an opportunity of expressing my views upon this question. And I can assure you, gentlemen, that this subject of famine prevention is one which will continue to engage the utmost attention of the Government of India. Guided by the report of the Famine Commission, and adopting it in the main, though with some exceptions, we desire, upon the lines of that report (and particularly in the light of the practical experience which has been gained here), to establish throughout the country similar departments to those which have existed now for several years in the North-Western Provinces. I do not say that in every part of India exactly the same system can be followed. I am, as I have already said a friend of decentralization; I am therefore a friend of leaving a large latitude to Local Governments in respect to the details of the mode in which they will apply the principles which the Government of India desire to adopt; but those principles which have been practically tried here are, as it appears to me, sound principles; and it is in the direction which has been successful in these provinces that we desire to proceed. And gentlemen, as I have mentioned this subject, I would desire to say that—although there is much in certain directions which the Government may be able to do in this matter—Government is very far from being able to do all; and that it is a very great mistake to suppose that only Government is capable of doing for the people of any country that which they can better do for themselves: and therefore it is to native gentlemen, to the great proprietors of India, to those who have a large stake in agriculture, that the Government must look to aid them in this work, to take the lead and to set an example to those who are less wealthy, have less means and less intelligence. And it is upon men

Address from the Agra Municipality.

of that description that we rely, and from whom we think we have a right to seek aid in a matter in which their interests, as well as those if their poorer fellow-countrymen, are concerned; and I have not the least doubt that they will come forward and help us, more and more, in what I believe to be one of the most important works that can be undertaken for the benefit of the great masses of the people of the country.

Then, gentlemen, you have, in the conclusion of your address, noticed the efforts which are being made now, by the Government of India, with a view to preserve intact and uninjured those splendid and beautiful monuments and buildings by which especially this part of the country is adorned. I am very glad indeed, gentlemen, to learn from your address that you appreciate the efforts of the Government of India in that direction. If I had any doubt (which I had not) of the importance of those efforts, it would have faded away before the beautiful buildings which I have seen since I came to Agra. You have, gentlemen, in the Taj a building which may be said truly to be among the most beautiful structures of the world; and I fully share the opinion, which I believe was expressed by my great predecessor, Lord Dalhousie, who is said to have remarked that it was well worth while coming to India for the purpose of seeing the Taj alone. Well, the journey to India in Lord Dalhousie's days was a much more serious matter than it is now; but I entirely agree that any man who has the means and opportunity would do well to visit Agra, if only for the purpose of seeing that beautiful building. Gentlemen, it appears to me to be the duty of the Government of this country to use every means to preserve the ancient records of the history and of the arts of India. There have been Governments, as we learn from history, which, ruling over other races, have thought in their blindness that their interest lay in suppressing the language, and, if it were possible, in blotting out the history and throwing into the shade the arts of the country over which they ruled. That, gentlemen, is not the principle of the English Government of India. I, for my part, can truly say that while, as Governor-General of India, I feel proud of all the great achievements of her history and of the splendid monuments which adorn her country, I desire that that history and those monuments should be appreciated by the people of India, and that that national art and that national feeling, of which those monuments are the beautiful outcome, should be cherished and preserved. I have no jealousy of any such feelings. I believe that the more you are proud of your past history, and the more you study it the better you will be inclined to appreciate what is good in the Government of the present day; and I can assure you that, in doing something to preserve those ancient monuments, I believe that I am doing as much to benefit my own country as I am doing to benefit yours.

Gentlemen,—I have only one word more to say, and that is to express to you once more my thanks for the kind address which you have presented to me; and to tell you, as the representatives of the people of Agra, how much satisfaction I have derived from my visit to the city this afternoon, and from the friendly and cordial reception accorded to me by the people.

VISIT TO THE St. PETER'S COLLEGE AND ORPHANAGE, AGRA.

13th Nov. 1881. [ON Sunday evening, the 13th November, the Viceroy visited the St. Peter's College and Orphanage. His Excellency, on his arrival, was received by His Lordship the Catholic Bishop of Agra and the Very Reverend Father Symphorien, the Principal of the College, and was conducted to the Boys' School, where an ode, addressed to the Viceroy and Lady Ripon, was sung by the scholars; after which, an

Visit to the St. Peter's College and Orphanage, Agra.

address of welcome was present, to which His Excellency replied as follows:—]

I am requested to say a few words to you who are here present to-day, and especially to those who are the pupils of this institution. I had no expectation, when I came here, that I should be called upon to make any remarks upon this occasion, although I confess that a long experience of occasions of this description has taught me that it generally happens that some insidious but seductive gentleman, like Father Symphorien, say to one at the end of the ceremonies—"Won't you be good enough to say a few words?" (*Laughter.*) Well, now, I cannot refuse to obey that call, and if anything that I can say will be of advantage to those who are the students of this institution, I am very glad to have the opportunity of addressing a few words to them. And I need no preparation for this purpose, because I have, throughout the whole course of my public life, been deeply interested in that which is the principal object of this inistitution—the advancement of the education of the young; and I have been convinced by a long experience that there are few questions of more importance in the days in which we live, whether it be at home in England, in India, or in any other part of the world, than the question of education. Now, my young friends, I feel the very greatest interest in being able to visit this institution to-day, because there are connected with it memories which reach far back into the historic past of India; for, as you all know, this establishment connected with the Catholic Church dates from the reign of the great Mogul Emperor, Akbar, and is one of the most ancient European institutions in the whole of the Indian Peninsula.. Now let me suggest to you, my young friends, that the very fact that this is an ancient institution, founded here in the midst of the Mahomedan Empire long before the English race ruled in this part of India, ought to make you very proud of belonging to an institution of such antiquity, surrounded as it is by

Visit to the St. Peter's College and Orphanage, Agra.

such celebrated memories. And you who are brought up here in this College at Agra ought to remember that you have an especial call to maintain the reputation of the College, and to see that, having existed now for some hundreds of years, it does not fall back in its reputation or in its rank amongst other educational institutions in India through any neglect, on your part, of the advantages it affords. As I said before, I believe that the question of education is one of the most important public questions of the times in which we live ; and do let me entreat of you, the pupils of this institution, to avail yourselves earnestly and zealously of the advantages which it affords to you. It is very likely that you young boys, when you hear me say that, will say to yourselves, "Oh ! it is all very well for him to talk so ; he is an old fellow, with no further interest in play and amusement ; and it is all very well for him to preach to us and tell us that we ought to attend to our studies." Well I assure you that it is not because my limbs are a little stiff, and I am not as skillful at games as you are, that I give you that advice; but it is because a long observation of the world, in many parts of it, and in many quarters of the globe, has convinced me that in these times if you wish to live advantageous, honourable, and happy lives in the future—and I trust that God may grant to you all many years yet in the world—if you wish to make those years, which He in his mercy gives you, useful for your fellow-men, calculated to promote the glory of God, and advantageous to yourselves,—you must avail yourselves of the opportunities which you have now in this institution. Your faculties are now young and bright; you can learn things with comparative ease which later on in life you would learn with great difficulty ; and which perhaps you would not have the opportunity of learning at all, because you must make your way in the world ; and in these times you will not make your way in the world—you will not take that position which your intelligence and characters

Dinner at Jeypore Palace.

would entitle you to occupy—unless you cultivate that intelligence and develope those characters by attention to your studies here, and by availing yourselves to the utmost extent of the advantages which an institution of this kind affords. Therefore do let me entreat you—I do not wish to detain you longer now—but do let me entreat you earnestly, one and all, to put your shoulders to the wheel and cast aside the lassitude which may sometimes come over you in the trying climate of this country, and devote yourselves zealously to derive from this establishment the many and great benefits which it is calculated to confer upon you. And now, as I have obeyed Father Symphorien, I have asked him to obey me, and he has been kind enough to say he will; and the request I have made is that, as I have given you a preachment on the advantages of study, he should make amends to you for that infliction by allowing you a holiday.

[His Excellency then inspected the College and the Girls' School and Orphanage, where the children, all neatly and prettily dressed, were drawn up and sang a hymn of welcome. Two bouquets of artificial flowers were presented to His Excellency, and, as he passed down the line, a pretty child stepped forward and delivered a short and simple address of welcome in French. After leaving the schools, His Excellency and party proceeded to the Roman Catholic Cathedral near by, where a Benediction was pronounced.]

DINNER AT THE JEYPORE PALACE.

[THE Viceroy left Agra on the morning of the 16th, at 8 o'clock, for 17th Nov. 1881. Jeypore; breakfasting at Bhurtpore *en route* as the guest of the Mahárájáh. Her Excellency Lady Ripon followed by the ordinary mail in the evening. The Viceroy arrived at Jeypore at 5 o'clock, and was received at the station by the Mahárájáh, with whom were nine of his principal Sirdars; Colonel Bannerman, the Resident; and a large number of officials. The Viceregal Party were driven in the Mahárájáh's State carriages through the city, and thence to the Residency. The road along the line of route was lined by sowars and sepoys of the Deoli

Dinner at the Jeypore Palace.

Irregular Force, by the Raj soldiers, and by the mounted retainers of the various Thakurs and Chiefs of the States of Rajputana. The scene was most picturesque and impressive; the people thronged to witness the procession of carriages through the broad streets, which were gaily decorated with flags, bannerets, and triumphal arches. The city streets were lined by the Raj troops and large numbers of Nagas, many of whom performed a wild sword-dance in front of the procession. Sixty-two State elephants in trappings of gold and silver brought up the rear of the procession, which, entering by the Sanganir Gate, traversed the chief steeets and debouched by the Ajmere Gate. On the morning of the 19th, the Mahárájáh paid His Excellency a formal visit at the Residency. The Viceroy returned the visit in the afternoon, the Mahárájáh receiving His Excellency in the Durbar Hall of the Palace, where were assembled over 300 Sirdars and Chiefs—those of superior rank being presented to His Excellency by the Resident. A large number of officials and ladies were also present to view the ceremony. In the evening a dinner was given by the Mahárájáh in the Dewan-i-Khas (Hall for Nobles) in the Palace, at which the Viceroy and Lady Ripon were present. The Mahárájáh was also present and received the guests (about 60) on their arrival, but did not take his place at the table. At the conclusion of dinner, the Mahárájáh took a seat next to the Viceroy, when the health of the Queen-Empress was proposed by Colonel Walter, on behalf of His Highness. The toast having been honoured, Colonel Walter, on behalf of the Mahárájáh, proposed the health of their Excellencies the Viceroy and Lady Ripon. His Highness expressed the pleasure it gave him to receive their Excellencies in his capital; he hoped that they were pleased by what they had seen in Jeypore, that they would carry away pleasant reminiscences of the place, and that on a future occasion their Excellencies would revisit the city. The toast was drunk with all heartiness, and His Excellency replied to it as follows:—]

Ladies and Gentlemen,—I am most grateful to His Highness for having asked Colonel Walter to propose my health and that of Lady Ripon upon this occasion; and I am still more grateful to the Mahárájáh for the splendid hospitality with which he has been good enough to entertain us. I can assure you that I have derived—and I think I may say without hesitation, that Lady Ripon has also derived—the very greatest satisfaction and enjoyment from our visit to this beautiful city. I have seen, since I came to India,

Dinner at the Jeypore Palace.

many beautiful, many interesting and striking sights; but I can say most truly that nothing which I have witnessed has surpassed that which I have seen since I came to the city of Jeypore. I have been immensely struck by all that has come under my notice since my arrival here yesterday, and in no respect have I been more struck than by the spirit of noble and princely hospitality which has marked the reception given to us by His Highness. You, Colonel Walter, have been good enough to express, on His Highness's behalf, the hope that it may possibly be in our power to visit this city and State again. It is impossible for me to give any promise upon that subject now. All I can say is, that if it should be my good fortune during my stay in this country to be able to come once more to Jeypore, the reception which I have met with now will certainly make me desirous to do so. And now, ladies and gentlemen, before I sit down, I have to discharge the pleasant task of proposing to you a toast which I am sure all those who are assembled in this Hall to-night will drink with the utmost satisfaction; and that is the health of His Highness the Mahárájáh. (*Applause.*) We, his guests, owe him many thanks for the manner in which we have been entertained. But, ladies and gentlemen, I must be permitted to take another view of the toast which I am now proposing, and to express my earnest hope— as one charged with a great responsibility in connection with the government of this country—that His Highness may, through God's blessing, have a long, prosperous, and happy reign; that he may walk in the footsteps of that distinguished Prince whose successor he is; that he may confer upon the people of his State, benefits such as those which the late Mahárájáh conferred upon them; and that in the course of a reign which, as I have said, I trust may be prolonged, he will devote himself zealously and earnestly to promote to the utmost of his power the welfare of the numerous people entrusted to his care. (*Loud and prolonged applause.*)

DISTRIBUTION OF PRIZES AT THE MAHÁRÁJÁH'S COLLEGE, JEYPORE.

18th Nov. 1881. [ON Friday, the 18th November, Their Excellencies visited Amber the ancient capital of Jeypore, and in the afternoon Lady Ripon inspected the Girls' School, while the Viceroy distributed the Northbrook medals to the boys at the Mahárájáh's College.

In reply to an address presented to him by the Teachers of the College, His Excellency spoke as follows :—]

Gentlemen,—I beg to thank you most heartily for the address which you have just presented to me. I can assure you that I am much pleased to be able to visit this institution upon the present occasion. Since I came to this city of Jeypore, I have witnessed many interesting and striking sights, but I do not know that any thing I have seen (even amongst those remarkable sights which recall so many recollections of a long distant past) has filled me with greater gratification and interest than is afforded to me now by a visit to this institution, founded in the heart of a native State, for the promotion of the combined education of the East and of the West. Since I came yesterday to this city, I have received many proofs of the enlightened wisdom of the late Mahárájáh and his deep interest in the welfare of this city and of its inhabitants, and of those of the whole State of Jeypore; but I do not know that I have received any proof so convincing, of that wisdom and that enlightenment, as that which is afforded by the fact of his having established an institution of this description for the education of the people of his State. You are quite right, gentlemen, when you remark in the address which you have presented to me, that I feel a deep interest in the subject of education. I have done so now for many years of my life, and I have not forgotten that interest since I came to India, for I am convinced that there are few questions at the present time of greater importance to the welfare of this country than those questions which relate

Distribution of Prizes at the Mahárájáh's College, Jeypore.

to the progress and advancement of public education. And, gentlemen, holding those opinions, there can be no more gratifying circumstance to me than to find that the principles which I have so long advocated at home, and upon which it is my intention to act here, have been so well and so fully recognised in this native State. I can assure you that I feel the deepest interest in the welfare of the native States of India. I believe that their prosperity and advancement are of as great importance to the British Government in this country—to the Goverment of our gracious Sovereign the Queen-Empress—as they are to the inhabitants of those States themselves; and I desire their maintenance and their well-being as heartily almost as you can do. Therefore, gentlemen, it is to me a source of infinite pleasure that by the wisdom of your late ruler—the representative of one of the most ancient races of the world—a step has been taken so well calculated to advance the prosperity and the true progress of the State of Jeypore as that which he took when he founded the Mahárájáh's College in this city. Gentlemen, I have in the course of to-day had the advantage of reading the last report of this institution, and I have read that report with very great satisfaction. I have been extremely pleased to note the progress which this institution has made from year to year. I have been glad to observe the character of the studies which are pursued here, and the success which has been obtained by the students of this institution in the competitions into which they have entered. I have also been well satisfied to perceive that this College is, as I understand it, a centre of other educational institutions in the Jeypore State; and I must say that there was one feature in that report which gave me even more gratification, I think, than any other, and that was to find the steps which are being taken in the State of Jeypore in the direction of female education—the education of girls. Now, gentlemen, I am well aware of the many difficulties which beset that subject of female education in India; but I do not think that I

Distribution of Prizes at the Mahárájáh's College, Jeypore.

could have received a more convincing proof—a proof which I hail with the utmost satisfaction—that those difficulties can be, and in the course of time will be, overcome, than that given to me by the fact that here, in this native State, by the wisdom and the enlightened course freely pursued by a native prince, measures have been taken for the establishment of girls' schools, which are already doing, as it seems to me very valuable and important work. I rejoice also to learn the facts which have been brought before me in that report as to the progress of primary education in the mofussil districts of this State. That is a subject in which I take a very special and peculiar interest. I know well that it is impossible in this vast country to proceed very rapidly in that matter, or to hope to do after many years even a small portion of the work which ought ultimately to be accomplished; but here again I am much encouraged in the efforts which I hope to make in that direction, in the districts of India under the immediate administration of the British Government, by the example which has been afforded by the State of Jeypore. These things I look upon, gentlemen, as subjects upon which I may most heartily and unfeignedly congratulate you. I may congratulate you upon the past—upon this as upon the other great benefits which your late Mahárájáh conferred upon his people. I may congratulate you, I think, with every confidence upon the future, from the proof which the interest I know the present Mahárájáh feels in this and kindred institutions affords, that he will walk steadily and firmly in the steps of his distinguished predecessor; and that he will support, maintain, and extend the measures which that prince took for the prosperity of his country.

And now let me say one or two words to those who are students in this institution—and I am very glad that, through its means, its students are able to understand the words which I desire to address to them. I am very glad indeed that there is a regular English branch in this institution;

Distribution of Prizes at the Mahárájáh's College, Jeypore.

and that in another branch also English instruction is given. I am confident that that is a very great advantage, and I appreciate it especially as it enables me to speak to you in a language which you can understand; for I can truly say, gentlemen, that I would have given a great deal when I came to India if I had been able to speak the language of Hindoostan; but you at least can understand me in my own language, and I would therefore very briefly ask you, students here, not to neglect the great advantages which an institution of this kind affords. If you desire to make your way successfully in life—nay, my friends, if you desire not to fall back in life and find yourselves beaten in the race and falling ever into a lower and less advantageous position,— you will, if you are wise, avail yourselves to the utmost of the advantages which this College affords you. You may rely upon it that the young generation of India, who are now just rising, or have just risen, to manhood, will find that if they neglect their education and are without that instruction which an institution of this kind happily places within their reach, they will be beaten in every walk of life and passed by their competitors on every side. And gentlemen, students of this institution, I for one shall do my best, so far as concerns those parts of India which I directly administer, to beat you in that competition if you do not avail yourselves of the advantages here offered to you, for it is one of the objects of my Government to promote to the utmost of our power the spread of education in India. Well now, you owe it to your late Mahárájáh, you owe it to the famous race of Rajputs to which you belong, that you should not be beaten in that or any other contest; you owe it to this city and this institution that you should use to the utmost those advantages so freely brought within your reach. I am sure that you will do so if you only think of—only reflect upon —all the personal motives, and motives yet higher, the love of knowledge and the desire to understand all those great

134 *Speeches by His Excellency the Marquis of Ripon.*

Address from the Municipality of Ajmere.

facts of science and history which you may learn in an institution of this description. I am confident that you will not waste such rich opportunities as time goes on ; and that hereafter, when I have left India and gone back to my own country, I shall be able to watch the progress of the Mahárájáh's College at Jeypore, and find that it has gone forward steadily advancing in that noble career of progress which it has so well commenced. (*Loud cheers.*)

[Other public institutions were then visited, and the Viceregal party, having united, drove to the Futteh-Teebah, to witness a display of fireworks. The whole city was brilliantly illuminated in the evening.]

ADDRESS FROM THE MUNICIPALITY OF AJMERE.

19th Nov. 1881. [THE Viceroy, accompanied by Colonel Walter, Agent to the Governor General for Rajputana, and Colonel Bannerman, arrived at Ajmere at 4 P.M. on the 19th November ;—Lady Ripon followed in a special train later in the day. His Excellency was received at the Railway Station by Mr. Saunders, Commissioner, Brigadier General Carnegy, the Mahárájáh of Kishengurh, the Maharao Rajah of Ulwar, the Nawab of Tonk, the Rana of Jhallawar, the representative of the Maharao Rajah of Bundi, the Tazili Istumrardars of Ajmere, and all the local civil, political, and military officers. His Excellency drove to the Residency through the public park, the road being lined with soldiers, police, and native levies. Lord and Lady Lawrence joined the Viceregal party at the Residency. Here an address of welcome was presented by the Municipal Committee, in which they congratulated the Viceroy on the termination of the Afgan war, as allowing of attention being given to the internal administration of India ; thanked the Government of India for the loan in aid of local works of improvement, and hoped the advantages of the decentralization policy would shortly be extended to Ajmere. His Excellency, in replying, spoke as follows :—]

Gentlemen,—I am much obliged to you for the address which you have been good enough to present to me, and

Address from the Municipality of Ajmere.

I am especially gratified to observe the expressions of loyalty and devotion—of deep affection and profound loyalty—in your own words—which are contained in this address when speaking of our beloved and illustrious Sovereign, the Queen-Empress. It will be my agreeable duty to communicate that expression of your sentiments to Her Majesty, and I know that she will be greatly touched, because she cherishes deeply the affection and the loyalty of her Indian subjects.

You speak of the new Park which has been laid out in the neighbourhood of your city, and which is now approaching completion. I was very glad to find that my route to this house lay through a portion of that Park, and to observe how much it will conduce to the beauty of this neighbourhood and I trust to the enjoyment of the inhabitants of Ajmere. I can assure you, with reference to that paragraph of your address which alludes to the loan which has been made by the Government of India in order to confer upon the inhabitants of this district the great benefit of a plentiful supply of pure drinking-water, that it is the earnest desire of the Government to see the blessings of pure water and good drainage, and all sanitary improvements, extended as widely as possible to the cities and towns of India.

Gentlemen,—You have spoken of a recent Resolution of Government upon the subject of local self-government. I have had occasion to make various remarks upon that subject very recently, in reply to addresses from bodies similar to your own in other parts of the country, and as in these days the words which are spoken by a Governor General upon such occasions find their way by some mysterious process into the pages of the newspapers, I will not repeat what I have said before. You have especially spoken in this address of one portion of the recent Resolution of Government in which we express our desire that, so far as may be possible, the funds raised by municipal bodies should be devoted to objects over which those bodies can, with advantage to themselves and to the country, exercise a direct

Address from the Municipality of Ajmere.

control. We attach, gentlemen, great importance to that principle, first, because we believe it to be in itself a sound principle of taxation, and secondly, because we feel sure that by, as far as may be, devoting the funds raised by municipal taxation, to local purposes in which those who pay them have a direct interest, we shall best promote self-government, and we shall best secure that those who are charged with the representation of their fellow-citizens, as you are, will pay on earnest and intelligent attention to the various objects over which their control and administration is extended. I rejoice to find, from the remarks which you have made upon this occasion, that that principle is one which commends itself to your judgment.

And now, gentlemen, I do not know that I need detain you longer, except once more to thank you very heartily for the good wishes which you have expressed for me and for my wife. I can assure you that I feel those good wishes very deeply, and that it is my earnest desire that, when my administration of affairs in this country comes to an end, I may have the good fortune to carry away with me to my own country those good wishes which you are now so kind as to convey to me. But, gentlemen, I cannot conclude what I have to say to you to-day without adverting for one moment to another topic : for how would it be possible for an Englishman, speaking to the Natives of India, not to ask you to join with him in giving this the first and earliest welcome to one who is present in Ajmere to-day. We have with us now, gentlemen, the son of a great father ; the son of a man who gave all his energies—and they were wonderful—all his talents—and they were great—all that purity of character by which he was distinguished, to the service of India and of England. We have here to-day the son of Lord Lawrence, and I am sure that you, Europeans and Natives alike, will join with me in tendering to Lord Lawrence our hearty congratulations on his visit to this country. I know that he will find in India many objects of interest,

Distribution of Prizes at the Mayo College, Ajmere.

recalling to him the recollections of his youth; and I know that I speak the sentiments of all in India when I say that we honour him for the name he bears, and that that name, and the memory of John Lawrence will never fade from the recollections of the Europeans and Natives of this country. I esteem it a fortunate circumstance that I am the first Governor General of India to whose lot it has fallen to welcome Lord Lawrence to this country, because I set before myself, from the very first hour when I undertook the great task of the administration of India, the noble example of Lord Lawrence as that which I should endeavour to follow; and it will be the proudest object of my ambition to walk, so far as I am able, in his footsteps. (*Applause.*)

DISTRIBUTION OF PRIZES AT THE MAYO COLLEGE, AJMERE.

[THE Viceroy distributed the prizes to the students at the Mayo College, Ajmere, at half-past 12 on the 21st of November. The ceremony took place in one of the large class-rooms, which was crowded with European residents and visitors, and native gentlemen. His Excellency having taken his seat, Captain Loch, the Principal, read the annual statement, from which it appeared that there were now more students in attendance than on any previous date, more admissions during the past year than in any former one, and more competitors in the final examination. He urged the importance of impressing upon the parents the necessity of enforcing regular attendance.

His Excellency then addressed the assembly as follows :—]

21st Nov. 1881.

Mahárájáhs, Princes, Ladies and Gentlemen,—I can assure you that it affords me great pleasure to be able to be present upon this occasion and to discharge one of the duties—and a most agreeable duty it is—which falls to the lot of your President when he visits this college. I am very glad to be able to be present to-day, for more reasons than one: first, because of the great interest which I feel in

S

Distibution of Prizes at the Mayo College, Ajmere.

the success and welfare of this institution; and secondly, because there are some circumstances of rather an especial nature connected with the assembly of to-day. We have here on the present occasion not a few persons whose names are connected with the first design, with the foundation, and with the commencement of this college. We have present here to-day, in the first place, my friend Colonel Walter, by whom it may truly be said that the first idea of this institution was suggested; for you will find in his Report for the year 1868-69 the germ of that idea which was subsequently seized upon by my distinguished predecessor, Lord Mayo, with the instinct of a statesman, and from which this institution took its rise. And then we have to-day present amongst us, the first Principal of this College, Colonel St. John, and I am quite sure that all here present will join with me in welcoming him back to India, to which he has returned after having discharged with marked energy and ability the very important duties entrusted to him by the Government of India, in Afghanistan. (*Applause.*) And then, ladies and gentlemen, we have the distinction of having amongst us to-day, the first boy pupil whose name was entered on the rolls of this College, in the person of the Maharao Rájáh of Ulwar (*applause*), who has gone forth from your ranks to rule his state, and who already gives the fairest promise that he will do honour and justice to the training of this institution. (*Applause.*) But, gentlemen, when we thus recall those who are present here to-day how is it possible that we should not bear in mind one who is not here—one who, cut off by the hand of the assassin, was removed from the government of this country in the flower of his age, but not before he had had time to perform great services for India, and to win for himself the respect and attachment of the European and native population of the country. I believe I am right in saying that the late Lord Mayo was regarded with special feelings of respect and attachment by the Princes and Chiefs in

Distribution of Prizes at the Mayo College, Ajmere.

Rajputana ; and I am sure that, while we of England shall long lament a public man whom we so prematurely lost, you in India will not easily forget the name of one who had the interest of this country ever at heart. (*Applause.*) Now, ladies and gentlemen, when we turn from considerations connected with the past to the present state of this College, it is satisfactory indeed to find how much cause for congratulation it supplies. The report which has just been read by Captain Loch shows the steady progress which this institution has made during the six years of its existence ; and I rejoice to find that it is at the present moment in a condition which must afford so much gratification to all who are interested in its work. That condition is due very much to the zeal, ability, and tact of Captain Loch (*applause*), of whose government of this College I hear the highest praise from those who have the amplest means of judging of it. And I may also say with what great personal satisfaction I heard from Captain Loch the words which fell from him with respect to the present Head Master, Mr. Johnstone. (*Applause.*) When it became my duty, last summer, to select an officer to fill the post which Mr. Johnstone occupies, knowing well the importance of this institution, I felt the reponsibility of the choice, and I looked round to find a man who seemed to me, among possible candidates, the fittest person to select. I rejoice to find that your experience of Mr. Johnstone up to the present time has confirmed my judgment in selecting him. (*Applause.*) I cannot avoid expressing my entire concurrence in the remarks which fell from Captain Loch with respect to the great importance of regularity of attendance, and I trust that the parents of the boys in this College who may have heard these remarks, or to whom the knowledge of them may come, will lay them deeply to heart, for it cannot be disputed that the full advantage of an institution of this kind can only be obtained by the steady and assiduous attendance of the students throughout the course of the period of instruction. It is an error of the gravest kind to throw away the advantages of an institution like this by irregularity of attendance; it is fair neither to the institution nor, what is much more important, to the boys themselves; and I trust that those charged with the duty of looking after the students of this College will for the future be most careful, as far as circumstances will permit, to insist upon regularity of attendance. (*Applause.*) Now, ladies and gentlemen, I said a few minutes ago that I felt a very strong personal interest in the success and prosperity of this College, and I will tell you why I feel that interest. I am deeply impressed with the belief that it is of the greatest importance to India that the Native States of this country should be prosperous and well administered. I am firmly convinced that the maintenance of those Native States is of no less political importance to the Government of England than it is to the people of those States themselves (*applause*), and it will always be the aim of my policy, so long as I fill the office which I now occupy, to maintain the integrity and the dignity of the Native States of India (*applause*), and to promote to the utmost of my power their prosperity and wellbeing. (*Applause.*) But at the same time I am especially impressed with the deep responsibility which rests upon the Government of India in regard to the welfare of the people of those Native States. The British rule in this peninsula has established throughout the length and breadth of the land an uninterrupted and unbroken peace. It is one of the greatest claims which we can put forward to the attachment of the chiefs and inhabitants of India, that that peace is maintained by the power of the English name; but the very fact that we thus enforce tranquillity throws of itself the great responsibility upon the Government of India of seeing that the inhabitants of the Native States do not suffer from misgovernment, or from oppression (*applause*); and it is undoubtedly a task of no small difficulty and delicacy to reconcile that freedom from all harassing and needless interference which we desire to secure to the Native Princes

Distribution of Prizes at the Mayo College, Ajmere.

and Chiefs with that protection from injustice and wrong which we are bound to afford to the people who dwell in their territories. (*Applause.*) Now, it seems to me that there is no better mode of effecting this object and discharging these responsibilities than by encouraging the work that is done in an institution of this kind, and by promoting among the youth who are hereafter to become Princes and Nobles in the States of India, that education and that training which will best fit them to discharge the responsibilities of the important positions which they will ultimately fill; and it seems to me that this College is admirably fitted for the performance of that important work. (*Applause.*) For, as Captain Loch has explained, it is the object of this College to afford at one and the same time the means of sound education and intellectual development, and to give also to the students a manly training. (*Applause.*) Now, we do not wish to turn those who are educated here into mere imitations of Englishmen; that would be a very foolish desire, and calculated not to benefit, but to injure, the future prospects of the students. Nothing can be further from our wish than to weaken their connection with their families, or their attachment to their country, or their respect for its traditions. What we desire is, as far as possible, to combine what is best in the education which we give to our own English boys with an entire respect for the customs and feelings of the people of this country. We set before us as the end and aim of our efforts here, so to train the students that they may be enabled hereafter, efficiently and successfully, to discharge the important duties which, in all human probability, will fall to their lot. In short our object is to give you all that we possess in the learning and the civilization of the West, while at the same time we wish you to retain all that is good in your own traditions and customs (*applause*), and therefore it is our most earnest desire, and my strongest hope, that the students will do their best to profit by the advantages which it affords to them.

Distribution of Prizes at the Mayo College, Ajmere.

You, my young friends, can do more for yourselves than we can do for you. Your future must be—do what we may—very much in your own hands. If you learn here to value knowledge and to seek it, to lead manly and honourable lives, to despise all that is low and sensual and unworthy, you will earn for yourselves the respect of the Government of India and the love of your own people. Many of you here will no doubt be called to fill great positions, full of temptations and of responsibilities, and will have depending upon you many thousands—indeed, as in the case of some of the great States of Rajputana, some millions of your fellow-countrymen looking to you for their happiness, their well-being, and in good truth for their lives. *(Applause.)* You, my friends, come of an ancient and noble race, whose origin is hid in the mists of time; and you are born to fill the great position of Princes and of Nobles. There is a French proverb which has come down to us from old days, and which tells us *noblesse oblige*—that is to say, that he who claims to be of noble birth must prove that he is so by noble deeds. Let that proverb be your motto. You know that we Englishmen are all proud to call ourselves gentlemen, and that we prize that simple name more than any high-sounding titles. Now, what is the meaning of the word "gentleman"? It means a man of courteous, gentle and refined manners, such as are possessed in an eminent degree by many of the Native Princes and Chiefs of India; but it means something more—something higher and better than that. It means a man whose courtesy and gentleness and refinement are not a mere matter of outward grace only, but rather a matter of the heart also—a man who is honourable and truthful, and manly and just; who lives not for his own selfish enjoyment, but to do his duty faithfully to God and to those who are dependent upon him—whose aims are high and who scorns an ignoble life. Be then, my young friends, true Rajput gentlemen. On you and on your conduct depends in a very large measure the future of your country. When I look upon the bright faces before me, I have great hope of that future, and, as one who has your welfare and the interest of India deeply at heart, I earnestly pray you not to mar that fair promise by neglecting the opportunities which you here enjoy of fitting yourselves for the high and responsible positions which in all probability most of you will be called upon hereafter to fill. (*Applause.*)

[His Excellency then distributed the prizes to the students, and in conclusion requested the principal to grant the boys a holiday,—a request which was readily complied with. The Viceroy then visited the various houses in the grounds, each State having a separate building devoted to the boys sent up by the Chief and his subjects ; and was afterwards present at a luncheon in the Mayo Hall, given by the Chief Commissioner, to which a large number of guests had been invited.]

DINNER AT CHITTORE.

[HIS Excellency the Viceroy, accompanied by his personal Staff, 23rd Nov. 1881. Mr. Saunders, the Commissioner of Ajmere, Lord and Lady Lawrence, and others, arrived at Chittore by special train shortly after 4 o'clock on the afternoon of the 22nd November. The occasion of His Excellency's visit to Chittore was the holding of a Chapter of the Star of India, at which His Highness the Maharana of Oodeypore (or Meywar) was to be formally invested with the insignia of a Knight Grand Commander of that order. The reception in state of His Excellency by the Maharana, and his Sirdars and the principal officials in camp, was conducted with all the pomp and ceremony befitting the occasion, and was very impressive. At noon on the 23rd November, the ceremony of investing the Maharana was performed by His Excellency in a temporary pavilion erected in the camp, before a large assembly of ladies and gentlemen and feudatory Chiefs. Her Excellency Lady Ripon was present, having arrived at Chittore in the morning.

On the evening of the same day, the Maharana entertained the Viceroy and all the guests in camp at dinner. At the conclusion of dinner, Colonel Walter rose and read the following address :—

"*Ladies and Gentlemen,*—On behalf of His Highness the Maharana, I beg to propose the health of His Excellency the Viceroy and

Dinner at Chittore.

Marquis of Ripon, and in doing so I will use His Highness's own words; they are as follows :—' I wish sincerely to express the great pleasure I have experienced in meeting Your Excellency to-day, along with my Sirdars, in this time-honoured city of Chittore, which is considered by one and all of us so famous and so very dear, for the defence and possession of which so many of my ancestors have in years gone by sacrificed their precious lives. In commemoration of this, the Sesodia Chieftains of Meywar have all since borne the title of "Chittoda." (*Cheers.*) Our meeting to-day is the outflow of the mutual feelings of regard which have existed between the British Government and the Meywar State ever since the year 1818—(*cheers*)— and in proof that this kindly feeling still exists, Your Excellency has invested me, on behalf of Her Majesty the Queen-Empress of India, with the honourable insignia of the Star of India, of which Most Exalted Order Her Majesty has been graciously pleased to appoint me Knight Grand Commander—(*cheers*)—a title which will tend to increase and make enduring our mutual bonds of union. (*Loud cheers.*) I receive this honour with the greatest pleasure, and beg most heartily to thank Her Imperial Majesty and Your Excellency, being fully confident that this distinction will conduce to the welfare and prosperity of my State and people. (*Cheers.*) I have been looking forward with great pleasure to an opportunity of meeting Your Excellency ever since I heard of your invariable kindness and other many excellent qualities, and rejoice that my wish has now been gratified. (*Cheers.*) May Her Majesty the Queen-Empress have a long, happy, and prosperous reign; and may Your Excellency's management of Indian State affairs be as beneficial to the people as creditable to yourself, and thereby leave in the hearts and minds of the people of India a lasting memorial of Your Excellency's Viceroyalty.'"

Loud and continued cheers greeted the conclusion of the Maharana's speech. His Excellency the Viceroy, in responding, said :—]

Ladies and Gentlemen,—I assure you that I am deeply grateful for the toast which has just been proposed on behalf of the Maharana of Oodeypore; and I am greatly touched by the language of His Highness himself, in which that toast has been offered. (*Cheers.*) I am sure, ladies and gentlemen, that there is no one present on this occasion who will not have rejoiced at the terms in which the speech read on behalf of His Highness was couched, and who will not have felt proud, as an Englishman, that such

Dinner at Chittore.

words should have proceeded from one of the Native Princes of India. It has been to me a source of great gratification to be able to be present upon this occasion, and I particularly rejoice that the first time that I have been called upon, by the command of our gracious Sovereign, to confer upon any native Prince in this country, with the full and complete ceremonial which attatches to that duty, the distinction of a Knight Grand Commander of the Star of India, should have been the occasion upon which that distinction was conferred upon His Highness the Maharana of the State of Meywar. (*Cheers.*) I rejoice that that should be the case, because His Highness is the foremost representative of the ancient and noble race of Rajputs—(*loud cheers*) —one of the most famous races in the history of Hindustan —(*continued cheers*)—and I rejoice yet more because His Highness is distinguished not only by those noble manners and that gracious bearing which we should expect in one of his illustrious birth, but by the wisdom and by the moderation with which he rules the people entrusted to his care— (*cheers*)—and therefore it seems to me that it was peculiarly appropriate that such a prince should be the first upon whom I should be called during my Viceroyalty to confer this distinction in the name of our Sovereign. There appears to me also to be a peculiar suitability in the locality in which this ceremonial has taken place. Ladies and gentlemen, His Highness has reminded us in touching terms of the memories with which Chittore is rife. Those memories recall deeds of gallantry which with difficulty can be paralleled in other history—deeds of gallantry which marked not men only, but the ladies of his illustrious house. (*Loud cheers.*) There are gathered round the summit of that famous rock, the memories of the chivalry of Rajahstan; there are to be found there, as I saw to-day, those touching memorials, those simple stones so humbly adorned, but adorned with the pious hands of the Rajputs of the present time—(*cheers*)—those stones

Dinner at Chittore.

which recall to us the recollection of the men who, when they knew that they had lost all but the honour of their country, died to make that honour secure. (*Loud cheers.*) Well, then, ladies and gentlemen, surely we may all of us congratulate ourselves that we have been present upon an occasion so full of interest upon every ground, and it was to me a very pleasant task to be charged with the duty of placing round the neck of this distinguished prince the very same insignia which are worn from time to time by our gracious Sovereign herself—(*loud cheers*)—the very same insignia which are borne as a proud distinction by the members of the Royal Family of England; and I rejoice, indeed, to find how very correctly and justly His Highness has interpreted the true meaning of the decoration of the Star of India. (*Cheers.*) It might perhaps have been thought by some that the descendant of a race so ancient would have regarded the Order of the Star of India as a recent creation, but His Highness has judged more justly. He has seen that, modern though it may be, that order was established to mark the closer tie which now binds our gracious Sovereign to her Indian dominions—(*loud cheers*)—and to bear unfaltering witness to the affectionate regard on the one side, and the loyal attachment on the other, which unites—and which I trust will ever more and more firmly unite—the Crown of England and Princes and Chiefs of India. (*Loud and continued cheers.*)

Ladies and Gentlemen,—I need say no more. I have to ask you to drink a toast which I know you will drink with the utmost enthusiasm. I have to ask you to show your gratitude for the princely hospitality with which we have been entertained—(*cheers*)—and to wish to our illustrious host that long life and that unchanging prosperity which he so richly deserves.

[The toast was drunk enthusiastically, followed by three cheers for the Maharana" and one cheer more."]

ADDRESS FROM THE BENARES MUNICIPALITY.

[THE Viceroy arrived at Benares on the morning of the 28th November. Her Excellency Lady Ripon was detained by illness at Ajmere. His Excellency took the opportunity, during his three days' stay, of visiting the principal public institutions and places of interest in and around Benares. On the afternoon of the 29th, the Viceroy visited the Town Hall, where the Municipal Committee were assembled to welcome him, and where an interesting collection of the arts and manufactures of Benares was laid out for his inspection. On His Excellency's arrival, he was conducted to a seat, when Mr. Hercules Ross, the Chairman of the Municipality, addressed His Excellency in a short informal speech, in which he expressed the gratification of the Municipality at His Lordship's visit; referred to his interest in municipal institutions and their advantage to the country and concluded by hoping that His Excellency would be induced on a future occasion to re-visit Benares. Lord Ripon, in reply, spoke as follows :—] *29th Nov. 1881.*

Gentlemen,—I am very glad indeed to meet you upon this occasion, and I thank you very much for the kind welcome which you have just accorded to me. Mr. Ross, in the remarks which he has made, has so accurately expressed my sentiments with respect to municipal institutions in India, that it is needless that I should detain you by dilating upon that topic. I can only assure you that it is always a satisfaction to me to meet gentlemen who are, like yourselves, the representatives of their fellow-citizens in the various towns and districts of India ; and certainly it gives me great pleasure to meet to-day the representatives of this ancient and famous city. I have heard, I need not say, a great deal, all my life, of the city of Benares ; and I am very glad indeed that it has at length fallen to my lot to visit it. I can assure you that, so far as I have yet had an opportunity of seeing the various objects of interest in this city, I have been very much gratified by what I have seen ; and I am specially gratified by the circumstance that I now meet you here, gentlemen, in your own Municipal Hall—a hall which has been presented to this body by the munificence of the late

Address from the Bengali Community of Benares.

Maharajah of Vizianagram. I recognise very highly the public spirit of that distinguished person, and I only hope that the example which he set may be largely followed in future by other native chiefs and gentlemen of wealth and distinction. There are few monuments which a man can raise to himself better than one which will recall continually the recollection of his munificence to the minds of his fellow-country-men when they meet for the transaction of public business. Mr. Ross has been good enough to express a hope that my visit here may induce me to return again on some future occasion, before I leave this country, to Benares. Of course, I cannot say whether it will be possible for me to do so or not; but there is one circumstance which would make me more than usually anxious to pay another visit to this city—and that is, that unfortunately, in consequence of an attack of illness, Lady Ripon was unable to accompany me on this occasion, as she had hoped to do. She is very anxious to see a city of which she has heard so much, and I can truly say that it will afford me gratification if on a future occasion I can accompany her here, to see the various objects of interest with which Benares abounds, and which I myself have so much enjoyed. (*Applause.*)

ADDRESS FROM THE BENGALI COMMUNITY OF BENARES.

29th Nov. 1881. [ON leaving the Town Hall, His Excellency visited the temple of Vishwanath, the Vizianagram Female School, and the Manmandira Observatory—the latter an ancient and celebrated stucture, overlooking the Ganges. After His Excellency had gone over the building, an address of welcome was read to him on behalf of the Bengali Community of Benares, to which he replied as follows :—]

Will you be kind enough to express to the gentlemen who have concurred with you in presenting me with this

Dinner at Nandesur House, Benares.

address, my best thanks, and say that I am very much obliged to them for this proof of their good feeling towards myself. I have heard with particular satisfaction the just appreciation, to which you give expression in your address, of the benefits which the people of this country receive from British rule. I am very glad to observe that those who have drawn up this address so thoroughly enter into the spirit by which the Government, acting under the direction of Her Majesty the Queen-Empress, will always be animated. I am also very grateful for the sentiments expressed towards myself, and for the manner in which you have spoken of the course which I pursued during the time I have been in this country in charge of the great and responsible office which I now fill. I can assure you that I appreciate very highly such marks as this, of the good feeling of any portion of the native community of this country. I cannot hope that, in a vast country like India, all the acts of the Government will meet with the approval of all the various sections of the people; but I trust that, like those whom you represent, all classes in India will do me the justice to believe that, whether they approve or do not approve of the course which I may feel it to be my duty to pursue, I shall constantly be animated by the warmest desire for the interest of India and of the inhabitants of the country, and that I shall make it the main object of my administration to promote those interests to the utmost.

[His Excellency then drove to the Sigra Church Missionary Society's School, where another address of welcome was presented, to which he briefly replied.]

DINNER AT NANDESUR HOUSE, BENARES.

[On the evening of the 29th November, the Maharajah of Benares entertained the Viceroy and about 150 guests, who had been invited

29th Nov. 1881.

Dinner at Nandesur House, Benares.

to meet His Excellency, at dinner in a large hall adjoining Nandesur House, which was specially erected for the occasion. The hall was brilliantly lighted with chandeliers, and the walls effectively decorated with flags and banners and swords arrranged in various devices. At the conclusion of dinner, the Maharajah appeared and took a seat beside the Viceroy, when Mr. Sladen, the Commissioner, on behalf of His Highness, proposed the toast of "The Queen." The toast hving being duly honoured, Mr. Sladen again rose and said :—

"*May it please Your Excellency, Ladies and Gentlemen,*—The next toast that I have been asked by His Highness the Maharajah of Benares to propose is the health of his distinguished guest the Marquis of Ripon, Viceroy and Governor General of India. (*Cheers.*) The Maharajah of Benares has desired me to express the great honour that he feels conferred on him, and the pleasure which he has derived from His Excellency's visit; and he trusts that he may be excused for expressing his regret that at the last moment Her Excellency Lady Ripon was prevented by indisposition from accompanying him. The Maharajah trusts that his Excellency has been pleased with what he has so far seen of the ancient city of Benares and its surroundings; and he hopes that he may not have had any cause to regret having given up the idea of the shooting trip to His Highness' preserves that he once projected, in order that he might have a better opportunity of becoming acquainted with Benares and its neighbourhood. (*Cheers.*) The Maharajah hopes, too, that at some future date His Excellency may be able again to visit this place, and in that case he trusts that he may still have the opportunity of showing him some sport in these jungles." (*Cheers.*)

The toast was drunk with enthusiasm—three Pipers of the 78th marching round the hall and playing a national air. His Excellency the Viceroy, in rising to return thanks, was received with cheers. He said :—]

Ladies and Gentlemen,—I beg to return my best thanks to His Highness the Maharajah of Benares for having requested Mr. Sladen to propose my health, and to you, ladies and gentlemen, for the cordial manner in which you have received that toast. I can assure the Maharajah that it has been a very great pleasure to me to partake of that hospitality for which I have long heard that His Highness is famed. I knew, indeed, by an almost personal experience, that the report of that hospitality was fully substantiated by the fact, because of the kindness which His Highness

Dinner at Nandesur House, Benares.

was good enough to show to my son last year when he paid a visit to this part of the country—(*cheers*) and I was therefore particularly glad to have this opportunity of personally thanking His Highness for that kindness, and of making his acquaintance myself. I have, ladies and gentlemen, derived great pleasure from my visit to this ancient and interesting city. All who had ever heard anything about India have heard of the fame of Benares, of that holy city on the Ganges which has been described by travellers and by historians, and which has been depicted by painters—(*cheers*)—and therefore it has been of course very agreeable to me to have had an early opportunity during my stay in this country of visiting this place; and I can truly say that so far as I have been able during the course of yesterday afternoon and to-day to visit Benares and its neighbourhood, I have derived very great pleasure from the sights which I have everywhere seen. Few things can be, I think, more striking than the contrast which is afforded by the various races of India which are gathered together in the early morning upon the ghats on the Ganges, as I saw them to-day. Few things can be more curious than those ancient temples, instinct with the memories of many ages, and around which so many interests are gathered in the minds of the Hindu community of this country. I am very well aware, ladies and gentlemen, that in a tour such as that which I have been making in various parts of India, it is very possible to over-estimate the amount of information and of knowledge of the true condition of the people of any country which may be gathered from a rapid progress of that kind. I am very well aware that it is not easy to judge of the real state of a population from seeing them, as a Viceroy necessarily sees the inhabitants of those parts of the country through which he passes, in their gala dress; but at the same time I cannot doubt from the experience which I have recently had, that, even in passing rapidly

Dinner at Nandesur House, Benares.

from one part of the country to another, it is in the power of a person in my position to learn much that may be very valuable to him in the course of his administration of a great Empire like this—(*hear, hear, and cheers*);—and if there was nothing else which would be an advantage to one in the position which I fill, it cannot, I think, be doubted that it must be most useful to a Governor-General of this country to have such opportunities as are afforded by occasions like this of making the personal acquaintance of distinguished natives of this country like my friend, the Maharajah of Benares. (*Hear, hear, and cheers.*) I am sure, ladies and gentlemen, that we have had to-night a proof of the princely hospitality which is displayed by His Highness when he assembles his friends around him. We have in this building itself a proof of the almost magic results which can be attained in this country, for I am told that this commodious hall in which we have just been dining, and which might well form a portion of the magnificent palace, has been raised, by some of those arts of legerdemain for which India is famous, within the space of four days. (*Cheers.*) Well, then, we have very much to be grateful to the Maharajah for upon this occasion; and I am sure, ladies and gentlemen, that you will all heartily join with me in drinking the toast with which I am about to conclude, and heartily wishing long life and health to the Maharajah of Benares; and in expressing the earnest hope which I entertain, that he may soon be entirely delivered from the illness under which he has been recently suffering. (*Loud and continued cheers.*)

[After a short interval, the Maharajah rose in person and returned his best thanks to His Excellency, saying that he was only too pleased to feel that his unworthy reception had met with the Viceroy's approval.]

OPENING THE PRINCE OF WALES' HOSPITAL AT BENARES.

[On the afternoon of the 30th November, His Excellency the Viceroy opened the Prince of Wales' Hospital. The ceremony took place in a tent in the central enclosure of the Hospital, in the presence of a large assembly of ladies and gentlemen, and of the leading native gentlemen of Benares. The Viceroy, on his arrival, was received by the Hospital Committee and conducted within the enclosure, where there was a guard of honour of the Ghazipur Rifle Volunteers with the Band of the 10th N. I. The Viceroy inspected the Volunteers and was afterwards conducted over the wards by the President and Secretary of the Hospital Committee. He then proceeded to the dais within the tent, and here he was received by the Maharajah of Benares, the Koomar Maharajah, Syed Ahmed Khan, Sir Herbert Macpherson, Mr. Sladen, and others. On His Excellency taking his seat, with the Maharajah on his right, Mr. Sladen the President of the Hospital Committee, read a brief statement of the circumstances under which the hospital was erected. This was followed by a statement by Rajah Shumbu Narayana Sinha, the Joint Honorary Secretary to the Hospital Committee, giving particulars of the cost of the undertaking and naming the principal contributors. Syed Ahmed Khan having read a translation of this statement, in the vernacular, His Excellency, at the invitation of the Maharajah, rose and addressed the assembly as follows:—] 30th Nov. 1881.

Maharajah, Ladies and Gentlemen,—I very gladly comply with the request which has just been made to me by His Highness the Maharajah, that I should undertake the duty of declaring this Hospital to be open. I am sure that there is no one here who will not agree with me that there can be few works for the material benefit of man of greater importance and value than the erection of a new Hospital; and certainly if there was any part of India in which the establishment of a good institution of that description would seem to be peculiarly fitting, it appears to me that that place is this city of Benares—not merely on account of the large population which is gathered within the city walls, but also because, year after year, as we all know, the city of Benares (deemed so sacred by the Hindu

Opening the Prince of Wales' Hospital at Benares.

community throughout India,) is visited by thousands of pilgrims from every part of this peninsula. It is not, therefore, ladies and gentlemen, surprising that His Highness the Maharajah of Benares, who is so distinguished alike by his public spirit and by his generous charity, and those other native gentlemen who are associated with him in the commencement of this undertaking, should a few years ago have felt the want of an institution of this kind and determined that that want should exist no longer. The statements which have been already submitted to you inform those who might not have been previously acquainted with the circumstances, of the course which has been adopted and the steps which have been taken for the purpose of establishing this institution; and this Hospital had the singular honour that the first stone of it was laid by his Royal Highness the Prince of Wales, during his visit to this country. Now, it seems to me, ladies and gentlemen, that it was specially appropriate that, if His Royal Highness was to lay the foundation-stone of any public Hospital in India, one of those which he should have selected should have been this Hospital at Benares, because, in consequence of the circumstance to which I have already alluded, this building will be tenanted not only by the inhabitants of this large city and its neighbourhood, but by the representatives of every portion of Her Majesty's Indian dominions. Under such circumstances, I need not say with how much pleasure I find that it falls to my lot, during this my visit to your ancient city, formally to open this Hospital. A building of which the first stone was laid by the Prince of Wales can receive no additional distinction by being opened by any lesser person; but it is perhaps only fitting that I, who am at the present time the representative in this country of our gracious Sovereign the Queen-Empress, should put, as it were, the finishing touch to a work which was so well commenced by His Royal Highness, our Sovereign's son. Ladies and gentlemen, the

Visit to the Government College, Benares.

work of establishing an hospital is one in which men of all races and of every creed may equally share, and I rejoice to find that that has been the case in this instance. At the head of those who founded this institution we find His Highness the Maharajah—the worthy and public-spirited representative of the great Hindu community of India ; and we find among those who have been his zealous co-operators in this work, one who is a not less worthy representative of the Mahomedan community—my friend Syed Ahmed. This is as it should be, for it proves that the memory of past animosities and of religious differences the most deep-seated, have melted away before the warm sun of that charity which thinks nothing human alien from its care, and which in an institution of this description is able to unite the sympathies of all varieties of feelings and of opinions in one common effort to alleviate those sufferings to which men, as men, are all alike subject. This is but a portion of that work of union and concord among every section of the community of India, which it ought to be one of the foremost objects of English rule in this country to develope and promote ; and therefore it is that I hail the establishment of this Hospital, not only on account of the great and undoubted benefits which it is calculated to confer upon this important community, but also because of the generous spirit by which those who have founded it have been animated ; and it is consequently, your Highness, ladies and gentlemen, a very great satisfaction to me now to declare that this, the Prince of Wales' Hospital of Benares, is open. (*Applause.*)

VISIT TO THE GOVERNMENT COLLEGE, BENARES.

[His Excellency, after leaving the Prince of Wales' Hospital, drove to the Government College. Here he was received by the Principal, 30th Nov. 1881.

Visit to the Government College, Benares.

Dr. Thibaut, who took him through the various class-rooms, after which the Viceroy was conducted to a seat, and one of the students stepped forward and recited the following verses :—

> A look of joy the ancient city wears,
>   Fair Kashi, emerald set in waves of green,
>   And tower and dome and pinnacle are seen
> Beneath the outspread light ; brown Gunga bears,
> Sin-laden, to the sea his weight of cares
>   Laid down by weary man ; while from afar,
>   Fretting the glowing sky, the tall Minar
> The glory of the restless world declares :
> This bright and happy day, in which we greet,
>   In thee, great England, long shall cherished be
> In the still halls of learning, when we meet ;
>   And oft remember that we owe to thee,
> When thought greets power in this of thought the seat,
>   That power is ever kind, and thought is free.

To this and other addresses of welcome in the vernacular His Excellency replied as follows :—]

Mr. Principal and Gentlemen,—I find it rather difficult to respond to the greeting which you have given to me upon this occasion. If I had been possessed of the great poetic talent which distinguished my predecessor, Lord Lytton, I might have made an appropriate reply to the poems which have been addressed to me in due poetic form ; but unfortunately I am only able to thank you in plain prose. I can, however, assure you that I am none the less grateful for the reception which you have given to me upon this occasion. It is a great pleasure to me to visit this institution and to find it installed in a building so beautiful and so commodious. I understand that the College of Benares is one of the oldest educational institutions in this country, connected with the British Government ; and it is to me, therefore, peculiarly interesting to be able to visit it on this occasion. It may be known to some of you that I have, for a very much longer period than, perhaps, I should like to recall, felt the deepest interest in all that concerns the progress of education, whether in my own country in England or here in India ; and therefore, to visit an institution of this kind, dating back for a long period of years, and to find it

Visit to the Government College, Benares.

continuing to flourish, and numbering (as I understand it does at the present moment) almost one thousand students, is a matter of very great satisfaction and gratification to me. I will not now detain you long, but would venture to express my hope that I may draw from one of the expressions contained in the English poem which has just been read, an indication of the spirit in which the studies of this place are pursued. I observe that in this poetical address you speak of "the still halls of learning." Now, I am very glad to find that you apply that adjective *still* to these halls of learning, because I trust that it shows that the students of the Benares College feel that they are not here for purposes of display—feel that the end and aim of their studies is not to be that they may know a little about a great many things, and may, when they go forth from this institution, flourish their limited amount of knowledge in the faces of those who know less than themselves; but that they feel that their studies here are to be conducted in that earnest, quiet, zealous spirit which I hope may be indicated by your use of the words "the still halls of learning." Rely upon it that it is better to know one thing well than to know a little of many things; that it is better that your studies should, so far as they may reach, be deep and real, than that they should appear to the outward world to be varied and extensive; and I trust that it is in that quiet spirit of true students that you pursue your labours here. If you do, you will win from Knowledge those great secrets and those glorious gifts which she can give you; but if you seek first and foremost to make her subservient to little ends and mean purposes, I can tell you that that fair Dame cannot be won by homage like that, and that those to whom she reveals her secrets are those who seek her for herself. It is my earnest hope that it is in this disposition that you approach and prosecute your studies, under the able guidance of your Principal. If I am not mistaken, he was once engaged in warfare of another kind; I trust that in the peaceful campaign which he is now carrying on against ignorance, he will win laurels far purer than those which in his earlier days crowned the standards of his country. (*Loud and prolonged applause.*)

DISTRIBUTION OF PRIZES AT ST. XAVIER'S COLLEGE, CALCUTTA.

9th Dec. 1881. [ON Friday afternoon, the 9th December, the Viceroy presided at the annual Distribution of Prizes to the Pupils of St. Xavier's College, Calcutta. His Excellency, on his arrival at the College, was received by His Grace, Archbishop Goethals, and the Rector of the College, and conducted to the hall set apart for the ceremony, which was filled by a large assembly. At the conclusion of a dramatic exercise by the boys, seats were placed on the stage for His Excellency, the Archbishop, and others. The Viceroy then distributed the prizes, after which an address was read by one of the students, to which His Excellency replied as follows :—]

Ladies and Gentlemen, Professors and Students of this College,—I can assure you I have received the address which has just been presented to me by the students of this institution with great satisfaction. I must, however, say, ladies and gentlemen, that I find myself upon this occasion in a somewhat difficult and unusual position, for I am not accustomed, I confess, to tread these boards, and we all know the fate of those who upon any stage are called upon, with inferior talents, to succeed consummate actors. However, I must do the best I can in the trying circumstances in which I am placed, and I feel that I may hope to be able to discharge my duty more efficiently than those circumstances would appear to render possible, because, at all events, I have at heart very deeply the cause which this institution is intended to promote. It had been my hope that I might have distributed these prizes last December, but I was prevented on that occasion by a severe illness from fulfilling the engagement I had made. I rejoice, however,

Distribution of Prizes at St. Xavier's College, Calcutta.

that it has pleased God to enable me to discharge that duty to-night, and I am very glad to have the opportunity of performing it, first, because of the high respect which I entertain for the Reverend Fathers who are doing in this College such good work for this great town, and for India; and secondly, because I have this day had an opportunity of witnessing a display of the talent possessed by the students of this College, under circumstances which, in many respects, afford a fair test of the extent to which those who have appeared before us to-night possess many, at all events, of those qualities which will enable them successfully to enter upon the contest and the hard business of life, to which they will so soon be called. I trust, however, ladies and gentlemen, that our young friends will not in the future altogether take as their model that famous Scapin who has been so well represented to us to-night with an ability and talent which are highly remakable (*applause*), but whose peculiar talents it would be better to imitate on the stage than in real life; while at the same time, I can form no better wish for my young friends, the pupils of this institution, than that all the events of their lives may end as happily, and, above all, that their matrimonial speculations may be as successful as those of Octavio. And again, ladies and gentlemen, I am glad to have this opportunity of marking by my presence the interest which I feel in this institution, because I am strongly convinced that a good work is being done here. It appears to me that this College of St. Francis Xavier may be justly considered a real place of education. There are many circumstances in the present time, which tend to make men often think that the mere cultivation of the intellect represents the full and complete idea of education. I am very well aware that, in the days in which we live, it is impossible, under many circumstances and in many institutions, to attempt more than the cultivation of the intellect in some or all of its branches : but the idea of a full and complete education

Distribution of Prizes at St. Xavier's College, Calcutta.

means the training of the whole man—not intellectual training alone, but moral training also (*applause*); and that we know, from the testimony of those who are best acquainted with the work which is being done in this College, is the aim successfully carried out in the institution on behalf of which we are assembled to-night. I am very glad to learn, from the information which has been placed at my disposal, that this institution is at the present time in a flourishing condition, and that its numbers have of late years been steadily increasing, and its sphere of usefulness extending; and it is my earnest hope that it will go forward in the good work in which it is engaged, and that, under the zealous guidance of those Reverend Fathers who preside over it, it will extend still further its sphere of utility. I am desirous to avail myself of this opportunity, however, of pointing out to those who are the students of this institution that, if we interpret that great word "education" as I have interpreted it just now, we must all of us bear in mind that education of that kind,—the real complete training of the man,—does not terminate when his school period, or when his University studies, are ended. Education in that sense is a thing which for all of us ends only with the end of our lives. But there is this difference between the education which may be received here, and that which you will have to get for yourselves in after-life,—that here you have provided for you good masters, able professors, and a sound method of teaching; but when you go forth from this College (when your student's life is ended, but your education still goes on) you will in the world be surrounded by teachers of every kind, —by teachers of evil as well as of good, and of error as well as of truth; that you will then be without the guidance which you here possess, and that it will rest with yourselves to say which of these teachers you will choose. For in that long education of the life of man, every circumstance is in some way a teacher, every companion and every friend; and

Assam Emigration Bill.

it rests, then, with yourselves, relying upon God's aid and His holy guidance, to determine whether you will choose that path which will ever lead you on to further developments of your intellectual and moral nature, or whether, turning away into the broad road that leadeth to destruction, you will undo the work which has been done for you here. Here there is laid, as I believe, a solid foundation, but it is a foundation only, and it will depend upon yourselves, when you go forth amidst the trials of life, to say whether you will build upon that foundation the beautiful edifice of a pure and noble life, or whether you will leave its stones bare, or overlay them with the foul mud of an ignoble existence. (*Applause.*) You have said, my young friends, in the kind address which you have presented to me, that the prizes which I have just distributed have been contested upon a peaceful battle-field. I have no doubt these prizes have been well fought for, and have been won in a real and honourable competition. If the idea that I was to present you with these prizes to-day has been any encouragement to you in that strife, I sincerely rejoice; but you have pointed out most truly that the primary incitement to earnest exertion and good work should ever be found, not in any earthly patronage, nor in the hope of any personal distinction, but in the desire to please God, to develope those faculties with which He has so largely endowed you, that you may use them for His service, and faithfully to do your duty to Him and to your fellow-men. (*Loud applause.*)

ASSAM EMIGRATION BILL.

[IN the Legislative Council, held on the 15th December, Mahárájá Jotíndra Mohun Tagore made a statement regarding the Bill to amend the Law relating to emigration to the labour districts of Bengal and Assam, in which he asked that the Bill might be referred

Assam Emigration Bill.

back to the Select Committee for further consideration, with special reference to a memorial from the British Indian Association, which criticised in detail many of the provisions of the Bill, and in view of the fact that native opinion was strongly opposed to its becoming law in its present form. The Hon. Mr. Thompson (the Member in charge of the Bill) expressed himself willing to accept the suggestion, on the understanding that the Bill should he brought up again in Council at its first meeting after the Viceroy's return from Burma for final consideration and passing into law.

His Excellency the President said:—]

It seems to me that the course suggested by my honourable friend who has just spoken is the right one in this case. The question has been carefully considered by the Government of India, and it is a mistake to suppose that they have not given consideration to the interests of both the parties who are concerned in this legislation. But, on the other hand, I do not think it would be desirable that any portion of the public should labour under the impression that the interests of those who are least able to represent their views in this matter have not been fully considered; and, under these circumstances, and in order especially to meet the views of the British Indian Association, I concur with my friend Mahárájá Jotíndra Mohun Tagore, that the Bill should be referred back to the Select Committee with the addition of the Honourable Members proposed (Mahárájá Jotíndra Mohun Tagore and the Honourable Mr. Inglis), but on the distinct understanding that the Commitee's final report on the Bill shall be taken into consideration on the first day on which the Council sits after my return from Burma, ; which will probably be the 5th of January.

5th Jan. 1882. [The Bill came up again before the Legislative Council, for final discussion, on Thursday, the 5th January 1882. Mr. Thompson presented the further report of the Select Committee, and moved that it be taken into consideration. He addressed the Council at some length, and was follwed by Mr. Inglis, Mahárájá Jotíndra Mohun Tagore, Mr. Reynolds, Sir Ashley Eden, Mr. Stokes, Sir Donald Stewart, and Mr. Thompson again, in reply to points raised by

Assam Emigration Bill.

Mahárájá Jotíndra Mohun Tagore and the Lieutenant-Governor. His Excellency the President spoke as follows :—]

I have listened with great interest to the discussion which has taken place, and am very glad that, on the occasion of the last meeting of this Council, we agreed to the postponement of the consideration of the Bill before us to-day. I think that the alterations made in the Bill by the Select Committee are decided improvements—improvements which have been suggested by the public discussions which have taken place and the interest which has been taken in the question by my honourable friend Mahárájá Jotíndra Mohun Tagore. I am also very glad that this measure has been now fully discussed by the public, and carefully considered by the members of this Council at a very full meeting such as that which has assembled on the present occasion.

I do not think there is the slightest necessity for me to take any notice of what our American cousins would call the " tall talk" which has gone on about this Bill. We are all very well aware of the value of that sort of thing, and it is not my intention to occupy the time of the Council in making any answer to the very exaggerated statements which have been made in respect of this measure. But one thing has struck me in regard to it, and that is, the great change which has taken place in the view taken of this kind of legislation in regard to emigration to Assam.

Some persons speak now as if this was the first step which had been taken in this direction, and as if the whole object of the Bill was to advance the interests of the planters, at the expense of the coolies ; but the statement which was made by my honourable friend the Lieutenant-Governor, and the extracts which have been read by him from his remarks when he had charge of the Bill in the Bengal Council, will show that when this system of emigration was originally introduced, it was brought forward entirely in the interests of the coolies, and that the object

Assam Emigration Bill.

was to restrict the system of emigration, which was then open to great abuses, and in which serious evils existed. The orignal Bill was introduced to regulate that system. That was not only the opinion of Sir Ashley Eden; but I find, on reference to the discussions in 1862, that a gentleman who is well known to all present here—Nawab Abdul Latíf—on that occasion took precisely the same view of the objects and purposes of this legislation. That gentleman said, he "thought that the proposed measure was very proper and very much called for. There was great propriety in the interference of the Government in a matter which daily concerned the welfare of thousands of its subjects." Therefore, it was admitted at the very inception of this business, that the distinct object and purpose of this legislation was the protection of the cooly against the evils to which he was subject under the emigration arrangements of the time. I feel, as strongly as any one can, the difficulty which exists with regard to legislation of this kind. The moment you come to interfere between the employers of labour and those whom they employ, you enter into a most difficult field of legislation; for it is the duty of Government to look into the interests of both parties. In many respects it may undoubtedly be said that those interests are identical; but at the same time it cannot be denied that there are other respects in which they are antagonistic. And it is a very difficult task to draw the right line in legislation of this description, so as to deal with perfect fairness to both parties. I, therefore, shall greatly rejoice when the time arrives—and I think, with several here, that it may not be very distant—when special legislation with regard to this question may be dispensed with, and the whole subject of emigration from India, and immigration into Assam, may be left to the operation of the ordinary laws of the country. We are approaching that time, I think, somewhat rapidly, because I hope we may very soon improve our communications with Assam; and I can say for myself and my honourable colleagues, that it is

Assam Emigration Bill.

our earnest desire to do everything we can to promote the improvement of those communications, whether by rail or by water, and the great object we have in view is to arrive at a period when this matter may be left entirely to the ordinary laws of the country.

Now it has been said that there is something inconsistent in maintaining side by side a regulated system of emigration, such as is provided for in this Act, and in admitting at the same time the free engagement of labourers in Assam when once they get there. I confess I think that is not a valid objection, because there is no doubt that the difficulties of communication and the cost of bringing labourers to Assam are still great, and form the ground of a reasonable desire on the part of planters to have the security of a contract of some duration to recoup them for the expense to which they are necessarily put in bringing coolies to the tea districts from such considerable distances. If contracts of long duration are to be sanctioned by law, it becomes necessary, in the interest of the cooly, to have a system for his protection. But as communications have already improved, and from various circumstances the time appears to be approaching when a system of free emigration may be adopted in Assam, it seems, extremely desirable and natural that you should make a commencement at the present time. It should be borne in mind that all that has been done is to give labourers who go to Assam, or who are there, the same rights in respect of their labour as would be enjoyed by them under the general law of the country, and to put them on precisely the same footing as any man who enters into a labour contract in the Punjáb or anywhere else. I am bound to say I think a very strong case ought to be made out before the Government of India would be justified in continuing to refuse persons in Assam the same right to enter into arrangements for their own labour which are already enjoyed by persons in other parts of India. I have taken a great deal of interest in

Assam Emigration Bill.

this question, because, as I said before, it is a question of very great difficulty, in which you have to deal with the interests of two distinct parties, one of which is much more able to represent his feelings than the other,—consequently, one of the great objects I have had in view has been to ascertain what is the real state of things in Assam under the present law. You have heard the statement of my honourable and gallant friend the Commander-in-Chief as to the impressions left on his mind by the result of his recent visit to Assam; and I am certain that nothing can be more satisfactory than what my honourable and gallant friend has gathered from such inspection as he has been able to make, as to the condition of coolies on tea plantations. He has said that their condition is not only as good, but certainly better than, the condition of similar labouring persons elsewhere in India. But the opportunities I have had of acquiring information are not confined to the statements I have just referred to, for I have had the great advantage of consulting, in the various stages of this Bill, with the Chief Commissioner of Assam, Mr. Elliott, who, as everybody who knows him can testify, is a singularly able and energetic officer. He has been very careful in giving his opinion on the subject. When he was first called upon, he declined—and I think very rightly—to express any decided opinion till he had the opportunity of looking into the matter himself and seeing what was the real condition of affairs; but, having done so, Mr. Elliott tells me now that he is perfectly satisfied that the condition of the coolies in Assam is generally highly satisfactory; that they are not subjected to oppression, and that, as a rule their employers, though there may be individual exceptions, are most anxious to treat the coolies well, and that the arrangements for their housing, medical attendance, and general comfort, and the relations which exist between the planter and his coolies, are of as satisfactory a character as can be expected to exist anywhere.

Assam Emigration Bill.

Now, when we look at this question, we ought to look at it from a practical point of view, and such testimony as I have just adduced has therefore a very important bearing on that matter. This Bill has been treated to a certain extent as if it were new legislation, and several at all events of the criticisms sent in to Government by those who have made representations in connection with the Bill, have been criticisms, not upon the new provisions of this measure, but upon the provisions of the Bill, which are re-enactments of the existing Bengal law. Now, no doubt, any Government which adopts what I think is the best system—and certainly the most convenient system in a case of this kind —and, when it wants to alter the existing law, repeals that law so as to embody the whole law on the subject in one new measure, is exposed, not here only, but at home, to the inconvenience of persons looking at the Bill, not as a re-enactment of the existing law, but as something entirely new, and proceeding to find all sorts of faults with provisions which have been, in fact, in operation for many years. That has to a certain extent been the case with this Bill. The fact of the matter is, that the far greater portion of the Bill is a re-enactment of the existing law. If any one will turn to the Bill and look carefully at the new provisions it contains, he will find that the major part of them are distinctly in favour of the cooly, and intended to increase his protection and improve his position. I will not trouble the Council by going through the details of those provisions. I have done so carefully, and I can say that the statement I have made, that the majority of those provisions are in favour of the cooly, is undoubtedly correct.

There are certainly provisions in which alterations have been made at the instance of the employers, and not of the employed. The principal changes in that direction to which I will advert have been, first, the, prolongation of the period of the contract from three to five years. My honourable friend Mahárájá Jotíndra Mohun Tagore objects to that,

Assam Emigration Bill.

and it is a very fair subject for discussion. All I have to say is, that it is a point which, in the original memorial of gentlemen interested in the tea industry, was most pressed on the Government. It does seem to me to be extremely hard to say to them, "You shall not be allowed to enter into a contract of the same length as persons engaged in the British colonies, and as the French and other foreign Governments are allowed." I do not think that is a position which this Government can occupy; but we have provided that during the last year of the five-year contract, the wages paid to the coolies shall be steadily increased. There has been some misconception, I think, with regard to the provision regulating the minimum wages to be paid to the cooly. A good deal of the controversy has been worded, at all events, as if those who entered upon it had thought that what was fixed was the maximum, not minimum, of wages. As I understand the nature of the industrial arrangements of Assam, every able-bodied cooly will undoubtedly earn, as he dose now, a much larger amount of wages than he would be entitled to as a minimum. The fact of the matter is that by the system of task-work, I believe the wages of the coolies are far higher than they are in many other parts in India, and the labourers in Assam have also the advantage that their wives and children are able to be employed on the light labour of picking tea-leaves in certain seasons of the year. So that the total amount of wages of the family is very much larger than what we can, I fear, state to be the income of the labouring classes in other parts of India, and it is quite unreasonable to treat figures which are strictly a minimum as if the intention of the Legislature was to fix wages at that amount. The object of that figure is to prevent a sick or weakly cooly from being employed below a certain rate. It is always expected that able-bodied men will earn a great deal more, but we have felt ourselves bound to protect the weaker coolies against their being placed in a position which would leave them with means

Assam Emigration Bill.

wholly inadequate for the sustenance of themselves and their families.

I now come to the question which has been raised with respect to the measure which has been proposed, in order to make sure, before the cooly is moved from his place of residence, that he is really acquainted with the nature of the contract into which he has entered. I have before me a very fair and temperate representation which has been made by the Indian Association within the last two or three days. They have argued the subject very fairly, and they have put forward objections to certain parts of the Bill which are well entitled to consideration. They press upon us in their memorial, this point of the ignorance of the cooly, and give a curious extract from a book published by a missionary of the Brahmo Somáj, to show how very ignorant a great number of the coolies who engage to go to Assam are. I have no doubt that that is a perfectly fair statement of the knowledge of many of these coolies; but I do claim for the Bill that it takes the utmost possible care that the labourer should thoroughly understand the nature of the engagement he is about to enter into. I know that my honourable friend Mr. Rivers Thompson has considered this point to be one of great importance, and we are aware that the British Indian Association has made some useful suggestions upon it: there are also other useful suggestions in their memorial, but this one is to my mind the most important. They suggest that it should be made perfectly clear that it is the duty of the registering officer to explain the contract to the cooly. It was always intended that that officer should make that explanation to the cooly; but it is much better to make it plain and explicit, and to put into specific words that it is his duty to do so. The registering officer has therefore been directly required to explain the terms of the contract to the coolies, and, as pointed out by Mr. Rivers Thompson, the Bill provides that the officer shall assure himself that such person is competent to enter into such contract,

Assam Emigration Bill.

and understands the same as regards the locality, period and nature of the service, and the rate of wages and the price at which rice is to be supplied to him; that the terms thereof are in accordance with law; that he has not been induced to agree to enter thereunto by any coercion, undue influence, fraud, misrepresentation or mistake, and that he is willing to fulfil the same. I do not know how you can cover wider ground than this.

If a cooly, as in the case mentioned in the memorial of the Indian Association, has been told that he is being taken to the house of a European in Calcutta to work as a servant there, he has been clearly engaged under a misrepresentation. The registering officer is also to satisfy himself that the cooly, at the last moment, after the fullest explanation has been given to him of all the particulars of his contract, is then and there willing to enter into the contract. That, I think, is an answer to the point which has been suggested by my honourable friend Mahárájá Jotíndra Mohan Tagore, because, if a man is not really willing, the contract is void.

There is only one more point of detail in regard to which I will say a word. My honourable friend alluded to the power which the Bill confers, of arresting an absconded labourer without a warrant. I am not the least surprised that he should view this power with suspicion. It is a power which ought not to be conferred without the greatest possible care, and I myself shared the suspicion of my honourable friend, and viewed it with considerable doubt and hesitation; but it is also true, as has been shown by my honourable and learned friend Mr. Stokes, that this is a power which has been granted, not only in this case and in that of British Burma, but is conferred in certain cases in England; it is a power that has hitherto been worked without complaint, so far as I know, in Assam. The Commission which was appointed to enquire into the matter recommended that the limit of ten miles which exists in the

Assam Emigration Bill.

Bengal law should be entriely done away with, and that the power should be altogether unrestricted. I did not feel myself free to accept that proposal. I consider that this is a power which requires to be carefully watched, and I do not think that it will be right to abolish the limit altogether, or that a man should be liable to arrest without a warrant, close to the door of a Magistrate from whom a warrant might be obtained. But I became convinced, and the members of the Government were convinced, after careful and prolonged consideration, that, as a matter of fact, the ten miles limit is altogether illusory; that it is not, generally speaking, paid attention to, and that there is a much better chance of the check upon arrest without warrant being made practically effective if the limit is reduced from ten to five miles—that being a reasonable distance within which you may require that a person should go to a Magistrate to obtain a warrant. And therefore it was, though not without reluctance, that I consented to the modification of the limit from ten miles to five. I can assure my honourable friend that I should be the last person to agree to anything that was calculated to extend unnecessarily a power so open to objection as that of arrest without warrant; but in a country where communications are so difficult, and the number of persons exercising magisterial powers are necessarily so restricted, as at present in Assam, a provision of this sort appears to be called for.

I do not think that I need detain the Council with any further remarks, except to say that the real question which we have to consider in regard to this Bill is, whether the time has come when it is possible at once to leave emigration to Assam to be carried out entriely under the ordinary laws of the country; or whether it is necessary to continue for a time a system of special regulation. That is the first question we have to consider. It certainly seems to me that the time has not come in which, in the interests of the coolies

Assam Emigration Bill.

themselves, we can allow them to be engaged in Bengal and the North-Western Provinces and taken to Assam at the expense of the planter, without taking on their behalf proper precautions for their good treatment when they arrive there. And there is another reason why the present system should not be abandoned at this moment, and that is, that we shall be selecting a very unfortunate period for disorganising the existing arrangements for cooly-labour for Assam. The tea industry, as we all know, has been for the last few years in a suffering condition. Things are rather improving at the present time; prices are rising, and the English public are becoming sensible of the good quality of India teas; and this time of transition seems to me to be most inopportune for making any great change in the law regulating the organization of the tea industry. I am sure the Council will be of opinion that it is of the utmost importance to the interest of the great mass of the people that we should encourage as much as possible the application of capital for the opening out of the resources of the country and the promotion of a fresh means of employment for the people. And it cannot be gainsaid, that it is in itself a great advantage that we should drain off a portion of the overcrowded population of some parts of the country to other parts where it is sparse. I am told that, in the case of many coolies who go to Assam, they are able at the termination of their engagement to procure land for themselves, and to settle down to cultivate it, and can also get employment for themselves and their wives and children, on fair terms, on the tea plantations. It is an enormous advantage to relieve the crowded districts of Bengal and the North-Western Provinces—where population increases, as the census shows, from year to year, from decade to decade—and to induce a portion of the inhabitants of those districts to pass away to other parts, where their condition will be materially improved. It is better for those who remain and for those who go.

Distribution of Prizes at La Martinière.

These are the questions of general consideration connected with this matter. If it has been asserted that the Government of India has, in regard to this measure, been actuated by any desire to promote the interest of one class in preference to another, I do not care to answer such an accusation. I am quite prepared to leave the judgment of my own conduct to those who know anything of my character; for if I did not believe that this measure would improve the condition of the tea industry in Assam and conduce greatly to the welfare of the coolies, I should certainly not give my consent to it.

[The Bill was then passed.]

DISTRIBUTION OF PRIZES AT LA MARTINIÈRE.

[ON Thursday afternoon, the 15th December, the Viceroy distributed the prizes to the pupils of La Martinière Schools, in the presence of a large assembly of ladies and gentlemen. Owing to indisposition, the Marchioness of Ripon was unable to attend. His Excellency, on his arrival, was received by His Honor the Lieutenant Governor, the school authorities, and by a Guard of Honor of the Martinière Cadet Corps, whose band played the National Anthem. The Head Master having read the Annual Report, the Viceroy distributed the prizes, after which His Excellency addressed the assembly as follows :—] 15th Dec. 1881.

Your Honor, Ladies and Gentlemen,—I can assure you that I am very glad to have been able to attend here to-day, because the name of La Martinière is one well known to all those who are at all acquainted with India, and has certainly been known to me long before I came out to this country. I am glad to be able to offer to the Governors, to the Head Master, to the other teachers of this institution, and to all friends of La Martinière, my congratulations, upon the satisfactory report which has been read to us to-day, and upon the pleasing and agreeable character of all we have seen and listened to upon this occasion.

Distribution of Prizes at La Martinière.

Ladies and Gentlemen,—I am deeply impressed with the necessity that exists for schools of this description, which provide a sound and useful education for large numbers of the children of Europeans and Eurasians, upon conditions which are consonant with the feelings and wishes of their parents. You, sir, in the report which you just now read alluded to the school as coming within the category of "schools established in the plains," and you spoke of the difference which exists with respect to the advantages of hill schools. Well, I am not about to enter now into any argument on the subject, and that for one very obvious reason—that I believe there is ample room for schools of both descriptions. I feel strongly that, particularly for children of European race, schools in the hills present undoubted advantages; but it is, on the other hand, perfectly evident that, in a great city like Calcutta, and in many other large towns of India, there is ample room and an unquestionable necessity for schools such as this, on whose behalf we are assembled to-day; and the need of such schools, and their public utility, has been recently acknowledged in the Resolution of the Government of India to which the Head Master alluded in the report. That Resolution deals with a part only,—if you look to the numerical proportion of the population with which it deals—with but a small part of the great question of public education in India. But it appears to me that, in the careful abstinence which characterises that Resolution, from all interference with religious instruction; in the earnest respect which the Government of India shows for the conscientious feelings of parents, and in our readiness to employ all existing educational machinery, to the utmost of our power, to aid in the great work of education in this country, that Resolution is founded upon principles of general application.

I, for one, ladies and gentlemen, have never been an advocate for strict uniformity in any educational system; and I have never been one of those who desire that a

Distribution of Prizes at La Martinière.

system of public education in any country should be directed to train up men after one single type alone. On the contrary, I attach great importance to securing a variety of educational institutions and systems, because I believe it is of very great value that those varying characteristics which distinguish classes and races and individuals should all have their appropriate training, so that the educational system of any country should secure to the people the full and rich development of all shades of the national character.

Now, there are many circumstances in the present day which tend in the direction of producing a greater amount of uniformity among men, and to the getting rid of, and diminishing, originality of mind. This I think to be a tendency against which we ought to contend, and I am, therefore, no advocate, in this or in any other country, for any unnecessary interference on the part of the Government in the matter of education. What the Government does—what any central Government does—is necessarily of an uniform character, and tends to become more and more stereotyped as time goes on. A system originally well established, may possess the very best features of the educational system of the time; but as it continues, it is likely to fall behind and to make little use of new views and further educational developments, unless we find side by side with the system maintained by the Government, independent institutions like this, which enter into rivalry with the institutions more directly connected with the administration of the country; a rivalry which is perfectly friendly —a rivalry for the promotion of one noble object —a rivalry from which Government institutions have nothing to fear, and from which, in my judgment, they have much to gain. (*Applause.*) When I say that I am no eager advocate for the extension of Government interference in education, I say that upon one condition, and with one proviso, and that is, that the work of education, in this country shall be efficiently done. That I hold to be a *sine quâ non*; and it

Distribution of Prizes at La Martinière.

is quite clear, I think, that in no country, whether in Europe or here, can that work in these days, in all its width and extension, be adequately carried out independently of the assistance and of the funds of the central administration. And if this be true of European countries—if it be true of England—I am inclined to think that it is much more true of India; and I trust, therefore, that none of you, who have listened to the observations I have just made, will carry away with you any idea that it would be the tendency of my policy, as Viceroy of this country, to restrict the aid of Government in the promotion of public education. On the contrary, I desire to extend that assistance and to carry it deeper down into the lower ranks of the population; but it is for that very reason, and because I feel that the work to be done in regard to public education is a work of such great magnitude, and because I recognise that if it is to be done efficiently, it will involve a larger amount of expenditure than it is possible for the Government of the country at present to embark upon—that I accept heartily the coöperation of institutions of this kind (*applause*); and therefore I am glad to have had this opportunity of expressing the deep and sincere interest which I feel in the work which is being done here, and in other kindred colleges and schools.

And, ladies and gentlemen, if I have seized this opportunity of giving expression to that sentiment, there is also another feeling to which I cannot help alluding upon this occasion. I cannot help availing myself of the opportunity now afforded to me to return my best thanks on behalf of myself, and I may say of my colleagues of the Government of India, to Archdeacon Baly, for the great services which he has rendered to the cause of European and Eurasian education in this country. (*Applause.*) We owe Archdeacon Baly our best thanks. But there are others, too, who owe him thanks yet greater and deeper— the European and Eurasian inhabitants of this country, for whose interests in matters concerning the education of

Address from the Municipality of Rangoon.

their children he has done so much, in whose cause he has spent so much time and study, and worked so unceasingly. They owe him a debt of the deepest gratitude. (*Applause.*)

And now, ladies and gentlemen, I do not know that I need detain you longer upon this occasion. I have to say, on behalf of Lady Ripon, that she deeply regrets that she was not able, on account of not being by any means strong, to be present here on an occasion which would have afforded her so much interest and pleasure.

I have only, in conclusion, most heartly to wish prosperity to the Calcutta La Martinière. It has nearly fifty years of good work to show, and I earnestly desire that for many half centuries, and for centuries still to come, it will continue to furnish and to train up successive generations of young men and young women like those who have appeared before us to-day—whose lives, when they go forth from this institution, will bear bright witness to the moral and intellectual fruits which result from the culture which this place affords. (*Applause.*)

ADDRESS FROM THE MUNICIPALITY OF RANOOGN.

[On Friday evening, the 16th of December, Their Excellencies the Viceroy and Lady Ripon embarked on board the *Tenasserim* for a visit to British Burma. The party accompanying Their Excellencies was composed of the Hon. E. Baring ; C. Grant, Esq.; E. C. Buck, Esq.; H. W. Primrose Esq.; the Rev. H. S. Kerr ; Surgeon-Major Anderson ; and Captains Brett, Muir, and Durand, Aides-de-Camp. The *Tenasserim* arrived at Rangoon on the afternoon of the 20th December, Their Excellencies being met at the mouth of the river by Mr. C. E. Bernard (the Chief Commissioner) and a small party of gentlemen, in one of the steamers of the Irrawaddy Flotilla Company. At a quarter past 4 the Viceroy landed at the Phayre Street Wharf, where he was received by the Chief Commissioner, accompanied by all the Civil and Military Officials of Rangoon, by the Municipal Committee, the Port Trust

20th Dec. 1881.

Address from the Municipality of Rangoon.

Commissioners, the Chamber of Commerce, and the principal residents. The wharf had been decorated for Their Excellencies' reception by a Committee of the people of Rangoon. Ladies of the Principal Burmese families of Rangoon and its neighbourhood were assembled in a part of the wharf set apart for them, and welcomed the Viceroy and Lady Ripon after their national custom. On His Excellency entering the covered part of the wharf, Major Poole, the President of the Municipality, read an address of welcome, which concluded by expressing the satisfaction of the Municipality at the recent Resolution of Government, favouring the policy of recognising and encouraging the independence of municipal bodies.

His Excellency replied as follows :—]

Gentlemen,—I am much obliged to you for your address, and for the sentiments which it contains. I thank you sincerely for the congratulations which you have been good enough to offer me upon my arrival in this your city. I can assure you it is a source of great pleasure to me to visit a province of Her Majesty's Indian dominions, so marked by its advancement and progress as the province of Burma; and I expect to derive both gratification and advantage from the opportunity I shall have of seeing some portion of so interesting a part of India. Gentlemen, I rejoice to find that you hail with satisfaction and approval a recent Resolution of the Government of India upon the subject of decentralisation, and the extension of local self-government; and I am very glad to learn from my friend Mr. Bernard that measures have already been taken for extending the principle of election to the chief municipalities of Burma, and that, at all events as regards the population of Rangoon, that proposal has been received with favour. I sometimes hear it said that the natives in many parts of India are indifferent to the system of election, and that the best men in the various cities are not willing to come forward and to offer themselves to the choice of their fellow-citizens. With respect to the modes and forms of election to be adopted in any part of the diversified dominions of our Queen in this country, what the Government of India would desire is that such systems should be selected as

Address from the Municipality of Rangoon.

may be deemed most suited to the indigenous habits of each portion of the empire, and most in accordance with native feeling. And with respect to any hesitation (if any such does exist) in the minds of the best men of the European or Native community to offer themselves to the choice of their neighbours, all I can say is that for my part I regard a man who is selected by his fellow-townsmen to represent their interests in a municiplity, as one who receives a high distinction; and that I should always myself be inclined, as Viceroy of India, to mark by other honours my sense of the position of any one who had been for a series of years honoured by the confidence of his fellow-countrymen. Gentlemen, as I am speaking upon this topic, I may be permitted to say that I have read with very great satisfaction the remarks upon this question of Municipal Government, which are contained in a recent Administration Report of your Chief Commissioner. Mr. Bernard has shown that he thoroughly and rightly appreciates the objects and the intention of the Government of India in this matter; and I may in truth say, briefly, that the views which are expressed in that Administration Report appear to me to be a model of those by which the Government of India would desire that Local Governments should be animated. (*Applause.*)

Gentlemen,—We have present here with us to-day my honourable colleague Major Baring, the Financial Member of Council, and I am glad to take this opportunity of acknowledging the large share he has borne in the preparation and development of the Resolution to which I have been referring, and the deep interest which he feels in all that tends to extend local self-government in this country. What we desire is, to see local interests managed by local bodies representing local opinion. In our opinion it is a distinct credit to any district officer if he is found to work through, and with, the Municipality with which he has to do; and it seems to us that it is better that even useful

Address from the Burman Community.

reforms should be postponed for a year or two, and ultimately carried out with the consent of local bodies, and in the form most acceptable to them, than that they should be adopted at once, with a disregard of the feelings of the municipal body. We desire to respect the independence of such bodies, and to encourage them to speak their minds freely; but at the same time, we should not be justified in permitting a backward and obstructive municipality permanently to stand in the way of the welfare of their fellow-citizens, to postpone indefinitely necessary measures of sanitary reform, education, water-supply, improvement of roads, or the like. We do not do so in England. In many cases, the Government at home takes the power to itself of enforcing the necessary measures on municipalities who show themselves unworthy of the trust reposed in them: in short, the principle on which the Resolution is founded may be said to be this,—We wish to use local bodies to the utmost, in the management of local affairs; we desire to secure them from hasty or needless interference; we desire to deal with them with the utmost patience; but, on the other hand, we do not intend that they should be permitted to obstruct the solid good of their fellow-citizens in any case in which they may show themselves permanently unwilling to discharge the duties entrusted to them. I have thought it desirable, as you are about to enter, more widely than before, on the course of municipal self-government, to take this opportunity of explaining the views of the Government of India in this matter. It only remains for me to thank you once more for your kind welcome.

ADDRESS FROM THE BURMAN COMMUNITY.

20th Dec. 1881. [THE Viceregal Party then proceeded up the wharf, at the outside of which the Burmese section of the community presented an address of

Address from the Burman Community.

welcome, of which the following is a translation:—"May it please Your Excellency,—We the undersigned members of the Burmese Community respectfully beg to state:—" That, owing to the just and upright Government exercised over the people of the country in consequence of the good will, sympathy, and other kindly feelings entertained by Your Excellency for them, without distinction as to race, they are free from anxiety and dread, and, like fresh blossoms, they live in exceeding contentment and happiness under the shelter of the British flag. They longed, previously to Your Excellency's arrival, to behold the face of him to whose attention and care they are indebted for this peaceful security. And now that Your Excellency has graciously been pleased to visit these shores, and they are enabled personally to behold and pay their respects to Your Excellency, their delight and amazement at the favour vouchsafed them are unbounded. They know plainly that Your Excellency has at heart the contentment and happiness of various races under Your Excellency's government, and that Your Excellency exercises just government over them accordingly. They earnestly pray, therefore, that the life of Your Excellency may be prolonged, that the glory, might, and honour of Your Excellency may day by day increase, and that the just government of Your Excellency may continue to be exercised over them as heretofore."

His Excellency's reply, which was translated for the audience, was as follows :—]

Gentlemen of the Burman Community,—I am very much pleased by the terms of the address which you have presented to me, and I can assure you that I am very glad that I have been able to visit this interesting province so soon after the time of entering upon my duties as Viceroy of India. I am well aware that Burma is one of the most progressive provinces of India, and I therefore rejoice, indeed, to have this opportunity of seeing its condition with my own eyes. The Government of India regards the races and creeds upon a footing of perfect equality ;—that is one of the fundamental principles of the Government of Her Majesty the Queen-Empress in this country. Therefore, we regard you, who belong to a race so different from those with which other parts of India are peopled, with as much interest as we do those who inhabit the more ancient portions of Her Majesty's Indian Empire, and it will be equally our object to promote your interests.

DINNER AT GOVERNMENT HOUSE, RANGOON.

20th Dec. 1881. [AFTER His Excellency had replied to the Burman address a procession was formed and proceeded towards Government House. Various triumphal arches were erected along the line of route by different sections of the community (Persians, Chetties, Fokien Chinese and Surates), each of whom presented an address of welcome, to which His Excellency replied briefly. In the evening, the Chief Commissioner gave a dinner at Government House, to which a large number of guests were invited to meet Their Excellencies. Mr. Bernard proposed the Viceroy's health, and His Excellency replied in the following speech :—]

Mr. Bernard, Ladies and Gentlemen,—I thank you very sincerely for the manner in which you have received the toast which has just been proposed to you, in such kind terms, by my friend the Chief Commissioner. I can assure you that it is a great pleasure to me to have been able to visit this distant province of Her Majesty's Indian dominions, and to find myself here in a portion of those dominions marked by such evident and unmistakeable signs of prosperity and progress. It is due to that fortunate existence of peace at the present time (that peace to which you, Sir, have alluded in terms so just) that I have been able to come thus far from the ordinary route of Governors-General; and I, for one, accept entirely the congratulations which you have been good enough to offer me upon the establishment of that peace, and I shall always consider that if I have had any hand in furthering the settlement to which that peace is due, it is one of the acts of my political life of which, throughout what remains of my time upon earth I may be most justly proud. (*Applause.*) You are quite right when you say I am a friend of a peaceful policy ; not

Dinner at Government House, Rangoon.

because I should not be prepared upon any occasion when the true interests or the honour of England or India were at stake, to strike a blow—a quick and ready blow—for the defence of those great interests (*applause*), but because I believe, as was stated by the great and distinguished English statesman, Lord Derby, that the true interest of England is peace, and hold that that saying is yet more true of India; and it is to the continuance of peace that we must look for the advancement of that progress which, great and remarkable here in Burma, yet shows signs of its existence and its advancement in other parts of India in the present day. Here, ladies and gentlemen, these signs are unmistakeable. Whether we look to the population, or to trade, or to railway returns, or to shipping; or take any other test of prosperity, and compare the conditions of Burma at the present day with what it was ten years ago, I may truly say, without exaggeration, that the progress of these ten years has been enormous. And that progress has not been merely the result of some great leap which might have been made from accidental circumstances in the course of that decade of years; but it has been a steady progress, advancing continually and going on step by step down to the present day; a progress which is marked as between last year and the present year in due proportion, as it is between the present year and ten years ago. I have been reading with the greatest possible interest the very able Administration Report of my friend the Chief Commissioner, and I find in that Report that the year which is just closing shows a noble record of good work done. Whatever may be the branch of administration to which you may turn, you will see in it manifest signs of progression and advancement. If you look to railway communications, you will see there that you have one railway in Burma which is in the happy and fortunate condition of already, within a few years, paying four and a half per cent upon its capital cost; and I rejoice indeed to have

Dinner at Government House, Rangoon.

been able to induce the Secretary of State very readily to sanction the creation of that new railway from this place to Toungoo, which I hope will also have a very great effect in developing the resources of the country. (*Applause.*) But railway communications could do little if they were not aided and supplemented by road communications, and I was therefore exceedingly glad to find, from the Report of my honourable friend, that his attention was being closely turned to that question of road communication and that it was his intention to devote for the future a considerably larger sum for the development of roads in this province than had hitherto been devoted to that great and important object. I have already, this afternoon—in which I believe I have made some eight or nine speeches, to a great variety of races, though happily they were not so long as that with which I am detaining you now—had occasion to allude to the progress which is being made in the development of Municipal institutions in Burma, and I shall say nothing on that subject now, except to repeat my thanks to Mr Bernard for the admirable manner in which he has dealt with the subject in his Report.

But there is one subject in which I have felt a great interest for a number of years—a greater number, perhaps, than it is agreeable to recall—on which I should like to say a word or two; and that is the subject of public education. I rejoice to see, also, that there is good work being done in this province of Burma. The higher schools are doing their work, and I trust they will continue to do that yet more successfully. I was, however, glad to observe, from the Report to which I have alluded, what valuable results were obtained from the labours of the Christian Brothers in their School of St. Paul. (*Applause.*) I was glad also to see the position which was occupied by the School of St. John, and to find how zealously and earnestly the Baptist Missionaries in this country were labouring for the cause of education among the wild tribes of Karens.

Dinner at Government House, Rangoon.

But, as you may be aware, I attach a very special and peculiar importance to the progress of primary education in India; and it seems to me to be a very interesting feature of your educational system in Burma, that you have been able to use, to so large an extent, the indigenous educational establishments of this province in connection with that branch of education; and that there is a great hope of enlarging, extending, and making yet more useful the native indigenous education which is afforded by the Bhuddist Monasteries throughout this land. That seems to me to be dealing with this question on its true and sound basis, endeavouring to use every national and native means to encourage and develope it, and so to make it useful for the purposes of modern science and modern civilisation. I was, however, a little disappointed with two points which came out in regard to education, in that Report. The first was that, although something is being done (more, perhaps, than in any other part of India) in the matter of the education of girls, yet it seemed to me that there was considerable room for doing a great deal more in that direction in this province, because, if I am not mistaken, you have not, here in Burma, to encounter the great difficulty which lies in the way of female education in other parts of India. You have alluded to the freedom of the women in this part of the country, and their unrestricted intercourse in society; and that in itself is a feature which ought to make female education much more easy here than in other parts of India, and which will, I hope, lead to a great development of female education in the course of coming years. The other point was that I, who am so much interested in the development of Municipal institutions, regret to observe that the Municipalities of British Burma devote what seems to me far too small a portion of their funds to the promotion of education. That fact was alluded to in the Report, and I am quite sure that, so far as may be consistent with the legitimate independence of those bodies,

Dinner at Government House, Rangoon.

they will be encouraged by you, Sir, to appropriate a larger portion of their funds to the purposes of primary education.

There is one other topic upon which I would say a word, and that is, the development and extension of the vast agricultural resources of Burma. You are aware that the Government of India have lately re-established the Revenue and Agricultural Department, which was first set up by my distinguished friend—for I had the honour of his friendship—the late Lord Mayo (*loud applause*), and which, having suffered a temporary eclipse, has been wisely, in my judgment, re-established by the present Indian Government. And one of the first measures in connection with that resuscitation of the Agricultural Department in India was to obtain the sanction of the Home Government to establish an Agricultural Department in Burma, upon the recommendation of your Chief Commissioner. Well now, I hope that from the establishment of that Agricultural Department many benefits may result to this province. Happily, the Burmese Agricultural Department will not have to discharge those duties which must ever be the foremost duties of an Agricultural Department in any other part of India, because you enjoy in Burma a complete, or almost quite complete, immunity from the great evil of famine. But there is a great deal to be done towards the development of the agricultural resources of this rich province, and although I am not one of those who think it is in the power of Government to take upon itself vast and extended duties in respect to agriculture or commerce, which can be better done by the people for themselves, yet there are many things which can be done here, under the auspices of the Department which is about to be established, which will tend to develope agriculture, which will tend to procure a larger supply of labour—one of the great wants of Burma at the present day—which will tend to introduce labour-saving machines

Dinner at Government House, Rangoon.

more largely into this country, and to aid in the establishment of new branches of agriculture yet in an undeveloped state, like that of tea, coffee, and tobacco; and the development of those which already exist here, but perhaps in a comparatively undeveloped state, like that of sugarcane. These are great and important objects in regard to the permanent prosperity of this province, and it is with the view of discussing with the Chief Commissioner the best mode in which we can labour to attain those objects that I have asked Mr. Buck, the able and energetic Secretary in the Agricultural Department, to accompany me on this occasion, that he may advise me and Mr. Bernard in our conference as to the best mode of attaining these great and useful ends.

It only remains for me to thank you very heartily, on behalf of Lady Ripon, for the kind manner in which you have spoken of her on this occasion. Yes, ladies and gentlemen, Mr. Bernard is quite right; he speaks doubtless from his own experience (*applause*) when he sets that high value upon a good wife; and no one knows the worth of a good wife, and the aid she may be to a man in the hard work of official business, better than I do. (*Applause.*)

And now, before I sit down, I must ask you to drink one more toast. I know well there are many I see before me who are waiting for the conclusion of my speech; but I am quite sure they will heartily join in supporting me in the proposition I am about to make, for I am about to ask you to drink the health of the Chief Commissioner. (*Applause.*) When Mr. Aitchison—who now, by that well-earned recognition of his long, able, and eminent services to the Government of India, which was conferred on him by the Queen is Sir Charles Aitchison—when he was called last year to take his place in the Governor General's Council at Simla, I had to consider to whom I could entrust the duties of his office. I knew that Burma was a progressive province; I knew it was a province which needed at its head an able, energetic man, and I looked round to see where I could find the fittest man for the position. I was told on all hands, by those whom I consulted, that I had better choose Mr. Bernard. (*Applause.*) It was a trial to me to give him up, because, though I had only worked with him for about a month, that month was quite time enough to tell me the value of his services at the Home Office; but I felt it my duty to look to the interests of this great province—I felt in my duty to choose a man distinguished by earnestness of purpose and zeal for the public service, by marked abilities, and by untiring energy; and, above all, to choose a man who would have a deep and heartfelt sympathy for the people over whom he was called to rule; and, ladies and gentlemen, I rejoice to find that, after some ten months of experience of the results of my choice, Mr. Bernard's conduct in this administration has fully proved the justice of my judgment. *(Applause.)*

RECEPTION OF BURMESE GENTLEMEN.

22nd Dec. 1881. [ON the 21st December, the Viceroy held a Levée at Government House, Rangoon, which was largely attended. In the afternoon, His Excellency paid a visit to the Thayettaw Monasteries, where he was received by about seventy Buddhist monks. At 1 P. M. on Thursday, the 22nd December, His Excellency held a reception of native gentlemen, at which decorations—gold medals and chains—were distributed to a number of Burmese officials, in recognition of long and faithful service to the Government. His Excellency then received several memorials from the inhabitants of Rangoon, on various local matters, and afterwards addressed the assembly as follows :—]

Gentlemen,—I am very glad to have this opportunity of meeting you, the representatives of various sections of the native community of this city, and in acquiring, through the memorials which you have presented to to me, a knowledge of your wishes upon matters of local interest.

Reception of Burmese Gentlemen.

I consider, gentlemen, that in thus fully making known your wishes to me you are taking a very useful course, and setting a good example, which I trust will be more and more followed on similar occasions in other parts of India. It is the foundation of my policy as Governor-General of this country, and the great end and object of my administration, to advance the interests of the people of every part of the Indian dominions of our Queen-Empress, and to keep constantly in view the promotion of their welfare. It seems to me that this ought to be at all times the great aim of the English Government in India, and that it is the plain duty of that Government and the best justification of its existence. Now, gentlemen, it helps very much towards the attainment of this object, that the inhabitants of different parts of the country should make known their wishes to the Government as you have done to-day; and I shall always be ready to give to those wishes my most careful and considerate attention. It may not—indeed, it may be assumed that it will not—be possible to comply with all of them; but I am most anxious that the people of India, of all races and all classes, should understand that any expression of their desires will always receive the fullest consideration from the Government of India, and that if in any instances the requests so made to us cannot be granted, they will never be rejected through indifference or neglect.

I am much pleased to have had this opportunity of recognising, by the decorations which I have just distributed, the services which have been rendered to the Government by the various gentlemen who have received those distinctions. It was also a satisfaction to me a short time ago, upon the recommendation of my friend the Chief Commissioner, to appoint a native gentlemen of this province, Moung Ba Ohn, as a probationer in the covenanted civil service. He is the first Burman who has been admitted to that service, and I trust that by his zeal, energy, and

Reception of Burmese Gentlemen.

devotion to his duties he will prove himself worthy of the confidence which has been placed in him, and will thus encourage me, or future Viceroys, to give, from time to time, to the people of this province, their fair share of appointments of this kind.

The Government of India received, some time ago, representations from the Chief Commissioner pointing out the necessity of improving the position of Native Officials in this province. Those representations have received the most careful consideration from the Government, and although I am not at this moment in a position to communicate to you the detailed conclusions at which we are likely to arrive, it is a pleasure to me to be able to say that we recognise the importance of bettering the position, not in British Burma only, but throughout India, of those uncovenanted servants of the Government, upon whose zeal and good conduct the good administration of the country so largely depends; and that I hope that it may be in our power shortly to make known the measures we propose to adopt for that purpose, and which will, I have every reason to hope, meet the wishes of the Chief Commissioner.

And now, gentlemen, it only remains for me to thank you very sincerely, on my own behalf, and on that of Lady Ripon, for the very hearty welcome which you have given to us. We were greatly delighted by the variety and beauty of the various arches which were erected by Native bodies and by the Chinese residents along the road through which we passed on the day of our arrival, and it has been to me a pleasing duty to report to our gracious Sovereign the proofs of loyalty and cordial good will by which the reception of her representative has been marked. I shall, I assure you, always retain a very lively and agreeable recollection of my visit to British Burma, and of all the circumstances which have attended it; and it will be at all times my earnest desire to do everything in my power to promote your happiness and prosperity.

MEMORIALS FROM THE MERCANTILE COMMUNITY OF RANGOON.

[AT 1 P. M. on the 23rd December, the Viceroy received the Recorder and the Judicial Commissioner of Rangoon, and discussed the question of the establishment of a High Court. At 3 P. M., a Deputation of the leading merchants of Rangoon waited on His Excellency and presented memorials regarding the re-establishment of monopolies in Upper Burma, and praying that if no more effectual steps could be taken, a strong remonstrance should be addressed to the Burmese Government on the subject. The memorials also drew attention to the necessity for the establishment of a High Court of Judicature at Rangoon, to be presided over by not less than three Judges, two of whom would sit on appeals from any one of the Judges. After the presentation of these memorials, a discussion ensued:—] 23rd Dec. 1881.

His Excellency :—I have already received copies of these memorials, and made myself acquainted with their contents. The first is from the merchants and others in Rangoon, and relates, I think exclusively to the trade with Upper Burma; and the second is from the Chamber of Commerce, and relates also to that subject and to the question of the establishment of a High Court at Rangoon. It will be better to keep the two subjects quite distinct in the conversation we may have, as they have no connection with each other.

With respect to the first—namely, the monopolies which have unfortunately been recently established by the Mandalay Government, and which are inflicting evidently so serious an injury upon our trade with Upper Burma,—I am quite sure I need not tell you that I regret extremely that any circumstances should have arisen to check the progress of the trade whith now amounts to so considerable a sum, and was of growing importance to the country. It is the foremost object of my policy as Governor-General of this country, and the policy of my colleagues (especially in the

Memorials from the Mercantile Community of Rangoon.

Financial Department as represented by Major Baring), to do everything that can fitly and properly be done by a Government to develope the commercial and industrial resources of all parts of India. I look upon it as a very great object for the Government in this country, at the present time, to encourage private enterprise and the investment of private capital in India to the utmost extent that it is possible for us to do so. You know very well that the resources of this country (especially of the province of Burma) are great, and there are many sources of wealth only waiting to be developed by the application of capital; and everything we can do to render it easy for private capital to be applied to the development of the resources of the country, you may rely upon it, it will be our object to do, in every way in our power. Entertaining these views, I need scarcely tell you that I regard with very great regret the obstacles which have been lately interposed in the way of freedom of trade with Upper Burma. It is a matter of a very serious character, which has already occupied the attention of the Government, and will continue to occupy our very close attention. At the same time, the circumstances of that country are such as to render it a task of difficulty and delicacy to decide what steps (if any) it would at the present moment be possible to take with a view to endeavouring to remove the obstacles which now so seriously interfere with and fetter our trade. Upper Burma is in a very disturbed condition, as you are aware—indeed, the latest information in my possession seems to point to a state of things which leaves one to suppose that a serious crisis is likely to arise very shortly in the country. How far that may be the case, time will show; but that seems the most probable result of the present condition of affairs at Mandalay. With respect to anything the Government can do at the present moment to relieve you from the difficulties in which you are placed in regard to your trade, I shall be very glad indeed to learn the views of the gentlemen

Memorials from the Mercantile Community of Rangoon.

who are present, as to what, in their opinion, could be done by the Government with a view to better the present condition of affairs. Looking at these two memorials, I find that the first memorial merely states very clearly, fully, and forcibly the difficulties under which you are suffering, and leaves the remedy to be discovered by the Government. I am very much obliged to you for the confidence which you place in us, but it would be a great advantage to us to learn what you think would be the best course to adopt. The second memorial states one step, at all events, which might be taken, in a sentence the first part of which is undoubtedly most true, and represents very fairly indeed the difficulties of the situation :—

'In a case of this kind, it is less difficult to describe the grievance than to suggest a remedy ; but we would respectfully submit that, if no more effectual steps can be taken, a strong remonstrance, at least, should be addressed to the Burmese Government.'

I shall say a word about that presently, but, in the first place, I should be very glad if any gentlemen present would express freely and openly their views upon the subject, and what steps they think it would be possible for the Government to take, to put an end to this most unsatisfactory state of affairs. I hope you will kindly give us your advice with the utmost freedom. I have asked you to come up here to this room (which I am using as an office, through Mr. Bernard's kindness), that we might not have a formal, but a friendly, interview ; and I should be very much obliged if you would explain to me whatever views you entertain on the matter.

Mr. Kennedy observed that they wished to leave the matter entirely to His Excellency, to adopt any steps he thought advisable to extricate them from the difficulty.

His Excellency:—As regards the suggestion which is made in the memorial of the Chamber of Commerce, I should wish to say this,—that we have already addressed a remonstrance to the Mandalay Government (which, in fact,

Memorials from the Mercantile Community of Rangoon.

I need scarcely tell you, for it was obviously our duty to do so) upon the first establishment of the earlier monopolies, pointing out to them the grievous injury which was inflicted on our trade, and the view which we took of the unfriendly character of measures of that kind. Since then, as I understand—indeed, quite recently—additional monopolies have been established. Is that not so? Our letter was written in September.

Mr. Kennedy remarked that the Mandalay Government was going on creating fresh monopolies from time to time.

His Excellency:—It seems to me that it is a very fair question for us to consider whether we should not make a further remonstrance in strong and decided terms, pointing out the great objections which there are, in our opinion, to the establishment of these monopolies; and I will consult my colleagues when I get back to Calcutta on that point, as I understand that is the step you would wish to be taken. I feel very much indeed that our great interest—in fact, I might almost say, our only interest—with regard to our relations with Upper Burma is the interest of our trade. As long as the trade stands on a reasonable and sound footing, that is all we want with the Mandalay Government; reasonable and friendly relations, with full freedom for the development of trade. That is all along the view which I have taken of it, and I should desire to direct my course towards that object, which I look upon as the fundamental point which we ought to have in view in our relations with the Government of Upper Burma. I do not know that I can say anything further as regards the steps to be taken. If there is any point you could call my attention to, or any step you could suggest, I should be glad to hear your views. You are men locally acquainted with the matter, and knowing the course of trade, and knowing much more than I can possibly do about the state of things at Mandalay.

Memorials from the Mercantile Community of Rangoon.

Mr. Binning asked, supposing a remonstrance were ineffectual, if any further steps could be taken.

His Excellency :—Well, that is precisely what I wanted to know,—whether you had any further steps to suggest. You see, I have always held the opinion (not only in regard to this question, but in regard to political questions generally) that nothing is more unwise and undignified for a Government than to threaten if they are not prepared to act on those threats. That I will not do. If I said to the Mandalay Government or any other Government, 'I shall do so-and-so if you do not do something else,' I should feel bound to do what I had said, if occasion arose. Threats, therefore, are a serious step, and I do not know if anything of that kind is desirable at the present moment. I should like, however, the Mandalay Government to understand clearly that there is nothing so serious to us as anything affecting our trade; —that is, as I have already said, our principal interest there ; and a concession on this point is the first (perhaps, at present the only) proof they can give us of their desire to be on friendly terms.

Mr. Grieve said he thought they would be quite satisfied if His Excellency decided on addressing the Mandalay Government again ; and Mr. Binning asked what were the views of the Government with regard to a fresh treaty.

His Excellency :—Of course, the making of a fresh treaty must depend on the opportunity. If a fair opportunity opened, and there was any point on which you thought the present treaty could be improved, we should be glad to consider any suggestion you could make ; but the state of the country does not point to anything like that at present. If the Mandalay Government approached us, we should be glad to receive any reasonable offer they might make. It is not for us at the present moment to go to them, but, should they come to us, we should endeavour to negotiate upon a basis which would benefit our trade.

Memorials from the Mercantile Community of Rangoon.

Mr. Grieve said all they desired was a free trade with Upper Burma. At the same time, the opinion among them was that a treaty with Burma was not likely to be carried out, and, as things were just now, the commerce of Rangoon was in a state of stagnation altogether.

His Excellency :—Yes, I was sorry to see that the trade had fallen off very much. We must watch events. For months my attention has been directed to the matter—in fact, ever since I became acquainted with the circumstances of the case ; and I look upon it entirely in the light of our trade interests, and I shall not lose any favourable opportunity that may arise of putting things on a better footing.

Major Baring, on being referred to by His Excellency, stated that the rice-trade was quite independent of the treaty, and that the falling off there was due to increased production in Upper Burma.

His Excellency :—It seems to have fallen off very largely.

Mr. Grieve said this was not the subject of complaint ; he added that Rangoon merchants would of course prefer that rice should pass through their mills, rather than go unmilled to Upper Burma.

His Excellency :—With respect to the other point which the Chamber of Commerce have alluded to in their memorial, regarding the judicial arrangements of the province and the proposal to establish a High Court or Chief Court, I cannot at the present moment express any decided opinion.

It is one, no doubt, of importance, and, in consequence of communications which reached us from Mr. Atichison before he left you, and from the present Chief Commissioner, it has already received a good deal of attention from the Government of India ; and it would now seem to be ripe for a decision, at all events as to what should immediately be done, for, in a progressive province like this, arrangements suitable for one time may have to be

Memorials from the Mercantile Community of Rangoon.

altered sooner than we expect ; and I can assure you that we shall give the greatest weight to the opinions which you have expressed. I have made it my business here to confer with the Recorder and Judicial Commissioner, and I am also acquainted with the views of Mr. Bernard ; and I shall thoroughly discuss the question with him before I leave ; and you know that in the Government of India we have the advantage of the advice of Mr. Rivers Thompson, one of your former Chief Commissioners, who has not lost his interest in Burma, and who concerns himself very much with any questions that affect the welfare of this province. Perhaps, however, some of you might kindly point out to us the chief practical objections you have to the present arrangement. You briefly allude to them here, but, as I have heard what is to be said by the executive authorities, I should like to hear what you, as the representatives of the public, think are the objections to the present arrangements.

A pause followed.

His Excellency :—The Chamber of Commerce speak of delays. Do you find much delay arising from the circumstance of these gentlemen being occupied with other duties.

Mr. Dickson stated that there had been delays.

His Excellency :—We may take it, I suppose, that there is a general feeling that the present arrangement is not satisfactory, but is that founded upon practical inconvenience which has been felt by gentlemen attending these Courts ?

Mr. Dickson :—I believe it is so.

His Excellency :—You also mention that it would secure greater uniformity in the decisions of the lower Courts. Is it felt that at present there is practically a want of such uniformity ?

One of the Deputation replied in the affirmative.

Ball at Rangoon.

His Excellency :—Very well, I promise you we shall consider the question very carefully, and pay all due attention to your wishes as representatives of this important community. I must thank you for the kind words you have said to me individually in your address. I have enjoyed my visit here very much,—indeed, as much as anything I have seen in India. It is pleasant to be in a country which shows such signs of progrress, and I shall carry away very pleasant recollections of my visit here. I am also much obliged to you for your visit, as it is a great advantage to learn the views of those who are directly interested in questions of trade and commerce.

[The Deputation then thanked His Excellency for the courteous reception he had given them, and on the Viceroy's rising, withdrew.]

BALL AT RANGOON.

23rd Dec. 1881. [IN the evening a ball was given in honour of the Viceroy and Lady Ripon, by the people of Rangoon, at which Their Excellencies were present. In reply to the toast of his health, proposed at supper—]

His Excellency said that he tendered his most hearty thanks to all for the cordial manner in which the response to the toast of his health had been given. He felt keenly the warmth and loyalty of the welcome which had been extended to him in Rangoon, and he must say that each succeeding reception he was called on to attend seemed more kind and more enthusiastic than the former one. He had been called upon to make many speeches lately, and, as he did not see any reason to unsay anything that he had already said (nor had he anything new to say), he must confine himself to thanking the people of Rangoon for the welcome they had given him on this occasion. With regard to what Major Poole[1] had said

[1] The Deputy Commissioner and President of the Municipality.

Visit to St. John's College, Rangoon.

about the Town Hall, he felt that he should be honoured by having his own name connected therewith, especially as the hall would remain a monument of such a widely respected townsman as Mr. Fowle. He thanked those present, in the name of himself and Lady Ripon, for the way in which they had been received; and assured his audience that his visit to Burma would ever remain among the most pleasant among his recollections.

[Three hearty cheers were then given for the Marquis and Marchioness of Ripon, and 'one more' for Mr. Fowle.]

VISIT TO ST. JOHN'S COLLEGE, RANGOON.

[ON Sunday afternoon, the 25th of December, the Viceroy visited St. John's College, Rangoon. In reply to an address read by Dr. Marks, the Principal, His Excellency spoke as follows :—]

Mr. Bernard, Dr. Marks, Ladies and Gentlemen,—It affords me great pleasure to visit St. John's College, and to be present on this interesting occasion. You, Dr. Marks, have rightly interpreted my visit as an indication of my deep interest in the education of the youth of this country, more especially of the class to which you have alluded. Measures are now being considered by the Government of India, which it is hoped will give a fresh impetus and support to their education. As I look upon the faces of the pupils before me, I am struck with that remarkable admixture of races which I have noticed everywhere in Rangoon—different nationalities all working side by side in perfect harmony and accord. I feel sure that this institution is doing really good work in this city; and I earnestly hope and pray for the continued success and prosperity of St. John's College. To you boys I would say,—value and improve the opportunities here offered to you. All the instruction and education that you receive in this place you will need in later life; and if you do but make good use of your time

Addresses of Welcome to the Viceroy at Moulmein.

at school, let me assure you that you will reap benefits great and numerous hereafter. I thank you all for the very kind reception which you have given me, and I wish you every happiness and success.

[At 3-15 P.M. on the 26th December, His Excellency and party embarked from the Phayre Street wharf, on board the *Tenasserim*, and proceeded to Moulmein, accompanied by the Chief Commissioner and Mr. G. D. Burgess, and attended by the I. G. S. *Enterprize*, with part of the Suite on board. The troops, the Volunteers, the principal residents, the officials, and the public of Rangoon attended, to do honour to Their Excellencies on their departure, in the same way as on their arrival. The Viceroy expressed his hearty approval of the arrangements, non-official and official, made for his reception and his entertainment at Rangoon; and directed that this expression of his feelings, which the Marchioness of Ripon fully shared, should be made known to the people of all classes, non-official and official, European and Native, to ladies as well as to gentlemen.]

ADDRESS OF WELCOME TO THE VICEROY AT MOULMEIN.

27th Dec. 1881. [THEIR Excellencies the Viceroy and the Marchioness of Ripon arrived at Moulmein at 11 o'clock on the morning of the 27th December, and disembarked at the Main Wharf at 11-30 A.M. At Half-way Creek, on the Moulmein river, the Viceroy's party removed from the *Tenasserim* to the I. G. S. *Irrawaddy*, which had been sent over to Amherst to await His Excellency's arrival. The Viceroy and Lady Ripon were received at the wharf by Colonel Duff, Commissioner of Tenasserim; Colonel Jenkins, Commandant; Major Furlong, Mr. Macrae, Mr. Birks, and other officials, Consuls of Foreign States and representatives of the various Communities. On landing at the wharf, an address of welcome was presented to the Viceroy by the English-speaking inhabitants of Moulmein, to which His Excellency replied:—]

I am much obliged to you, gentlemen, and I can assure you that it has given me great pleasure to come to Burma; and I quite made up my mind, when I thought of going to Rangoon, that I would make an effort to visit your town.

Addresses of Welcome to the Viceroy at Moulmein.

I had heard much of its beauty; and certainly what I have seen in the approach along the river fully confirms the anticipations I had formed. I am grateful to you for your kind and cordial welcome, and I am glad to find you fully appreciate the recent Resolution announced by the Government of India, with respect to the encouragement of private enterprise, and think it is calculated to develope the trade of this place. I trust those who are capable of undertaking works of a commercial and industrial character in this country will start the work of developing its resources; for when we say we desire to encourage private enterprise, it is, of course, understood that private enterprise will be ready to accept the offer, and to do its part; and I trust it will be so both with respect to capital from Europe and to local capital—for it is mainly in regard to local capital that we desire to encourage private enterprise.

[An address was next presented by the Burmese and Talaing residents of Moulmein, to which His Excellency replied:—]

I thank you very much for your kind welcome, and am very glad to see you. I have been very much pleased with my visit to British Burma, and with all I have seen; and I shall always retain pleasant recollections of my visit, and shall devote my utmost efforts to develope and promote the welfare of this province.

[In reply to addresses presented by Deputations of the Persian and Mahomedan communities, His Excellency said:—]

I am very much obliged to you, gentlemen. It is very pleasant to see so many different races living together under the shadow of the British Government, and labouring to promote in unison the welfare of the country.

[To an address presented on behalf of the Chetties, His Excellency replied:—]

I thank you very much. When I came out to this country, I was commanded by Her Majesty the Queen-Empress to display towards her subjects in India and her Eastern

Addresses of Welcome to the Viceroy at Moulmein.

dominions, of all classes, and races, and creeds, a strict impartiality; and it has always been my endeavour to act on that principle. I shall communicate to Her Majesty the expressions of loyalty which have just been conveyed to me, and which I am happy to say are the same as those which I have received in all parts of the country. I am glad to accept what you have said as to the interest I feel in the cause of education. I can assure you that that is a subject which I have very much at heart, and that I desire very much to promote, by every means in my power, the education of all classes of the community.

[In reply to an address from the Chinese Community, His Excellency said:—]

I thank you, gentlemen, and I am very much obliged for your kind address. I can assure you I appreciate highly the presence of the Chinese Community in this province, and I am well aware of the advantage the province derives from their presence, and of the industrial habits which they display. I have already had occasion, in connection with my visit to Rangoon, to assure the Queen-Empress of the loyalty of her Chinese subjects; and I shall be very glad to repeat that assurance in connection with your address.

[At 3 P.M. the Viceroy held a Levée, which was largely attended; and at 4 P. M. His Excellency held a reception of Burmese gentlemen, at which decorations were given to a number of officers, in consideration of their long and faithful services to Government. After the presentations had been made His Excellency addressed the assembly as follows:—]

Gentlemen,—I am happy to meet you, and to have an opportunity of expressing to you personally, as I have already done to the inhabitants of Rangoon, the interest which I feel in the people of British Burma. I am much pleased with my visit to this province, and am particularly struck by the natural beauties of Moulmein. I regard the cordial reception which you have given me as a proof of your loyalty to the Queen-Empress and your

Addresses of Welcome to the Viceroy at Moulmein.

respect for her representative. I and my colleague in the Government of India, Major Baring, have conferred with the Chief Commissioner on many questions connected with the condition of the province, and it has been especially pleasant to me to be able to inform him that the Government hope before long to take measures for improving the position of our native officials. We have also discussed various measures for the improvement of agriculture and the development of the resources of the country. The Government will do all that they can for this purpose; but you, who are the leading men of the Burman community, can do much more yourselves. I do not ask you to abandon those methods of agriculture which long experience may have proved to be well suited to your soil and climate; but I trust that you will see the advantage of availing yourselves of such improvements, suggested by European and American experience, as may appear likely upon trial to be advantageous in this country. It is in this way that you may derive the largest amount of benefit from your connection with England. I need not tell you, who know well how zealously Mr. Bernard devotes himself to everything connected with the advancement of your interests, that he is sure to carry out in the most earnest manner the wishes of the Government of India in regard to these matters.

I rejoice, gentlemen, to find the province is prospering. The well-being of the people of Her Majesty's dominions is the first object of my care, and it is a gratification to me to hope, from your friendly reception, that you recognise that this is the principal end of my administration. Lady Ripon desires me, on her behalf, to express the pleasure which she has derived from the greeting you have given her, and, for her and for myself, I once more sincerely thank you.

MEMORIAL CONCERNING THE TIMBER DUTY, MOULMEIN.

29th Dec. 1881. [ON the morning of the 29th December, a Deputation of the Merchants of Moulmein, both English and Burmese, waited upon His Excellency at Government House, to petition against the present tax on timber, regarding which a memorial had been submitted to Mr. Bernard, the Chief Commissioner. Mr. Henderson acted as spokesman for the Deputation, and stated the case of the memorialists at length. He said the complaint was that they found the amount of the tax at present too heavy; but their principal grievance was that they were at a disadvantage as compared with Rangoon, where all the timber from foreign and British territory was imported free of duty. He thought that they ought to be put on the same footing as Rangoon; and he urged that if the revenue derived from the timber duty could not be given up, some means should be taken by which the trade in Rangoon should be made to bear its share of the burden.

His Excellency, in replying, spoke as follows :—]

I have had the advantage of having before me the memorial which is addressed to Mr. Bernard, the Chief Commissioner, and of fully considering the subject with him and with my honourable friend, Major Baring, the Financial Member of the Council of the Governor General. And of course you will not think it unreasonable that in dealing with a question involving such a considerable sum of revenue, we should have considered prominently whether we could afford to dispense with the amount of money connected with this duty; and, after fully considering the question, we came to the conclusion that it would be possible for us to dispense with that amount without any serious inconvenience to our financial position. Under these circumstances, we were free to consider the general bearings of the question, and I confess that I cannot myself resist the strong arguments which you put forward in this memorial, and which have been enforced by the remarks of the gentleman who has just sat down,—that you are undoubtedly by this tax placed in a disadvantageous

Memorial concerning the Timber Duty, Moulmein.

position, and are unduly weighted in your trade as compared with the port of Rangoon. Now, gentlemen, it is my desire and that of my colleague to see that every port and every town in any part of the Indian dominions should be placed upon a footing of equality. I entirely admit that it is a hardship which you have a right to complain of, that you should be placed at a disadvantage with regard to Rangoon ; and the desire of the Government of India in such a case is to deal on the most perfect footing of equality with all ports and towns and districts of the country. Under these circumstances, it is obvious, if that principle is to be adopted at all, then, as you say, either the duty imposed on timber coming down here must be removed, or else an equal duty must be imposed on timber going down to Rangoon.

There is one remark in the memorial, on the question whether it would be impossible to impose a duty on timber coming down to Rangoon, which I think involves an error. You say, the treaty with the Government of Upper Burma has now lapsed. This is not my view of the question. I have no doubt that the existence of monopolies imposed by the King of Ava (which have been, I regret to say, recently increasing in number) is inconsistent with the spirit and intention of the treaty ; but, on the other hand, the treaty cannot be said to have lapsed. It might be open to argument, whether the imposition of these monopolies, so inconsistent with the spirit of the treaty, would justify the Government of India in abandoning the treaty ; but until we have thought fit to take a step of that kind, and given due warning to the Government of Ava, the treaty cannot be said to have lapsed ; and, for my own part, I am not at present inclined to take the step of denouncing the treaty, whatever may be ultimately necessary, under circumstances which I hope and trust may be amended before long. But, until that step is taken, the treaty cannot be justly said to have lapsed ; and consequently, we are still bound on our

Memorial concerning the Timber Duty, Moulmein.

part by the provisions of the treaty, and cannot withdraw from it without due and proper notice to the Government with which the treaty was made.

Besides that, although I should like to leave the Government of India free in regard to the question of maintaining that treaty, I have no desire to impose a tax of this kind upon the people of Rangoon. It would be open to objection in our own interests, and I am therefore happy to feel that, as we can afford to make the sacrifice of the revenue, it is in my power to say that we will remit the duty, reserving only such portion of it as may be necessary at present for the purpose of amply providing for the arrangement to which allusion has been made. What I am prepared, therefore, to do is to reduce the duty at once to one per cent. We desire to keep that one per cent. of duty on, to cover the expenses connected with the arrangement which has just been described; but Mr. Bernard will consider, in consultation with you gentlemen who are interested in trade, whether it is necessary to keep up such an arrangement or not. It would, however, obviously disorganise trade to dispense with such an arrangement at the present moment, and you could not expect us, after making such a considerable sacrifice, to perform that operation gratis: we therefore propose to keep on a duty of one per cent. at present.

The question has arisen, as to when this concession should take effect. The natural thing to have done would have been to have brought it into operation from the commencement of the next financial year—that is, from the 1st of April; but we have felt that to announce the decision now, at the end of December, and to postpone carrying it into effect till April, would greatly disorganise the trade; and under these circumstances, we are prepared to reduce the duty from the 1st of January next. I hope you will see in this a proof that the Government of India desire to encourage trade by every means in their power, and to

Deputation on the establishment of a High Court.

deal with this and all other ports and districts in the country on the fair footing of equality.

[Major Baring briefly explained that under ordinary circumstances, half of the loss of revenue would be borne by the Provincial, and half by the Imperial, Government ; but in the present instance, it was proposed to make a grant of an extra lakh to Burma for the next two years, and it was hoped that, at the end of that time, the elasticity of the revenue, which was one of the features of the revenue of the province, would enable the province to bear its share.

The Deputation then thanked His Excellency, and left.]

DEPUTATION ON THE ESTABLISHMENT OF A HIGH COURT.

[A Deputation waited on His Excellency the Viceroy at noon on the 29th December, regarding the proposed establishment of a High Court. Mr. Law, who acted as spokesman, explained the views of the Deputation on the subject, and concluded by saying that, owing to the short time he had had, he was unable to speak with more precision, or to furnish statistics in support of what he had said ; but if necessary he would be happy to forward any information that was required. His Excellency replied as follows :—]

29th Dec. 1881.

I have had the advantage of seeing, last night, a report of the proceedings of the meeting held in the Town Hall, and learning the object of this Deputation. Perhaps you go a little too far in supposing that a superior court is about to be established here immediately. It is quite true that I—and I think I may say, the rest of the Government of India, are favourable to the establishment of what I should prefer to call a Chief Court, mainly upon the grounds of the representations made to us by the commercial community both here and at Rangoon, and our great desire to meet the wishes of that community as far as possible. But the question will have to be referred Home to the Secretary of State, and, after that, will require legislation : therefore the fact that the Court will be established is not so very near.

Deputation on the establishment of a High Court.

A certain amount of necessary delay will take place, and I cannot answer for the view that will be taken of the matter by the superior authority to whom it must be referred. With respect to the point to which you have specially referred, it will receive careful consideration. No doubt, suggestions have been made in the direction of abolishing the superior court existing here, so far as superior jurisdiction is concerned; but no decision has been come to upon that point, and I can promise you that the representations you have made will receive our best consideration. It will also greatly facilitate our consideration if you will kindly furnish us with those further facts and statistics to which Mr. Law referred, and which you might send in through the Chief Commissioner. I should be very sorry to take any hasty step in the direction of abolishing the court which exists here, and my present impression as an individual is, that it would be wise to allow the existing arrangements to remain until we have had an opportunity of seeing how the establishment of a Chief Court worked.

[In the afternoon, Their Excellencies and Party embarked on board the *Irrawaddy*, and proceeded down the river to Amherst, where a change was made to the *Tenasserim*, which proceeded at 5 P.M. direct to Calcutta. His Excellency expressed himself as highly satisfied with the arrangements made for his reception and entertainment at Moulmein, and desired that an expression of his feelings on this point should be conveyed to the public and to the officials of Moulmein and of the Tenasserim division.]

OPENING THE EXHIBITION OF INDUSTRIAL ARTS AT CALCUTTA.

[On Saturday afternoon, the 4th January, the Viceroy opened the **4th Jan. 1882.** Exhibition of Industrial Arts, Calcutta, in the new Museum. The Hon. H. T. Prinsep, the Secretary, having conducted His Excellency to a seat, delivered an explanatory address, to which His Excellency replied as follows:—]

Sir Ashley Eden, Ladies and Gentlemen,—It affords me great pleasure to be able to be present on this occasion, and to assist and take part in the opening of this, the first Exhibition which has been established in Calcutta.

I do not wish to detain you with any lengthened remarks of my own in declaring this Exhibition open. The objects of the Exhibition have been so well and clearly explained in the remarks which have just fallen from Mr. Justice Prinsep, that I need not go over the same ground which he has traversed.

I believe that Exhibitions of this description, especially when they are held successively in different towns throughout the country, are calculated to afford a very useful encouragement to the development of arts, and also to advance the artistic character of our manufactures. It also appears to me that great advantages are likely to be derived from the opportunity thus given to make known to the public, more fully than was formerly the case, the beautiful and interesting products of indigenous art, and by affording the wealthy classes of the community in this country the opportunity of purchasing these products, instead of objects (often of a commoner description and of inferior beauty) brought from Europe. Again, it is of no small importance that an Exhibition of this kind offers to manufacturers the means, at one and the same time, of attracting the public taste to their productions, and also of learning what is the style of goods most likely to meet public approval; and further,

Opening the Exhibition of Industrial Arts at Calcutta.

there will arise, I hope, another benefit from these Exhibitions in the stimulus given by them to Indian manufactures—an advantage to which I attach, for my part, great importance.

No one who considers the economic condition of India can doubt that one of its greatest evils is to be found in the fact that the great mass of the people of the country are dependent almost exclusively upon the cultivation of the soil. This circumstance tends at one and the same time to depress the position of the cultivators, to aggravate the evils of famine, and also to lower wages generally. I always hail, therefore, with great interest, everything which is calculated to open new sources of employment for the people, or to develope those which already exist. This is work which can only be accomplished by the co-operation of a variety of agencies. The Government can do somethings towards it, and private individuals can take their share. The owners of capital, whether Indian or European, have a great and valuable part to perform in the promotion of this great work. Such Exhibtions can aid also, in their own way, in the promotion of this important object.

I was very glad to hear, from the remarks which fell from Mr. Prinsep, of two novel features which distinguish this Exhibition. Arrangements have been made, it appears, to give facilities for ordering reproductions of any of the articles exhibited, which purchasers may wish to possess; and I cannot doubt that these arraugements will prove a great convenience both to manufacturers and to the public. The other feature alluded to is one to which I attach great importance, and of which I hear with special pleasure. Mr. Prinsep has told us that you, Sir Ashley Eden, have offered to pay the expenses of the poorer artizans and workmen of Bengal, who may wish to visit the Exhibition. Now, ladies and gentlemen, my experience since I came to India has generally shown me that the Lieutenant-Governor of Bengal generally knows how to hit the right nail on the head (*cheers*), and he has certainly done so on this occasion

Repeal of the Vernacular Press Act.

(*cheers*); for, according to my ideas, one of the most important uses to which such an Exhibition as this can be put is to afford to the working classes and to the smaller manufacturers the means of improving and widening their taste, and of expanding their ideas. I trust, therefore, that this grant of Sir Ashley Eden's will be largely made use of by those for whose benefit it is intended.

Ladies and Gentlemen,—I do not think that I need detain you any longer, as you are all, no doubt, anxious to pass from this place into the Exhibition itself, and to see the very beautiful objects which await you there. It will be sufficient for me to say that I heartily wish success to this Exhibition, and I trust that the example set here in Bengal will be followed widely in other parts of India.

In accordance with the request made to me by the Committee, I now declare this Exhibition to be open. (*Cheers.*)

REPEAL OF THE VERNACULAR PRESS ACT.

[ON the occasion of the repeal of the Vernacular Press Act by the Legislative Council, the Members of which unanimously spoke in support of the Bill introduced with that object, the Viceroy made the following remarks :—] 19th Jan. 1882.

I do not wish to detain the Council by any observations of my own; nor do I think that I am in any way called upon to review the reasons or motives for which this Act was originally introduced. All I desire to say is, that it will always be a great satisfaction to me that it should have been during the time that I held the office of Viceroy that the Act was removed from the Indian Statute-book.

THE TRANSFER OF PROPERTY BILL.

26th Jan. 1882. [THE Legislative Council assembled on the 26th January, to discuss the Transfer of Property Bill. The primary object of this Bill, as explained by Mr. Stokes when he introduced it five years before, was to complete the Code of Contract Law (Act IX of 1872) so far as it related to immovable property, and thus to carry out the policy of Codification which the Government of India had resumed. Its secondary object was to bring the rules which regulated the transmission of property between living persons into harmony with certain rules affecting its devolution upon death, and thus to furnish the necessary complement of the work which the Legislative Council commenced by passing the Law of Succession (Act X of 1865), continued by passing the Hindu Wills Act (XXI of 1870) for the Lower Provinces and the Presidency Town, and would soon, it was hoped, end by extending the latter Act to Hindus and Bhuddists in the rest of India. Another object of the Bill was to amend the law of mortgages and conditional sales, which had, at least in Madras and Bombay, got into a somewhat unsatisfactory condition. Mr. Stokes now presented the final Report of the Select Committee on the Bill, and moved that the further and final Reports of the Committee be taken into consideration. He explained at some length the nature of the amendments described in those Reports, and went fully into the history of the Bill, which in its present form, he argued, was a systematic and useful arrangement of the existing law, and which he hoped would speedily be passed. The Hon. Durgá Charan Láhá, Sayyad Ahmad, Rájá Siva Prasad, Messrs. Crosthwaite and Evans, and Mahárájá Jotindro Mohán Tagore spoke in favour of the Bill, and the motion was put and agreed to. Mr. Plowden next addressed the Council, arguing that sufficient publicity had not been given to the Bill, that a lengthened postponement was desirable, in order that the Native Community might have a fuller opportunity of expressing their views, and finally moved "that the Bill as amended by the Select Committee be re-published." The Lieutenant-Governor (Sir A. Eden) thought that the Council would be acting with undue haste in passing the Bill at once, and suggested its postponement for a few weeks. Mr. Rivers Thompson considered the suggestion a reasonable one, upon which Mr. Stokes stated that he was prepared to postpone the passing of the Bill for three weeks. His Excellency the President spoke as follows :—]

There seems to be a very broad distinction between the

The Transfer of Property Bill.

suggestion thrown out by my honourable friend the Lieutenant Governor and the motion of my honourable friend Mr. Plowden. That motion is one for delaying the passing of this Bill for a very lengthened period. Most of the observations made by him in support of that motion consisted of criticisms, which may be perfectly just in themselves—though I am not convinced that they are—against the whole mode of the procedure of this Legislative Council in regard to the publication of Bills. He says that our methods of publication fail to secure effectual publicity, and that a very small number of persons in the country know what legislation is going on in this Council.

That, I dare say, broadly speaking is very true, and even with all the publicity of Parliament and the Press at home, I would venture to say that a very small numerical proportion of the people of England know what Bills are passed in Parliament. No doubt, that proportion is very much smaller in this country, and my wish is that the utmost publicity should be given to every measure brought into this Council. But when my honourable friend says that these Bills are only published in certain Vernacular Gazettes, and mentions the number of persons who take in those Gazettes, it appears to me that he omits from his calculation the rest of the Vernacular Press. Now, the Vernacular Press, at all events, should be acquainted with those Bills as published in the gazettes; and if such Bills do not come into the hands of the writers in that Press then I venture to say that those gentlemen do not give sufficient attention to an important part of their public duties. Be that as it may, however, of course the Government, and the Legislature particularly, can only take certain recognised methods of affording to the public the opportunity of knowing what is going on in this Council; and it rests with the public to avail themselves of that opportunity, or not, as they think desirable. All we can do is to give to the Press and the public sufficient means

The Transfer of Property Bill.

of informing themselves in respect to such Bills as are before this Council; and I confess that I do not at present see how it would be possible to materially change a practice which has been in existence for a very long time in regard to the publication of such Bills.

If, however, my honourable friend Mr. Plowden will make suggestions with a view to obtaining greater publicity for Bills brought into this Council, we shall be glad to consider them, provided they are such as the Government can adopt.

As regards this particular Bill, the fact is that leave was given to introduce it on the 31st of May, 1877, and that we have now arrived at the 26th of January, 1882, which is very nearly five years since the Bill was introduced. I find that the Bill has been published four successive times in such newspapers or gazettes as the Local Governments thought fit, and it seems to me that, according to the ordinary and general modes of publication, and to the course followed with regard to other legislative measures during that period, this Bill has had a large amount of publication and has been for an unusually lengthened period before the public. I therefore very much doubt whether any further publication would be likely to elicit any additional opinion regarding the measure. I quite understand the advantage of such a delay as my honourable friend the Lieutenant Governor suggests, because public attention is now directed especially to this matter, and, no doubt, within a period of three weeks, a considerable expression of public opinion, favourable or unfavourable, may be brought forward; and I think it therefore perfectly reasonable to accede to that proposal. On the other hand, I consider that such a proposal as my honourable friend Mr. Plowden makes would fail to secure the object which he desires. If, as he proposes, the measure is postponed for another year, the result will probably be that in the interval people will not have attended to it any more than they have hitherto, and that, when it comes up again, at the last moment they

The Transfer of Property Bill.

will examine it as a perfectly fresh matter and start all the same objections to it over again.

Now, I am very sensible of the necessity for affording every opportunity for the expression of public opinion on a measure of this kind; but of course no one can conceal from himself that it is perfectly possible, by postponing the consideration of such a measure till the very last moment and then asking for an indefinite delay, to bring about the same result as would be accomplished by moving for its rejection, or practically to shelve the Bill altogether. I do not for a moment say that this is the case here. Nevertheless, I quite admit that, if a case has arisen for postponement—and my honourable friend the Lieutenent-Governor says it has—we ought not unduly to press on the progress of the measure.

In conclusion, I would only point out that, so far as the discussion upon the Bill has gone to-day—and it has been discussed by men of great talent and large experience,—that discussion has been favourable to the Bill as it stands. This debate will be of great advantage to the public; it will guide their opinion in respect to the Bill; it will tend to remove certain impressions which appear to exist in the public mind; and therefore, though I cannot agree to the motion of my honourable friend Mr. Plowden for a lengthened postponement, I am quite willing to agree that the Bill should be postponed for three weeks.

[After some further discussion, Mr. Plowden withdrew his motion and the motion for the passing of the Bill was postponed for three weeks.

The Bill came before the Council again on the 16th February, when after the consideration of some minor amendments, Mr. Stokes moved that the Bill be passed. Babu Durgá Charan Láhá and Mr. Inglis drew attention to the inexpediency of the principle embodied in the first section of the Bill, which permitted its extension by mere executive order of the Local Governments to territories to which it did not at present extend; such extension, they thought, should only be permitted by an Act of the Legislative Council. Mr. Plowden

The Transfer of Property Bill.

explained that he had come to the Council intending to oppose the passing of the Bill, but that his opposition had since been removed by the first of Mr. Stokes' amendments (above referred to), postponing the period at which the Bill was to come into operation from "April" to "July." His Excellency the President said :—]

Before this Bill passes, I should like to say a few words with respect to what fell from my honourable friends, Bábú Durgá Charan Láhá and Mr. Inglis, regarding the mode in which it is proposed, in accordance with precedent, to extend this Bill to other parts of the country than those to which to has been made immediately applicable. If any notice of amendment on that point had been placed on the paper, it would have most certainly received the careful attention of the Government; but as no such notice has been given, the point cannot now be practically considered. With regard, however, to the general question, I do not wish to lay down any hard-and-first rule, or to pledge the Government as to the course which it may take in regard to future Bills. That course must be regulated by the nature of each particular Bill and the circumstances of the time at which it may be proposed to the Legislative Council. I have also one other point to mention. In the course of the discussion three weeks ago, there appeared to be some doubt in the minds of Members of Councill as to what was the opinion of a very distinguished person in this city —the Chief Justice of the High Court—with reference to this Bill[1]. Of course, any opinion entertained by Sir

[1] In the course of his speech on the 26th January, Mr. Plowden had remarked—"He (Mr. Plowden) also saw a note the other day, which he supposed was the same which had been just referred to by the Honourable Member in charge of the Bill, and which contained the opinion of the Honourable the Chief Justice of the Calcutta High Court; and what did the Chief Justice say ? The Council had heard that Sir Richard Garth was in favour of the Bill, and Mr. Plowden concluded he was, as the Honourable Member in charge of the Bill said so. But he did not gather, from what he saw of that opinion, that the Chief Justice was absolutely in favour of that Bill. Sir Richard Garth said in effect that he could not say he quite approved of the principle of the Bill as it had been framed. It went far too much into details, and would perplex mufassal Judges in the consideration of many difficult questions."

The Transfer of Property Bill.

Richard Garth is entitled to so great weight by the Government, that I felt it my duty to ascertain what his opinion in regard to this measure was. I accordingly addressed to him the following note :—

" MY DEAR SIR RICHARD,—There appears to be an impression in the minds of some persons that you disapprove of the Transfer of Property Bill now before the Legislative Council.

" It would greatly assist me in deciding what course it would be desirable to pursue with that measure, if you would let me know what you think of it in its present shape, and whether, in your opinion, it ought to be passed into law without further delay, or should be postponed for another year.

" Yours sincerely,
"(Sd.) RIPON."

" *Calcutta, 8th February,* 1882."

To that letter I received the following answer :—

" MY DEAR LORD RIPON,—I beg to acknowledge the receipt of your letter, and to say, in reply to it, that on the whole I do approve of the Transfer of Property Bill, and trust that it may be allowed to pass into law without further delay.

I feel grateful to Your Excellency for having given me an opportunity of expressing this opinion. I fear that my views on the subject were somewhat misrepresented on the occasion of the late debate upon the Bill ; and I should be extremely sorry if any critical remarks which I may have made in my note of November last were in any degree the means of retarding the progress of a measure which, I believe, will prove a real blessing to the people of this country.

" The remarks to which I allude applied rather to the principle upon which the Indian Law Commissioners in England have been in the habit of framing laws for India, than to any special defects in this particular Bill.

" I have no desire to criticise the numerous objections which have been made to the Bill by my good friend and colleague Mr. Cunningham. Suffice it to say, that for the most part I do not agree with him, and I believe that, if a Bill were framed in accordance with his views, it would not be nearly so good a measure as that which is now before Your Excellency's Council.

The Transfer of Property Bill.

"A perfect Bill upon such a subject is probably out of the question, and it is as difficult in codification, as it is in other things, to please everybody ; but, having regard to the length of time during which this Bill has been under consideration, the careful and repeated discussion which it has undergone, and the pains which have been bestowed upon it by the highest authorities in the land, I think that any further postponement of the measure can lead to no profitable results.

"No man, I believe, has ever protested more strongly than I have against hasty and ill-considered legislation in such matters ; and I am afraid that my excellent friend Mr. Stokes has often looked upon me as one of his most determined opponents. But it can hardly be said with any show of reason, that this Bill has not received its due meed of consideration ; and I was indeed rejoiced to find that Sir Michael Westropp, although not approving of the Bill for the Presidency of Bombay, paid a just and generous tribute to the ability and earnest industry which has been displayed in the preparation of it, and which, whether we agree with him or not, we must all feel that our friend the Legal Member of Council most fully deserves.

"I am,
"My dear Lord Ripon,
"very sincerely yours,
"(Sd.) RICHARD GARTH.

"33, Theatre Road ;
"15th February, 1882."

[The motion was then put and agreed to.]

THE EASEMENTS BILL. CODIFICATION.

[IN the Legislative Council on the 16th February Mr. Stokes moved 16th Feb. 1882. that the Bill to define and amend the Law relating to Easements and Licenses, as amended, be passed—this motion following one that the consideration of the further report of the Select Committee be taken into consideration, and certain amendments proposed by the Lieutenant-Governor, which were agreed to. Mr. Stokes explained briefly that the object of the Bill was to state clearly and compactly the law relating to Easements, which was now (in the words of the Chief Justice of Bombay) "for the most part to be found only in treatises and reports practically inaccessible to a large proportion of the legal profession in the mufassal and to the subordinate judges." In reply to the objection that the Bill was not necessary, Mr Stokes supplemented his previous remarks on the point by quoting a minute of Mr. Justice Field's in favour of the Bill. The Hon. Sayyad Ahmad Khan and Messrs. Evans and Crosthwaite then addressed the Council, after which His Excellency the Viceroy spoke as follows:—]

I should like to say a few words—not upon the merits of this particular Bill, because I have nothing to add to what has fallen from those who have preceded me, and whose authority on the mere legal aspect of the question is much greater than any which I possess. I merely wish to say, in respect to the observations made by the Honourable Mr. Crosthwaite, that I do not feel the objections which he indicated in the commencement of his speech to the passing of a Bill of this kind for a limited area. I think that, in a country so large as India, that is a very judicious course to pursue, because different parts of the country are in different conditions of progress, and might require to be dealt with in a very different manner by legislation; and therefore I cannot say that is an objection which weighs with me, that a Bill of this kind should be passed in connection only with those Local Governments who desire to have the advantage of it. What I am anxious to speak about is not the subject of this particular Bill, but the general question of which this measure is a part—the question of what is

The Easements Bill. Codification.

known by the name of 'Codification.' My friend Sayyad Ahmad, on a late occasion, addressed the Council on that subject, and expressed his views in favour of the extension of codification in India, and his belief in the advantages it was calculated to confer on the people of the country. This is the last of a certain number of measures which were introduced into this Council a few years ago by the Government of India, and at that time the subject of codification was discussed in some speeches which were then made; and I hope, therefore, that my colleagues will pardon me if I now occupy some little time with remarks upon the general question involved in all these measures.

I am not about to argue on the general merits of codification. The question of codification has now arrived at a stage at which most questions in course of time arrive, in which those who are opposed to any principle, finding that the arguments against them are strong, and rest upon very high authority, no longer profess themselves enemies of that principle. You no longer hear, or very rarely hear, people in public argument, whatever they may think in private, say that they are opposed to codification in general. On the contrary, what they say is, that codification is an excellent thing; that the arguments of Bentham, Austin, Field, and others are quite conclusive, and that they entirely agree in the propriety of codification, but that they are altogether opposed to this particular measure. It is against the measure, not against the principle of codification, that their arguments are directed. All persons who have had experience of legislative bodies are quite aware of that phase of public questions, when it is no longer possible to contest the general principle, and when the battle is confined to a war of posts and of details. This question has been so thoroughly threshed out by the eminent men I have just named—and I would add by Sir H. Maine, who is well worthy to be placed by their side—that I am only anxious now to say a few words as to the applicability of this principle to India. It has been often

The Easements Bill. Codification.

said that this principle is very good in itself and very applicable to Europe, or to America, or to countries in which Western civilization exists and dominates, but that it is not applicable to the circumstances of India, because the natives of this country are a peculiarly conservative people; that they have their own customs, which are well known and recognised; and that the best possible course is to leave these customs alone, and allow them to operate in accordance with the traditions which have come down to them from a distant period of time. I confess that that argument has pressed a great deal at times on my own mind, and if the state of things in India were really such as that argument supposes it to be, then it may fairly be said that it is premature to attempt to introduce measures laying down general principles of written law upon varied and important branches of legislation. But I venture to think that the statement to which I have alluded is founded upon a misapprehension of what is the real condition of affairs in this country at the present time. I will not rest my opinion on my own authority. I have attended for a considerable number of years to Indian affairs, but I have been only a short time in this country, and I should be sorry to rest an opinion of that kind upon my own limited experience. But if the Council will pardon me, I will read a long quotation from a very great authority, Sir H. Maine, which appears to me to put the actual state of things with regard to the influence of English law in India upon the existing condition and circumstances of the customary laws of the country, in a light which has very much impressed me, and which I think is well worth the consideration of the Council when they are dealing with questions of this kind. I hope the Council will pardon the length of the quotation, because the views to which I desire to direct attention are much better expressed in it than it would be in my power to express them, and also because they are set forth by a gentleman whose authority is much greater than any I can

The Easements Bill. Codification.

pretend to. The quotation is from a book very well known —Sir H. Maine's *Village Communities in the East and West*,—and is as follows:—

"You may therefore, perhaps, recall with some surprise the reason which I assigned in my first lecture for making haste to read the lessons which India furnishes to the juridical student. Indian usage, with other things Indian, was, I told you, passing away. The explanation is that you have to allow for an influence which I have merely referred to as yet in connexion with the exceptional English Courts at Calcutta, Madras, and Bombay. Over the interior of India it has only begun to make itself felt of late years, but its force is not yet nearly spent. This is the influence of English law—not, I mean, of the spirit which animates English lawyers and which is eminently conservative, but the contagion, so to speak, of the English system of law,—the effect which the body of rules constituting it produces by contact with native usage. Primitive customary law has a double peculiarity : it is extremely scanty in some departments; it is extremely prodigal of rules in others; but the departments in which rules are plentiful are exactly those which lose their importance as the movements of society become quicker and more various. The body of persons to whose memory the customs are committed has probably always been a quasi-legislative, as well as a quasi-judicial body, and has always added to the stock of usage by tacitly inventing new rules to apply to cases which are really new. When, however, the customary law has once been reduced to writing and recorded by the process which I have described, it does not supply express rules or principles in nearly sufficient number to settle the disputes occasioned by the increased activity of life and multiplied wants which result from the peace and plenty due to British rule. The consequence is, wholesale and indiscriminate borrowing from the English law—the most copious system of express rules known to the world. The Judge reads English law-books; the young native lawyers read them; for law is the study into which the educated youth of the country are throwing themselves, and for which they may even be said to display something very like genius. You may ask, What authority have these borrowed rules in India? Technically, they have none whatever; yet, though they are taken (and not always correctly taken) from a law of entirely foreign origin, they are adopted as if they naturally commended themselves to the reason of mankind ; and all that can be said for the process is, that it is another example of the influence, often felt in European legal history, which express written law invariably exercises on unwritten customary law when they are found side by side. For

The Easements Bill. Codification.

myself, I cannot say that I regard this transmutation of law as otherwise than lamentable. It is not a correction of native usage where it is unwholesome. It allows that usage to stand, and confirms it rather than otherwise; but it fills up its interstices with unamalgamated masses of foreign law."

Well, now, I am bound to say that I was extremely struck with that passage the first time I read it after I came to India, and that it has made a considerable impression on my mind ever since; and that I have had a good deal of evidence, since I read it, to show the accuracy of the statements contained in it. It appears to me that it contains two statements: in the first place, that there is in Indian customary law, and in the customary law of all countries, in its original condition, an element of progress,—namely, that it was applied by those bodies which Sir H. Maine described as *quasi*-legislative as well as *quasi*-judicial, and that there was then a means, while preserving the customary law, of applying to the changing circumstances of the time a change in the interpretation of the principles of that law, and even of extending and altering them sensibly. But, of course, the moment you crystallize—if I may say so—these customs by the operation of a series of legal decisions which, when they have once been given, become fixed, that element of progress and modification to meet changing circumstances is destroyed. On the other hand, Sir Henry Maine points out that, in that large domain of law in which primitive customs give no light and provide no remedy suitable to the circumstances of advancing civilization, the practice of our Courts necessarily and inevitably introduces and fills up, as he says, the large and wide interstices of that law by an unamalgamated mass of English law. Therefore, we are not in the position, as it seems to me, of being able to maintain unchanged, without the operation of English law upon them, the ancient primitive and traditional customs of the country. There is a great change inevitably going on by the operation of English law and English Courts—a change which is

The Easements Bill. Codification.

steady, and at the same time almost unconscious; and the question which we have to deal with is, what is the best mode of meeting a state of things of that kind?—whether it is better to leave that change to go on by the introduction of the principles of English law, gathered here and there as the case may arise; or whether it is better from time to time to lay down in carefully-prepared and well-considered statutes those principles which appear most nearly to combine the general principles of native law with the best principles of modern jurisprudence. I am bound to say that I am very much impressed by the strength and force of Sir Henry Maine's argument in the passage which I have quoted, and I believe that it distinctly proves that it is not correct to suppose that there is no change whatever going on by the ordinary operation of English law in this country in native custom, and that it is far better to legislate from time to time with a careful regard of the character and nature of that custom, as far as it is now operative and alive, and to fill up the interstices which exist in it, not with what might be called the accidental importation of portions of English law to meet particular cases, but by deliberate and well-considered legislation. That is the principal reason which has led me to think that the general course of legislation which has been followed now by the Government of India for a long series of years, in the preparation of measures of this kind, is a course suitable to the existing circumstances of this country, and which may be pursued from time to time with the greatest advantage, and without which you will find what is valuable and living in native customs passing away more rapidly, through possibly more insensibly, than would be the case under the operation of any distinct legislation on which public opinion could be brought to bear, and which could be discussed in this Legislative Council.

Now, there is, of course, I know very well, in the minds of a good many persons, an alternative to such a

The Easements Bill. Codification.

system as that of which I have been venturing to express my approval, and that is, the system of practically leaving judicial officers throughout the country to act according to their own unfettered judgment in these matters. And I think that the preference for the system, which was adopted in many parts of India in former days with great advantage, lies very much at the root of some of the objections felt by some persons to what is called codification. On that point I should like again to refer to the authority of Sir Henry Maine, and in doing so, I shall read from a letter of his which was quoted by my honourable friend Mr. Stokes on a previous occasion in connection with this very Bill in its earlier stage. The name of the writer was not then attached to it, but I have Mr. Stokes' authority for now mentioning it. Sir Henry Maine writes :—

"The true alternative to codification is the course hinted at by a certain school of administrative officials,—that of having no law at all, but of giving the fullest discretionary powers to functionaries of every class. I do not at all deny that a great deal may be said for it. If the history of India could be begun again, and if Parliament were not disposed to do what it did in the old Statutes, and to force law upon us by the Courts it established, I am not at all sure that a wise Indian legislator would not go in for universal discretion. But the very Indian officials who denounce law do not seriously believe that it can be got rid of; and the only effect of their objections is to prevent its being improved in the only rational way. Great undigested lumps of English law are finding their way into the law administered by the Courts to the people. I doubt whether in India there are a dozen copies of some of the books from which this law is taken ; and these are, of course, written in language unintelligible to the bulk of the natives and to the great mass of Englishmen."

I do not, I confess, agree myself with the opinion here expressed by Sir Henry Maine, which is more a political than a legal opinion, when he says that he is not at all sure that a wise Indian legislator would not go in for universal discretion. That is, I confess, not my view of what is desirable in India in its present condition. I entirely admit that there have been men in past times, able rulers, no doubt, and who have been able to administer to the people a law extremely acceptable to them, because they possessed those rare qualities of sympathy with the natives, and that intimate knowledge of their feelings, traditions, and habits, which enabled them to discharge duties of so much difficulty in a manner acceptable to those whom they governed. But such men are always rare. You cannot supply the ranks of our judicial service in any number with men possessing these rare qualifications. I have the very highest possible opinion of the ability of the Indian Civil Service, but of course it is out of the question to find many men possessing those peculiar qualifications which have marked the career of some of the most distinguished members of that service in times past; and, even if we could find them, I feel bound to say that it would, in my judgment, still be a distinct advantage to the country that we should pass out of that patriarchal stage so far as concerns the more advanced and civilized parts of the country. Doubtless there are many tribes and races in a very backward—some of them almost in a savage—condition, who must be governed on principles different from those which are applicable to the great mass of the people of India; but, speaking of the country in general, I say that it is a good thing that you should pass away from the condition of affairs in which, instead of having settled law, the decision of judicial cases was left to the arbitrary and unfettered judgment of the particular individuals who tried them. I do not use the term 'arbitrary' in a disparaging sense, but I hold that it is a clear benefit to the people of this country that they should advance from the stage of arbitrary discretion to one of written and settled law. Sir Henry Maine, in the book from which I have just now been quoting, says that the fact that natives of India are becoming more acquainted with their rights as individuals is a source of serious difficulty to the Government of this country. There may, of course, be difficulties in such a state of advance

The Easements Bill. Codification.

from one stage of civilization to another. You cannot pass from one stage of civilization to another in any country, or at any time, without peculiar difficulties; but whatever may be the nature of those difficulties, I say distinctly that it is well for the people themselves that they should acquire an increased knowledge of their rights; that they should be more and more ready to enforce those rights, and should be able to appeal to the law and to distinct Statutes. Under any circumstances, I should think it a great misfortune if we were to fall back upon that patriarchal system which has been so largely abandoned in most parts of India from time to time.

Again, I think that, when we consider that a very large number of our judicial officers in this country are necessarily men who have had none of that special legal training which barristers at home possess, and who consequently perhaps are not so well up in law-books and cases as barrister-judges might be, it seems to me that that in itself constitutes a strong argument for the embodiment in distinct and clear Statutes of the principles and rules with which officers of that kind have to deal.

I have myself been a judicial officer at home, as a magistrate and justice of the peace, with no judicial training; and I know perfectly well that I should be entirely at sea if, having to decide cases when sitting in such a capacity, instead of having a distinct law to refer to, I had to search through a vast mass of cases for guidance. The result would be that I should be entirely in the hands of the magistrate's clerk, from whom I should have to take my law. I cannot but think, therefore, that it must be a great advantage to the judicial officers of this country to have the rules by which they are to be guided embodied in clear and definite language in Statutes framed with the utmost care and deliberation.

I must beg pardon of my colleagues for having detained them so long. But I now come to the last point upon

The Easements Bill.   Codification.

which I have anything to say, and that is, to the charge sometimes made against the Acts passed by the Government of India—the charge of what is called technicality. The drafting of Acts of Parliament is, in fact, a science, and the language of all science is necessarily technical. It is impossible to avoid it. What is called the absence of technicality is in reality the absence of precision; it is impossible to draw up laws with care and accuracy without the employment of technical language, and that system of definition which has been introduced of late years both in England and here, with, as it seems to me, such great advantage to the precision and intelligibility of our Statutes. That objection is one which I am very well used to at home, where I have had a pretty long administrative and political experience of the preparation of Acts of Parliament, and with their discussion in both Houses; and I know very well how frequently that objection to what is called technicality is raised, and I know also how often it is listened to in the House of Commons or in the House of Lords, with the result that, when the technicality to which objection is taken is avoided, the Act becomes in many respects altogether unintelligible, and has to be amended in a very few years, just because language has been imported into it during the course of debate by gentlemen who object to technical language, who bring in what they call common sense, and which really turns out afterwards to be a puzzle to the Judges sitting in Westminster Hall. I, therefore, myself do not see the force of that objection to technicality. I have had long experience of questions of this kind, have had intimate personal knowledge of some of the ablest draftsmen in England, and I can truly say that I have never had to do with any one who surpassed my learned friend, the Legal Member of the Governor General's Council, in zeal, in wide knowledge, in the accuracy and precision of language with which his Bills are drawn. I therefore, must say that I think the charge of want of

The Easements Bill. Codfiication.

clearness, of accuracy, is one which, as far as my experience goes, can be brought less against the Bills drawn by my honourable and learned friend than against many of those which have been drawn by men of great distinction at home. As Sir Richard Garth truly says, in the letter which I read earlier in our proceedings, men will always differ about questions of wording and drafting, but all experience goes to show that, if you have got a really competent draftsman, on whom you can place real reliance, the best thing to do is to trust him with regard to drafting, whatever opinion you may entertain with regard to political questions about which the Executive Government is bound to exercise the fullest discretion, and which are of course matters for discussion in this Legislative Council.

I must again beg pardon for detaining the Council so long, but I was anxious on this occasion, when the last of the measures of codification introduced some time ago was about to pass, to take the opportunity of expressing my general views on the subject. I think I may say that I am always accustomed to say plainly what I think on any subject, but I do not know how far my opinions may be acceptable to the members of this Council; but they are founded upon the honest conviction which I entertain, that these measures will tend to promote the best interests of the people of this country.

[The motion was then put, and the Bill was passed.]

DISTRIBUTION OF PRIZES TO THE CALCUTTA VOLUNTEERS.

[ON Saturday afternoon, the 25th February, the Viceroy presided at the annual Distribution of Prizes to the Calcutta Volunteers. After inspecting the Corps, His Excellency delivered the following address :—]

Colonel Graham, Officers and Members of the Calcutta Volunteer Corps,—It is a great pleasure to me to meet you once again upon this annual occasion ; and I rejoice to find, from the reports which have been laid before me, that the progress of this Corps during the past twelve months has been altogether satisfactory. And especially was I pleased to be informed that the shooting of the Corps, during the year which has just concluded, has been superior to that of the previous twelve months. The principal event of that period in connection with this Corps has been the establishment of a mounted company. I can assure you that it afforded me great pleasure, in union with my colleagues in the Government of India, to give my sanction to the formation of that mounted company ; and I trust that, as time goes on, the company will increase in numbers and in efficiency. In many respects a body of mounted volunteers have greater difficulties to encounter than infantry volunteers. It is more difficult to attain an equal amount of efficiency in that branch of the service than it is in the infantry; but I feel very confident that the members of the mounted company of the Calcutta Volunteers will recollect that the character of the whole Corps is in their hands, and that it behoves them to take care that the general standard of efficiency of the body is not diminished by any neglect on their part; and sure I am that this consideration will stimulate their efforts and encourage their exertions, and will induce them to devote themselves yet more earnestly to the special duties which they have undertaken in the Corps.

Distribution of Prizes to the Calcutta Volunteers.

Besides the addition of this mounted company during the last year, two new cadet companies have also been added to the Corps. Now, Colonel Graham, I attach much importance to the existence of cadet companies in connection with bodies of Volunteers. Some persons, perhaps, may think that difference of size may somewhat impair the appearance of a corps; but in the case of Volunteers we have to remember that in cadet companies we have the nucleus of many a future Volunteer Corps, and that it is a great advantage, not only to the youths themselves, but to the country at large, that in the early period of life they should obtain the training which is afforded by a corps of that description. Hereafter they may enter the ranks of your other companies, or perhaps they may go forth from Calcutta to reside in other parts of India; and if they take the latter course; then this Corps will be able to feel that you have done your part in training volunteers, not only for your own Corps, but it may be for many other Corps throughout the length and breadth of the country.

I was very glad to learn that you were for a few days in camp a short time ago. I have always felt that there were few things which tended more to promote the true efficiency of a body of volunteers, than that they should from time to time go into camp. By going into camp, even for a day or two, Volunteers are brought, not for a few hours, but for a more lengthened period, under the rules of discipline; and we all know that discipline is the essence of every military body. Many things may be learnt in camp in a few days which could not be acquired in many days of ordinary drill, and I am quite sure that under a commanding officer so able and so zealous as Colonel Graham, who has the interests of the Volunteers so fully at heart, there are no advantages which can be derived from camp experience which you will not have the opportunity of securing.

I do not think that I need detain you much longer; but there is yet one remark which I desire to make. I have

Distribution of Prizes to the Calcutta Volunteers.

said more than once since I came to India, that the Government of India placed great confidence in the Volunteers. I was accustomed by my English experience to feel a deep interest in the Volunteer movement, and to fully recognise its value; and I am happy to say that nothing which I have learnt during the twenty months in which I have had the honour to hold the great office I now fill, has in any degree diminished the confidence that I was naturally inclined to place in the Volunteers of India. But I desire to impress upon you that the fact that such confidence is reposed in you by the Government casts upon you great and especial obligations. It would indeed be a grievous thing if the hour of trial should ever come, and the Government, acting upon that confidence, should find that it had been misplaced. I have no fear that that will be the case, but I should wish you always to keep before your mind the truth that, just because the Government *does* place that confidence in you, you are bound to do your best to justify it. Volunteering is not a thing of handsome uniforms or pleasant meetings; t has in it a deep and true reality, and it is only in proportion as you realise that you have undertaken duties to your country which you cannot shirk, that you will be able to fulfil those expectations which the Government and which your countrymen have formed concerning you.

Colonel Graham,—I regret extremely to say that Lady Ripon is unable, in consequence of slight illness, to be present on this occasion. Up to the middle of the day she had fully hoped to be able to come, and had done her best to bring about that result ; but her inexorable medical adviser positively forbade her to leave Government House, and I should not have been a good husband if, under those circumstances, I had not supported him. I am happy, however, to say that she has prevailed upon Lady Stewart to take her place upon this occasion, and I am quite sure that you who have won prizes will be proud indeed to receive them from Lady Stewart's hands, not only on account of those

Criminal Procedure Bill.

many qualities which so well entitle her to "rain influence, and adjudge the prize," but also because you will remember that she represents one who is so well fitted, by his great and eminent services, to hold with the greatest advantage to India the command of that gallant army which our Sovereign has entrusted to his care.

It now only remains for me to ask Lady Stewart to be good enough to present these prizes.

CRIMINAL PROCEDURE BILL.

[THE Report of the Select Committee on the Criminal Procedure 2nd Mar. 1882. Bill was taken into consideration by the Legislative Council on the 2nd March. Two amendments to the Bill, proposed by Mr. Stokes, were adopted; a third amendment, proposed by Mahárájá Jotindra Mohán Tagore, the object of which was to expunge from the Bill the section which gave power to the Government to appeal against an acquittal, gave rise to lengthened discussion. The Hon. Durgá Charan Láhá, Sayyad Ahmad Khan, and Rájá Siva Prasád spoke in favour of the amendment; the Hon. Messrs. Reynolds, Plowden, Crosthwaite, Gibbs, and Stokes spoke against it. His Excellency the President said :—]

I have listened very carefully to the discussion, in which opinions have been expressed on both sides of the proposal submitted to us by the Mahárájá; and I am bound to say that my own opinion is that it would not be desirable to adopt the amendment moved by my honourable friend the Mahárájá, at all events on the present occasion. My honourable friend was good enough to inform me a few days ago that he desired to bring this question before the Council, and I then told him that I would give my attention to the subject, and would not fail carefully to consider it. I need not say that I have not had time to do that up to the present moment. The question is obviously not a new one. The statements brought forward to-day show that it has been considered on various occasions by the Government of India

Criminal Procedure Bill.

and by the Local Governments, and it is certainly not a question on which I should feel myself justified in taking action without further inquiry than we have yet been able to institute. It is evidently a matter upon which the opinion of the Local Governments ought to be called for before any step is adopted which would be contrary to the opinions which they have expressed on previous occasions. I do not think that anybody is likely to suppose that I have an inherent objection to reform; but, at the same time, I am quite of opinion that it is the duty of the Government of India while it is always ready to consider any proposals for the amendment of the law, or for the improvement of the administration of the country, to proceed cautiously and without undue haste. I have endeavoured, since I have been in this country, to adopt that principle, and, even in cases about which I might individually have had no doubt, I have felt it right carefully to inform myself as fully as possible as to the facts and circumstances of the case, as it relates to this country, before I attempted to act upon any preconceived notions which I might have derived from my English experience.

I believe that a steady progress of reform is the only wise course which in these matters, the Government of India can adopt; and I frankly say that I have not had an opportunity of giving to this question that full consideration, and consulting all those persons whose opinion, it appears to me, I am bound to take into consideration before I adopt a change involving the abandonment of a principle which has evidently been adopted most deliberately by the Legislature of this country, acting in accordance with the sanction of the Secretary of State.

Under these circumstances, my counsel to the members of this Council is not to adopt this amendment. I have the fullest intention of fulfilling the promise made to my honourable friend the Mahárájá, that I will give the subject my consideration as soon as opportunity offers; but if I am asked

Criminal Procedure Bill.

to say 'aye' or 'no' upon this motion at the present moment, I have no alternative but to oppose it.

[The motion was put and negatived.

The Honourable Durgá Charan Láhá then moved an amendment to Section 456 of the Bill, which related to the rights of a European British subject to apply for an order directing the person unlawfully detaining him, to bring him before the High Court. The object of the amendment was to apply the provisions of that section, without distinction, to all persons. In justification of it, Bábu Durgá Charan Láhá read some extracts from a letter in the *Englishman* newspaper, showing an abuse of power on the part of Executive Officers, and expressed his apprehension that there were many cases of the same kind which had not reached the public. Messrs. Crosthwaite, Stokes, Gibbs, and Major Baring opposed the amendment, mainly on the ground that ample security to the liberty of every class of Her Majesty's subjects was provided by the Bill. Rájá Siva Prasád and Mahárájá Jotindra Mohán Tagore supported it.

His Excellency the President said:—]

It has often been my fate, in discussions in Parliament and elsewhere, to find that, when I spoke late in a debate, I was placed in a most unfortunate position; because most of what I was going to say—all my best arguments—were taken away from me by those who had preceded me on the same side. I have very great cause of quarrel in this respect with my honourable friend Major Baring, because he has stated so fully and ably the views which I hold on this subject, that there is very little for me to say, beyond what the gentleman at Bristol said when he and Mr. Burke were canvassing for that city—"I say ditto to Mr. Burke." Nevertheless, at the risk of repeating some of the arguments he has used, I will, for a few moments, go over the ground traversed by him and others who feel that it is not advisable to adopt this amendment on the present occasion. In the first place, I think it is quite clear that the particular case to which my honourable friend Durgá Charan Láhá alluded, and in respect to which he read an extract from a letter in the *Englishman* newspaper, is, if I understand the extract that he read, met by the amendments

Criminal Procedure Bill.

made in the existing law by the Bill now before us; because the difficulty which arose in the cases in the Panjáb, to which my honourable friend referred, appeared to have arisen because the Court could not inquire into any proceedings on the part of magistrates which were not in the nature of judicial proceedings. The word 'judicial' does appear in the existing code, but has been removed from the clause as it stands in this Bill. At the present moment, the words are 'in any judicial proceeding.' The word 'judicial' has been taken out, and that will, I hope, meet the particular case quoted by my honourable friend from the *Englishman*.

Besides this, however, section 100 of the Bill provides greater security than at present exists against anything in the nature of arbitrary or illegal imprisonment. Now, I certainly cannot think it necessary that I should say that no one can be more opposed to anything of that kind than I should be; and I desire to give every person in this country, of whatever race he may be, the fullest security against suffering so grievous a wrong as that which would undoubtedly result from anything in the nature of illegal or improper imprisonment. I venture to hope, however, that sufficient provision has been made in this Bill, by the changes to which I have alluded, to give reasonable and adequate security against danger of that kind. I must, however, admit that I sympathise a good deal with what I think is the feeling at the bottom of the amendment moved by my honourable friend Durgá Charan Láhá. I think the real meaning of the amendment is that he feels a certain amount of disinclination to there being such a chapter as the 33rd chapter of this Bill—a chapter providing a special mode of procedure for Europeans and Americans. I should be very glad if it was possible to place the law in regard to every person in this country, not only on the same footing,—for that the Bill will, I hope, practically do,—but to embody it in the very same language, whether it relates to Europeans or Natives. But no one who

Criminal Procedure Bill.

recollects the history of questions of this kind in this country can doubt that to deal with that special chapter which regulates the procedure with regard to Europeans and Americans in the manner that has been suggested would be to deal with very difficult and very delicate questions. Cases have arisen—not under this particular clause, but of a kindred nature—in which the Government of the day has been beaten in this Legislative Council. We all know the agitation that has taken place and the strong excitement which has arisen in past times upon questions of this sort. They are certainly matters not to be entered upon without very full consideration, or as my honourable friend Mr. Stokes remarked, without consultation, not only on the part of the Government here, but also with the Government at home. Under these circumstances, I would strongly recommend that that particular section and that particular portion of the Bill be left alone now. Whether any alterations can be made in them from time to time, will always be a matter of interest to the Government—certainly to me, —and I will not fail to consider this particular subject of *habeas corpus* when opportunity offers; but I think that it is impossible to open a question of that magnitude, complication, and difficulty without a great deal more thought and examination than it would be possible for the Council and the Government to give to it at the present time.

Then there is the point upon which my honourable friend Major Baring touched, namely,—whether, as this amendment is proposed, and as other amendments might easily be proposed, in this Code of Criminal Procedure, we should not wait until all the possible amendments have been got together and considered, instead of adopting the more limited amendments which the Bill proposes at the present time. I must say that I earnestly hope the Council will not take that course, for I confess to a great personal interest in some of the amendments which it is proposed

Criminal Procedure Bill.

to make in the law by this Bill. The three amendments to which special attention has been drawn by my honourable friend Major Baring, and the amendments in the direction of greater security for personal liberty, are all amendments to which I myself attach great importance; and I think that it would be a great misfortune—at all events, if that is too strong a term, I should greatly regret—if those amendments were not introduced now, and if the country were to be deprived for another period of twelve months of the advantage of those amendments. Take one of them,—the queston of enhancing a sentence upon appeal. That is a thing which is going on from time to time, and, in fact, instances of such enhancement have only very recently been brought under my notice; and I think it is a very undesirable power to entrust to the Courts, if it were only for the reason that it is evidently a distinct discouragement to a man who thinks he has been aggrieved, to resort to appeal; and I should be very sorry to deprive the people of India of the advantage of that and other amendments for twelve months longer, simply because there are some further amendments which might, in the opinion of some of my honourable friends, be introduced.

I am always glad when discussions like this take place. I think that they do a great deal of good. They bring points under the attention of the Executive Government, which it is very desirable we should consider; but, as I said before on the previous motion, it is not reasonable to expect that the Government should deal hastily with questions of this magnitude. What they ought to do is to proceed steadily and with caution in the improvement of the law and the administration of this country in those respects in which they are capable of amendment. Of course, there is always difficulty, as my honourable friend Major Baring has pointed out, when we are dealing with one of our great codes. Nobody can doubt—indeed, I do not believe that there is anybody in the country who does

Criminal Procedure Bill.

not admit—that it is a great advantage that we have this Code of Criminal Procedure, and the Penal Code, and the other great codes of India, which have been elaborated now for a series of years with so much care by the most eminent men, in the form of a regular code; that is to say, of a book which may be put into a man's pocket, and which contains all the information required upon questions of criminal procedure, the penal laws, and other matters. But if you are to pass small amendments of these codes without re-enacting the whole code, then in a short time your whole code as a body would become obsolete, and would be surrounded by a quantity of confusing satellites which would entirely obscure the vision of those who had to look at the great central planet itself. Now, we know very well that there is a certain amount of inconvenience in throwing a large Bill of this kind on the table of this Council, and saying, "We are going to pass this Bill of four or five hundred clauses for the sake of a comparatively small number of amendments;" but, unless you wish to give up the advantage of having these great codes, that appears at present to be the only mode in which we can proceed, though I think it quite worthy of consideration whether some other mode ought not to be devised, which might obviate that difficulty. I saw a criticism the other day in a public journal, as to the great expense said to be incurred in the printing of all this matter for the purpose of making a few amendments. That is a subject which has attracted my attention, and I think it is desirable that we should see whether any other system could not be safely adopted.

I wish only to make one other remark, and that is, that the necessary mode of procedure being, for the present at all events, to re-enact the whole code, it must not be taken that, because the Government in the year 1882 re-enacts the whole of this code, it therefore expresses the same deliberate opinion upon every single clause contained in it which it would be expressing if it were enacting it for the

Criminal Procedure Bill.

first time. Technically, it is a re-enactment; in reality, it is a reprint with certain amendments. The only points on which the definite opinion of the Government is expressed are the points to which these amendments relate. The Government is perfectly open to re-consider any other portion of this code at any time, and must not be taken to imply any opinion upon any of its general provisions. As I have said, it is practically a reprint and a re-arrangement of the code with certain amendments, and those are the only portions of it upon which the opinion of the Government is now deliberately pronounced. Those amendments, though few in number, appear to me calculated to confer considerable advantage on the people of this country, and to improve our methods of criminal procedure in a liberal and generous spirit; and therefore it is that I trust that, without adopting the amendment of my honourable friend Durgá Charan Láhá, because it raises large and difficult questions which we are not in a position to deal with at the present moment, the Council will pass this Bill, in order that the people of India may have without delay the advantage of those other improvements of the law which will result from the amendments which the Government has submitted.

[The motion was put and negatived, and the Bill was subsequently passed into law.]

ADJOURNMENT OF THE COUNCIL

[At the close of the discussion on the Criminal Procedure Bill, His 2nd Mar. 1882. Excellency the Viceroy made the following remarks.:—]

Before the Council separates, I wish to state that I propose to hold a special meeting of the Legislative Council on Wednesday next, the 8th instant, in order that my hon'ble friend Major Baring may make his Financial Statement. Members of Council are of course aware that in regard to these financial proposals it is of the utmost importance, both for the Government, as regards its revenue, and for the convenience of those engaged in trade, that when final alterations are once announced, they should be carried into effect as speedily as possible. That is the course which has always been followed in the British Parliament, in order to prevent the loss to Government and the inconvenience to trade which otherwise would result. At the same time, it appears to me that to propose that the Bills which will be submitted by my hon'ble friend Major Baring, in connection with his proposals, should be passed on the same day, by suspending the standing orders of this Council, would be to go further than the requirements of the case demanded. What I would suggest is, that the Council should assemble on Wednesday to hear the Financial Statement, and that it should again meet on Friday, instead of Thursday, which will give Members of the Council a whole day to consider the financial proposals of the Government. The consideration of the Bills which my hon'ble friend will present on Wednesday will then be taken up on Friday, and the Bills passed if they meet with the approval of the Council; and afterwards the ordinary business, which would in the usual course of things have come on Thursday, will be proceeded with. There will be no sitting on Thursday.

DISTRIBUTION OF PRIZES AT THE BARRACKPORE PARK SCHOOL.

4th Mar. 1882. [On Saturday afternoon, the 4th March, His Excellency the Viceroy distributed the prizes to the students of the Barrackpore Park School, and addressed the boys as follows:—]

My young Friends,—I am very glad to welcome you once more upon this occasion, and to see you again assembled in the Park at Barrackpore for the distribution of the prizes of the school. I have listened with much interest to the report which has been read by your Head Master, and have been sorry to find the untoward circumstances against which the school has had to contend during the last twelve months. I trust, however, that you have passed through this time of trial successfully, and that neither the influence of the sad sickness which has prevailed so largely in this neighbourhood, nor yet the competition of another school which has recently sprung up, will, in the end, be found to interfere seriously with the prosperity and the progress of the Barrackpore public school. Against illness no school or teachers, and no zeal of students, can contend ; but competition, though it may be disagreeable, has undoubted advantages in the stimulus which it administers to the school to which it is applied ; and I have great confidence from what I have learned of the past of this school, that it will be able to hold its own, by means of increased exertions on the part alike of the teachers and of the students, against any competition that can be brought to bear. I have listened with very great pleasure to the recitation which has just taken place. Comparisons are proverbially odious, and I do not wish to institute a comparison between the recitation of this year and that of last year ; but at least I may be permitted to say—and I think that all who have listened to-day to that recitation will agree with me—that the result shows no falling off whatever in that respect ; and I can

Distribution of Prizes at the Barrackpore Park School.

assure you that I thought the parts both of Brutus and Cassius were played with great skill by those who performed them. I have also had much pleasure in delivering to-day, in addition to the prizes properly belonging to the school, the two prizes which, in accordance with the promise which I made last year, I myself have given ; and I was very glad to learn from Mr. Primrose, who looked over the papers submitted in connection with these prizes, that in his opinion (and he is a very competent judge on educational matters) the papers show the ability of those who had contended for the prizes, especially in arithmetic. There were also many proofs of skill in the letters which were sent in, though, of course, it is not likely that, written in the English language, those letters should possess all the qualities which they would have possessed if they had been written in the native language of those who drew them up. I shall be most happy to continue these prizes for another year, and I do not know that any better subjects could be chosen than those for which the prizes have been offered upon this occasion. But I should like to reserve to myself the right, if I should be here to offer prizes next year, to change the subjects for which they are offered, according to what might then seem to be the requirements of the school.

In the report with which these proceedings commenced an allusion was made to the desire which your Head Master feels for the adjunction to this school of a vernacular department. That, as you know, is not a question upon which at the present moment I can pronounce an opinion. It is a matter which must be considered by the Local Government, upon the report of its own educational officers. I can only say that if those who are so competent to judge of the matter as the educational officers of the Bengal Government, should be of opinion that the addition of such a department will be advantageous to the school, I shall be very happy to bear my part in assisting towards the necessary expenses required for setting it up.

Financial Statement, 1882-83.

I do not know that I have anything more to say to you to-day. I always think that upon these occasions, which are intended for the enjoyment of the pupils of a school, the less time which is taken up by speeches, the better, and I have no doubt that you will much prefer to enjoy yourselves in this Park so long as light permits. I will therefore no longer encroach upon the short time of daylight which still remains, except to express to you my hearty good wishes for your happiness and prosperity during the next year.

FINANCIAL STATEMENT, 1882-83.

10th Mar. 1882. [THE Legislative Council assembled on the 8th of March, when Major Baring (Finaucial Member of council) made his Financial Statement, and in connection with his proposals, obtained leave to introduce three Bills, namely,—(1) to amend the law relating to Customs duties and for other purposes ; (2) to regulate the Duty on Salt and for other purposes ; and (3) to amend the law relating to Kánúngos and Patwárís in the North-Western Provinces and Oudh. The discussion of the Financial Statement took place on Friday, the 10th of March, the motion before the Council being " that the Bill to amend the law relating to Customs duties, and for other purposes, be taken into consideration." At the close of the debate, His Excellency the Viceroy spoke as follows :—]

The discussion which has taken place in this Council today has been, on the whole, I think I may fairly say, so satisfactory to the Government, as indicating the judgment pronounced by the Members of this Council upon their financial proposals, that I might almost have dispensed myself from the necessity of occupying the time of this Council with any remarks of my own ; but, considering the important nature and the large scope of the proposals contained in the Budget of my hon'ble friend Major Baring, it would not, I think, be altogether right that I should permit this discussion to be brought to a conclusion without giving briefly the reasons which have induced me to accord my

Financial Statement, 1882-83.

cordial concurrence to the proposals which have been submitted to the Government by my hon'ble friend; and, therefore, I will ask the permission of my hon'ble colleagues to occupy their attention for a short time while I make a few observations upon the principal points with which this Budget deals.

I will begin by speaking of the proposed repeal of the customs duties. I need not recapitulate the convincing evidence brought before this Council in the statement of Major Baring, to show that the existing state of things in respect to our customs revenue is one which it was impossible to continue longer than was absolutely necessary. That that is the case, I think I may fairly say is admitted on all hands, and no one appears to contest that the steps which were taken with respect to our customs tariff under the government of my predecessor, Lord Lytton, left that tariff in a condition in which it was impossible that it could permanently remain. And, in making that statement, I am not saying anything of which my hon'ble friend Lord Lytton would complain; because, in a recent speech which he has made in England, he distinctly admitted—and he took credit to himself for the fact—that the partial measures of customs repeal adopted by his Government were intended to bring about that result which they have undoubtedly now produced, and to render the continuance of the chief customs duties in this country altogether impossible.

It was, therefore, as it seems to me, absolutely imperative that the Government should take the earliest opportunity of dealing with this question of the customs duties, and I must say for myself that it was a strong motive with me to seize that opportunity as soon as it arrived; because, by dealing with this subject in a permanent and final manner, we may cherish the hope that we shall thus put an end to those differences of opnion upon the questions which have unhappily now for several years existed between the people of England and the people of India, and in which I must

Financial Statement, 1882-83.

frankly say that I think neither party to the controversy has been just to the other.

I think that, in India, men have been apt to overlook the feelings which must naturally be entertained upon this subject by those who have all their lives been the earnest and conscientious advocates of the principles of free trade. No doubt it is perfectly true that, when Manchester manufacturers ask for the repeal of the cotton duties, they are asking for something which will confer benefit upon themselves; but I venture to say that it is almost impossible for those who stood beside my friends the late Mr. Cobden and Mr. Bright in the great free trade controversies of the past, to understand how men can possibly accuse them of selfishness because they desire to confer upon the people of India those benefits from which they and the people of England have derived so many blessings. And, again, I think that in England men have not understood that strong—I had almost said, that vehement—dread which exists in this country in connection with the imposition of direct taxation. Neither, I think, have they adverted to the fact of the limited extent to which economic principles are either studied or understood here, and, therefore, this controversy might have continued, and might have been made the subject of more and more misunderstanding between two great branches of the subjects of our Queen-Empress, who ought to feel that they form but one people under the shadow of her august throne. But I should mislead my hon'ble colleagues and the public if, in consequence of my allusion to the present condition of this question of the customs tariff and the impossibility of continuing the existing state of things, they were to suppose that I was attempting to shelter myself behind the special circumstances in which we are now placed, and was attempting to represent that, in adopting the policy of repealing the customs duties, I have been only brought to that conclusion by the mere necessities of the particular situation in which we are placed. I desire

Financial Statement, 1882-83.

upon all occasions to be frank both with my hon'ble colleagues in this Council and with the public of India, and therefore I am bound to say that it has been with great satisfaction that I have seized the present opportunity of repealing these customs duties; because I earnestly believe that that repeal will be found beneficial to the general interests of India. My hon'ble friend Mahárájá Jotindrá Mohun Tagore dropped some words about neglect of justice to India in consideration of the interests of Manchester manufacturers. I am quite sure that my hon'ble friend did not mean those remarks to apply to me, and, indeed, if my hon'ble friend has done me the honour of paying any attention to the course which I have pursued during a public life which has extended now over more than thirty years, he will know that, from the earliest period of that public life, I have been an earnest and consistent advocate of the fiscal principles of the free trade party; and I have been so because I believe that those principles were principles of general application, calculated to confer the largest benefits upon the great mass of the community of any nation to which they might be applied. And, therefore, no man can be surprised that, holding those opinions strongly and firmly, and having advocated them throughout the whole course of my political career, I should be desirous, when a fitting opportunity occurred, of having a hand in conferring upon the people of India the benefit of the application of principles which I believe to be calculated to conduce to their permanent advantage and prosperity. And I can say that if I did not entertain that opinion,—if I thought that the course which the Government is about to take with respect to these customs duties was a course which would benefit England at the expense of India, I would not have been induced by any consideration to be a party to such a proceeding. I desire, so long as I may hold the position which I have now the honour to fill, to govern India in the interests of India and for the benefit of her people and

Financial Statement, 1882-83.

I would not consent to be a party to any measures which I did not honestly believe would conduce to that great end.

The policy of the Government in this respect is a policy which has been pursued, as we all know, at home now for a long series of years, and which can quote in its support the names of the most illustrious financial statesmen of England, from the time of Mr Husskinson, or the days of Sir Robert Peel, down to the long and eminent financial administration of my right hon'ble friend Mr. Gladstone. That policy has been founded upon a belief—I should rather have said, an absolute conviction—that anything in the nature of protective duties is highly injurious to the country in which they exist, and also upon the belief that small customs duties, which hamper trade and produce very little revenue, are highly mischievous and objectionable; and I am bound to say, especially with respect to the last of these objections—the objection, namely, to small unproductive duties, which interfere greatly with trade and fetter its operation—that it applies more strongly to India then to other countries; because I believe there is scarcely anything of more importance to the future prosperity of this great peninsula than that we should do all in our power to promote and to increase commercial progress and industrial advance, and that everything which tends to check or fetter the commerce or industry of this country has an especially baneful influence upon the general interests of the population.

It must be borne in mind that this customs revenue, speaking broadly, was not an increasing revenue. It had not those elements of growth which exist in many of the great sources of revenue in England, and, from its very nature, it was not calculated to possess those growing elements; whereas it may fairly be hoped that, by thus removing the trammels which press upon the springs of trade, we may stimulate enterprise and may derive direct financial benefit from increased railway receipts, which are a growing

Financial Statement, 1882-83.

element—and which, I believe, will prove in the future to be a very growing element—in the revenue of the country. But while I say this, and while I express my strong opinion that the course which the Government is taking now is opportune and calculated to be highly beneficial to the country, I am yet bound to say that I should not have been a party to the repeal of the cotton duties, or to the repeal of the other customs duties, if it had been proposed to repeal them in the face of a deficit, or if it had been necessary, in order to repeal them, to impose other taxation upon the country. I am not at all unaware of the great examples which might be quoted in favour of carrying out an important customs reform under the shelter of the imposition of a direct tax. We have all heard of the famous budget of Sir Robert Peel, in which he made a large reform of our complicated, antiquated, and troublesome English customs system, and recouped himself by means of the imposition of an income tax; but I do not think that that would have been a wise course to pursue in India. I am very well aware, as I have just said, of the strong feelings entertained in this country with respect to direct taxation. I am not going to enter now upon that thorny question; but it would have been, in my judgment, highly unwise, for the purpose even of so large a benefit as the repeal of these customs duties, to have shown that want of consideration for a large and strongly-expressed public opinion which would have been involved in such a proposition as one by which fresh taxation would have been imposed upon the people for the purpose of repealing these customs duties. It was on that very account that, in spite of all the anomalies of some portions of our present customs system—in spite of the exceeding absurdity of the results which followed from some of the arrangements made in regard to grey goods by previous alterations, the Government of India abstained from touching this question last year. We were then not completely free from the

Financial Statement, 1882-83.

expenditure and the trammels of the Afghan War, and we determined that no consideration, even of public convenience should induce us to deal with this question, except at a time when we could take it up and could proceed to settle it on a general and permanent footing, and in a condition of the finances which, as has been recognised by my hon'ble feiend the Lieutenant-Governor of Bengal, would justify the large remission of the customs duties proposed this year.

And now I will pass on to a consideration of the arrangements proposed with respect to the salt tax. I can really add very little to what has fallen from my hon'ble friend Major Baring with respect to that matter. I confess that I am a very strong advocate of this portion of the Budget. I think that the large reduction we propose in the salt tax is very desirable, both upon general grounds and upon financial grounds. My hon'ble friend Major Baring has dealt with the financial portion of the question, and I can add nothing to what he has said in that respect; but I desire to express the difficulty which I feel in adopting the view which has been put forward by some of my hon'ble friends in the course of this discussion, that this tax upon salt—which is a tax upon a necessary of life; which is a tax of many hundred per cent. upon the natural price of the article; which is paid, as I believe I am justified in saying, for or on behalf of every person in this country, of all the many millions gathered under the sceptre of our Queen-Empress—is not a tax which is felt by those who pay it; is not a tax which it is desirable to reduce apart from the financial considerations which lead to its reduction, in order to confer a benefit upon the great mass of the population of this country. My hon'ble friend Rájá Siva Prasád has stated his opinion that this salt duty is felt by the people, that it does press upon them, and that they will obtain considerable relief by the reduction now proposed. I confess that I find it very difficult to suppose that that is not the case, and that

Financial Statement, 1882-83.

a tax of this kind, paid by men whose annual income is as low, or nearly as low, as the figure mentioned by my hon'ble friend Major Baring, does not press heavily upon those who are least able to contribute to the necessities of the Government.

I know that it has been sometimes argued, in favour of the reduction of this tax, that no man can consume more than a certain amount of salt, and that, therefore, the tax presses most unequally upon the poor as well as the rich. That is an argument which in India may, I admit be pressed too far, because, as we all know from the habits and the charity of the people of this country, the wealthier classes have always a very large number of persons depending upon them, and the salt tax they pay is not a tax upon what they consume themselves only, but also upon the salt consumed by the large number of human beings dependent upon them for their existence. Nevertheless, when every allowance is made for that consideration, I am at a loss to understand how it can be argued that this tax is a peculiarly equable tax; because, however great the number of dependants a rich man may have, it is quite impossible that the amount of salt duty he pays can bear to his revenue anything like the same proportion which the amount of duty paid by one of those poor raiyats. described by my hon'ble friend, bears to his small and miserable income.

My hon'ble friend Mr. Inglis remarked that we should not repeal the salt duty, but equalise it. 'Take off,' he said, 'the differential duty in Bengal.' That would have been in many respects a good thing to do, if we had done nothing else. If, however, we had taken off the differential duty on sea-borne salt in Bengal, and left the salt duty as it was in other parts of India, there would have been plenty of people to tell us that we had taken off the duty for the benefit of the Cheshire manufacturers. That is exactly the style of argument which would have been used, and it would undoubtedly have been true as regards the effect of

Financial Statement, 1882-83.

the repeal of the duty on sea-borne salt, though not as regards the intention of the Government.

Then there is another point which presses with me very much in respect to this salt tax, and that is, the effect it has on agriculture. We all know that the consumption of salt is very necessary for cattle, and, in the papers to which my hon'ble friend Major Baring referred (and very remarkable papers they are) in connection with this subject—namely, the reports from Rájputána with respect to the result of the recents salt arrangements in that part of the world—particular attention is drawn to the fact that in many cases, while the consumption of salt by the people themselves is not diminished, the amount of salt given to the cattle has diminished greatly. It is, no doubt, contrary to public policy to maintain at a high rate a tax which has a practical tendency to discourage and interfere with the progress and advancement of agriculture. Then, again, it must be borne in mind that, as my hon'ble friend Major Baring said, this tax, when lowered in other parts of India a few years ago, was raised in Bombay and Madras, and the quotation he has made from a very able newspaper on the Bombay side shows that the people of that part of the world have not forgotten that fact, and that they are of opinion that the tax raised against them has pressed upon them heavily, and that they will undoubtedly rejoice in a reduction which will bring down the tax nearly to what it was before it was raised a few years ago.

Now, it seems to me that, with respect to this salt tax we are in this position. If the salt tax does not press upon the people—if it is a tax which they do not feel at all and do not object to pay, then it does form, without doubt the best possible financial resource you can have, and, the lower you can bring it down, the greater is the security to the people of India against other forms of taxation. If on the other hand, the salt tax does press upon the poorer classes of the country, then surely it is only right and just

Financial Statement, 1882-83.

that the Government should give those—the poorest classes —a share of the prosperity which the country is enjoying at the present time, even although it may at some future period of financial difficulty and disaster be necessary to re-impose the duty temporarily, in order that we may recoup ourselves for the loss which such a condition of affairs would impose upon us. But, then, my hon'ble friend says that all experience shows that this reduction does not reach the people. I can really add nothing to what my hon'ble friend Major Baring said upon that subject. I cannot say what may be the experience of this country. I can only say that the experience of all other countries is precisely the other way, and I am altogether unconvinced that large reductions of taxation will not ultimately reach the consumer, and will not be found here, as everywhere, to benefit the consumer at large. With respect to that, I may say that it is the intention of the Government to use every effort in their power to make known as widely as possible this reduction of the salt duty. We propose to address Local Governments on the subject, with a view to their taking measures to make the reduction everywhere known to the actual masses of the people themselves; and I would also ask the aid of the Vernacular Press in regard to that matter, and beg them to make the reduction as widely known as possible among their readers in every part of the land.

I pass now from the salt duty to the question of the license tax. My hon'ble friend Major Baring has stated very distinctly and unmistakeably in his Financial Statement the policy of the Government upon that subject, and the position which we take up. He has told to this Council and to the public that we reserve to ourselves entire freedom to deal with the license tax hereafter as we may think right. It is perfectly open to us, as he explained, to repeal it, re-cast it, or leave it for a time in its present position, although undoubtedly we acknowledge and admit that in its present form it is open to just and important

Financial Statement, 1882-83.

objections. But, when the choice is put to me as a choice between getting rid of the license tax and of the salt duty, I personally must honestly say that I can have no hesitation as to the choice which I would make. I prefer the salt duty, because, in the first place, as I have said, it presses upon—at all events, it cannot be disputed that it is paid by—all the poorest people in this country; whereas, as shown in the Budget Statement, the license tax is paid by only between 200,000 and 300,000 persons. Therefore, in respect to numbers, I cannot for a moment doubt that the course the Government is taking in this respect will afford relief from taxation to a far larger number of people in the country than would have resulted from the repeal of the license tax. And it must be recollected that there is in this Council very little representation, if any, of those poorest classes—indeed, no representation at all, except such as may be found in those who take an interest in their situation and are prompted to speak on their behalf. Those classes, as my hon'ble friend Rájá Siva Prasád remarked are in this country practically dumb; their voices do not go to swell the chorus of public opinion; they are little heard, even in the echoes of the Press; and, therefore, it is the bounden duty of the Government to guard their interests and to provide for their benefit. But there is another reason why I prefer on this occasion to deal with the salt duty rather than with the license tax, and that is, because I certainly hope and believe that it will be found that, when this salt duty is reduced as largely as we propose to reduce it, the loss of revenue will be in the course of time recouped, and that that recoupment will enable us hereafter to proceed to further reductions of taxation; whereas, if we had dealt with the license tax and simply abolished it, there would have been no opening for recoupment—no prospect of a revenue growing up again from that source.

Then it may be said—'You are going to take off something like £1,400,000 of salt duty. Why do not you take

Financial Statement, 1882-83.

off a less amount of salt duty and repeal the licence tax—or, (as my hon'ble friend Mr. Inglis suggested) 'take off the export duty on rice?' I will tell you why. Because we are convinced that, with respect to this question of the salt duty, a bold policy is the only sound policy for the Government to adopt. If you make a small reduction of the salt duty, it is very possible it will not reach the people. It is extremely possible that they will derive little or no benefit from it, and then the revenue will not be recouped. You can only hope to obtain all the benefits we desire from this reduction of the salt duty by making a large and bold reduction in it, which will afford a fair prospect—and, I venture to hope, a great deal more than a fair prospect—that the great mass of the people will benefit by it; that benefiting by it, they will increase their consumption of salt, and that, from that increased consumption, our revenue will gradually recover from the loss first accruing to it from the partial remission of this duty. That would not have been the case if we had made a small reduction. We should never have obtained the object we had in view, and it would have practically resulted in a dead loss of revenue without the advantages which, under present circumstances, we may hope to obtain from it.

Then, again, with respect to the license tax, my hon'ble friend Major Baring, in his Budget Statement, has set out a variety of considerations which introduce elements of uncertainty into our financial position in regard to the future. I hope and believe that they are all those elements of uncertainty which will turn out for our benefit, and which will be ultimately solved in a manner calculated to confer financial advantages upon the country. But it is very necessary that, under such circumstances, we should proceed cautiously, and that we should wait, while those grounds for uncertainty exist, until we can see our way more clearly in regard to them, before making any larger remissions of taxation than those very considerable ones which this

Financial Statement, 1882-83.

Budget proposes. I think nothing could be more unwise than that we should propose to repeal a tax which is undoubtedly, and I may at once admit it, an unpopular tax, unless we had been perfectly certain we should not be obliged to have recourse to it again within the space of a few years. The history of direct taxation in this country, as explained by my hon'ble friend Major Baring, gives most striking proofs, as it seems to me, of the unwisdom of dealing rashly with this question—of making constant changes and proceeding without those elements of certainty which, as I say, are at the present moment in some respects wanting to us.

With respect to opium, I have really nothing to add to the very able statement made upon that subject in the Budget speech of my hon'ble friend Major Baring. That statement has, I think I may say, been received with general satisfaction by all who have heard it. My view on the subject of opium is a very simple one. I do not deny that there are objections of various kinds to the opium revenue I do not deny that it is not a satisfactory branch of our revenue, in many ways; but I say distinctly that I will be no party to abandoning that revenue unless I can clearly see my way to replace it by some other form of taxation which would be neither oppressive to the people nor strongly repugnant to public opinion. Well, I can see nothing of the kind. I have considered the question very carefully. I have considered it with the utmost respect for the opinion of those excellent men who take a different view of this subject from that which I take, and who are moving at home in the matter; and I have been totally unable to discover the taxation by which our opium revenue could be replaced, and by which, without oppression, without incurring a great, and, I may say, a just, unpopularity, we should have the slightest chance of recouping ourselves if we were to abandon that revenue in whole or in part. As I said before, it is, in my judgment, the first duty of the Government of

Financial Statement, 1882-83.

India to consider the interests of the people of India; and it is from that point of view that I look at this question; and, looking at it from that point of view, I can have no doubt that the course which the Government of India have determined to take,—namely, that of maintaining our position with respect to the opium revenue—is a just and right one.

But, then, I have heard it said, ' If you cannot make up for the loss of this revenue by fresh taxes, you can make up for it by reduction of expenditure.' Well, there is no one more anxious for reduction of unnecessary expenditure than I am. There is no person who desires to see every item of expenditure which is not needed in the interests of the country got rid of than I am. That is the view of the Government, and we are most anxious to reduce expenditure wherever it is possible. Some reductions of military expenditure we have already made, as has been explained to you, and we hope that yet further steps in that direction may hereafter be taken. As you know, the whole of this subject was very carefully considered a year or two ago by an Army Commission, composed of very able men, who examined this question with the greatest care and made an admirable report. That Commission was presided over by my hon'ble friend, Sir Ashley Eden; and, as I have mentioned his name, I cannot help availing myself of this occasion to say how strongly I recognise that, by his services on that Commission, he has added to the many great claims he has established by his long and distinguished career in India to the gratitude alike of the Government and of the people of the country; and I cannot but express the regret which I feel, and which I know will be heartily shared by all here, that it will not now be many months before we shall lose him from amongst us. But this I have to say in respect to this matter of expenditure, that it seems to me that every rupee of that expenditure which may be saved from unnecessary or unproductive objects is urgently needed for purposes of the highest importance to the people,—public

Financial Statement, 1882-83.

works, education, sanitary questions,—questions that I can scarcely number, but all of which make most urgent demands upon the Government for money, and I can hold out no hope that, by any reduction of aggregate expenditure, we can save, not seven or eight millions, but one or two millions, out of the necessary expenditure of this country for great objects of public importance.

The opium estimate for the coming year has been framed, as you are aware, upon a somewhat different principle from that upon which the estimate of last year was framed, and I am bound to say that, for myself, I prefer the course taken upon this occasion. I believe that estimate to be a very cautious one. It would be extremely unwise, I entirely admit, that our opium estimate should be anything but very cautious. All estimates of revenue should be low; all estimates of expenditure should be high; and I go further in regard to opium, and say that our estimate of the opium revenue should always be (on account of the peculiar circumstances connected with that branch of the revenue) a specially cautious and low one; but I believe that we have fulfilled that condition in the present year, and, as far as I myself can judge, I am of opinion that the amount placed by my hon'ble friend in the Budget is one which, saving unforeseen accidents of the season, or circumstances of trade, is likely to be realised.

I do not know that there are any other points connected with this Budget upon which I need express my opinion now. I have touched upon the principal matters with which it deals, and I have laid before my hon'ble colleagues in this Council some, at least, of the reasons which induce me heartily to concur in the proposals of my hon'ble friend. But I cannot conclude the remarks I have made on this occasion without tendering my warm thanks to Major Baring for the great care and labour which he has bestowed upon this Budget. No one who has not had the advantage I have had of watching him at work upon this subject for the last

Financial Statement, 1882-83.

twelve months can know how hard he has worked; what wide and varied consideration of the whole field of past and present taxation—what close and careful examination of our whole fiscal system and of the resources of the country—he has gone through in order to produce in this final form the proposals now before us. Whatever any man may think of those proposals, they are, I venture to say, so far as my hon'ble friend is concerned, the outcome of deep thought, of minute care, and of honest conviction; and I must say that to me they seem well worthy of the high reputation as a financier which he had already procured for himself before he came to India.

I must also express my best thanks to Mr. Hope.* It is needless for me to speak of his ability, or of his really wonderful industry. They are known to all, but they have, I venture to say, never been more conspicuously displayed than in connection with the preparation of the present Budget.

Allusion has been made once or twice in the course of this discussion to certain enquiries made last year by Mr. Barbour,† and I should be very ungrateful if I failed to notice the great assistance the Government has received from him; the manner in which he has conducted those enquiries has been marked by much ability and skill.

It only remains now for me, in conclusion, to say that it is my earnest hope that this present Budget, while it will unfetter trade and lighten the burden of taxation that presses upon the poorest in the land, will be found, when it has passed through the test of experience, to have dealt with our financial arrangements in a manner consistent alike with sound economical principles and calculated to confer large and increasing benefits upon all classes of the people.

[The Motion was put and agreed to, and the three Bills before the Council were passed into law.]

---

* Financial Secretary to the Government of India.
† Officiating Secretary to the Government of Bengal, General and Revenue Department.

CONVOCATION OF THE CALCUTTA UNIVERSITY

1th March 1882. [THE Annual Convocation of the Calcutta University, for the purpose of conferring Degrees, was held at the Senate House on Saturday, the 11th March, at 4 P. M. His Excellency the Viceroy, the Chancellor of the University, presided. There was a large attendance of the members of the Senate and of the general public. After the presentation of the Degrees, His Excellency, whose speech was frequently interrupted by applause, addressed the assembly as follows :—]

Mr. Vice-Chancellor and Gentlemen,—It is no light task for any one to be called upon to address an assembly like this, and to occupy, even for a brief space, the attention of such a body as the University of Calcutta ; and if the undertaking be an arduous one for those who have ample leisure to prepare themselves to accomplish it with all the thought and deliberation which it demands, what must it be for one who can only snatch a few scattered half-hours in the midst of the absorbing duties of such an office as that which I now fill in this country. I feel, therefore, gentlemen, in presenting myself before you to-day, that I have more than ordinary need of that indulgence which is always so readily accorded by the learned to those who can lay no claim to that honourable title.

It is a quarter of a century, almost to a day, since the Act of 1857 laid the foundations of this Institution and appointed as its first Chancellor that distinguished statesman, Lord Canning, who had hardly entered upon his duties in connection with this peaceful and beneficent work when he had to encounter, with that calm courage and that deep sense of justice for which he was so eminent, the most terrible storm which ever swept over India since she came under British rule. But that storm, of which so many of the traces are scarcely yet effaced, left the Calcutta University uninjured and ready to start forth upon the great work entrusted to it the moment the return of quiet enabled it to do so ; and when our minds recur to the date at which

Convocation of the Calcutta University.

the University took its rise, we cannot fail to be struck by the thought that the object which this Institution has in view was one pre-eminently needed at the moment when the dreadful transactions of the Mutiny were closed; for that object is, in the main, to bring together and to unite the European and the Native in the common pursuit and the common love of knowledge. We may then, I think, say, gentlemen, that on this occasion, when we commemorate the termination of the twenty-fifth year of the life of this University, we are met together to celebrate the Silver Wedding of Western and Eastern Learning, and to offer our best and most earnest wishes for the long and fruitful continuance of an union which is capable of conferring so many benefits upon East and West alike.

Such, then, was the origin and purpose of this University; but when we speak of it by that high title, we must always remember that it discharges only a portion of the functions of a complete University. It is in the main an examining body; it is not a place of study, so much as a place where study is tested. When I say this, however, it is not for the purpose of disparagement or complaint, but for the sake of accuracy. We have the example of the University of London to shew us that very good work may be done by an institution of this kind, and, indeed, we need no further proof that it is so than that which is afforded by the experience of the Calcutta University itself. It is not, however, solely by the direct operation of its examinations that this University takes part in the general educational work of the country. Standing at the head of the system of education of this side of India, it exercises a great and controlling influence over the teaching of the Colleges and Schools below it. It tests their work, and consequently it practically directs their studies, and in this way it constitutes a most important portion of our educational organisation, and is largely responsible for the tone and character of the studies carried on in the lower institutions. Such an influence as this

Convocation of the Calcutta University.

grows with the growth and popularity of the University, and becomes day by day more and more potent for good or for evil. It might be easily used for the mischievous purpose of reducing all our Colleges and Schools to one single type, and of checking all variety of education and training. This is a danger which I earnestly trust that the authorities of the University will always bear in mind, and against which they will, I hope, take every possible precaution. Measures have lately been adopted having that object, among others, in view; and it is very satisfactory to know that those in whose hands the government of the University is placed are fully alive to the importance of leaving the utmost possible freedom to the subordinate institutions, both for the development of the faculties of their pupils, and for the preservation of the influence of the personal character of their teachers.

There is also another direction in which, not this University alone, but all the educational establishments in the country, of which the management is in any degree directly connected with the Government, fail, and necessarily fail, to afford the means of a full and complete education. The Government of India is required by solemn pledges, strictly binding upon it in honour and good faith, to do nothing calculated to interfere directly or indirectly with the religion or the religious feelings of the native population; and it is therefore impossible for that Government, in any of its places of education, to attempt to give anything in the nature of religious instruction, or to interfere with that great branch of education at all. I fully recognise that it is only in this way that the British Government in this country can fulfil the engagements into which it has entered, and which form part, so to speak, of the constitutional arrangements of India; but I could not refrain from alluding to the limitation thus placed upon the scope of our education, because it is one of my deepest convictions that a system of education which makes no provision for

Convocation of the Calcutta University.

religious teaching is essentially imperfect and incomplete. I do not hold that such a system does no good, or that, when its existence is the necessary result of the circumstances of the time and country in which it is to be found, it is not deserving of encouragement and support. All truth is one, and one portion of it cannot be in real conflict with another. I hail, then, every effort to develop the minds of men and to store them with sound knowledge of every kind. I look upon it as an object of the highest interest and importance to the Government of this country to promote to the utmost the intellectual culture of the people of India of all races and creeds, among whom are to be found in all classes so many men of high intellectual qualities, who are eminently capable of profiting to the full by the best mental training which can be supplied to them. But I should not express my whole mind upon this great subject of education if I were to conceal my belief that what in the language of the day is called a purely secular education is not a complete education in the highest and noblest sense of the word.

This question of education is, as you are aware, gentlemen, occupying at the present time a large share of the attention of the Government. We are deeply impressed with its importance; we desire to advance further along the path which our predecessors have followed, and to spread the benefits of elementary instruction more widely than has yet been done among the masses of the people without retarding the development of that higher instruction in which, up to this time, the chief progress has been made. We have appointed a Commission, on which we have endeavoured to secure, as far as possible, representatives of all interests and opinions; and we trust that its inquiries will result in the collection of much valuable information and the proposal of such measures as are required by the present condition of the country. We have not included, in the duties entrusted to the Commission, any

Convocation of the Calcutta University.

examination into the state or working of the Indian Universities, because there is ample evidence before us that they are discharging their special functions with an amount of success, and of satisfaction to the public, which justifies us in placing a large confidence in those to whom the management of these institutions is entrusted. It is not at the summit of our educational system that improvement is most urgently required, but at its base. Our Universities are constituted and are drawing ever-increasing crowds of students to their examinations, till we are forcibly reminded of the multitudes which flocked to the Universities of Europe in the Middle Ages: and until it is doubtful, as Sir Henry Maine once remarked on an occasion similar to this, " whether there is anything founded by, or connected with, the British Government in India which excites so much practical interest in native households of the better class, from Calcutta to Lahore, as the examinations" of our Indian Universities. A large number of Colleges and Higher and Middle Schools exist, and, though there may be many points in which their management and the instruction given in them may be improved, it is to those points, rather than to any large increase in the number of such institutions, that our attention should be especially directed.

But in regard to Primary Education, there is a vast field before us. I am not at all inclined to underrate what has been already done in that branch of our educational system. Speaking here in the chief city of Bengal, I should be very ungrateful if I did not note, by way of example, the important measures by which Sir George Campbell laid—deep and solid, as I hope and believe—the foundations of Elementary Education in this province. It is one among the many claims of that distinguished person to the gratitude of Bengal and of India. But when we make the largest and fairest allowance for all that has been already accomplished, the work which remains to be done, if judged by

Convocation of the Calcutta University.

European standards, is so enormous, when compared with the resources at our disposal at present, as almost to make us despair of the accomplishment of the task. Yet, apart from the general importance of popular education, there are special circumstances connected with the particular stage of general education at which we have arrived in this country, which makes the wide extension of sound elementary instruction among the people at large a matter of peculiar urgency. We have now in India, as the result of the spread of Middle and Higher instruction, an educated class increasing in numbers from year to year, but still a mere handful when compared with the great mass of the people, for whom the means even of the most rudimentary instruction are very limited, and of whom a large proportion are not brought within the civilizing influence of the school at all. This does not seem to me to be a healthy state of things. It is not desirable in any country to have a small highly-educated class brought into contact with a large uneducated mass; what is wanted is, that instruction should be more equally distributed, that the artizans and peasants of the land should have brought within their reach such opportunities for the cultivation of their faculties as may be possible under the circumstances of their condition, and that there should be no sharp line drawn between the educated few and the ignorant and untrained many. The circumstances of India under British rule have led to the establishment in the first instance of places of Higher and of Middle Education; and our progress has been marked by what has been described as a process of filtration downwards. I make no complaint of this, but I feel strongly that the most difficult, and yet the really most important, part of our task lies before us, and it has become urgently necessary that we should address ourselves to its accomplishment.

But when we do so, we are met at the very outset by a difficulty of a formidable kind. To establish a real and

K 1

Convocation of the Calcutta University.

effective system of general Primary Education requires a very large expenditure. Where are the funds to come from? We all know that the financial resources of the Government of India are strictly limited, and we know also that the demands upon them are very great. Supposing the Government to devote to this object of Primary Education every rupee which it can spare from other purposes, the total amount will inevitably be found to be comparatively small, and it is therefore absolutely necessary that the friends of education should avail themselves, to the utmost of their power, of every other source of income which may be open to them. We must have recourse to all classes of men, and make use of every variety of motive. We must appeal to private individuals, to public bodies, to patriotic feeling, to religious zeal, and to the desire of personal distinction. I do not know that I can better illustrate the kind of aid which may be derived from these sources than by inviting you to consider with me for a moment what is done in this way in England. It is a very general practice—I should not be very far wrong if I were to say that it is an almost universal practice—for the wealthier land-owners to maintain the village school very largely, often entirely, at their own cost, with the exception of what they receive from the Government grants-in-aid, and from the small payments made by the parents of the children. These schools are under Government inspection, the scholars are regularly examined by Government officers, and, as I have said, grants-in-aid are given; but the whole management is in the hands of the local land-owner, or of a committee of local subscribers, who take a keen interest in the efficiency of the school and the progress of the children. Is there not here an example which might well be followed more largely in this country than it has hitherto been? In England the case is still stronger in regard to Higher and Middle education; towards the support of Primary Education the Government

Convocation of the Calcutta University.

contributes largely; towards that of Higher and Middle Education it does not, broadly speaking, contribute at all. Sir Henry Maine, in one of those remarkable addresses which he delivered when he held the office of your Vice-Chancellor, reminded his hearers how the great English Universities were founded—not by grants of public money not even, except to a limited extent, by kings and queens from their personal resources, but by the liberality of private individuals, many of whose names are now remembered only because they are enrolled upon the honoured lists of the benefactors of Oxford and Cambridge; and as it has been with the Universities, so has it been with the Colleges, Public Schools, and Grammar Schools of England ; they are the foundations of private men ; they date back to days when England was not a wealthy country as we count wealth at present—when the proudest of English nobles would have been but a poor man indeed, by the side of many of the great Chiefs and Zemindars of the India of to-day. I know no reason why that which has been done in the past, and is done every day now, not by great nobles, but by private gentlemen in England, should not be done by gentlemen of wealth and station in this country. I am not one of those who think that my countrymen possess a monopoly of all the higher qualities and all the virtues of mankind. I decline to believe that the patriotism, the public spirit, the charity, the interest in their poorer neighbours, which have prompted men to these deeds in England have no counterpart in this country. There may have been times when the gentlemen of India did not come forward to aid in such undertakings, because they thought that the Government did not wish them to be active in public affairs and preferred to keep the control of everything in its own hands , but, whatever may have been the case in the past, at all events such an excuse cannot be urged now. We invite you to come forward, we desire your co-operation, we wish to see you taking a larger and

Convocation of the Calcutta University.

larger share in public affairs of all kinds, and we esteem it a great help to the Government, as it is undoubtedly a great advantage to yourselves and to the people at large, that you should employ your wealth and strengthen your influence by public services, such as those which I have here described, freely rendered and gratefully received. If I mistake not, such benefactions are entirely in accordance with the spirit both of Hindoo and of Mahometan traditions. We have noble examples of them down to the present day. All I would ask is, that an increasing share of the available private wealth of the country may be devoted to a work so noble and so urgent as the spread of sound education among all classes of the people. The Roman poet boasted *Exegi monumentum cere perennius, regalique situ pyramidum altius;* and so it will be with you. A single school founded, a single college aided,—nay, I will say also, a single scholarship provided,—will do more in the times which are before us to uphold the honour of an ancient name, or to create the reputation of a new one, than any outward show of dignity or any personal display of wealth.

But if I thus earnestly ask aid from native gentlemen in this great work of education, it is not solely, nor even mainly, in order to obtain the funds which we so urgently need; it is yet more because I believe it to be of the very highest importance to give to our educational system that variety which alone can secure the free development of every side and aspect of the national character. It has often been the dream of despots to establish a system of education which would cast the whole of a great people in one mould and train them up in a blind and unreasoning submission to the will of a central power. This was the aim of the first Napoleon when he founded the University of France and gave it complete control over the whole education of the country. All Frenchmen were to be brought up exactly alike, and taught to believe that their first duty was to love and obey the Emperor, whoever he

Convocation of the Calcutta University.

might be, and whatever he might command ; and no one who is acquainted with the subsequent history of French education can fail to be struck with the deep root which this pernicious system, once established, has taken in France, and the strange way in which it has survived all political changes and been adopted by almost all political parties in succession, because it afforded them a powerful engine for the compulsory propagation of their own opinions. Now, such a scheme as this is alien from the genius of the English people and contrary to the policy which it would be wise for the English Government to pursue in India. We are here in the midst of ancient peoples, possessed of civilization, of literature, and of art of their own ; and our business is not to try and force them to reject their past, to forget all that is characteristic in their history and their traditions, and to convert themselves into bad imitations of modern Englishmen ; but to place without stint, at their disposal, all the riches of Western science and Western culture, that they may blend them in one harmonious union with the treasures of their own Oriental learning. If ever there was a country in which educational variety was a necessity, it seems to me that India is that country, It is a land of many races and many creeds. Hindoo, Buddhist, and Mahometan traditions are essentially different. and have each given rise to a different literature and a varied form of civilization. If we leave things to take their free and natural course, Western learning will combine with each of those great forms of Indian thought in a different and characteristic manner ; and, though its ultimate tendency may be to unity, it will reach that unity by varied means and along separate paths ; and in the midst of that unity, when it is at length attained, it will, like the great forests of tropical climes, preserve that rich and infinite variety which is one of the principal sources of the beauty of nature. How, then, can this great end be attained ? It seems to me that it can be attained only by securing for

Convocation of the Calcutta University.

our educational work the co-operation of the great indigenous influences which are still living and active in the country. No purely Government system can do this. The inevitable tendency of Government education is to become stereotyped; to take up definite lines and to follow them; to fall into certain grooves and never to get out of them; and therefore, if you want variety, if you want free growth and unfettered development, if you want to see various experiments tried and ignorance attacked on every side, you must frankly call in the aid of the public, you must encourage their efforts and give them ample scope. Your educational system will in this way not be so symmetrical, but it will be more natural; its results will be less uniform, but they will be more full.

But it may be asked, why do you make this appeal so urgently now? What is there in the circumstances of the present time which leads you to hold a great educational effort to be so necessary? I have already given you some reasons for the view which I take of the matter, but there is one which especially weighs with me, and to which I will now advert. I often heard it said in England, before I came out to this country, that there was nothing like real and effective public opinion in India, and that the want of it was one of the special difficulties which the Government of India had to encounter. Few things have struck me more during the time that I have been here then the various proofs which I have seen of the existence of a substantial public opinion, which is evidently growing and strengthening from day to day. I do not mean to say that there yet exists in India that general, widespread, constraining public opinion which is to be found in European countries, and which, when its voice is clearly heard, is the irresistible and unresisted master of Governments and Parliaments. Public opinion here is still to a great extent split up into sections, and represents very often only the views and interests of classes or of coteries; while the great mass of

' *Convocation of the Calcutta University.*

the people, the operatives of towns and the cultivators of the rural districts, are still unhappily without direct means of making their voices heard ; but with all these drawbacks and shortcomings, the power and influence of general public opinion, which is of course in the main native opinion, is obviously extending and advancing with a sure and steady step. No prudent Government and no wise statesman would despise or disregard it, while at the same time it has not yet arrived at that condition of solidity and depth which would make it the powerful instrument for warning and enlightening the administration which it is in England and other Western countries. My experience has also taught me the great difficulty which often exists on the part of Europeans on the one side and natives on the other in understanding each other's point of view. What seems a self-evident proposition to the one often appears to be almost incomprehensible to the other ; not, certainly, from want of intelligence, but from entire difference of habits of thought ; and yet as we, the men of both races, have to work together for a common end—the good of India and the well-being of her people,—it is of the utmost importance that every obstacle which prevents us from entering easily and fairly into each other's mode of regarding the many questions with which we have to deal in common, should be removed. How, then, can this be done ? How can public opinion be made more intelligent, more wide, more just, and more united, and therefore more powerful and effective ? By the spread of solid education alone. By education, the writers in the Press, who have in these days so large a share in the formation of public opinion, will learn to judge events more wisely, to weigh rumours more accurately, to reason more soundly, and to appreciate more justly the real value of words ; while by the same means the public, to whom they speak, will become every day less liable to be misled by absurd reports, or carried away by hollow declamation, and more capable

Convocation of the Calcutta University.

of forming their own independent judgment on what concerns their own interests, and impressing it upon those who profess to speak in their name. This is a process which must be gone through in every country before public opinion can obtain that powerful influence on public affairs to which in its full development it is justly entitled ; and the best mode of hastening the completion of that process is to promote the spread, throughout all classes of the community, of an education calculated to strengthen the mental faculties and to steady the judgment.

And now, gentlemen, I should like, with your permission, to say a few words with reference to the general purpose of all education and to the spirit by which the true student should be animated. The purpose of real education I take to be, not merely to fill the mind of the student with a large number of facts, not to enable him to talk glibly about a variety of sciences, not even to secure his passing all the examinations of his University, but to cultivate, to develop, and to strengthen the various faculties with which he has been endowed. If I am right in this, the first thing needed in education is thoroughness of knowledge ; the mental powers can be better trained by knowing a few things thoroughly than by knowing many things superficially ; and yet there are many circumstances in these days which tend to tempt men, and especially young men, to superficiality and to turn them aside from depth. The very extent and variety of the subjects of study which are offered to us in modern times, the many new sciences and branches of science which have been opened out to us within the last half century, the natural eagerness of youth to sip, one after another, at the beautiful flowers which grow so richly in the garden of learning, and last, but not perhaps least, the inevitable tendency of a wide and varied curriculum of examination,—all tend in the same direction ; and yet, if you measure the result of the education which a man has received, not by the number of topics upon which

Convocation of the Calcutta University.

he talks fluently in ordinary society, but by the number of those of which he has a real firm grasp; not by the books which he has read, but by those which he has digested; not by the facts which he has laid up in his memory, but by the accuracy of his judgment, the strength of his reasoning powers, and the force of his intellect,—you will soon be convinced that more real mental training is to be derived from the thorough study of a single subject than from a skin-deep acquaintance with a hundred sciences. I would say, then, to every student—Be thorough; know what you know as fully and completely as you can; use the fruitful spring-time of youth, when your intellectual powers are fresh and full of growth, to strengthen, to widen, to develope them on every side, rather than to fill your mind with miscellaneous knowledge which you can gather, as far as may be needful for you, much more easily in after-life, if while you are young you have improved to the utmost the instrument by which all knowledge is obtained. Spring is the time for working the ground and putting in the seed; autumn is the time for gathering in the harvest and storing it in barns.

And then, again, I would say to you, while you know accurately what you do know, while you are thoroughly acquainted with the true extent of your knowledge, keep also constantly before you, with no less care and accuracy a true sense of your ignorance. Few things are more useful to a student than that he should constantly recall to mind how many subjects there are of which he knows nothing; the more he realises this, the surer will be his hold of the subjects which he has fully mastered; the juster will be his appreciation of the real nature of solid learning, and the more sure will be the growth within him of that modesty which is the prime mark of the true student. And lastly, let us ever remember that the end of life, after all, is not to know, but to be. The usefulness of knowledge depends upon the use we make of it. If we use it for

Laying the Foundation-stone of the new Lecture Hall and Observatory of the Indian Association for the Cultivation of Science.

selfish objects or ignoble purposes, we had better have been without it. Those high and noble faculties of mind and will which are the exclusive inheritance of no age, or race or country, have been given to us, not that we may employ them for our own benefit alone, or cultivate them merely for their own sake, but that, developing them to the utmost, we may apply them all to advance the glory of Him whose gifts they are, and to promote the welfare of our fellow-men, who, wheresoever they may dwell, and whether they be rich or poor, learned or ignorant, are all alike the children of one common Father.

LAYING THE FOUNDATION-STONE OF THE NEW LECTURE HALL AND OBSERVATORY OF THE INDIAN ASSOCIATION FOR THE CULTIVATION OF SCIENCE.

13th Mar. 1882. [ON Monday afternoon, the 13th March, the Viceroy laid the foundation-stone of the new Lecture Hall and Observatory of the Indian Association for the Cultivation of Science. There was a large assembly of European and Native Gentlemen. His Excellency, on his arrival, was received by the President (Sir Ashley Eden) and the members of the Association, and conducted to a seat within the *shamiana* erected for the occasion. The Honorary Secretary (Dr. Mahendra Láll Sircár) gave a short history of the Institution, with an account of the subscriptions received, and concluded with an urgent appeal for the further necessary funds in aid of building-expenses. Sir Ashley Eden, in a brief speech, then requested the Viceroy to lay the stone, which being accomplished, His Excellency addressed the assembly as follows :—]

Sir Ashley Eden and Gentlemen,—It has, I assure you, afforded me much pleasure to have been able to be present upon this occasion, and to lay the first stone of this building, because I can truly say that I sympathise very heartily with the objects for which the institution which is here to be housed has been founded. I look upon it as an object

Laying the Foundation-stone of the new Lecture Hall and Observatory of the Indian Association for the Cultivation of Science.

of great importance that there should be established in the heart of this great city an institution which has, for one of its chief purposes, to provide the means by which students of science may pursue their delightful studies after they have left college or school; for we all know that in the case of many youths, little more can be done during their scholastic period than to place in their hands the tools with which they may afterwards acquire knowledge for themselves, and to teach them how to use those tools efficiently and well. And much, in truth, has been done if during school-life the efficient use of those tools is thoroughly taught. I had occasion a short time ago, when addressing another educational institution in this city, to remark that it was a great error to suppose that a man's education ended when he left school or college, and therefore naturally I feel a deep interest in the work and the labours of an institution which has for its purpose to provide the young men of this city (who, when they leave their colleges, are still animated by the noble desire of pursuing the studies that they have there commenced) with the means of continued self-education under the guidance of competent teachers. And again, it appears to me to be a great advantage that in this country, the people of which are animated by so strong a taste for science and so marked a love of scientific pursuits, this Association should be the instrument for bringing together a body of lecturers so learned and able as those who give their services to it, and of providing them with the means (whether of building or of apparatus) by which they may impart to their fellow-citizens the knowledge for which they are themselves so eminent.

But, Sir Ashley Eden and gentlemen, there is another circumstance connected with the proceedings of to-day, which affords to me a deep sense of gratification. It was only on last Saturday that I expressed my strong and

Laying the Foundation-stone of the new Lecture Hall and Observatory

earnest conviction of the great importance to the future o India, that her wealthy classes should come forward and take a large part in providing the means of education for her people; and I come here this afternoon, and I am told, to my great satisfaction, of the noble liberality which has been displayed by those who support this Association. (*Applause.*) We have heard of the munificent donation of Bábu Káli Kishen Tagore, a member of a family eminent among the families of India for their public spirit (*applause*), and we have heard the names of others who have in a lesser degree, yet probably according to their means, come forward to help in this great work. You can easily believe how gratifying it must be to me to receive so marked a proof that those to whom I appealed last Saturday are animated—not in consequence of that appeal, for those gifts date from an antecedent period, but from their own motion and their own love of knowledge—by that spirit to which I ventured to make my appeal. (*Applause.*)

Your admirable Honorary Secretary drew, I fear, rather a gloomy picture of the present condition of India in respect to learning. I hope and believe that he took a view somewhat too gloomy of your real condition; but I am not sorry to see a man of spirit and energy like my learned friend take that low view of your present condition, because it is only by being thoroughly discontented with what you have done that you have the chance of doing that which, we all hope, you will yet accomplish (*applause*); and I would venture to throw in my voice with Dr. Sircar's in the appeal which he made to you for the endowment of professorships. It seems to me that that is a matter of very great importance; it is important because it will give to this association a permanent establishment; it is important because it will tend to maintain and to keep up the high character of its professoriat; and it is important also for another and a general reason,—because, as your Honorary Secretary well pointed out, the fact of gathering around

of the Indian Association for the Cultivation of Science.

this institution a body of able scientific men will be not only that they will be here to teach the five hundred students who are to be gathered within the walls of this new building, but that they will form a body of learned and scientific men leavening the society of Calcutta, giving a tone to its learning, and pursuing in the midst of this city those scientific investigations and enquiries which can alone be thoroughly followed by men who have an assured independence, and which will, I trust, before many years are past, enable the natives of this country to take their proper place among the scientific men of the world. (*Applause.*)

I am very glad, therefore, gentlemen, to have had it in my power to be present here to-day, and to have been asked to have the honour—for an honour I esteem it—of laying the first stone of this building, in which I trust will be displayed to many generations of students the wonders of physical and of natural science. Here, astronomy will lay bare to them the sscrets of other worlds ; here, chemistry will show them the composition of the substances which they handle every day, and will point out to them the astonishing and exact harmony with which the elements of those substances are combined ; and here will be revealed to them all the mysteries of those mighty energies or forces which the discoveries of the last half century have been unfolding to us ; and then there will grow up for them the lofty conception of law—of law, wide-spreading and harmonious, binding together and restraining the exuberance of nature, and leading the mind of the true student onwards and upwards to the very foot of the throne of the great Law Giver himself, in whom we live, and move, and are, and from whom flow down for the delight of his creatures all those marvels and beauties of this outward world, which it is the part of science to explore. (*Loud and continued applause.*)

LECTURE BY COLONEL CHESNEY.

31st May 1882. [HIS Excellency the Viceroy presided at a lecture delivered by Colonel Chesney, Secretary to Government in the Military Department, at the United Service Institution, Simla, on Wednesday evening, the 31st May. The subject of the lecture was " Taking Stock." There was a large audience, the Commander-in-Chief, the Lieutenant-Governor, and a number of high Military officials being present.

The Lecturer contrasted the vicissitudes of Continental armies in international quarrels one with another, showing how supremacy passed to the Prussian army 120 years ago ; how that was shattered by the march under Napoleon ; and how that again fell before the German troops a dozen years back. Noting these changes and their momentous consequences, he advised " taking stock" of our military resources. The secret of success lay, he believed, in the originality and energy of the General directing the operations, and, illustrating his ideas by the incidents of the American war, he gave the highest praise to the masterly strategy of General Grant, and his vigour in crushing or capturing the enemy's forces. He extolled the value of discipline, not necessarily always of the conventional type, but the higher discipline of that fortitude and courage which endured to death by starvation or by wounds. He concluded by declaring that the first secret of success in war was courage, the second courage, and the third courage.

In rising to return thanks to the Lecturer, the Viceroy, who was received with cheers, spoke as follow :—]

I do not know whether there is any gentleman who would wish to make any remarks on the lecture which we have just heard. [*After a pause, His Excellency continued.*] If no one is bold enough to take that course—although we have been exhorted to display courage, and courage, and yet again courage *(laughter)*, I will request those present to perform a duty which I am confident they will discharge with the utmost readiness, and to return their cordial thanks to Colonel Chesney for the very interesting lecture which he has delivered. (*Applause.*) Nothing would be more out of place than that I, who am a mere civilian, should attempt any criticism, or venture even on any general remarks, upon the lecture we have

Lecture by Colonel Chesney.

heard from such a distinguished military officer as Colonel Chesney; but at the same time, there are one or two observations which suggest themselves to me, which perhaps I may venture without impropriety to submit to you in connection with that lecture. Colonel Chesney has laid it down that the secret of the success of the great generals who have successively followed each other in the world's history, and who, one after another, have won triumphant positions for their own countries, has lain in the possession by those generals of originality, vigour, and energy of character. Now, it seems to me, ladies and gentlemen, that there is every antecedent probability that that dictum must be true; because I believe it to be just as applicable to all other professions in life as Colonel Chesney insists that it is applicable to the profession of the soldier. (*Applause.*) I believe that the secret of success, whether of the public man, of the civil gevernor, of the great head of an industrial undertaking, or of any who are engaged in any of the great walks of life, lies, as Colonel Chesney has said, in the possession of those great qualities,—originality, vigour, and energy. It is by originality to conceive, by firmness to pursue the plans which he has conceived, and by untiring energy in that pursuit, that the statesman attains his ends (*applause*); and it is by the possession of like qualities that success may be attained in any other of those undertakings to which men may devote themselves. (*Applause.*) But then, Colonel Chesney said—turning from the generals of whom he had been speaking, to that other branch of the army (namely, the officers and private soldiers) without whose skill, and endurance, and courage the greatest generals of the world could effect nothing (*hear, hear*)—Colonel Chesney said that the second great secret of military success is to be found in discipline as he has defined it; and it seems to me, speaking with all due diffidence in the presence of distinguished soldiers, that the definition which he has given of true and high

Lecture by Colonel Chesney.

discipline is a very sound and correct one. (*Applause.*) He says, what you want is, that you should have an army which is prepared, if need be, to cast aside its communications, to advance boldly to the attack of the enemy, without counting its own risks, and to be prepared to endure, not only the hazards of battle, but the trials of sickness and the weariness of the long march. (*Applause.*) Ladies and gentlemen, I accept that definition of true discipline, and I have only to go back some two years to find a brilliant example of it in the annals of the Indian army. (*Applause.*) Was there not a famous Division which, upon a great occasion, cast aside its communications to an extent which frightened not a few members of a distinguished assembly across the water (*aplause and laughter*), and which, setting out without any means of communicating with its rear, endured the trials of a long and weary march in the climate of Afghanistan—cut off from all communication with the outer world for some weeks, to come forth at last from all its dangers to a signal and glorious victory. (*Loud and continued applause.*) At least we may say that that column of European and native troops, prepared by the skill, and forethought, and the noble self-denial of my gallant friend the present Commander-in-Chief (*loud and continued applause*), and led forth with his accustomed energy, originality, and vigour, and his no less remarkable good fortune, by my distinguished friend Sir Frederick Roberts—not only re-established the fame of the army of India, but fulfilled all the requirements in regard to discipline of the gallant Lecturer himself. (*Applause.*) I ask you now to accord, as I know you will, your heartfelt thanks to Colonel Chesney for a lecture most interesting in itself, and possessing what I take to be one of the most distinguishing features of a really good lecture—that it was in the highest degree suggestive—that it brought forward points upon which the Lecturer touched only as he passed, but which, I venture to think, may produce much fruit in the minds of those who heard and will read it, if only they will reflect upon and develope the hints which Colonel Chesney gave. *(Applause.)*

THE JHANSI ENCUMBERED ESTATES BILL.

[IN the Legislative Council, on Thursday, the 18th May, the Hon. Mr. Crosthwaite presented the Final Report of the Select Committee on the Bill to provide for the relief of Encumbered Estates in the Jhansi division of the North-Western Provinces ; and applied to His Excellency the President to suspend the Rules for the Conduct of Business,—explaining the necessity for passing the Bill at once, and the reasons for the delay that had occurred in dealing with it. His Excellency made the following remarks :—]

I think that quite sufficient grounds have been advanced for suspending the Rules of Business in this case. There is an additional circumstance which has led to some delay in the matter, to which my honourable friend did not advert, namely, that it was necessary in the last stage of the Bill to refer it home for the sanction of the Secretary of State. We have now received that sanction by telegram ; and, as everything connected with the measure is completed, and all the persons interested appear to be agreed to it in its present form ; and as, moreover, it deals with circumstances so exceptional and so difficult, I think we are justified in passing the Bill without delay. I may explain that some of the defects of the Bill, as it was originally introduced, struck my honourable friend, now the Lieutenant-Governor of the Punjab, when he was a Member of Council ; and a note of his on the subject led me to look carefully into the matter, when I certainly agreed with the view of it which His Honour then took, namely, that the Bill, as introduced in the Council early in 1880, was not framed in a manner which was likely to secure its satisfactory working. My honourable friend Mr. Colvin also

The Jhansi Encumbered Estates Bill.

shared the same opinion. Under these circumstances the whole of the Bill was re-cast—an operation which took a considerable time, especially as it involved financial considerations of no small importance. I am very glad, however, that the matter has now been brought to a satisfactory conclusion, and I have therefore no hesitation in declaring that the Rules are suspended.

[Mr. Crosthwaite then moved that the Final Report be taken into consideration. He explained the main provisions of the Bill, and dwelt upon the necessity of altering the revenue system. Mr. Plowden, while supporting the Bill, regretted the delay which had occurred in placing it before the Council, and thought that the difficulties of the Jhansi landlords were the result of a defective revenue system which it was in the power of the Local Government to prevent. His Excellency the President said :—]

With respect to the delay that has taken place, I should like to make one or two further remarks. I, of course, have no personal experience of the delay which took place before the time when I came out here, two years ago. At that time the position of the matter was this : The Bill as originally brought in—which, as my honourable friend Mr. Crosthwaite has explained, was a very different Bill from the present one—was then before the Council. It was under reference to a Select Committee, who went into it very carefully, and, as I have already explained, towards the end of the time when we were at Simla in 1880, Sir Charles Aitchison spoke to me upon the subject, if I mistake not. At all events, he recorded a note in which he expressed doubts as to the propriety of adopting the Bill in the form in which it then stood. As soon as I was able to resume business at Calcutta, after my illness, I looked carefully into the matter. It seemed to me that the views put forward by Sir Charles Aitchison were very just, and I conferred with Mr. Bazett Colvin upon the subject at the commencement of last year. He then said that he should himself have preferred a Bill upon the lines of the present Bill, rather than upon those on which it was introduced

The Jhansi Encumbered Estates Bill.

under Lord Lytton's Government; and I then requested him to draw up the Bill in the form which he thought that it should assume. That Bill involved a very important principle,—that of advances upon the part of the Government— a principle which it is impossible to adopt all over the country, because of the enormous cost; and it therefore required to be considered with very great care, in order that we might see whether the circumstance of Jhansi would justify the adoption of such a measure, so clearly exceptional in its character. Well, Mr. Colvin prepared his draft, conferred with Sir George Couper on the subject, sent up the draft here, and it was then very carefully considered by the Financial Department. My honourable friend Major Baring very handsomely accepted the principle for this particular case, thinking that there were sufficiently exceptional grounds for doing so. The measure was therefore, in fact, in a condition in which it might have been passed last session at Calcutta, if it had not been necessary, under the orders of the Secretary of State, to refer it home to him before passing it. He lost no time in considering the matter, and in conveying his sanction to it by a telegram; and it is on that telegram that we are now acting. I mention these facts merely to show that the subject is one of a very difficult character, requiring to be treated with very great care; and that, although there has been more delay than would have been desirable, the matter has not been neglected, and that the delay has not been the result of any carelessness on the part of the Government in regard to it, but may truly be said to have arisen from the intrinsic difficulty of dealing with a question of this kind as we propose to deal with it in this Bill. I think the public should understand that that is the position of the case.

With regard to the question of the alteration of the revenue system, referred to by my honourable friends Mr. Crosthwaite and Mr. Plowden, that is a question which I

The Petroleum Bill.

will not attempt to discuss upon the present occasion. I can only say that it is a matter of great importance, and that it is receiving the careful consideration of the Government.

[The Motion was put and agreed to, and the Bill was passed into law.]

THE PETROLEUM BILL.

31st May 1882. [IN the Legislative Council, on the 31st of May, the Hon. Mr. Ilbert obtained leave to introduce, and introduced, a Bill to modify temporarily certain provisions of the Petroleum Act of 1881. He explained briefly the object of the Bill, stated that it was introduced at the special request of the Secretary of State, and that he did not now propose to ask for a suspension of the Rules of Business in order to carry the Bill at once through the Council. His Excellency the President said :—]

I think that the course which my honourable friend proposes to adopt is the correct one. Some representations in respect to this Bill have been made to the Government of India only quite recently—in the course of yesterday; and, although the Bill is introduced at the request of the Secretary of State, I think the circumstances are not such as to justify its being passed with the extreme rapidity which would result from the suspension of the Standing Orders of the Council. The introduction of the Bill will have brought it to such a stage as will admit of its passing, if necessary, at the next sitting of the Council. That, I think, will be sufficient to meet all the requirements of the case, and will give the public and the Government a somewhat longer time to consider the nature of the arrangements to be made under it.

THE PUNJAB UNIVERSITY BILL.

[THE Punjab University Bill was passed in the Legislative Council 5th October 1882. at Simla on the 5th October 1882. After Mr. Gibbs, Sir Charles Aitchison, and Mr. Ilbert had addressed the Council on the subject of the Bill, His Excellency the Viceroy spoke as follows:—]

After the very full exposition we have heard of the objects of the Bill in its present shape, and of the mode in which those objects will be attained under this measure when, as I trust, it becomes law, it would be quite unnecessary for me to enlarge upon the questions now before the Council; but I cannot let this Bill pass without expressing my great satisfaction that it should have fallen to my lot to occupy the position of Governor General and President of this Council at the time when this measure became law.

Somewhat less than two years ago, on the occasion of my first visit to Lahore, I received more than one address from bodies in that city upon the subject of the proposal to create a University in the Punjab. I then stated that I would give to the subject my careful consideration, and that I was very anxious to comply as far as possible with the strong wish evidently entertained by the leading men in the Punjab that an institution of this description should be established in their midst; and I have fulfilled that pledge. I did not then state—for I had not sufficient information to enable me to state—what would be the result of the consideration given to this subject by the Government of India; but I am exceedingly glad that that result has been one which will, I trust, be greatly to the advantage of the population of the Punjab and satisfactory to those who have, during the lengthened period to which my honourable friend the Lieutenant-Governor alluded, devoted themselves to further this great and important object.

I entirely agree with one remark among many which fell from my honourable friend Mr. Ilbert, when he said that it

The Punjab University Bill.

was not a disadvantage, but, on the contrary, was to be regarded with approval, that this University would differ in some respects from the other Universities in this country. I think that that variety in the character of the various educational institutions of the country is in itself a very great advantage, and, so far from considering it any drawback, I view it with great satisfaction.

I also desire to express my very deep sense of the obligation under which the Princes, the Chiefs, and the Native Gentry of the Punjab have laid the Government and the public by the manner in which they have come forward to support and endow this institution. The efforts which they have made are entirely in the direction in which, as it seems to me, it is most desirable that educational proceedings in this country should move; and I regard it as a most auspicious event that they should have come forward so liberally and based the foundation of this University, not upon Government contributions, nor even upon Government support, but upon the free and magnificent gifts of those who are the natural chiefs and leaders of the people of the Punjab.

I do not think I need now trouble the Council with any further observations. I hope ere long to have an opportunity of addressing the new University when it meets under the auspices of the law about to be passed. It only, therefore, remains for me to offer my hearty congratulations to the Lieutenant-Governor on the fortunate circumstance that it has been during the period of his administration—from which I anticipate so many benefits to the Punjab—that the coping-stone, as he has said, has been put upon an institution, in laying the foundation of which he himself so many years ago took a part.

OPENING THE NEW RIPON HOSPITAL AT SIMLA.

[On Friday afternoon, the 20th October, the Viceroy laid the foundation-stone of the new Ripon Hospital at Simla. Her Excellency Lady Ripon, Sir Donald and Lady Stewart, and a large number of people of all classes, European and Native, were present to witness the ceremony. Mr. A. O. Hume, the President of the Hospital Committee, opened the proceedings with an eloquent and amusing speech, after which His Excellency spoke as follows :—]

Mr. Hume, Ladies and Gentlemen,—I can assure you that it is a great satisfaction to me to have been able to accept the invitation which was given to me a short time ago, that I should lay the first stone of this new Hospital at Simla. I have taken, now for some time, a strong interest in the undertaking in which the Committee of this Hospital are now engaged; and, ladies and gentlemen, I must confess that the first source from which that interest was derived was that source from which, I venture to think, very many of the best inspirations of men have flowed: it was Lady Ripon and her interest in this work (*loud cheers*), which first drew my attention to the great want of hospital accommodation in Simla; and acting, as I always do, in obedience to my wife's commands (*cheers and laughter*),—which I am sure all the ladies present will think a very judicious course of proceeding (*laughter*),—I have done what little lay in my power to forward this enterprise. Ladies and gentlemen,—I am quite sure that any of you who may have visited the existing building which is called the Simla Hospital, and which ill deserves the name, will have been as strongly impressed as I have been with the necessity of erecting a more suitable dwelling for that institution. You cannot look at the rooms—wards I cannot call them—which are contained in that incommodious hospital, and not see, after all the efforts that have been made to improve them, how ill-suited they are for the purpose to which they are

Opening the new Ripon Hospital at Simla.

devoted—dark, imperfectly ventilated, grievously overcrowded, and possessing all the qualities which are least desirable in an hospital. (*Hear, hear.*) I am told that, properly speaking, making the due provision which ought to be made in a hospital for the accommodation of the patients, there is only room in the present building for, I think, eighteen beds; but that there are, even now, thirty patients in the hospital—that is to say, there are not far off, at the present moment, twice as many patients crowded into that building as those which can properly and suitably be accommodated; and I understand that there have been times when the number of patients to be received has so greatly exceeded the possibilities of accommodation in the rooms of the building, that they have overflowed, and that beds have been placed from time to time in the surrounding verandah. I need say no more, I think, to prove conclusively that the present building is utterly inadequate to provide for the requirements of this growing community; and, ladies and gentlemen, I believe that I am justified in saying that, in some respects, the efforts which have been made during the last year for the improvement of that hospital and its accommodation have really resulted in showing more conclusively how inadequate that accommodation is. I learn that the number of out-patients who were relieved last year, as compared with those who were relieved in the year 1880, was over 7,000, as against something over 5,000; and I understand that the number of in-patients last year was almost exactly double the number of in-patients received during the preceding twelve months. Therefore, the efforts which have been made to make the hospital better suited for its purpose—the labours which were commenced by Dr. Owen during the time that he was in charge of the hospital, and which have now devolved as a duty upon my friend Dr. Franklin—so able to discharge any duty of that description—those efforts, I say, have, in fact, resulted in producing a state of things in some respects almost more

Opening the new Ripon Hospital at Simla.

unsatisfactory and more imperfect than that which existed previously to the time at which greater attention was directed to this important object. Now, surely, ladies and gentlemen, that simple statement of facts—the truth of which you may ascertain for yourselves any day, if you choose to visit the present building—is in itself sufficient to show beyond dispute the necessity of the appeal which is now being made to you to assist in this great work of providing Simla with suitable hospital accommodation.

Ladies and Gentlemen,—We have heard from my friend Mr. Hume, in the course of his interesting address, mention of a very considerable sum of money which may be required before this work, in his opinion, can be completely and suitably finished. That whole amount will not at first be needed, and I think I may say that, whatever funds may be contributed for this purpose, will be spent upon really useful objects. I would earnestly recommend those who have the management of this undertaking not to strive to make their building ornamental outside, or ambitious in appearance; but to try to make it all that a hospital ought to be—a model hospital in its medical and sanitary arrangements. This brief statement of facts is, I think, all that need be brought before you now; because there can be no necessity in these days that any man should occupy the time of an assembly like this in producing arguments to prove that the creation of a public hospital is a great and noble work. (*Applause.*) We live in days, ladies and gentlemen, when science—and especially medical science—is making, daily, great and wonderful advances; we live in days in which the means of alleviating the physical sufferings of mankind are greater than they have ever been, and in which those means, through God's mercy, are increasing continually; but what is the use of the progress of science, of the advancement of medical skill, unless means are provided which will bring the poor and the suffering of every country within the reach of that science and within the touch

Opening the new Ripon Hospital at Simla.

of that skill? Surely we none of us, who look at the world around us, and who think at all of the deep suffering that exists close to us—though we may shrink from seeing it—can doubt that there is no more urgent, no more noble work, than to do what in us lies to bring close to the doors of those who suffer, those means of relief and of cure which science has provided for them. (*Applause.*) Can there be a stronger claim than that which our suffering fellow-creatures, of whatever race, are able to make upon us—upon us who have, in whatever degree, the means of affording relief to them out of the superfluities, be they great or be they little, which we ourselves possess? It is quite true, ladies and gentlemen, that there is something which is far more valuable than any pecuniary contribution for the relief of human suffering ; it is quite true that, where it can be given, personal service for the sick and the poor is of infinitely greater value than any pecuniary assistance, and that it brings alleviation and consolation to those who suffer, which money cannot bring. But it is not in the power of all to render that personal service to their suffering brethren ; and there are special difficulties in this country, and special reasons, which may make it less easy than it may be in other lands; but all of us who have the means, be those means great or be they little can, according to the measure of those means, give something for this object. I hope that the result of this day's meeting will be to show that there is here, in Simla and its neighbourhood, an earnest sense of what is due to those who suffer—an earnest sense of the vast claim which those who are huddled together in masses greater than perhaps we realise in the imperfect buildings around us, have upon us, who live in healthier buildings and enjoy larger incomes.

Ladies and Gentlemen,—There was one part of Mr. Hume's address to which I listened with very mixed feelings. I thought that my object, when I came here

Opening the new Ripon Hospital at Simla.

to-day—at least one of the purposes which I was expected to fulfil—was that I should make an appeal to the generosity of the Simla public to come forward with their contributions to this Simla hospital. But Mr. Hume shadowed forth, in powerful and eloquent language, another source from which funds might be derived; and he seemed to think that he would be able by his eloquence to touch even the stony heart of my honourable friend the Financial Member. (*Laughter and applause.*) Now, ladies and gentlemen, I have long entertained a very high opinion of the discretion of Major Baring. That opinion has been confirmed to-day; for I do not see him anywhere here (*laughter*); and I am told, on what I believe to be good authority, that, with that foresight for which he is remarkable, he went away into camp a few days ago (*laughter*); doubtless because he got wind of the appeal which my friend Mr. Hume intended to make to him. (*Continued laughter.*) Well, now, Mr. Hume remarked that he would entirely accept, and was quite certain that he would fully agree with all that I should say upon the subject of a contribution from the Government of India. Ladies and gentlemen,—I am an old trout *(laughter and cheers)*, and I am not going to take the fly which Mr. Hume has thrown over. (*Continued*) *laughter.*) The Government of India will do upon this as upon all subjects, that which is right *(hear, hear)*; my honourable friend Major Baring will act with a due regard to economy and with a proper attention to efficiency; and I have not the slightest doubt that when he reads Mr. Hume's speech, his heart will be touched, his feelings will be moved, and he will probably remain in camp till he has recovered from the attack. (*Cheers and laughter.*) Now, ladies and gentlemen, my advice is this,—upon every other question place implicit confidence in the Government of India; but not upon this (*laughter*); and I would say to you, fill up that paper, put down the largest

Opening the new Ripon Hospital at Simla.

possible sums you can—and the larger the sums you put down, the more likely it is that the Government of India will come forward and pay up the rest. (*Hear hear, and laughter.*) But, joking apart, I would venture to say that the first thing to be done is for the public to show a fair interest in this undertaking. It is a matter in which the public are interested; it is a great object of public utility; it is an undertaking in which it is an honour to any man to have a part; it is an undertaking which makes a clear and direct appeal to all who dwell in Simla and its neighbourhood;—nay, I will go further, for, looking to the fact that Simla is the residence of the Government of India for many months in the year, I will say that that appeal extends beyond the limits of Simla—beyond even the jurisdiction of my friend Mr. MacNabb, and goes far and wide throughout the land, to all who have any connection with the Supreme Government of this country. (*Cheers.*)

Ladies and Gentlemen,—I listened with great interest to the concluding portions of Mr. Hume's speech, in which he reminded us of the immense value which there is in any work which has a tendency to bring together men of all races and all classes in this country, in one common undertaking. Yes, ladies and gentlemen,—in this land, where there are so many differences of race, of creed, and of caste,—where there is so much which tends to keep men apart and to weaken and repress that sympathy which is the truest bond of civil society, it is a great recommendation in any undertaking, that it is one in which all men may unite, for which they may work together side by side, and may learn, through such co-operation, to cast away the animosities of the past, and to labour more and more with mutual respect and mutual forbearance, for the promotion of common objects of public and social importance (*applause*); and I rejoice to see here, to-day, ample evidence of such a union of classes and races and creeds—to

Opening the new Ripon Hospital at Simla.

see assembled around this stone, and gathered on this hillside, representatives of the Government of India; representatives, so fitting and so distinguished, of the Princes, Chiefs, and gentlemen of India; representatives of all classes and of all races: and I trust that we may find here, in this assemblage, a happy omen that this institution will not only tend to alleviate human suffering and diminish human misery, but also to bring together in the bonds of a closer union, the subjects of our gracious Queen-Empress in this Indian land. (*Applause.*)

Ladies and Gentlemen,—I have to make one personal apology to you this afternoon, because I believe that I am the cause of that which alone is wanting to this meeting—Sir Charles Aitchison is not here. You all know—you who know him—how deep is sure to be his sympathy with an object such as this; and I need not tell you that if it had been possible for him, he would have been present to-day. But when I was asked, not very long ago, to lay this foundataion stone, I named this day, I frankly confess, because it happened to suit best my own arrangements; and I forgot —though I was not ignorant of the fact, and remembered it after it was too late—to call to mind that Sir Charles Aitchison had made arrangements which he could not postpone, and which obliged him to leave Simla before this meeting took place; but I have his authority for stating that he feels the deepest interest in this undertaking, and it has his entire sympathy and approval. (*Cheers.*)

And now, ladies and gentlemen,—before I proceed to perform the special duty which falls to my lot, and to spoil as much as I can this beautiful trowel (for the gift of which I am very grateful to the Committee), it only remains for me, in conclusion, earnestly to invite your aid—to ask you, before you leave this place, to put your names down on that paper,—to use that ample supply of pens and ink to record the sums that you intend to give *(laughter)*; to remember that Major Baring is inexorable, that the Government of

Agricultural Loans Bill.

India is stingy, and that all that you have to look to is your own efforts (*continued laughter and applause*); that the great principle of the Government of India is self-help and local effort; that you must not trust to us, but to yourselves; and that the best thing you can do is at once to discharge your duty by recording your names in the manner I have suggested. (*Cheers.*) My earnest hope is that it may please God to bless these our efforts; that this building may grow up worthy of the place in which it is to be erected, and that it may prove, for many and many generations to come, a continual source of blessing to the inhabitants of Simla. (*Loud and continued applause.*)

[His Excellency then formally went through the ceremony of laying the stone, having previously placed, in a small cavity in the lower stone, a bottle containing a copy of the *Pioneer* of the 20th October. The trowel, which was a silver one, was handsomely chased and bore the following inscription:—

"With this trowel was laid the foundation-stone of the Ripon Hospital, by his Excellency the Marquis of Ripon, K.G., Viceroy of India, 20th October 1882.]

AGRICULTURAL LOANS BILL.

26th Oct. 1882. [IN the Legislative Council held on the 26th October, Mr. Crosthwaite obtained leave to introduce a Bill to consolidate and amend the Law relating to Loans of Money for Agricultural Improvements. His Excellency the Viceroy made the following remarks on the Bill:—]

I have only to say, in regard to this Bill, that it is not a very large measure. I believe, however, that it will remove many of the difficulties which now prevent the practical employment of the existing machinery for Governmen loans for agricultural improvements, and that, as far is it has that effect, it will, I cannot doubt, be beneficial to the agricultural community.

Central Provinces Local Self-Government Bill.

The difficulties found to exist in India in this matter are not confined to India alone. We find also at home that loans of this description are not taken advantage of to the extent to which one might naturally suppose they would be, for very much the same reasons as those which have deterred agriculturists from availing themselves of them in this country,—namely, the difficulties created by the very strict rules which have been laid down for the guidance of applicants for loans of this description. These rules have been found to be unpalatable to English landholders, and I am not by any means suprised to find that they have had the same effect in this country. The main object of this Bill is to simplify those rules to the greatest possible extent, to enable them to be applied to the different parts of the country as varying circumstances require; and it is my earnest hope that, although the measure is not one of a very extensive character, it will effect a small and useful reform in the present system of loans for agricultural improvements.

CENTRAL PROVINCES LOCAL SELF-GOVERNMENT BILL.

[On the 2nd November, the Hon. Mr. Crosthwaite laid before the Legislative Council the Report of the Select Committee on the Bill to make better provision for Local Self-government in the Central Provinces. He explained how the Bill originated, and described at some length the plan of it, and how it was proposed to work it. Mr. Plowden spoke strongly in support of the Bill and of the policy of local self-government which it embodied. His Excellency the Viceroy said:—]

2nd Nov. 1882.

I am very glad that my honourable friend [1] who has just spoken has addressed this Council on this occasion, because he has given the weight of his authority in favour of the policy of the Government of India in regard to

---
[1] Mr. Plowden.

Central Provinces Local Self-Government Bill.

local self-government. He has most rightly described his long and varied experience in matters of administration, and I am quite confident that the public will receive the testimony which he has given in support of the principles upon which the Resolution of the 18th of May was founded with the utmost satisfaction, and that it will go far to dispel any lingering doubts or suspicions which may be entertained as to the objects of that Resolution. There is really very little left for me to say, after the discussion that has taken place in regard to this Bill; but there are one or two points on which I should like to make a few observations.

My honourable friend Mr. Crosthwaite has pointed out that it is really due to an accident that this Bill is the first legislative measure brought forward in connection with that extention of local self-government which the Government of India are endeavouring to bring about; and must also be borne in mind that this Bill is not to be taken as a model on which all further Bills will be framed for other parts of the country. It is a Bill for the Central Provinces only; it has been drawn up in accordance with what the Select Committee believe to be the special requirements of that part of India, and it does not at all follow that, either in the particular organization which it is proposed to establish in the Central Provinces under this Bill, or in regard to the powers of control to be exercised over the local bodies in the Central Provinces, or in regard to the extent of the powers to be entrusted to those bodies themselves, that the provisions of this Bill, and the system on which it is founded, would be the best which could be adopted for other parts of the country. In drawing up the Resolution of the 18th of May last, the Government of India very particularly pointed out that they had not the slightest intention of laying down hard-and-fast rules of a uniform character for the extension of local self-government throughout the whole of this vast Peninsula. It would have

Central Provinces Local Self-Government Bill.

been an exceedingly absurd idea if it had ever entered into the heads of the Government to do anything of the kind. The circumstances of different parts of India are most various. We have in this country, races almost on the verge of the savage state; and we have, on the other hand, large populations marked by a very considerable advance, political and social, and counting among them men of very subtle and developed intellects. It is, of course, obviously impossible to deal with a country in that condition upon any uniform plan in regard to a system of local self-government.

Therefore, what we proposed was that laying down a few broad and general principles, those principles should be applied according to the peculiarities and requirements of the different parts of the country in different ways, so as to meet those requirements and to suit those peculiarities; and we especially and clearly pointed out that we thought it was very desirable that the mode in which the principles of that Resolution were to be carried out should be varied, not only from province to province, but in the different parts of each province itself; because we wanted to make trial of various methods of procedure, various modes of composing the local boards, and electing and controlling them, in order that, after experience, we might learn in the course of time what were the best methods of dealing with these matters, and what might be the system generally applicable, at all events to the great divisions of the country. Now, with regard to the Central Provinces, as my honourable friend Mr. Crosthwaite has said, we deal with a part of the country to a certain extent backward; speaking broadly, as compared with other parts of India—such as Bengal, Bombay, and elsewhere—it may be said to be a somewhat backward district. Consequently, you must so frame your measure as to suit the condition of such a district, and to meet the wants and circumstances of a population by no means far advanced in the social scale.

Central Provinces Local Self-Government Bill.

And, besides that, there are in the Central Provinces certain districts—in point of area, I believe there are very considerable districts—inhabited by a population which may be almost described to be in the savage state. Of course, in districts of that description no system of local self-government can be introduced; nobody ever thought of introducing it; it would be a very long time indeed before any measure of the kind could be introduced in parts of the country like that; and, therefore, the principle on which the Bill has gone is to leave to the Chief Commissioner the power of applying this Bill to such portions of the country as he thinks fit to receive it. Those portions of the country inhabited by specially backward populations will, of course, be omitted from the operation of the Bill; and, as my honourable friend Mr. Crosthwaite has pointed out, we have in Mr. Morris a gentleman so thoroughly acquainted with all the circumstances of the province which he has ruled for a long period with so much advantage to the public service, that we can fully trust him to apply this Bill in a cautious, wise, and discreet spirit.

There is one feature of this Bill to which I attach considerable importance; and it is that an effort is to be made to found the new local institutions which will spring up under it as much as possible upon the indigenous Native institutions of the country. The mukaddams or head-men of the villages are to form the basis of the local boards and councils, and I think it very desirable that here, as elsewhere, where there still may remain indigenous institutions of local self-government, that they should be made use of to the utmost possible extent; because what we want to establish is, not a system founded on English ideas or English ways, but a system consonant with the wants, habits, and even the prejudices, of the Native population.

Now, allusion has been made by my honourable friend Mr. Crosthwaite to the remarks made upon this Bill by those who have seen it in the stage in which it now is. Those

Central Provinces Local Self-Government Bill.

remarks contain only the criticisms of officials; but the Bill will now be published, and we shall have the advantage, before it becomes law, of receiving such observations upon it as the public of the Central Provinces may favour us with. I am happy to say that the Bill as now drawn has received the cordial support of Mr. Morris, the Chief Commissioner. Mr. Morris' Secretary, in writing to the Government of India in respect to this measure, stated :—

"In the first place, then, I am to say that the Chief Commissioner cordially accepts the principles on which this Bill is based, and heartily concurs in the desire of the Government of India to do all that can be done to extend self-government 'as an instrument of political and popular education.' This is a subject in which he has taken considerable interest in the past, although the sphere of operation has been very limited."

And then the letter concludes with these words :—

"The Government of India may rest assured that, should such a measure as this Bill become law, it will be patiently and carefully, but also boldly and loyally, applied; and the Chief Commissioner is persuaded that he will have the cordial co-operation of all local officers in carrying out the aims of Government."

You could not have stronger expressions of approval on the part of an officer than those contained in that letter from Mr. Morris; and I myself am—and I am sure my honourable colleagues also are—very much gratified to find that our proposals do receive the cordial approval of a man of such long experience, and so well known as an able administrator, as Mr. Morris; for what he approves of is not likely to be fraught with those dangers which, as my honourable friend Mr. Crosthwaite says, some people are of opinion that the policy of Government in this respect is likely to produce. It must also be borne in mind that Mr. Morris is especially qualified to speak on this subject, because he has done more, perhaps, than any other head of a Local Government in India to introduce into his province some portions of a general scheme of local self-government long before this question was taken up by the Government

Central Provinces Local Self-Government Bill.

of India. We have heard a great deal to-day about the backward condition of the Central Provinces. Well, my honourable and gallant friend near me (Sir Donald Stewart) remarked, when that expression was used,—" but I have understood that in the matter of primary education the Central Provinces stand almost at the head of the provinces of India." There is a great deal of truth in that remark ; and so it has been in the matter of local self-government, so far as the principle of election is concerned ; and therefore Mr. Morris knows very well from experience what he is talking about when he gives his sanction to the policy of the Government of India in this respect ; and I think we may rely upon it with the most perfect satisfaction that the Bill when it becomes law will be applied by Mr. Morris in the spirit in which he says he will apply it, and which is precisely the spirit in which the Government of India wishes this measure of local self-government to be applied, not only in the Central Provinces, but throughout the country generally—that is, patiently and carefully, but also boldly and loyally.

I do not think I need add anything more to what I have said about this measure ; but I am very anxious to make it clear that the fact that it is the first Bill of this kind which has been brought before this Council is due to exceptional circumstances ; that it is a Bill intended for the Central Provinces, and for the Central Provinces only ; and that, while it fully embodies the principles of the Resolution of the 18th of May, we do not in any way require other Local Governments to adopt its special provisions for themselves.

DISTRIBUTION OF PRIZES TO THE SIMLA VOLUNTEERS.

[ON Saturday afternoon, the 4th November, the Viceroy presided 4th Nov. 1882. at the distribution of Prizes to the Simla Volunteers. The proceedings took place on the Ridge near the Church, a large *shamiana* being pitched for the accommodation of spectators. His Excellency, accompanied by Mr. H. W. Primrose, Lord William Beresford, and other members of his Staff, arrived at 4-30, and, in addressing the Volunteers, spoke as follows :—]

Colonel Peterson, Officers, Non-commissioned Officers, and Members of the Simla Volunteer Corps,—Although I have risen to say a few words to you before the commencement of the prize distribution, it is not my intention to make anything in the nature of a speech this afternoon, because it does not seem to me that the occasion is one which calls for anything of that sort. But I am anxious, in the first place, to express to you, Colonel Peterson, and to your officers and men, Lady Ripon's great regret that she has been unable to fulfil her intention of being present upon this occasion to give away some of these prizes. Unfortunately, she has been suffering for some ten days or a fortnight from an attack very much in the nature of bronchitis, which, as you know well, is not a thing to be trifled with. She has been taking every possible care of herself, in the hope that she might have been able to come here to-day ; but her stern and inexorable medical adviser told her this morning that she must not on any account think of coming out in her present condition : and I am bound to say that I think his advice was very sound. She has not been out at all since the attack first came on ; and I believe it would have been very unwise if she had attempted to fulfil her earnest desire to come here to-day. I am quite sure, therefore, that you will all of you excuse her and that you will thoroughly believe that if it had been possible for her to be here she would have come, and thus testified to the deep interest she feels in the prosperity of the Simla

Distribution of Prizes to the Simla Volunteers.

Volunteer Crops. (*Hear, hear.*) And now, as I am speaking, I cannot help offering a few words of congratulation to Colonel Peterson on the present condition of this corps. From the reports which I have received, I am happy to believe that it is advancing steadily in the course of progress, and the Government of India have recently recognised, in the best way that they could, their sense of the progress thus made, in having consented to an increase in the number of drill-instructors attached to this corps, and in having agreed to allow the corps an Adjutant of its own. Those measures are, I am happy to think, fully justified by the condition and efficiency of this Volunteer Corps; and I hope that you will all see in that a proof of the interest which the Government of India feels in your prosperity and efficiency, and of their readiness to recognise the degree of progress which you have recently made. But I hope, also, that the Government of India having, in this respect done its duty towards you, you will see that, now that you are supplied with competent drill-instructors and with an able Adjutant all to yourselves, it is your duty to make the utmost use of those advantages, and not to stand still—not to rest contented with what you have, up to the present time, accomplished; but to go on step by step advancing in efficiency, from year to year. I believe, Colonel Peterson, that the true motto for every Volunteer Corps is "*Nil actum reputans, si quid superesset agendum*"—that is think nothing done if aught remains to do,—never stand still in the path of progress,—never rest upon the efficiency to which you have attained; but strive always to go forward and to reach a yet higher standard. And I hope that, as years go on, the numbers of this Corps will continue to increase. I rejoice to see you here to-day assembled in numbers so considerable; but I must say that when I look at the many active and stalwart young men whom I see in my walks about Simla, and compare them with the numbers in the Volunteer Corps, my expectations are not altogether

Distribution of Prizes to the Simla Volunteers.

satisfied. I think there are many young men here in Simla who ought to be in this Corps, and who would do themselves credit and derive great advantages from joining your ranks: and I earnestly trust that all those in high and important positions, who may be unable themselves to enter the ranks of this Corps, will use, so far as they legitimately may, that influence which they possess with others younger and more active than themselves, to induce them to show their interest in an institution which I am firmly convinced, if it is solidly established and widely extended, is calculated to confer great benefits upon the inhabitants of this district.

Colonel Peterson,—I do not know that I need detain you longer, except to express once more my most hearty desire for the progress and prosperity of the Simla Volunteers. (*Cheers.*) I am very well aware how very inadequate I am to represent the lady who was to have given the first of the prizes to those who have won them. I know how much their value will be diminished by being received from the hands so much less fair than hers, of which I am unhappily possessed. (*Laughter.*) But I stand here as her representative, and it is by her orders and on her behalf that I now present to you those prizes which she would have been so happy to have delivered to you herself. (*Cheers.*)

[The prizes were then distributed by His Excellency, Mrs. Baring, Mrs. Wilson, General Trevor, and others.]

ADDRESS FROM THE MUNICIPALITY OF LAHORE:

LOCAL SELF-GOVERNMENT.

h Nov. 1882. [THE Viceroy, accompanied by his Staff, left Simla on his autumn tour, on Monday, the 6th November. His Excellency arrived at Lahore on the morning of the 8th, and in the evening, after dinner, received a Deputation from the Municipality, who presented him with an address. The address, after welcoming His Excellency on the occasion of his second visit to Lahore, proceeded as follows :—

"When your Excellency first came amongst us, the country was still new to its Ruler, but the people had already learned to look upon him with strong regard and affection, from the sympathy displayed towards them, and from the promise held out of a policy, even then inaugurated, which tended to the improvement of their social, intellectual, and political condition. During the last two years, your Excellency has been unremitting in endeavours to fulfil that promise and to develope that policy. It would be impossible, within the compass of a brief address of welcome, to enumerate the benefits which have already resulted. The people of India have begun to feel how unselfish the aim of British rule may be when administered on the principles by which your Excellency is guided ; and they are becoming more loyal and devoted subjects of Her Most Gracious Majesty the Empress of India, because they feel not only that the Government is just, but that it desires to sympathise with them more fully ; to be their friend as well as their ruler ; and thus to raise them to a higher position than they have yet reached among civilised nations. In granting the boon of local self-government, we humbly trust and believe that your Excellency will not be disappointed in the result, and that the people of this province will display those qualities of energy, public spirit, civic virtue and self-help, which alone can enable them to reap the full benefit of the liberal measures of Government. It is gratifying to us to feel assured that His Honor the Lieutenant-Governor of the Punjab and the Members of His Government will spare no effort to carry out in its integrity the scheme proposed by the Supreme Government."

The Viceroy replied as follows:—]

Gentlemen of the Municipality of Lahore,—I am grateful to you for the address which you have just delivered to me. I am much gratified—nay, I may truly say, I am much touched—by the tone of that address, and by the proof

Local Self-Government.

which it affords of the manner in which you appreciate the spirit by which I have been guided in my administration of India. Gentlemen, you are quite right when you say that I feel a warm and heartfelt sympathy for the people of this country; and you are right also when you state in your address that it is my desire to act in the great office which I now fill, not merely as the ruler, but more as the friend of the people of India; and I can truly say that if I find, when my term of office draws to a close, that the sentiments expressed in your address are still those entertained by the public of this country, I shall feel that I am amply rewarded for any labours which may have fallen to my share, because I shall have done something to attain one of the great ends which I set before me when I came out here, namely, to do what in me lay to bind together, in closer union than heretofore, the British Government and the Indian people. (*Cheers.*)

Gentlemen,—You have touched in your address upon a question which is exciting much attention in this country at the present time, and in which, as you know, I myself feel a warm interest—I mean the subject of local self-government; and I will, therefore, for a short time address to you some observations in connection with that important question. I believe that you are aware that the main and primary object of the Government of India in the steps which it is taking at the present time for the development and extension of self-government in this country, is to advance and promote the political and popular education of the people, and to do what may be done, under the circumstances of these times, to induce the best and most intelligent men of the community to come forward and take a share in the management of their own local affairs, and to guide and aid and train them in the attainment of that important object. Gentlemen, we have not been led to adopt this policy at this time in consequence of any mere inclinations of our own, but I may truly say that we

Address from the Lahore Municipality:

have been almost forced to adopt it by the circumstances of the times with which we have had to deal. We had last year, as you are aware, to make arrangements for the renewal of those quinquennial provincial contracts which were originally introduced in the time of Lord Mayo, and which formed one of the distinguishing features of that great policy of decentralization which will always constitute one of the greatest claims of that distinguished statesman upon the gratitude of India. Those five years' contracts were running out, and we had to consider upon what terms they should be renewed; and when we came to turn our attention to that question, we thought it our duty to see whether the time had not come to apply yet more fully, and to carry out yet further, the policy which Lord Mayo had inaugurated; for it must ever be borne in mind that that policy, in its full intention, was not one only of provincial decentralization, but that Lord Mayo looked with the eye of a statesman to promote also the great object of self-government; and it seemed to us that we could not better apply the principles which he laid down than by carrying decentralization beyond the stage at which—not I believe, in accordance with his desire, but owing to circumstances which followed his unhappy decease—it had been arrested, and to advance it from decentralization as between the Government of India and the Provincial Governments, to decentralization as between those Provincial Governments and the local bodies within their jurisdiction. But when we came to look at this problem and to seek for a solution of it, we found that it would be essential to infuse new life and fresh vigour into those local bodies on which we desired to confer fuller and more extended powers.

These, then, gentlemen, were the principles which we have acted on; but I think that I may perhaps make more clear the views of the Government of India and remove some misconceptions which appear to exist in the minds of

Local Self-Government.

some persons if, having told you what was our object and our purpose, I tell you what we did not desire to do.

We did not desire, gentlemen, to introduce into India any cut-and-dried system framed upon an English model, or based upon specially English political theories. We did not desire to lay down any uniform system, to be adopted under all circumstances throughout the length and breadth of this great land, whether in regard to the composition of local bodies, to the extension of the franchise, or to the system of control. On the contrary, no one who reads the Resolution of the Government of India of last May can fail to perceive that what we wished was to see a variety of systems tried in different parts of the country, in order that we might find out by actual experience what was the system, or what were the systems, best suited to each province and to each portion of this great peninsula. (*Hear, hear.*) And we desired also, above all things, that the new arrangements of self-government should as far as possible be those which were most consistent with the habits and the customs of the people in the different parts of India; that they should be drawn up in close consultation with representative men of different classes and districts; that they should be based so far as may be upon the indigenous native institutions which still exist; and that we should avail ourselves to the utmost of those "organic groups"—to use the felicitous expression of my honourable friend the Lieutenant-Governor—which are still to be found amongst us, so that the system to be founded might be one consonant with the traditions of the country and the feelings and requirements of the people.

Then again, gentlemen, we did not require that the system which we proposed to inaugurate should be applied by the various local Governments to every portion of the territory under their respective control. We were not so foolish as to believe that all parts of India were fitted for a system of this description; we know very well that in

Address from the Lahore Municipality:

this great land there are men of many races and in many stages of civilization, and that while you may find, in the most advanced parts of India, men of developed intellects and great intelligence, skilled in the management of their own private affairs, and well capable of managing the public affairs of their own localities, there are also parts of the country which are inhabited by races still scarcely removed from the savage state ; and that it would be utterly absurd to introduce any system of self-government among Sonthals, or Bhils, or Khoonds. Again, gentlemen, we did not expect that the policy which we were adopting would have, as its immediate result, better practical administration. I will be very frank upon this subject, for, as we have stated plainly in our Resolution of last May, we are quite aware that it was very possible that, in many instances, better practical administration may not, at first at all events, result. We have another object in view—the education and the training of the people ; and we shall be content to put up, under due restrictions and for a limited time, with many failures in practical administration. (*Cheers.*)

Gentlemen,—It is a great pleasure to me to speak on the subject of local self-government here in the Punjab, because the Government of India has found in my friend Sir Charles Aitchison an able, an earnest, and an honest supporter of their policy in this respect. (*Cheers.*) And it is to me indeed a source of the highest gratification that a man of his experience and his talents should give the weight of his great authority to a measure with which I am so intimately connected. Sir Charles Aitchison at once apprehended to its full extent, and in its true meaning, the policy of the Government in this matter ; and if I were to seek for the best commentary and the best development of the Resolution of the 18th of May last, and for the best practical application and exposition of the principles upon which that Resolution is founded, I should

Local Self-Government.

need no other document than the Punjab Resolution of my honourable friend. (*Cheers.*)

Gentlemen,—I cannot doubt that this policy, laid down by the Supreme Government and endorsed to the full by the Lieutenant-Governor of the Punjab, will receive from all the officers who serve in this great province a cordial and loyal support. I see it sometimes intimated that there is something in this policy which might be taken to imply some want of confidence on the part of the Government in the administration of our District Officers. Now, there cannot be a grosser misrepresentation of the objects which we have in view. (*Hear, hear.*) No man can have a higher respect than I have—a respect which I inherited from my father—for the ability, for the zeal, and for the public spirit of the Civil Servants of India. No, gentlemen, it is not because we have found a great and glaring want of administrative ability on the part of those who have had the management of the existing system, that we propose this change. It is because we have another—a further, and in some respects a higher—object in view than the simple promotion of good administration; it is because we desire, as a great political object, to avail ourselves of the free and the ready assistance of those native gentlemen of influence and intelligence who are, as we believe, capable of taking, with great advantage, a large part in the management of their local affairs. (*Cheers.*) And, gentlemen, I believe that there cannot be a greater error than that of those who suppose that, by this system, the just and legitimate influence of District Officers will be diminished. I hold, on the contrary, it will be found that that influence will be increased. No doubt such a system as this will make a call upon somewhat different qualities from those which have been brought forward under the present system of more direct administration. I should say that, for the future, we shall require rather the qualities of the statesman than the qualities of the

Address from the Lahore Municipality :

administrator ; and, for my own part, I think that the qualities of the statesman are the higher qualities of the two ; and I cannot doubt that, when we make a demand for such qualities upon the members of the Punjab Commission, that demand will be fully answered. The Punjab Commission has been famous for many a long year for the ability of its administrators ; but, gentlemen, there are upon the proud list of that Commission many names, from those of Henry and John Lawrence, down to that of Sir Charles Aitchison, which may justly claim to take their place on the roll of English statesmen (*cheers*) ; and though it may be true that the qualities of statesmanship called forth by a policy of this description differ somewhat from those which have been exhibited in the past, yet I for one cannot admit that, in the guidance, the training, and the leading of a great and intelligent population in times of peace, there are not just as high qualities required as those which are brought to light in days of war and of diplomacy.

Gentlemen,—It seems to me, then, that in this matter the Government have done their part. We have laid down our policy ; your Lieutenant-Governor has heartily accepted it, and I am sure that he will be supported by those who are subordinate to him in this province. It remains, therefore, in the Punjab as in the rest of India, for the people to do their part; it remains for you, gentlemen, men of influence and education, to come forward in answer to the call of the Government, and to take your proper place in the administration of the country (*cheers*) ; it remains for you to say whether this policy is to be attended with success or failure. I do not doubt that the appeal thus made to you will be adequately answered on your part. (*Cheers.*) I feel no doubt that the promise held out in your address will be fulfilled, because I see, from the words that you have employed, that you justly appreciate the qualities on which we are about to make a demand, and

Local Self-Government.

that you are prepared to make that sacrifice of your time and of your convenience which you are required now to make in the interests of your neighbours and of the country at large. But, gentlemen, nevertheless, I do not doubt—as I have said already—that we shall have to encounter and have to lament not a few instances of failure. There will be much, I dare say, in many places, to try the patience of local officers and to disappoint the hopes of Government; but this is a matter in which, before all things, patience and gentle handling are required. If, having planted this small tree of self-government, we are always pulling it up to look at its roots in order to see how far they have got down into the ground, I venture to say that this experiment will be no more successful than those which have preceded it. (*Cheers.*) Twenty years ago, an eminent man—one of your Lieutenant-Governors, loved, I believe, alike by European and Native—I mean Sir Donald Macleod (*cheers*)—sketched out the whole of the policy which the Government of India have now adopted; and if, twenty years ago, his proposals had been accepted and carried out in the spirit in which they were made, the Punjab would now have been at the head of India in this respect. (*Cheers.*)

I say, therefore, gentlemen, that I have little doubt that, unless we are patient, we shall fail; that if we try to drive those who are to manage those local institutions too hard, and if we expect too much from them at first, we shall only make an ignominious fiasco. I therefore trust that ample time will be given to work out this policy to its true end, and we shall be prepared to accept many shortcomings, in the hope that they will teach, by the best of all instructors—experience—those who are entrusted with the administration, how to walk successfully in the path upon which they are about to enter. But at the same time, gentlemen, this also I must say,—that though I desire to see great patience exercised, and though I deprecate haste, or

Address from the Lahore Municipality:

undue and over-eager expectations of immediate results, I, on the other hand, am firmly determined that this experiment shall not fail through the pertinacious neglect, through the sloth, or through the continued incompetence of the local bodies that are about to spring up. (*Cheers.*) Not to do so would be to betray the policy which we are advocating, and to abandon those interests that we have most nearly at heart. We must therefore retain sufficient control over these local bodies—a control varying in different parts of the country, according to the advancement of the people and the circumstances of each district. We must maintain, I say, sufficient control over these local bodies to see that they do not permanently, obstinately, or slothfully neglect their duty towards their fellow-citizens: and that control, gentlemen, I, for my part, am determined to maintain; and I trust that it will be applied patiently, but still firmly, by local Governments. I believe it to be unnecessary to ask any greater powers of control than those for which ample precedents are to be found in the laws of England. You know that there is no country in which local self-government has taken firmer root, and has made a greater advance, than in England; and you may perhaps be aware that there is scarcely any country in the world in which men are more jealous of the interference of Government. When, therefore, I say that all the control we want is that which the English Parliament has given to the English Government over English Municipal bodies, I am confident that that is an amount of control of which no man can reasonably complain.

Gentlemen,—I need not detain you longer. You have touched in your address upon other subjects of interest; you have spoken of the new Punjab University, and of the extension of Primary Education; but I need not offer to you any observations on these topics now, because, in the course of next week, I shall be called upon to preside at the inaugural meeting of the University, and that will be the

Local Self-Government.

fitting occasion upon which to make any remarks which may suggest themselves to me upon that or kindred matters.

You have also told me of the successful result of your local efforts in regard to the water-supply and sanitation of this city. I have heard of that success with great satisfaction; because I attach very high importance indeed to all questions connected with sanitation. I do not think that the public is at all aware of the extent to which disease is preventible, and to which human misery may be alleviated, by adequate sanitary arrangements. (*Cheers.*) I am therefore very glad to find, from the language which you have addressed to me, that you are yourselves awake to the importance of this matter, and that you are likely to set a good example to the rest of the province in regard to it.

Gentlemen,—Once more I thank you for your friendly words. I see, with the greatest pleasure, that you understand the spirit in which I desire to work, and your address, delivered to me to-night, will do much to encourage me to continue to labour in order to promote, to the utmost of my power, the advancement, the well-being, and the happiness of the people entrusted to my care. (*Cheers.*)

ADDRESS FROM THE MUNICIPALITY OF PESHAWUR.

17th Nov. 1882. [THE Viceroy arrived at Peshawur on the morning of the 17th November, having left Lahore on the 9th and spent the interval in visiting the Salt-mines at Meanee, and shooting and fishing at Jelalpur and Tangrote. His Excellency was received at Khairabad, on the right bank of the Indus, by Mr. Cordery, Commissioner of Peshawur, and other officials, and proceeded by special train to Peshawur, arriving there at 10 A.M. At noon, Lord Ripon, accompanied by the Commissioner and His Excellency's Staff, drove in procession to the city, with an escort of the 9th Cavalry. At the Edwardes memorial gateway (recently erected by public subscription to the memory of the late Sir Herbert Edwardes) His Excellency was met by the Deputy Commissioner, who presented him with the key of the gate. After inspecting the gateway and having presented to him a number of Sirdars of the district, His Excellency drove to the new Egerton Hospital. Here, after inspecting the building, he received an address (written in high Persian) from the Peshawur Municipality, in which, after compliments, the Committee went on to say that although they resided in a frontier district, and far from the seat of Government, still, just as the different members of the body owe allegiance to the heart and obey its directions, whether they be near or distant, so they, the native residents of Peshawur, although they were at the remotest extremity of the Empire, were equal in loyalty to those who dwell under the shadow of the throne itself. They regretted the shortness of His Excellency's visit to Peshawur, but were grateful for his having consented to open the Egerton Hospital, an institution the benefits of which they hoped would be extended not only to the people of Peshawur, but to those of the countries lying beyond the frontier. His Excellency, in replying, spoke as follows :—]

Gentlemen of the Municipality of Peshawur,—I thank you for your address. It affords me much pleasure to have had this opportunity of visiting this interesting city. As you remark in your address, of which I have been provided with a translation, Peshawur is situated upon the extreme frontier of the British Empire in India, but nevertheless it is a place connected with many important memories, and it lies upon a route of commerce which I trust may, as time goes on, be more and more developed. I have been much interested to-day in having passed through the new gate of

Address from the Municipality of Peshawur.

your city, which has been erected to the memory of a distinguished man whom I greatly honoured—the late Sir Herbert Edwardes;—and who well deserves that his memory should be imperishably recorded in this district, which he administered so long, with such great advantage to the British Government and to those who were brought under his rule. I thank you, gentlemen, for the loyal expressions which are contained in your address, and for the attachment which you express to our gracious Sovereign, the Queen-Empress; and which I earnestly trust, and which I believe, represent the feelings by which you are truly animated. I regret that my stay in Peshawur should be so short; but, as you can readily believe, it is not easy for one in my position to find time to discharge all the duties which fall to his lot—certainly not to find time to visit all the remarkable and interesting places in India which he would desire to see; but I could not, as I was approaching the Northern frontier of Hindustan, omit to visit Peshawur, of which during my whole life I have heard so much. And especially was I tempted to come here when I learnt that one of the duties I should be asked to undertake was to declare this new Egerton Hospital to be open for the natives of this district. It is a great pleasure to me to take part in opening this Hospital, first, because it bears the name of one who has done such good service for the Punjab and for India,—my friend, your late Lieutenant-Governor, Sir Robert Egerton, —and who has carried away with him, I am confident, from every part of this great province, the affectionate regard of those whom he governed and with whom he has been associated. It is also a great pleasure to me to have taken part in handing over to this city a building from which I have every reason to hope that the people of Peshawur, for many generations, will derive very great benefit. I am very glad to observe from your address how thoroughly you appreciate the value of a good hospital, and how well you understand the advantages which an institution of that

Address from the Municipality of Peshawur.

description is calculated to confer on a district in the midst of which it is placed. I am glad to see that this building is admirably suited for the purpose for which it is intended; it seems to me to be laid out with great care and skill; the wards are commodious and well-ventilated; and I have no doubt that you will derive from the erection of this building in your midst, all the good which you anticipate. Gentlemen, I cordially share the sentiments which you express in your address when you say: " Not only do we hope that the people of Peshawur will derive great benefits from this Hospital, but we trust that these benefits will be received by those people who live in the more distant regions of Central Asia." It will be a great satisfaction to me if this Hospital is found to be of use not only to the subjects of the Queen-Empress, but to those travellers who may visit this country from distant portions of Central Asia, and from the districts immediately bordering upon the frontiers of India, whether they come here as traders for commercial purposes, or whether, as so many of them do, they pass through India in the character of pilgrims. It is my desire to live upon the best and most friendly terms with the various nations and tribes which surround the frontiers of Hindustan. The Government of India has not the slightest desire to interfere in any manner with the independence and the just rights of those neighbouring tribes, whether they be small and wild collections of people dwelling in narrow valleys on our borders, or whether they be the subjects of the greater kingdom of our ally, the Amir of Afghanistan. It is my earnest desire, so long as I fill the the office I now hold, to use my best efforts to promote the most friendly relations with those who dwell upon the confines of the dominions of the Queen-Empress; and it is my firm intention to respect their rights and to regard their just claims to independence, at the same time that I am determined with equal firmness to protect the rights of Her Majesty's subjects in India, and not to permit them to suffer in life, in

Address from the Municipality of Peshawur.

limb, or in property, from the inroads of those who ought to live in friendship with us, and with whom I, for my own part, desire to be on the most friendly terms. I trust, gentlemen, that, as you say in your address, those who come from other countries—whether Afghans or the inhabitants of Central Asia, or from whatever part of the Asiatic Continent they may come—to visit this city of Peshawur, and who, if they should be struck down with sickness, are comforted and cured and provided for, in this Hospital—I trust that, when they return to their native lands, they will go forth from India as messengers of peace and friendship, and that they will report to those among whom they reside, the manner in which they were treated and the good reception that they received at the hands of the inhabitants of Peshawur. Gentlemen, I can assure you that our gracious Sovereign the Queen-Empress feels the deepest interest in all her Indian subjects, of every race and class and creed, and it will be my pleasing duty—a duty which I shall perform by the next mail—to inform Her Majesty of the loyal sentiments which are embodied in this address, and to assure her that the inhabitants in the city of Peshawur may be numbered among her faithful subjects. For myself, gentlemen, once more I tender to you my hearty thanks for your friendly reception.

INAUGURAL CONVOCATION OF THE PUNJAB UNIVERSITY.

18th Nov. 1882. [THE Viceroy returned to Lahore on the morning of the 18th November, and at noon on the same day presided at the inaugural Convocation of the Punjab University, of which His Excellency is Patron. The University hall was filled with students and spectators of all classes, the seats to the right of Lord Ripon being occupied by the Nawab of Bhawalpore, the Raja of Kapurthala, and the Raja of Faridkote. In formally reporting to the Viceroy, the business to be transacted, Sir Charles Aitchison said—

"In reporting to Your Excellency the business before this, the inaugural Convocation of the Punjab University, I deem it a happy and auspicious circumstance that the Convocation should be presided over by Your Lordship. I deem it so not merely because the Punjab University Act has become law during Your Excellency's Viceroyalty, but much more because I know that the popular movement which culminated in the Act passed six years ago, has met with your cordial sympathy and support ; and because I also know that the principles upon which the University has been founded are in complete harmony with the enlightened policy of self-help and self-government which Your Excellency has recently so clearly and forcibly expounded. In a paper dated so far back as August 1865, the proposed University is described as 'the people's own department of public instruction.' The popular element has been a distinguished feature of the project from the very beginning, and explains to a great extent the prominence given to Oriental studies in the constitution of the University. One of the special objects of the University, as set forth in the Statutes, is 'to associate the learned and influential classes in the province with the officers of Government in the promotion and supervision of popular education.' The other special objects, as Your Excellency is aware, besides making provision for the highest study of English, are two,—'1 : To promote the diffusion of European science as far as possible through the medium of the vernacular languages of the Punjab, and the improvement and extension of vernacular literature generally. 2 : To afford encouragement to the enlightened study of Eastern classical languages and literature.' All these special objects are prominently set out in the preamble of the Act, and I have recently had the satisfaction of being assured, by those who were most intimately connected with the movement from the first, and to whose suggestions indeed the foundation of the University is due, that the Act in its present form is all that the founders and the public desired."

Inaugural Convocation of the Punjab University.

In addressing the Convocation, after the degrees had been conferred and the presentations made, His Excellency spoke as follows:—]
Mr. Chancellor, Nawab of Bhawalpore, Raja of Kapurthala, Raja of Faridkote, and Gentlemen,—It affords me, I assure you, very great satisfaction to have been able to be present as Patron of this University upon this auspicious occasion, and to have this public opportunity of offering my sincere congratulations to those who now for some eighteen years, I believe, have been labouring to secure the establishment of a University in the Punjab. You, Sir Charles Aitchison, were among the foremost of those who started this movement, and you and others who worked with you then were speedily aided by the generous assistance and the liberal contributions of the leading Princes and Chiefs and Gentlemen of this great province; and when I carry back my recollection to that time, so many years ago, of which I have only read, and look through the papers which have been brought before me, to see what has been the course which the promoters of this scheme have pursued from that distant date till now, I find beside those eminent names to which I have adverted, the name of another gentleman which will be always associated with the foundation of the Punjab University; for no man has worked harder, no man, I believe, has devoted himself with greater zeal to promote this great public object for the benefit of the Punjab and indeed of all India, than the Registrar of this University, Dr. Leitner. (*Cheers.*) To you, Sir, to you Princes and Chiefs, and to the Members of the Senate of this University, I therefore offer my hearty congratulations. It is now, almost to a day, two years ago since, on my first visit to Lahore, I received an address from the Senate of the Punjab University College, expressing their earnest desire for the establishment of a complete University in Northern India. Gentlemen, after I had made my reply to that address, it was whispered to me that those who

Inaugural Convocation of the Punjab University.

listened to it were somewhat disappointed with what I had said. They perhaps had expected that I should have made large promises before I was quite sure whether I could keep them. But that, gentlemen, is not my habit. I prefer to be better rather than worse to my word (*cheers*), and when I spoke to you in 1880, I had not had a sufficient opportunity of studying this question in all its bearings, of listening to the objections which might be made to the scheme which was then put before me, and of consulting, as I was bound to do, my colleagues in the Government of India. I therefore, though I deeply sympathised with your general object, thought it far better to speak words which may have seemed somewhat cold to you, than to raise hopes which I might not have been able to fulfil. But, gentlemen, I can assure you that it is a great gratification to me that, at length, this project has been carried to a successful issue. (*Cheers.*) It has been my duty in regard to it to consult many persons, to consult the Government of the Punjab, to consult the Secretary of State, and to obtain from the Legislative Council of India the necessary legal powers. All those operations necessarily took time, but at length, at the conclusion of two years, the work has been done, the law has been passed, and the University has been established upon a basis which I am happy to believe gives satisfaction to those who, for so long a period, have laboured for the attainment of this end. (*Cheers.*) Gentlemen, when I spoke to you two years ago, I think that if you had read between the lines of what I said, you would have seen how warmly I sympathised with the objects which you had in view (*cheers*), because I told you then, as I tell you now, that there were two features in the project put forward by the Senate of the Punjab University College which particularly commended themselves to my judgment and approval. One was that you proposed to base this University—the University which you desired to see established—upon a somewhat different

Inaugural Convocation of the Punjab University.

foundation from that upon which the other and older Universities of India are based; and the other was that this scheme had received the cordial support and the generous contributions of so many of the most leading natives of the Punjab. I, gentlemen, am one of those who believe that there is a great advantage in having educational institutions in a country founded upon different systems and presenting various methods of teaching. It is so in England, as many of you know, in the two great and famous Universities of that country—Oxford and Cambridge. There is a marked difference in the basis of their studies, Oxford placing the classics in the front rank of those studies, and Cambridge, on the other hand, giving the most prominent position to mathematics; and the same thing has occurred in the newest born of the English Universities—the recently established Victoria University of Manchester, with which I have the honour to be connected; for what classics are to Oxford, what mathematics are to Cambridge, science is to the Victoria University; and, therefore, when you make the foundation of your studies here, and their main, though by no means their exclusive object, the study of Oriental literature, you are only following the course which we in England have pursued for centuries, and from which we have derived the greatest advantage. (*Cheers.*) Now, gentlemen, it would be indeed out of place if I, who am unhappily ignorant of oriental literature and oriental learning, were, in the presence of so many distinguished and learned men, to say a word upon the subject of that literature, upon its scope and upon the many advantages which may flow from its study; but I have been very much struck within the last few weeks by reading a remarkable paper, written by one who has a right to speak about oriental literature—I allude to an article in a late number of the *Contemporary Review*, by Professor Max Müller. If I were to speak of Indian literature, Indian philosophy, and Indian science in the language in which

Inaugural Convocation of the Punjab University.

Professor Max Müller speaks of them in that essay doubtless I should be accused of exaggeration and partiality: but no man can bring any such charges against that learned person, who knows better than most people what he is talking about on this matter; and I commend to all those who have any doubt about the solidity of oriental learning and the lessons it has to teach, not to India and to Orientals alone, but to Europeans also—to study the short essay to which I have adverted. (*Cheers.*) Gentlemen, I thought it worth while just to put down a few words which Professor Max Müller employed in that article in reference to the study of Sanscrit. What does he say? He says:—"The study of Sanscrit will open before you" (he was especially addressing young students about to come out to India in the Civil Service) " larger layers of literature, as yet almost unknown and unexplored, and allow you an insight into strata of thought deeper than any you have known before, and rich in lessons that appeal to the deepest sympathies of the human heart." Gentlemen, I need no other proof of the soundness of the policy pursued in the foundation of this University than is contained in these words of the great Oxford Professor, and if Professor Max Müller is right, and if India has so much to teach us Europeans, as he tells us that she has, then the foundation of this University, which makes oriental studies its chief and foremost aim, is likely to conduce not only to the benefit of the natives of India—aye, and, as we have seen in the case of some of the men who have just come before us, to the natives of other parts of Asia also—but at the same time to the advantage of Europeans in this country and in the West. (*Cheers.*) The fact then, gentlemen, that this University presents a marked variety in the form and scope of its instruction, from those which distinguish the other Universities of India, leads me, without for one moment wishing to disparage those older institutions, to regard it as a fortunate circumstance that this

Inaugural Convocation of the Punjab University.

younger sister has sprung up in the Punjab. And then again, I hail with the greatest satisfaction the circumstance that this University has been established by the contributions of the Native Princes and gentlemen of this province (*cheers*), and that the management of this institution will rest so largely in their hands. (*Cheers.*) I have had occasion before to speak to other audiences of the strong desire which I entertain to induce native gentlemen of wealth and position to come forward and take their part in the promotion of public education in this country. I spoke at some length upon that subject at the beginning of this year, in an address which I made to the Calcutta University. But, gentlemen, my anxiety on this subject, and my wish to see native gentlemen take their proper part in promoting public education in India does not arise solely from financial considerations, or from the hope that we may thus be able to derive from private benevolence larger funds for the promotion of this great public object. I entirely admit that financial considerations do enter into the consideration of the question, and into my feeling in regard to it, because I know well that no widespread and general system of public education in all its branches—higher, middle, and primary—can be established in a vast country like this, except at a large cost; and I know, too, how narrow and inelastic are the resources at the command of the Government of India. This is, it seems to me, a case in which we may fairly make an appeal to those who have wealth themselves to greater or less extent, to help their poorer neighbours to develope those faculties with which God has endued them, and which He, in His mercy, has made the special inheritance of no class and no race. But, gentlemen, I attach importance to this matter yet more strongly because I believe that Indian education will greatly benefit from being largely conducted by natives of India themselves (*cheers*); because I believe that it is a great public object

Inaugural Convocation of the Punjab University.

to induce men like the distinguished Princes, Chiefs, and Noblemen whom I see around me in this assembly, to give not only their rupees, but their time and their personal attention to the great object of improving, of extending, and of developing national education in the country. (*Cheers.*) And, gentlemen, it is a great satisfaction to me to find that, in holding those opinions, I am once more in this case, as in regard to another important matter of great public interest at the present time, only walking in the steps of that distinguished man, your former Lieutenant-Governor, Sir Donald Macleod (*loud cheers*), for, in looking the other day over some old papers connected with the efforts which have been made from his day down to the present time for the establishment of this Punjab University, I found that Sir Donald Macleod, in an address which he had delivered upon the subject, laid down this as one of the great objects which he had in view in favouring the movement which was then commencing. He said that what led him to take the earnest part which he did in that movement was "more especially the conviction that in no other way can we so appropriately or effectively secure an object which I have long had much at heart, namely, the associating with us of the leaders of the people, in our endeavours to promote the progress of education and in our deliberations connected therewith." (*Cheers.*) Gentlemen, I can add nothing to these words; they exactly express my feeling upon this subject, and they express it with an authority to which I can lay no claim; and it is because I see in the system upon which this University is now founded an earnest and determined effort thus to associate with us in our educational projects, the leaders of opinion in this great province, that I so heartily rejoice to have been able to give my sanction, as Governor-General, to the Bill under which this University has been established. (*Cheers.*) And, gentlemen, I am glad to see some signs, at all events, that the example set

Inaugural Convocation of the Punjab University.

here in the Punjab is likely to be followed in a lesser or a greater degree in other parts of India. I have observed, with the very greatest pleasure, what has taken place recently with respect to the College at Agra. The Government felt themselves unable to maintain that College as a purely Government institution, because the cost of it was altogether disproportionate to the benefits which it was conferring upon the people; but there has been some misconception in the public mind in respect to the intentions of the Government in regard to this matter. We no doubt said that if arrangements which we should prefer could not be made, that then we should have to propose a system of distribution of the endowments of that institution, upon which we asked the opinion of the Lieutenant-Governor of the North-Western Provinces; but we distinctly laid down from the beginning that the arrangement which we desired to see adopted and carried out was that the gentlemen of Agra and its neighbourhood should themselves come forward and take over the College, with its endowments, and, with grants-in-aid from the Government, assisted by their own private subsciptions, should work it themselves. (*Cheers.*) That was the primary object and the first proposal of the Government, and I rejoice to think that that proposal has been accepted by the public spirit of the North-Western Provinces. (*Cheers.*) There is yet, gentlemen, another reason which I cannot altogether pass by to-day, why I rejoice so much to think that this Institution, and other institutions of education, whether they be Universities or Colleges, or even Primary Schools, should be managed and administered as far as may be by the leading men of the district in which those institutions are established, and that is that by this means many a useful practical lesson of self-help and self-reliance will be afforded, and a valuable training in the management of their own affairs will be given to those who have to do with the conduct of

Inaugural Convocation of the Punjab University.

institutions of this description, and that thus, that great political object which the Government of India of to-day have so much at heart, of aiding and advancing the political training of the people in the conduct of their own local affairs, will be greatly furthered and assisted. Gentlemen, there is a school of philosophers and political writers which tells us that the great and, indeed, the sole duty and object of Government is to maintain, in the largest sense of the phrase, the public peace. Now, gentlemen, I do not deny for a moment that that is the primary object and the first business of every government; and I venture to say that through that *pax Anglica* which reigns now throughout India, from Peshawur to Cape Comorin, the British Government has shown that it is able—and well able—to discharge that function; but I am far from thinking that that is the only, or the highest, aim and end of Government. It seems to me that when that foundation has been laid—as laid it has been now in India—and when peace is established throughtout the length and breadth of the land, it is the duty of the Government to-day, while upon the one hand it firmly and unhesitatingly maintains that peace, to endeavour, on the other hand to build up upon the solid foundation thus laid by the labours of its predecessors, a noble fabric of political and social institutions (*cheers*); and that the time has fully come when it should be one of the foremost objects of the British Government in India to provide, so far as a Government, within proper limits, can, for the intellectual training and for the social and political development of the people entrusted by God to its care. And, gentlemen, this is a work in which all we Englishmen in this country may take a part, from the Viceroy to the junior member of the Civil Service who has just landed on our shores. In that article of Professor Max Müller's to which I have already alluded, he says, addressing the students who were about to leave the Universities of England to take their place in the administration of India—"there are bright deeds to be done in India if only you will do them." Yes, that is my feeling. I believe that there are bright and noble deeds to be done in India by the English race, and that the time has come when it should be our object to promote those ends, not merely by the efforts of the Government or by the zeal of the Administration, but by associating with us in this great task the people of India themselves; and, gentlemen, I trust that this Institution, of which we have to-day laid the foundation,—firm, I earnestly hope, and enduring,—will conduce to that great end ; and that upon those foundations there may rise for future generations a beautiful structure of fair proportions, which may help to bind together Western and Eastern learning—the English race and the Oriental races; and if that aim should be realised, and if before I die it should be given to me to see some commencemnet of so noble a work, I shall indeed esteem myself fortunate in having been able to-day to take a prominient part in the inauguration of the Punjab University. (*Loud and continued cheers.*)

INSPECTION OF THE 20TH PUNJAB NATIVE INFANTRY.

[ON Friday morning, the 24th November, the Viceroy inspected the 20th Punjab Native Infantry, recently returned from service in Egypt, in His Excellency's Camp at Rupar, and addressed the regiment as follows:—] 24th Nov. 1882.

Colonel Rogers,—It is very gratifying to me to have this opportunity of greeting you and your regiment on your return from foreign service, and of assuring you in person how thoroughly this regiment has fulfilled the expectations of the Government of India. You, 20th, have shown yourselves worthy to fight beside the choicest troops in the British Army, and you have maintained unsullied the honour

Opening the Sirhind Canal.

of the Army of India. Your bearing on the 13th of September was all that Government could desire, and your march from your camp before Tel-el-Kebir to Zagazig has called forth the admiration of all who witnessed it; and throughout the late campaign you and the other Indian regiments associated with you have shown yourselves to be possessed of the three great qualities of a soldier—courage, endurance, and discipline. It has been your good fortune, on this occasion, to serve under the eye of a son of our Gracious Sovereign the Queen-Empress, and I am confident that the Duke of Connaught will tell Her Majesty how well her Indian soldiers did their duty. I am sure that those who have gone to England to represent this regiment will receive from Her Majesty the proof of her confidence and regard. I heartily welcome you home, and, in the name of the Queen-Empress, I thank you for your services.

[Colonel Rogers briefly acknowledged His Excellency's kind words, and the regiment was marched off.]

OPENING THE SIRHIND CANAL.

24th Nov 1882. [On Friday, the 24th November, the Viceroy opened the Sirhind Canal, in the presence of the Chiefs and visitors assembled at Rupar. These were received and accommodated, previous to the ceremony, in a large tent pitched near the Canal. His Excellency, who was preceded by the Lieutenant-Governor, arrived at 12 o'clock and took his seat on a raised *dais*, with the Chiefs on his right and the Lieutenant-Governor on his left. In requesting Lord Ripon to open the Canal, Colonel Home delivered an address, giving an account of its progress and the difficulties attending its construction since 1840, when the project was first suggested, up to the present time. The Canal he described as one of the largest in the world, and the second large work of its kind undertaken in the Punjab since the province came under British rule. Colonel Home warmly acknowledged the assistance ungrudgingly given by all the Chiefs through whose

Opening the Sirhind Canal.

territories the Canal passed, referring particularly to the support received from the late Mahárájá of Patiála and the present Council of Regency, the Chiefs of Jhind, Nabha, Faridkote, and Maler Kotla. The construction of the canal had afforded an opportunity of employing a large body of prisoners, whose discipline was admirable and whose aid was invaluable. The management of the internal distribution of the water would, Colonel Home explained, be left to the village communities, Government interfering only to advise or to prevent wilful waste. The duties of the administrative staff would thus be lightened, and the people educated to a more intelligent appreciation of the benefits derived from canal irrigation. The total length of the Canal was 502 statute miles. When the works were completed, 2,500 miles of channel would have to maintained. The Canal was designed to irrigate 522,000 acres from British and 261,000 acres from Native States branches. The total cost was estimated at 407 lakhs, 278 lakhs being defrayed by the British Government and 129 lakhs by the Native States.

The Viceroy, in replying, spoke as follows :—]

Sir Charles Aitchison, Mahárájás, Rájás, Chiefs and Gentlemen,—The address which has been just read by Lieutenant-Colonel Home gives a succinct but clear account of the history of this canal from the period when it was first suggested, more than forty years ago, to utilise the water of the Sutlej for irrigation purposes, down to the present day. It records the difficulties which have been met and at length overcome, the interest which has been felt in the scheme by the Chiefs of various native states, and the cordial support and liberal contributions which those Princes have accorded to the work. It also reminds us that this canal, the opening of which we celebrate to-day, is one of the largest works of the kind in the world, and shows that it is designed to provide the advantages of irrigation for an area of not less than 783,000 acers. We have, therefore, ample grounds for rejoicing at the success of this great work, for it presents all the features which we should desire to see combined in an undertaking of this description. Its magnitude is not unworthy of the Government of this great country. The benefits which it is calculated to confer will reach the present cultivator in the extended

Opening the Sirhind Canal.

districts within which its influence will be felt; while its construction is the result of the combined efforts of the Supreme Government and of Native Princes.

Of the magnitude of the head works of the canal, I need not speak; all here will have seen them for themselves, and will have been able to form at least some judgment of the skill and ability required for their construction, although we must bear in mind that it is not the works which we see now above the ground, and above the water, which have occasioned the greatest difficulties in this undertaking, but that, below the surface and hidden from the view, are to be found the fruits of the greatest portion of the skill and labour which have been devoted to this work; and when we remember that there will ultimately be 2,500 miles of channel to be supplied, and that water will be conveyed to more than three-quarters of a million of acres, we shall not wonder either at the cost of the whole work or at the difficulties which have been encountered in its execution. To my mind, also, this canal is invested with a special interest because its benefits will be confined to no class of the community, but will be shared alike by prince and by people, by landowner and by tenant, by rich and by poor. The waters of the Sutlej will no longer confine their blessings to those who dwell on the banks of that river so famous in Indian history; but, guided by the skill of man, will spread their fertilising powers over a vast extent of thirsty land, lying barren or scantily productive under the burning sun of India. To me it is a source of great satisfaction that the Rulers of the important states referred to in the address—Patiála, Jhind, Nabha, Faridkote, Maler Kotla, and Nalagarh—should appear as partners with the British Government in this great work of public utility. I esteem very highly such co-operation; I rejoice to see the Princes of India animated by a wise and far-seeing public spirit, such as they have displayed in regard to this matter; and I tender to those who have so generously aided in this

Opening the Sirhind Canal.

enterprise, my cordial thanks. They could make no better use of the wealth which God has given them than by employing it to promote undertakings of this sort, and they could adopt no surer means of winning both the loyal attachment of their own people and the grateful acknowledgments of the Government of the Queen-Empress. Colonel Home has specially alluded to the assistance given by the Council of Regency of Patiála under the presidency of my friend Sir Deva Sing, and by the Prime and Foreign Ministers of that State. All of these distinguished persons are entitled to our thanks and upon the two last named it is my intention to confer suitable titles.

There is also another circumstance connected with this canal which tends to increase the satisfaction with which I take part in to-day's ceremony. Colonel Home, at the conclusion of his address, alluded to the system of distribution which it is intended to put in operation as soon as the water has been admitted into the distributary channels; and he has explained that the principle upon which that system will be founded will be that of leaving the management of the internal distribution of the water to the village communities, and of interfering only to prevent wilful waste. I feel the greatest confidence that this principle is a sound one, and I shall watch its application and development with much interest. I believe that, by its means, not only will the labours of the administrative staff be lightened, as Colonel Home points out, but also that many practical evils and some abuses will be avoided, and that the system is likely to prove very advantageous to the cultivating communities themselves.

You will not doubt, gentlemen, after listening to what I have been saying, that I am a warm friend to irrigation and a firm believer in its beneficial results; but, at the same time, I must express my belief that, as in other cases so in regard to water, it is possible to have too much of a good thing; and I would therefore express a hope that those

Opening the Sirhind Canal.

within whose reach the water of this canal will be brought will use it not only readily, but wisely. If I am not mistaken, it is often found that though, for the first few years after the opening of a new canal, the increase in fertility of the irrigated soil is great and striking, a time comes when the crops often begin to fall off and the land begins to show signs of exhaustion. Why is this? Because an excessive use has been made of the water and too exclusive a reliance has been placed upon it. I would therefore strongly urge those to whom this canal is about to open fresh sources of prosperity, to make a cautious and a moderate use of the water which it will supply, and not to trust to it alone as a fertilising agent. Water is not a substitute for manure as a restorer of the powers of the soil. The two should go hand in hand, and, in proportion as they do so, it will be found that the land which this canal will irrigate will truly become a garden; but if water is used by itself for any lengthened period, it has a tendency in more ways than one to exhaust the productive powers which it itself calls forth; and it can therefore never supersede or take the place of those other restoratives which are required to complete its work and to secure the permanence of its benefits.

And now, gentlemen, it only remains for me to say that it will afford me great pleasure to comply with Colonel Home's request and to complete the formal opening of the Sirhind Canal. I trust that it will please God to bless the work which has been here performed, and to grant to generations upon generations of Indian cultivators the many advantages which this undertaking is designed to confer.

[After the applause which followed His Excellency's speech had subsided, Mr. Grant read a translation of the speech in the vernacular to the assembled Chiefs. His Excellency, accompanied by the Lieutenant-Governor, the Chiefs, and the rest of the assembly, then proceeded to a pavilion erected on the bridge over the canal, below which were the sluices; and here assisted by the Lieutenant-

Addresses from the Lucknow and Faizabad Municipalities.

Governor and the Mahárájás of Jhind and Nabha, he raised one of the sluices and formally declared the Canal open, once more expressing a hope that it would prove a blessing to the people and to the country through which it passed. A salute concluded the ceremony, and the great crowd of visitors and Chiefs, with their followers, returned to their respective camps.]

ADDRESSES FROM THE LUCKNOW AND FAIZABAD MUNICIPALITIES.

[ON Monday evening, the 27th November, the Viceroy held a Levée in His Excellency's Camp at Lucknow, at which a large number of gentlemen were presented. At the conclusion of the Levée, deputations from the Lucknow and Faizabad Municipalities waited on and presented His Excellency with addresses of welcome. The addresses referred chiefly to the subject of local self-government, and His Excellency replied to them as follows :—]

Gentlemen of the Municipalities of Lucknow and Faizabad,—I thank you heartily for the addresses which you have just presented to me. I can assure you that I am very glad to have had this opportunity of visiting the important province of Oudh, and of seeing the memorable spots which are included within the limits of the Lucknow Municipality, so full of most interesting and important historical recollections. I regret, gentlemen, that I shall not on this occasion be able also to visit Faizabad, but I am well aware that that town is one of much importance in this province of Oudh.

You, gentlemen of the Municipality of Lucknow, have chiefly touched (as was natural) in your address upon the important question of local self-government, which is now occupying so much attention on the part of the public; and you also, gentlemen of Faizabad, have alluded to the same subject. I have so recently had occasion to express in public my sentiments upon this question, that it is unnecessary that I should detain you long in reply to the remarks which you have made upon it; but I rejoice to

Addresses from the Lucknow and Faizabad Municipalities.

find from your addresses—and especially from that of the Municipality of Lucknow, which has entered more fully into the subject—that you rightly understand and appreciate the objects and intentions of the Government in regard to their policy in this respect.

Gentlemen,—It must, I think, be clear to every one, from the Resolution of the Government of India of the 18th of May last, that it is our desire, and a cardinal feature of our policy, to adopt in each province of India, and very often in the various districts within each provice itself, that system of local self-government which may be thought most consonant with the feelings and the habits of the people, and best suited to their peculiarities and idiosyncrasies. I attach, gentlemen, great importance myself to this point, and I have all along been most desirous that the leading inhabitants of each district should be consulted with a view to ascertain what are the arrangements most likely to suit their local requirements. It is, gentlemen, on the lines of an elastic system that the Resolution of the 18th of May was framed. As you, gentlemen of the Municipality of this city, have rightly said, we have had no desire at any time to introduce into India purely English theories or English ideas in this matter; and it is sufficient for me to quote a single sentence from the Resolution of the 18th of May, in order to make that fact perfectly clear; for we have said in that Resolution that "there may be methods unthought of in Europe which may be found suitable in India." That is ample proof that what we desire are not English—nay, not even European—methods in this matter, so long as the object which we have at heart is attained. What we want is, that the methods by which that object is pursued should be those most in accordance with the feelings and the customs of the country.

Gentlemen,—The Resolution, to which I have alluded, lays down a few broad general principles to which the Government firmly adhere; but the mode of their application we

Addresses from the Lucknow and Faizabad Municipalities.

wish to be varied in form and local in colouring, so that in this great peninsula, containing so many races, unlike in so many respects, those methods of carrying out our policy should be adopted which are most calculated to meet the various requirements of populations in many respects so different one from the other. I rejoice, gentlemen, to hear you say that you do not wish in this matter to lean upon the Government as upon a crutch, although you hope that at the first introduction of the new system the Government will give you assistance. I can assure you that the Government will be most happy—it will be indeed their duty—to afford you, in the carrying out of the principles of our Resolution, all the counsel and all the assistance that it may be in our power to give; but it is essential that that assistance should be given in the manner best calculated to preserve your freedom of action within the limits of your attributions, and not to weaken your self-reliance. The object we have had in view has been to induce the best, the most intelligent, and the most influential men in the country to come forward and take a larger part than hitherto in the management of their own local affairs, and gradually to train them to do so more and more. For this purpose it is essential that we should leave municipalities upon their new footing to walk alone to a great extent; that we should be prepared to see them not infrequently fall into errors; that we should set them free to learn the lessons of experience which in practical matters of this kind is the best of all teachers; and that we should do nothing which would tend to relieve the new local bodies from those responsibilities which must attach to any system of self-government in any real and honest sense of those words.

Gentlemen,—It seems to me that the policy of the Government in this respect, as laid down in the Resolution to which I have alluded, is clear and plain. Since the issue of that Resolution, nothing has occured to induce me to

Presentation of Colors to the 2nd B. L. I.

doubt, in the smallest degree, its wisdom or its propriety Here, in the North-Western Provinces and Oudh, you have a Lieutenant-Governor and Chief Commissioner—my friend Sir Alfred Lyall—who will, I am sure, carry out the policy of the Government in this respect wisely and liberally, with, at the same time, all due caution and the most careful consideration for local feelings and local requirements; and under his able administration it is my earnest hope, and my full expectation, that the foundation may be firmly laid of a system which, as it gradually extends and developes, will confer increasing blessings upon the people of this province.

Gentlemen,—I heartily thank you for your cordial welcome.

PRESENTATION OF COLORS TO THE 2ND (QUEEN'S OWN) BENGAL LIGHT INFANTRY.

28th Nov. 1882. [On the morning of the 28th November, His Excellency reviewed the troops in garrison at Lucknow, and afterwards presented new colors to the 2nd (Queen's Own) Bengal Light Infantry. Some 4,400 men were assembled on the Brigade parade ground, under the command of General Cureton, C.B., and there was a very large attendance of spectators. After the Viceroy had inspected the troops and witnessed the march past, the Division was formed up in three sides of a square, when His Excellency, accompanied by General Cureton, moved to the front of the regiment. The ceremony of trooping the colors was then gone through; the drums were piled, and the Viceroy received the colors and presented them to the two senior jemadars of the regiment. The usual consecration was omitted, as the regiment belonged to the native army. His Excellency then addressed the regiment as follows :]

Major Waterfield,—I have read with great interest the long and honourable record of the services of this regiment, which has now been enrolled in the army of India for a period not far short of a century. From the days of Lord Lake, from the battles of Delhi, Laswarree, and Deig,

Presentation of Colors to the 2nd (Queen's Own) B. L. I.

down to the late campaign in Afghanistan, the 31st Native Infantry (now the 2nd Queen's Own) have borne a distinguished part in a long series of warlike operations. During the Mutiny they were true to their salt, and their marked fidelity at that trying period was specially recognised at the time by the Government of India. In the late Afghan Campaign this regiment had to endure a trial far harder for gallant soldiers than the dangers of the field of battle. They had to bear up, day after day, against the wearying round of convoying stores and guarding the line of communications in a deleterious climate, which struck down men faster and in greater numbers than any encounter with a living foe. Throughout those weary months they did their duty, as they have always done it, faithfully and well. It is clear, therefore, that the Queen's Own Regiment has constantly displayed the great qualities of valour, fidelity, and patience. Faithful among the faithless, courageous, and enduring, to you I now may entrust these colors with the firmest reliance that you will keep them unstained. In the name of our gracious Sovereign the Queen-Empress I give them to you. Take them 2nd and guard them from all dishonour. Let them be dearer to you than your lives. Remember that you have in your hands the reputation of a noble regiment, and that it behoves you to uphold its honour and to maintain its fame; so that in coming years, when time, and it may be the bullets of your enemies, have once more wasted these silken tokens of your Sovereign's trust, some future Viceroy, when he comes to renew them, may feel, as I feel to-day that he may deliver the proud standard of England to this gallant regiment in the fullest confidence that he is entrusting it to men who are well worthy of the honoured charge.

[Major Waterfield replied to the Viceroy as follows :—

"*Your Excellency,*—In the name of Colonel Baker, whose unavoidable absence from this parade I greatly regret, as I know he does

Address to Regiments returned from Egypt.

himself, and in the name of the officers and men of the 2nd (Queen's Own) Bengal Light Infantry, I beg to offer you our most grateful thanks for the honour you have done us in presenting us with these colors. Your Excellency has noticed in the most flattering terms the past services and loyalty of this regiment. I trust that in future, should opportunity offer, we shall be able to maintain our good name, and to add fresh honours to the roll inscribed on these standards, and prove ourselves worthy of the honourable title lately conferred on us by Her Most Gracious Majesty the Queen-Empress."

Turning to General Cureton and the regiments recently returned from Egypt, His Excellency spoke as follows:—]

General Cureton,—I am now anxious to address a few words of greeting to those regiments who have just returned from the war in Egypt, and to offer to them my hearty congratulations upon the share which they have taken in those operations. The 2nd Battalion of the Derbyshire Regiment is not new to India. It served in the Mutiny, and I am glad to see it again in this country. If this regiment was not present at the crowning victory of Tel-el-Kebir, this was due to that fortune of war which not unfrequently relegates some of the best corps of an army to posts where the service to be performed is less brilliant, though it may be not less important, than that which falls to the lot of others; and I am confident that the Derbyshire Regiment would have proved itself in no degree unequal to the rest of the army of Sir Garnet Wolseley if it had been called to endure the trials of the earlier portion of the campaign, and to take part in the final assault of the enemy's position.

The Second Battalion of the Seaforth Highlanders carry back their Indian reputation to the beginning of the century, and record upon their colours the name of that victory of Assaye which laid the foundation of the fame of England's greatest soldier. This battalion was represented in the late campaign by only two companies, but those companies did their work as Highlanders are wont to do it, and they added yet another laurel to the wreath with which the brow of Scotland is adorned.

Address to Regiments returned from Egypt.

The 2nd Bengal Cavalry may well be proud to have formed part of that brigade which has given a world-wide reputation to the Native Cavalry of India, and their distinguished conduct is acknowledged on all hands, and their representatives have received the recognition of their services from our gracious Sovereign herself.

The 7th Bengal Native Infantry have on this occasion shown themselves well worthy of their ancient reputation. Like the 2nd, of which I have just been speaking, the 7th stood the shock of the Mutiny faithfully and firmly, and the memory of their services on that occasion will never pass from the grateful recollection of the Government of India. We could, as it seems to me, have given no greater proof of confidence in this corps than by selecting it for employment in Eygpt; and that confidence has been well repaid by the manner in which the 7th have borne themselves throughout the late campaign. They, too, through their representatives, will see the Queen-Empress, and will learn from her own lips how highly she values her Indian troops. By a happy accident, it so happens that the last mail brought me a letter from Her Majesty, in which she says—"The Queen is indeed proud and thankful at the splendid conduct all of her brave troops in Egypt." Officers of the Eygptian regiments, this is the message of your Queen-Empress. It will show you how carefully she has watched your actions—how she appreciates your conduct. To her praise I can add nothing. I can only cordially congratulate you on having won the approval of so gracious a Sovereign, and to tender to you a hearty welcome on your return from the war.

[His Excellency then drove off the ground, and the troops marched back to quarters.]

CANNING COLLEGE, LUCKNOW.

28th Nov. 1882. [ON Wednesday afternoon, the 28th November, the Viceroy, accompanied by the Lieutenant-Governor, visited the Canning College at Lucknow, and received an address of welcome. The address (which was read by Raja Amir Hussein, the leading Talukdar of Oudh) expressed gratitude for Lord Ripon's efforts in the cause of education; it explained that the object of the College—which was founded in 1864, by the Talukdars of Oudh, to perpetuate the memory of Earl Canning, their great benefactor—was to provide a course of instruction which would combine the depth and wide range of Oriental thought with the advanced ideas of Western science and literature, and to teach the rising generation to utilise the stores of intellectual wealth treasured up in their ancient records, by the aid of modern science. The records of the Calcutta University, the Punjab University College, and other examining bodies showed that the College had achieved success in giving effect to this aim. The address paid a high compliment to the zeal and ability of the Principal of the College (Mr. White) and his colleagues, referred to Sir Alfred Lyall's interest in their work, and quoted in terms of approval the sentiments expressed in the Viceroy's speech at the Calcutta University in March last.

His Excellency replied to the address as follows:—]

Sir Alfred Lyall and Gentlemen,—I thank you for the address which has just been read, and which I have received with much satisfaction. I can assure you that it gives me great pleasure to be able on this occasion of my first visit to Lucknow to have an opportunity of coming to see an institution of which I had already heard; and I rejoice to find, from the address, that the progress which that institution is making is of so satisfactory a nature; and that, during the eighteen years in which it has grown from a small school to the present extended and valuable establishment, its course has been attended by an ever increasing success. It also gives me much satisfaction to receive the assurance which this address contains, of the spirit by which the students of this institution are animated, and of the objects and aims which they set before themselves in the studies in which they are engaged. And I am very

Canning College, Lucknow.

glad also to observe the tone of affection and confidence with which the students appear to recognise the ability and zeal with which Mr. White, the Principal, and his colleagues, devote themselves to their important duties. When such feelings as these exist between teachers and students, it augurs well for the prosperity of an educational institution.

Gentlemen,—I am very glad to have this opportunity, of which I readily avail myself, to acknowledge the enlightened liberality with which the Talukdars of Oudh, as a body, have contributed, and are contributing, to the maintenance of this institution, so valuable to the province and so essential to the development and direction of the higher education of the people. I must, however, say, gentlemen, that I somewhat regret to learn that this College and the advantages which it so freely affords, are not made use of to a larger extent than appears to be at present the case, by the natives of this province, for whose benefit the institution has been established and endowed. I understand, indeed (and I am very glad to hear it), that a certain number of the sons and the relatives of the Talukdars have prosecuted their studies here, and in those studies they have won for themselves distinctions worthy of all praise. I trust that the example will hereafter be more widely followed, and that thus this valuable College may more and more perfectly and completely fulfil the main and primary object with which it has been so largely endowed, namely, the promotion and expansion of education in Oudh ; and I take the liberty of recommending this matter to the careful and earnest consideration of the Committee of this institution.

Gentlemen,—The framers of this address have been pleased to speak of the deep interest which I feel, and which I have felt now for many, many years, in the cause of public education. To that cause I have devoted much thought and much time, and I am only acting on those

La Martinière School, Lucknow.

principles which have guided my public life when, here in India, it is my earnest desire and constant endeavour to promote public education in all its branches—higher, middle, and primary. It is therefore to me a source of pleasure to be able to visit an establishment of this description in this famous city, and to receive from you, and from the students who are here devoting themselves to learning and cultivation, the hearty and cordial welcome which you have accorded to me to-day.

DISTRIBUTION OF PRIZES AT THE MARTINIÈRE SCHOOL, LUCKNOW.

29th Nov. 1882. [On Wednesday afternoon, the 29th November, Lord Ripon distributed the prizes to the pupils of the Martinière School at Lucknow. Sir Alfred and Lady Lyall, Sir Steuart Bayley, and a large number of ladies and gentlemen were present. The principal hall of the boys' school, in which the distribution took place, was prettily decorated with flags and banners, and garlands of green leaves and flowers. The Viceroy, who was accompanied by Mr. H. W. Primrose and other members of his Staff, arrived at the school at half-past 4 o'clock, and was received by the Governors and the Principal, and by a guard of honour of the School Volunteers, who numbered 130 boys, all well drilled and armed. On His Excellency being conducted to his seat at the head of the school-room, the Principal proceeded to deliver, an introductory address to the report on the School, in which he gave a sketch of the life of Claude Martin, the founder of the Martinières of Lucknow, Calcutta, and Lyons. Referring to the present position and prospects of the School, Mr. Sykes claimed for it that it holds its own with the best of the schools for Europeans and Eurasians in India, whether they be on the hills or in the plains. He alluded to the recent Resolution of Government, regarding the employment of Natives in the Public Works Department, and the practical closing thereby of the Roorkee College to Europeans and Eurasians, and hoped that it was not yet too late for the Government to reconsider the Resolution, and to throw open the College again alike to all classes. A hope was also expressed that the term "Natives of India," and similar terms, in the Resolution might hereafter be so defined as to

La Martinière School, Lucknow.

include in their import all Europeans and Eurasians domiciled in India. At the conclusion of this address, the prizes were distributed to the girls by His Excellency, after which the Head Master read a brief detail of the year's work. His Excellency then gave away the prizes to the boys, and afterwards addressed the assembly as follows :—]

Sir Alfred Lyall, Mr. Sykes, Ladies and Gentlemen,—
I have listened with great interest to the reports which have been read during the course of these proceedings. The interesting sketch of the career of Claude Martin, the founder of the Martinières of Lucknow, Calcutta, and Lyons which has been given us by the Principal shows the lively charity by which that remarkable man was animated, and how earnest was his desire that the wealth which he had acquired during his long and adventurous life should be made as useful as possible to his fellow-men. It is highly probable that the Principal was right when he said that General Martin little dreamt that the schools which he was founding by his will would attain the high position which they now occupy ; but he cast his bread upon the waters, and, under the fostering care of the British Government, the full benefits of his magnificent endowments have at length been realised. His name is worthy of all honour, and his example, of wide and constant imitation. It has been, ladies and gentlemen, a great pleasure to me to learn that this institution, in all its departments, is at the present time in so flourishing and satisfactory a condition. The Girls' School and the Boys' School seem alike successful, and the pupils of those institutions appear to make equal progress in their literary and their physical studies. It has been my fortune this year to visit both the foundations in India which were established by General Martin. In the spring I was present on an occasion similar to this, at the Martinière at Calcutta and there also I was glad to hear of the success of that useful institution. Since then, a great blow has fallen upon the College, and I cannot help availing myself of this opportunity to express here, in this sister institution,

La Martinière School, Lucknow.

my sincere regret for the untimely death of Mr. Biden, Principal of the Calcutta Martinière. He devoted himself to his duties there with the utmost zeal and earnestness, and even the single visit that I paid to the College was sufficient to show me that he had acquired the confidence and respect of his pupils. I sincerely lament his loss, and I am sure it will be deeply felt by all the friends of that institution.

Ladies and Gentlemen,—I listened with great pleasure to the record which has just been read, of the success which has attended the students of this College in the various examinations in which they have taken part recently; and I particularly noted the case of Walter Knight, whose name was specially mentioned. I observed also, in some papers connected with this College, which I was looking over before I came here, another remarkable instance of the excellence of the instruction which is here given, for I there found that a youth of the name of Joseph Adye had, at the earliest possible period, passed with great credit the examinations of the Calcutta University, and that then, going to England, he had been equally fortunate in the examinations of the London University, and had obviously laid the foundations of an honourable and hopeful career.

Ladies and Gentlemen,—Such examples as these show what it is possible for the students of this College to do, if they only avail themselves, as they ought, of the educational advantages which it provides. I think it was said that Walter Knight was not a boy of specially remarkable abilities; and it is, I am confident, within the reach of all those who devote themselves industriously and earnestly to the prosecution of their studies in an institution like this, to attain the same triumphs which he has gained. I trust that the youths of this College will ever keep in their memory the names of these and other boys who have gone before them and won distinction for themselves in after-life; and that they will strive to walk in their

La Martinière School, Lucknow.

footsteps along the path which they have trod with honour and advantage.

And now I would say just one word to those (be they girls or boys) who have been the fortunate receivers of prizes upon this occasion. I heartly congratulate you, my young friends, upon the distinctions which you have won, and I rejoice at the proof which they afford of the zeal and ability with which you are studying here. But I am anxious to remind you that, if a prize confers a distinction, it also imposes an obligation. It will do you no good hereafter to have secured a prize to-day unless you display in your future studies those qualities which have gained this distinction for you now. If you remain satisfied with what you have done, and rest upon your oars, then this prize will not profit you, will rather turn to your dishonour, because your teachers and your fellow-students will then be apt to say—"Oh! he got a prize in 1882, but ever since he has deceived our hopes and disappointed our expectations." Those who upon an occasion like this stand forth from the ranks of their fellows are bound in honour ever after to use their utmost endeavours to maintain the position which they have once won.

Ladies and Gentlemen,—I heartily wish success to this institution, and I trust that for long years to come it will continue to prove itself worthy of the wide aims and high purposes of its large-hearted founder. (*Cheers.*)

[His Honor the Lieutenant-Governor thanked the Viceroy for the honour which he had done to the institution in presiding on that occasion, and concluded by asking the boys to show their appreciation of His Excellency's kindness by saluting him with as hearty cheers as they could possibly give—a proposal which was enthusiastically responded to.]

ADDRESS FROM THE TALUKDARS OF OUDH.

29th Nov. 1882. [A Durbar for the reception of the Talukdars of Oudh was held by the Viceroy in His Excellency's Camp at Lucknow on Wednesday, the 29th November, at noon. The number of Talukdars present was about 200, and the spacious Durbar tent was filled with a large assembly of civil and military officials and ladies. After the ceremony of presenting the Talukdars individually to the Viceroy had been gone through, Rájá Amir Hussein Khan, the leading Talukdar of Oudh, read an address of welcome to the Viceroy, which, after referring with approval to the various progressive measures, inaugurated by Lord Ripon, proceeded:—"Twenty-three years have now elapsed since Lord Canning received us on the very spot where Your Excellency holds this Durbar, and we approach Your Lordship with the same sentiments of hearty welcome and admiration with which we waited on that illustrious Statesman. We repeat to your Excellency the assurance of our earnest desire to promote the prosperity of our country and our people. This has, we venture to say, been to us, as a body, our constant aim, and, in our humble efforts in this direction, we possess the great advantage of having in Sir Alfred Lyall a guide and adviser in whose wisdom and impartiality we have perfect trust. It would be ungrateful of us, if we were not to acknowledge before Your Excellency the debt we owe to the members of the Oudh Commission whose solicitous regard for the true interest of all classes of the people has earned for them our heartfelt thanks."

His Excellency replied as follows :—]

Accept, gentlemen, my best thanks for the address which you have just presented to me. I am extremely glad to have been able on this occasion to visit this province, famous alike for its historic recollections and for the fertility of its soil, and to have this opportunity of meeting you, gentlemen, in Durbar assembled.

I observe with satisfaction the loyal sentiments expressed in your address, and your ready acknowledgment of the benefits which have been secured to you by British rule. The deep interest felt by the Queen-Empress in the welfare of her Indian subjects of all classes and descriptions fully entitles her to that attachment and devotion which you have professed in just and well-chosen words.

Address from the Talukdars of Oudh.

I thank you sincerely, gentlemen, for the terms in which you have spoken of the measures which have been lately adopted by the Government of India. It is the earnest and constant desire of myself and my colleagues to govern India for the advantage of the Indian people; to promote their welfare and their happiness is our first aim. The task is a great and responsible one, requiring for its adequate performance abilities far higher than any to which I can lay claim; all that I can hope is, that I may be enabled to devote myself to the discharge of the functions of my great office in the spirit of that noble man whose name is inseparably connected with the history of this city, and who had written on his tombstone the touching motto, "Here lies Henry Lawrence, who tried to do his duty." An Indian ruler can set before himself no brighter example, and though I cannot hope to equal the great deeds which have conferred upon the memory of Sir Henry Lawrence an imperishable fame, I too, like him, will strive earnestly to do my duty alike to my gracious Sovereign and to the people whom she has entrusted to my care. In this difficult undertaking it is my good fortune to be surrounded and assisted by colleagues whose abilities, experience, and zeal help to supply my own defects, and upon whose ready help and wise counsel I can always rely with perfect confidence.

I will not detain you, gentlemen, by any allusion to the various measures of the present Government of India, of which you have spoken with approval, except to remark with respect to one of them, that it is very gratifying to me to find that a body of landowners like the Talukdars of Oudh have received with satisfaction the recent Resolution of Government on the subject of suspensions and remissions of revenue. India is, before all things, an agricultural country; agriculture is her greatest interest, and the occupation of the vast majority of her people; whatever, therefore, tends to promote the welfare of the agricultural

Address from the Talukdars of Oudh.

population must ever be an object of foremost interest to the Government; whatever is calculated to depress that population, or to lessen their well-being, must always be to us a cause of deep solicitude. I rejoice, therefore, to learn that in your opinion the recent Resolution of the Revenue Department is to be counted among the beneficial measures of my administration; it is my hope that it will prevent for the future some of those evils from which the owners and occupiers of land have from time to time suffered in the past; and I trust to you, gentlemen, loyally to pass on the benefits which you will, I hope, yourselves reap from this Resolution, to the tenants of all descriptions who hold land under you.

I accept with satisfaction the repetition of your assurance that it is your earnest desire to promote the prosperity of your country and of your people. I earnestly trust that this object will be kept steadily in view by the Talukdars of Oudh,—not so much because each Talukdar holds his land upon the condition entered in his sunnud, that he shall, so far as is in his power, promote the agricultural prosperity of his estate,—but because all Talukdars and Zemindars must be well aware that this condition only expresses the general duty and responsibility of all landowners unders the British Government. The primary and essential condition of agricultural prosperity is the well-being of the cultivators of the soil; the promotion of that well-being the Government has very earnestly at heart, and it attaches to it an importance of the highest kind. It is, moreover, a matter in which the interests of land-holders, and of the State under whom they hold their land, are identical. The State is bound to provide for the well-being of all classes of its subjects; while the landlord's estate can only be prosperous when it is cultivated by a thriving and contented tenantry, and when the relations between landlord and tenant have been adjusted upon a just footing of reciprocal consideration and mutual

Address from the Talukdars of Oudh.

advantage. If you are convinced of the truth of these principles, and are prepared to act in accordance with them, I shall confidently look to your co-operating cheerfully and loyally with the Government for their maintenance, extension, and advancement.

Gentlemen,—Your address affords me much pleasure by the assurance which it gives me that you appreciate so justly the spirit in which your Chief Commissioner, Sir Alfred Lyall, will conduct the administration of this province. You may confidently rely both upon his ability and upon his desire impartially to promote the prosperity and happiness of all classes in Oudh. His ripe wisdom and his long experience of affairs will enable him to give you the most judicious counsel in every difficulty. Look up to him as a friend, seek his advice, and follow it with the certainty that, in giving it, he has your true interests at heart.

It is also very agreeable to me to perceive that you are fully sensible of the zeal and earnestness with which the members of the Oudh Commission devote themselves to the interests of the province. They possess in a high degree, the confidence and respect of the Government, and I rejoice to learn that they enjoy so largely the gratitude and regard of those who come directly within the sphere of their administration.

I shall, I assure you, gentlemen, carry away with me very pleasant recollections of my visit to Oudh, and it will be my constant endeavour to advance by every means in my power the welfare of every class of the inhabitants of this fair and fertile province.

ADDRESS FROM THE RIFAH-I-AAM ASSOCIATION OF LUCKNOW

30th Nov. 1882. [On Thursday, the 30th November, the Viceroy received a deputation, consisting of 25 Native Gentlemen, representing the Rifah-i-Aam Association of Lucknow, who presented him with an address of welcome. The address, like others of a similar character, referred in terms of gratitude and approval to the various measures initiated and carried out by His Excellency's Government. Lord Ripon replied to it as follows :—]

Gentlemen,—I am glad to see you, and thank you much for the address which you have just presented to me. I have had so many occasions recently to express my views upon the public questions now occupying the attention of the Government and of the public, that it will not be necessary that I should detain you long in reference to the various points to which you have alluded in your address.

I am glad to find that the measures which you have enumerated are such as in your judgment are calculated to promote the advantage and prosperity of the country. It has been one of the great purposes of those measures, to advance the intellectual, social, and political development of the people. We have had that object in view in regard to local administration, in the measures which we have adopted and which we are now carrying out for the development of local self-government. We have had that object in view also in another of its branches, in the measures which we are preparing to adopt in regard to public education. It appeared to the Government that the time had come when the educational system of India, the foundations of which were laid nearly thirty years ago by the despatch of 1854, should be carefully inquired into and examined by a representative Commission. When that Commision has made its report, that report and the valuable evidence which the Commission have been collecting will receive the most careful consideration from the Government, our desire being to advance public education in

Address from the Rifah-i-Aam Association of Lucknow.

all its branches—higher, middle, and primary education. And, gentlemen, it was the same object of intellectual and social development that we set before us when we re-established in its plenitude the freedom of the press in India, because we believed that it was a great public advantage that all measures of the Government of every description, should be freely and fully discussed by the public in the press. The Government derives very great advantage from that discussion; any errors that may creep into its proposals are pointed out; suggestions, often very valuable, are made, and the Government has an opportunity of learning in what respects the public misinterprets or misapprehends the intentions by which it is animated, so that by timely explanation the real meaning of those intentions may be made plain.

These, briefly, gentlemen, are the principles upon which we have acted in regard to the various measures to which you have adverted in your address.

There is one measure which does not come altogether under the description which I have already given of the chief of those which you have mentioned—and that consists in the measures which we are now proposing and devising for the purpose of promoting the prosperity of those who are engaged in the cultivation of the soil. No questions can be more important than those which relate to agriculture, especially in a great agricultural district like this of Oudh; and I can assure you that everything which concerns the prosperity of the agricultural classes in all its branches—landowners and tenants alike—will continue to occupy the earnest attention of the Government.

Gentlemen,—I again think you for your address, and I am glad to have had this opportunity of meeting you.

DEKKHAN AGRICULTURISTS' RELIEF ACT (1879) AMENDMENT BILL.

22nd Dec. 1882. [IN the Ligislative Council, held on Friday, the 22nd December 1882, the Select Committee's Report on the Dekkhan Agriculturists' Relief Act (1879) Amendment Bill was, on Mr. Hope's motion, taken into consideration. Mr. Gibbs moved that, after section 10 of the Bill, a section should be inserted giving increased powers to Conciliators to compel attendance. A discussion ensued, Messrs. Hunter, Crosthwaite, and Ilbert speaking against the amendment, and Sir Steuart Bayley and Mr. Hope in support of it. His Excellency spoke as follows :—]

It is quite evident, from the mere fact that the members of the Executive Government differ in opinion upon this question, that it must be one of considerable difficulty, and at the same time, also, that it is not one of very vital importance, because if it was not difficult, they would be likely soon to come to an agreement upon it ; and if it had been a matter of very vital importance, they would have been bound to express an united opinion upon it.

My own view is that on the whole it would be better to adopt the amendment of my honourable friend Mr. Gibbs and I am led to that opinion by the fact that the amendment is supported by the two members of this Council representing Bombay, and is consistent with the wishes expressed by the Government of Bombay. The Bill is of a local character, and would not have been brought forward in this Council if it had not been for special reasons, to which I need not advert ; ordinarily, it would have been brought in in the Bombay Council, and there discussed with an amount of knowledge of local circumstances, which it is impossible to obtain here; but as that course has not been taken, we ought to look specially to the opinions expressed by the two able gentlemen who represent Bombay here, and to bear in mind that those views are in

Dekkhan Agriculturists' Relief Act (1879) Amendment Bill.

concurrence with the recommendations of the Bombay Government, who as Mr. Gibbs has shown, have very carefully considered the various proposals connected with the present Bill. I am also the more confirmed in my opinion —though I do not take a very strong view on the matter, one way or the other—that, on the whole, it would be better to accept the amendment of my honourable friend, because it appears to me that no objection whatever has been felt to this provision by the gentleman whose name has been frequently referred to in this discussion, and whose opinion on this question is of great importance— I mean Dr. Pollen. My honourable friend Mr. Ilbert has quoted Dr. Pollen's report in support of his view, but the most recent paper that I find among these documents, emanating from that learned person, is a letter or report of his, addressed to the Bombay Government and dated the 14th of last November. In that report Dr. Pollen says—

"When I was at Mahabaleshvar, on the 1st instant, I had an opportunity of reading the Bill, and I then stated my opinion that it was a great improvement on the original draft, and that its provisions seemed adequately to meet all the requirements of the case; but at the same time I expressed a wish to have a further opportunity of examining the details of the Bill more deliberately, so as to guard, as far as possible, against the chances of any latent errors which on a cursory perusal might have escaped observation. I have now the honour to submit, in accordance with the instructions of Government, the following remarks on the sections of the Bill which seem to require special notice."

Then Dr. Pollen, having prosecuted that further inquiry, proceeded to make comments at considerable length upon the various sections of the Bill, but makes no comment, and takes no objection, to the section now under discussion. Under these circumstances, I am inclined to draw the inference that Dr. Pollen does not think that this section would work unsatisfactory, and looking to the weight of local opinion, so far as we have it before us in these

Dekkhan Agriculturists' Relief Act (1879) Amendment Bill.

papers, I shall give my vote in favour of Mr. Gibbs'
amendment.

[The amendment was then put to the Council, and lost. Mr. Thomas
next moved the insertion of a section exempting certain instruments
from the provisions relating to registration, which, after discussion,
was also negatived. A protracted debate ensued on the motion of
Mr. Hope that the Bill as amended be passed, in which most of the
Council took part—the speeches being directed chiefly to attacks on
the Revenue System of Bombay, and to replies to them. His Excellency closed the debate with the following remarks :—]

I have not the least intention of detaining the Council
by entering into any discussion of this measure itself—indeed, the chief part of the debate now brought to a close
has turned on a question which, though connected with the
subject of the Bill, is distinct from it,—namely, the question of the Bombay revenue system generally. Not unnaturally, my honourable friends Mr. Gibbs and Mr. Hope
have intimated some doubt as to the regularity of that discussion. I myself entertained for a few moments some
hesitation on the point, but did not think it advisable to put
a stop, by the exercise of the powers of the Chair, to a
continuance of that discussion, because it partly arose out
of a circumstance which is of itself an anomaly,—namely,
that a Bill of this purely local character—affecting Bombay,
and, indeed, applying only to a limited portion of that Presidency—should have been brought in and passed, and subsequently dealt with by the Governor General's Council.
The discussion here, in this Legislative Council in Calcutta,
of the local affairs of Bombay would have been altogether
out of order if it had not arisen upon a measure in which
those affairs are directly dealt with ; but as that is the case,
a latitude of debate may fairly be allowed, which would
have otherwise been inadmissible.

But even if this had not been so, I should have been
quite unable to interfere after the circulation of the paper
written by an able and very intelligent Bombay officer, my
friend Mr. Lee-Warner, which relates to the question of

Dekkhan Agriculturists' Relief Act (1879) Amendment Bill.

the Bombay revenue system, and to nothing else. Of course, after that paper had been circulated to members of this Council by the honourable member in charge of the Bill, with special reference to this discussion, it would have been quite impossible for me to raise any objection to observations being made by members of this Council, which naturally arose out of a paper already in their possession, and under those circumstances I thought it advisable—being always anxious to determine any doubtful point in favour of freedom of debate —that I should not attempt to place any restriction upon the discussion which has just taken place. But I must at the same time say that I think it exceedingly inconvenient that we should attempt to discuss in this Council the strictly local affairs of the minor Presidencies, and that such a proceeding is, generally speaking, much to be deprecated, and might easily lead to serious difficulties. As regards the general question of the Bombay revenue system, I wish to reserve entirely my own opinion. My honourable friend Sir Steuart Bayley has explained the course hitherto taken with regard to that question, and has shown how revenue questions relating not only to Bombay, but to Madras also, fall in a special manner under the cognisance of the Secretary of State: so that any premature declaration of the policy of this Government would be clearly out of place. My own views on the question of suspensions and remissions of revenue are embodied in the recent Resolution of the Government of India on that subject; and, as regards the question of enhancement, I cordially concur with the views expressed by the Secretary of State, that, even when an enhancement may be reasonable in itself, it is not desirable that if it is heavy in amount it should be made at once, but that it should be introduced gradually, so as not suddenly to raise very largely the payment which the raiyats have previously been accustomed to make.

I do not think that I need detain the Council with any

Dekhean Agriculturists' Relief Act (1879) Amendment Bill.

further observations. I merely wished in the present instance to make something of protest against a course of proceeding with I think should be avoided as much as possible, and also to explain my reasons for not entering now upon the general question that has been raised, and reserving my opinion respecting it.

[The motion was put and agreed to, and the Bill was passed.]

PEOPLE'S EDITION.

SPEECHES

OF

THE MARQUIS OF RIPON,

VICEROY AND GOVERNOR GENERAL OF INDIA

1883.

VOL. II.

PUBLISHED

With the permission of His Excellency,

BY

KALI PRASANNA SEN GUPTA.

Calcutta:
PRINTED BY C. J. A. PRITCHARD, AND PUBLISHED
AT THE "STAR" PRESS,
19, LALL BAZAR STREET, CALCUTTA.

1883.

INDEX.

B.

BARRACKPORE SCHOOL. Distribution of prizes to the boys of the—	32
BENGAL TENANCY BILL.	37

C.

CALCUTTA MADRASSAH. Distribution of prizes at the— . .	4
CALCUTTA TRADES ASSOCIATION. Dinner of the— . . .	18
CALCUTTA VOLUNTEERS. Distribution of prizes to the— . .	38
CENTRAL PROVINCES. Local Self-government	1
——————————Tenancy Bill	68
CRIMINAL PROCEDURE CODE. Amendment Bill . . .	10 & 47

L.

LORD NAPIER OF MAGDALA. Unveiling of the Statue of . .	25

N.

NORTH-WESTERN PROVINCES AND OUDH. Local Boards Bill .	75

S.

SRIDHAR BANSIDHAR SCHOOL, NAWABGUNGE. Distribution of prizes at the—	20

V.

VISIT TO HER MAJESTY'S SHIP "EURYALUS"	43

SPEECHES

BY

THE VICEROY AND GOVERNOR GENERAL OF INDIA.

THE CENTRAL PROVINCES LOCAL SELF-GOVERNMENT BILL.

[THE Central Provinces Local Self-Government Bill was passed into 12th Jan. 1883. Law in the Legislative Council on Tuesday, the 12th January 1883.[1] In moving that the Bill be passed, Mr. Crosthwaite took the opportunity of explaining in detail the plan and the principles on which it had been framed, with the object of making the law clear and intelligible to those who would have to work it. The Honourables Syed Ahmed Khan, Mr. Hunter, Raja Siva Prasad, Mr. Ilbert and Mr. Gibbs spoke in support of the Bill. His Excellency the Viceroy said :—]

I really have nothing to add to the remarks which have been made by previous speakers in the course of this discussion. The Bill before us is, as has been pointed out, a Bill relating to the Central Provinces only, and consequently it is framed in accordance with the special circumstances which prevail in that district.

The Government do not put this Bill forward as a model measure which they would recommend to be followed by all the other Local Governments throughout the country. It might almost be said that the Central Provinces is one of the least advanced districts in India to which a system of local self-government can be considered to be at all applicable. It is therefore natural that a measure to be applied to a district of that description should be

---

[1] For a previous speech by the Viceroy on this Bill, see Vol. I., page 295.

The Central Provinces Local Self-Government Bill.

framed in a manner which might not be suitable to the circumstances of districts of a much more advanced description; and I desire that it should be distinctly understood that this Bill relates to the Central Provinces, and the Central Provinces only. It is a measure which we have reason to believe is well suited to the circumstances and people of those provinces; but, doubtless, many of the provisions which find a place in this Bill will not to be considered by the heads of Local Governments in other parts of India either necesarry or suitable for the populations under their charge. That being so, there is really very little necessity for me to make any remarks upon the details of this Bill. They have been ably explained by my honourable friend Mr. Crosthwaite, and commented on, with his full knowledge of such questions, by my honourable and learned friend Mr. Ilbert; and I do not think, therefore, that there are any matters upon which any further explanation with respect to the views, intentions, and objects of the Government can be required from me.

I will, however, make just one remark upon a single point of detail, alluded to by my honourable friend who introduced this discussion. He spoke of the section of the Bill—section 34—which relates to the framing of rules by the Chief Commissioner, and he said that some persons might think that a very wide discretion was left to the Local Government in respect to the framing of those rules. Now, it is very important that all persons who have to consider Bills of this description should bear in mind that the provisions which are contained in measures which will form part of the law of the land are hard-and-fast provisions which cannot be altered without referring again to the Legislature and passing a new Act. Now, in a matter of this kind, particularly at its commencement, it is very undesirable to lay down more hard-and-first rules than are necessary. What you want is, that the system should be elastic; and that you should ascertain by practical

The Central Provinces Local Self-Government Bill.

experiment what modes of self-government are most suited to the requirements and idiosyncrasies of the people in different parts of the country; for, if you tie the hands of the Government too tight by the regulations of an Act of the Legislature, that elasticity which is so desirable in order to arrive at the system best suited to fulfil the wishes and meet the requirements of the country will be altogether lost, and the Government will find itself bound, whether the measure is in practice found to be suitable or not, to enforce the provisions of the law, or else to go through the long and complicated process of again referring the matter to the Legislature. But those who are inclined to think that these rules are all too elastic, should bear in mind that we have, in this Bill, in fulfilment of the promise made in the Resolution of the Government, issued a short time ago, in respect to rules of this description, distinctly laid down that the rules issued under section 34 shall be published beforehand in draft and left for the consideration of the public for a certain period, in order that, if any objections are felt to them, those objections may be fairly represented to the Local Government.

And, certainly, if ever there was a case in which we may trust implicitly that the rules which will be made—I hope speedily—under the Bill about to become law, will be those best suited to carry out the provisions of this measure in a friendly spirit towards the spread of self-government, it is this; because it is due to Mr. Morris, whose time in the Central Provinces, I regret to think, is drawing to a close, but who nevertheless will have an opportunity of making the rules under this Bill, that I should say again what I said on the occasion of a previous discussion at Simla, that there is no civil servant in India who has shown himself, long before this question was taken up by the present Administration, more desirous of applying largely and wisely the principles of local self-government than Mr. Morris. The best thanks of the Government are due

Distribution of Prizes at the Calcutta Madrassah.

to that distinguished public servant for this part of his policy as well as for the ability with which he has so long administered the Central Provinces, over which he has been placed ; and I feel the most entire confidence that, in entrusting the initiation of the system established by this Bill to his hands, we are leaving it to one who fully and heartily approves of the principles of the Government on this subject as laid down in the Resolutions on local self-government.

DISTRIBUTION OF PRIZES AT THE CALCUTTA MADRASSAH.

17th Jan. 1883. [THE Viceroy presided at the annual distribution of prizes to the students of the Calcutta Madrassah on Wednesday afternoon, the 17th January 1883. The Madrassah was founded by Warren Hastings in 1781, with the view of enabling the Mahomedans of Bengal to acquire such a knowledge of Arabic literature and law as would qualify them for the Judicial Department, and was endowed by him with a zamindari yielding an estimated rental of Rs. 29,000. In July, 1819, the zamindari was resumed, and the rental was commuted to a fixed annual charge on the treasury of Rs. 30,000. The institution consists of two departments and a branch School. In the Arabic Department, Aratic and Persian literature, logic, rhetoric, and Mahomedan law are taught ; the course extends over six years.

The proceedings were held in a spacious open square in the centre of the building, Mr. Rivers Thompson, the Bishop of Calcutta, the Hon. J. Gibbs and Miss Gibbs, and other ladies and gentlemen, besides a large assembly of the leading Hindoo and Mahomedan gentlemen of Calcutta, being present. His Excellency—who was accompanied by Earl DeGrey, Mr. H. W. Primrose, and Capt Harbord, Aide-de-Camp—arrived shortly after 4 o'clock, and was received by the Lieutenant-Governor, Mr. Gibbs, and others. Dr. Hœrnle, the Officiating Principal, then read the annual report, after which the Viceroy distributed the prizes. His Excellency then addressed the assembly as follows :—

Mr. Rivers Thompson, Ladies and Gentlemen,—I am very glad to have learnt, from the report which was read at the commencement of our proceedings this afternoon

Distribution of Prizes at the Calcutta Madrassah.

that the progress which has been made by this institution during the past year is of such a nature as to be highly satisfactory to all who are interested in the welfare of this Madrassah; and I rejoice to be able upon this occasion to repeat those congratulations which were offered here last year by my friend Mr. Justice Wilson, when he said that the progress that this institution had made during the twelve months which were then drawing to a close had been such as might fairly satisfy all who were interested in its success. It is very pleasing to know now, after another year has passed, that that progress has still been fully maintainad.

This institution may claim a century of life, and it is, I believe, among the oldest of the educatioual establishments now existing in India; but, like all ancient institutions, it is essentially necessary that in a time of change and progress like that in which we live, the Calcutta Madrassah should maintain a steady advance, and should suit itself, as time goes on, to the changing circumstances of the period in which it has to discharge its important duties. What may have been a very satisfactory and sufficient education in the days of Warren Hastings, when this Madrassah was founded, would be regarded by all men as altogether inadequate to the needs of the present day; and while I am very glad to know that this institution has progressed with the advance of the time, I desire very earnestly to impress upon those who are concerned in its management, the necessity for steadily continuing that progress, and of making this college more and more fitted for the important work which it has now to discharge. And when I say this, I have not forgotten that this is specially a Mahomedan institution, and that it is not for me to express an opinion upon the peculiar educational needs of the Mahomedan community; but this, at least, I may say with great certainty,—that a wide, solid, and liberal education is necessary in these times for men of every race, creed, and class, if they desire to maintain

Distribution of Prizes at the Calcutta Madrassah.

their proper place in the battle of life, and to hold their own among their fellow-countrymen. (*Applause.*) As you all know, it is a cardinal maxim of the policy of the Government of India, that we should always preserve an attitude of strict impartiality towards all creeds and classes in this country. (*Hear, hear.*) What we have to do is, not to look to the race from which a man has sprung, nor to the creed which he professes, but to enquire what are his personal qualifications and what is his individual conduct; and, under circumstances like these, it behoves, as it seems to me, the leading men of every community in India to take care that their brethren in race and faith do not fall behind in the struggle of life, and to unite earnestly for that purpose. The educational task of to-day, gentlemen, is an arduous task, and for its full and complete accomplishment it requires the united action of forces of every description—of the Government on the one side, and of private individuals on the other—of public assistance and of religious zeal; and, above all, it is a task which needs that men should cast aside all mere regard for individual opinion or personal preference, and that they should unite, on all hands to accomplish one of the most important and greatest works which can be done in this day for the benefit of the Indian people. (*Applause.*) I can truly say, gentlemen that I feel a great interest in the welfare of this institution, as I do in that of all the institutions of higher and middle education in the land. You know very well that I earnestly desire to see the extension and improvement of primary education; but it would be a great error indeed if any man were to suppose that I did not desire, with equal earnestness, the maintenance and advancement of higher and middle education. (*Applause.*) And it seems to me that there are features in to-day's proceedings which may give the utmost encouragement to the friends of higher education, and especially to those who are interested in the prosperity of this institution.

Distribution of Prizes at the Calcutta Madrassah.

We have heard read out to us to-day a long list of donations of Mahomedan gentlemen who have come forward upon this occasion to testify to their deep interest in this place of education. I need not remind you of the names that are contained in this list, or of the important and many donations that have been announced. I need not recall to your recollection the Rs. 15,000 which have been given by the Amir-i-Kabir and the Rs. 6,000 by Syed Lutf Ali Khan, and the Rs. 3,000 by Syed Ali Khan, Bahadoor, and the other donations mentioned this afternoon. They show (and I am most gratified that it should be so) the strong interest that these Mahomedan gentlemen feel in the success of this institution for Mahomedan education, and their ready willingness to aid it with generous assistance. And, gentlemen, I esteem it an honour that many of the donors upon this occasion have thought fit to connect my name with the scholarships and prizes which they have established; and I can assure them and you that they could not have done anything more gratifying to me than to come forward, as they have done to-day, to contribute out of the wealth with which God has endowed them for the maintenance of this educational institution. (*Applause.*) But, gentlemen, there is another circumstance connected with to-day's proceedings which I have heard with yet greater satisfaction, and that is the contribution which has been announced as having been made by the Mahárájáh of Durbhungah. Gentlemen, that distinguished nobleman could scarcely have done a better deed than to give this proof of the sympathy which he and other Hindoos can feel for a Mahomedan place of education. We have heard, alas! on more than one recent occasion, of unhappy and disgraceful disturbances which have sprung up out of religious quarrels in more than one part of the country; and no man in India can do a better act than to set the example which the Mahárájáh of Durbhungah has set to-day, of that union in a work for the public good, which, if the

Distribution of Prizes at the Calcutta Madrassah.

example is widely followed, will tend more than anything else to put an end to these animosities which are a discredit to the country, and to bind together in close and intimate connection men of all creeds and classes in this wide land. (*Applause.*) I see, then, in these donations and in the interest which they testify as being felt in this college, a bright promise of future progress and continued prosperity for the Calcutta Madrassah ; and I can truly say that I shall watch with the deepest interest the advance of this institution. But before I conclude my observations, I want to say a few words to those who, after all, have more, perhaps, to do with the success and prosperity of this college even than the munificent donors whose gifts have been announced on this occasion. I would desire very earnestly to exhort the students of this Madrassah to do their part in promoting its prosperity. We have a homely proverb in England which runs to this effect—" You may take a horse to the water, but you cannot make him drink." So, gentlemen, you may bring students to this Madrassah : you may shower down before them all the rich stores of learning ; you may endow them with scholarships and offer them prizes; but if they do not exert themselves, if they do not do their part in the work which has to be done here, all that others do will be ineffectual, and they will obtain no benefit from the exertions of their friends. It rests, then, with you— the students of this institution—to determine whether, as years go on, it shall be a continued and increasing success. The character of the students determines mainly the character of every place of study, and the reputation of this college is in your hands. And in thus exhorting you to uphold that reputation, I might remind you that the success or failure of your career in life depends upon the use which you make of the few years of fertile youth which you will pass upon these benches. I might put before you in vivid colours how, if you waste your time here, you will be left behind in the keen struggle of these days, by those who

Distribution of Prizes at the Calcutta Madrassah.

value what you despise; and I might say with truth that worldly success and worldly fame will be the reward of your industry and will crown your efforts. But I prefer to set before you an aim less personal and less material, and to invite you to remember how great a place in the history of human learning has been, in past times, occupied by Mahomedan men of letters and men of science. Turn your eyes to those famous schools from whence so many branches of knowledge spread over Europe in the Middle Ages, and see what was then accomplished by men with whom you claim community of thought and of opinion (*applause*); and then determine that it shall not be your fault if you do not do something, little though it may be, to raise the standard of your own special education, and to make its future somewhat less unworthy of its brilliant past. (*Loud and continued applause.*)

I have one more word to say, which will perhaps not be altogether unacceptable to my young friends here. I want to ask Dr. Hœrnle whether he will be good enough to grant a holiday for the rest of the week to the students of this Madrassah.

[The students were then called upon to give three cheers for the Viceroy, which was warmly responded to. The proceedings then concluded.]

CRIMINAL PROCEDURE CODE, 1882, AMENDMENT BILL.

2nd Feb. 1883. [IN the Legislative Council held on the 2nd February, Mr. Ilbert moved for, and obtained, leave to introduce a Bill to amend the Code of Criminal Procedure, 1882, so far as it relates to the exercise of jurisdiction over European British subjects. Mr. Ilbert explained the existing law on the subject, which had been settled in 1872, and the principles by which the Government had been guided in framing the proposals which he was now asking leave to lay before the Council. "The Government," he said, "are of opinion that the time has come when the settlement which was arrived at in 1872 may with safety, and ought in justice, to be re-considered; we are of opinion that, if this question is re-opened, it ought to be settled on a permanent and stable foundation; and, finally, we are of opinion that no change in the law can be satisfactory or stable which fails to remove at once and completely from the Code every judicial disqualification which is based merely on race distinctions. . . . . . The only object which we have in view is to provide for the impartial and effectual administration of justice. It is by that test that we desire our proposals to be tried. If they are tried by that test, I am not without a confident hope that they will commend themselves both to the European and to the Asiatic subjects of Her Majesty as reasonable and just."

Mr. Evans, who said that he was not well acquainted with the rules of debate in the Council, wished to know whether the principles of the measure were to be debated on the present occasion or at a later stage. Most of the non-official members of the Council had like himself, heard for the first time to-day, what the proposed measure was. The question involved was one of the gravest importance to the English community in India, and he would ask His Lordship if he considered that it was more convenient to debate the principle of the Bill on the motion for leave to introduce it, than that the motion should be postponed so as to give time to the non-official English community in India, which was scattered far and wide in the various provinces, to make their voices heard: at any rate, he thought that it should be postponed to-day, as he felt that otherwise he could not give full consideration to it.

His Excellency the President said:—]

Nobody is pledged in the smallest degree by the introduction of this or any other Bill, and it would be obviously very unfair that Honourable Members of Council should be called upon to express an opinion on the principle of a

Criminal Procedure Code, 1882, Amendment Bill.

Bill which they have not seen. Nothing could be more lucid than the statement made by my honourable and learned friend who proposes to introduce the Bill, but, until the Bill itself is in the hands of the public, it would be unfair both to them and to the Government that any opinion should be expressed upon it, or that any discussion should take place upon the measure in this Council.

No one knows better than my honourable and learned friend Mr. Evans how difficult it is to understand a Bill, even with the clearest explanations of its provisions, until you have the Bill itself before you; and the public are sometimes perhaps a little too much inclined to criticise by anticipation measures of which they know nothing and have seen nothing; and I myself should not be in the smallest degree inclined to give any sort of encouragement to a procedure which, as I have said, is unfair both to the Government and to the public.

I need not, I am sure, say that the Government has no desire to push this matter forward without giving full time for its consideration. The proper occasion, I think, for discussing the principle of the Bill will be on its reference to a Select Committee. I look upon that stage of the procedure as standing in the place of what is called 'the second reading' in Parliament at home. In the House of Lords, a Bill is often brought in and put on the table without saying a word; in the House of Commons, this is not the case, but the occasions on which discussions arise on the introduction of a Bill are rare, and debate on the principle of the measure takes place on the second reading.

What I would, therefore, suggest would be that leave should now be given to bring in this Bill; that it should be brought in at the next meeting of the Council, and then published; and that due time should be given, before the motion is made for its reference to a Select Committee, in order to enable Members of Council to consider it

Criminal Procedure Code, 1882, Amendment Bill.

when they receive it in print, and to be prepared to discuss it fully after they have acquired a perfect knowledge of its provisions.

[Mahárájá Sir Jotindra Mohan Tagore having asked permission to address the Council on the subject of the Bill, the Viceroy remarked :—]

Although, according to strict rule, the Mahárájá has lost his turn for speaking, I am sure that this Council would wish me to give him leave to address them. And, in doing so, I should like to take the opportunity of expressing the great regret I feel that this, I believe, is the last occasion on which we shall have the presence in the Council of our honourable colleague Mahárájá Sir Jotindra Mohan Tagore. During the long period of his service in the Legislative Council, the Mahárájá has distinguished himself by his fairness, his enlightened views, and his remarkable courtesy towards all the Members of this Council.

The Government of India have derived very great advantage from the presence of my honourable friend in the Council, and it is a source of deep regret to me that the fair rule of giving a chance to others to take their place in this Council, and, therefore, of not unduly prolonging the presence in it of any one particular member, added to the Mahárájá's own desire to be relieved of duties which clash with his other engagements, has necessitated his retirement, and occasioned the great loss to the Council which must result from his absence from it.

[Mahárájá Jotindra Mohan Tagore expressed the grateful thanks of himself and his countrymen, to the Viceroy, for redeeming the promise, held out last session, to amend that portion of the Criminal Procedure Code relating to the trial of British-born subjects, and thus to remove an anomaly which had been a source of standing complaint to his countrymen. He felt, on leaving the Council, an honest pride in having occupied a seat in it while this and other great measures of reform had been either initiated or passed under the auspices of Lord Ripon ; and he concluded by tendering His Excellency his grateful thanks for the manner in which he had referred to his services.]

CALCUTTA TRADES ASSOCIATION DINNER.

[THE annual dinner of the Calcutta Trades Association took place at the Town Hall on Tuesday evening, the 6th February, the Viceroy being present for the first time on such an occasion. Upwards of two hundred gentlemen, of whom nearly one hundred were invited guests, sat down to dinner, including the Lieutenant-Governor of Bengal, the Chief Justice, the Bishop of Calcutta, the Hon. Sir Steuart Bayley, the Rev. Dr. P. Goethals, the Hon. Mr. Ilbert, the Hon. Mr. Hunter, Lieutenant-General T. F. Wilson, Archdeacon Baly, the Hon. H. S. Cunningham, Major-General Greaves, Sir Jotindrá Mohan Tagore, Babu Kristo Dass Pal, Nawab Abdul Latif, Sir Walter DeSouza, the Hon. C. Macaulay, Mr. H. W. Primrose, Lord William Beresford, Messrs J. Westland, A. Mackenzie, D. Barbour, Horace Cockerell, &c., &c.

After the toast of " The Queen-Empress and the Royal Family" had been proposed and drunk, the Master of the Association (Mr. D. Zemin) rose to propose the toast of the Viceroy's health, and in doing so was received with loud and prolonged cheering. Mr. Zemin expressed the great pleasure it afforded himself and the Association to welcome the Viceroy for the first time at their annual festival,—a pleasure which was greatly enhanced by the fact that Lord Ripon was so trusted, respected, and so highly regarded by all ranks and classes in India. He reviewed briefly the principal measures of the Viceroy's administration and dwelt upon the ultimate and lasting good which must result from His Excellency's rule in India. The Viceroy, on rising to respond to the toast, was received with much cheering He said :—]

Mr. Master, Mr. Rivers Thompson, and Gentlemen, —I thank you most sincerely for the kind and cordial manner in which you have received the toast that has just been proposed to you ; and I thank you, Sir, exceedingly for the terms in which you have been good enough to speak of the course which I have pursued since I first took upon me the duties of the great office which I have now the honour to fill. You have told us, Mr. Zemin, that this is the first occasion upon which any Viceroy or Governor-General of India has been present at this annual dinner of the Calcutta Trades Association. I cannot but think that that circumstance

Calcutta Trades Association Dinner.

must be to a great extent the result of accident, for I am quite sure that any of those distinguished men who have preceded me in the office which I now hold, would have been very glad to have come here on previous occasions of this kind, for the purpose of marking the respect which they must have entertained for this Association, and their sense of the services which it is calculated to render to the trade of this great city. (*Applause.*) But there is perhaps, in one respect some propriety in the fact, accidental though it may be, that I am the first Viceroy who has been present on an occasion of this kind ; because when I look back to my past public career I remember that I have, perhaps, been more intimately connected in England with great trading communities than any of those who have preceded me in the Government of India. (*Applause.*) I have never been connected with trade myself, but during the time that I had a seat in the House of Commons, I always represented great trading and manufacturing constituencies ; and I have therefore learnt from the earliest commencement of my public life to take a deep interest in all that concerns the development of trade, commerce, and manufactures, and to make a close and careful study of questions connected with the industry of the country (*applause*) and of the principles which ought to guide the legislation of India quite as much as they have guided the legislation of England. (*Hear, hear, and applause.*)

Sir,—I will not follow you through the catalogue of the acts of the present Government of India which you have passed in review. To do so would take too long, and it would be out of place upon this occasion ; but there is one subject which has occupied a large portion of our attention, and with which we have had a good deal to do, upon which it seems to me that I may with propriety say something on an occasion like the present. You have said with great truth, that it has been, and is, the earnest desire of the Government of India to encourage, by all legitimate

Calcutta Trades Association Dinner.

means, the development of private enterprise in this country. (*Applause.*) I remember to have heard it said, now many years ago, in the days of the East India Company, that there was a feeling that the policy then pursued in India was one which discouraged private enterprise, and looked coldly upon the investment of private capital in this country. I do not pronounce any opinion upon this occasion as to the justice of that view; but whether it was true then or whether it was not, this at least I can say without any hesitation—that the Government of India of the present day regards it as a matter of primary importance that private enterprise should be developed in this country to the utmost possible extent, and that it looks with the highest satisfaction upon every increase in the investment of private capital in Indian undertakings. (*Loud applause.*) Nay, gentlemen, I will go further, and I will say that I shall always regard it as a subject of congratulation if I see any opportunity of handing over to private enterprise any of the work which is now performed by the already overburdened Government of this country. (*Continued applause.*) I am not one of those, it is true, who believe that there is very much which any Government can do directly for the encouragement of industry or commerce; I am apt to think that any Government in any country is much more capable of doing injury than it is of giving effectual encouragement to trade. I believe that the first duty of a Government is to remove all unnecessary restrictions and to abstain from all irritating and needless interference with industry and commerce (*loud applause*); but when that has been done, and when that principle is steadily applied, there doubtless are ways in which it may be the legitimate function of Government to do something for the promotion and advancement of commerce and trade; and no doubt in this country—where the Government is accustomed, and is obliged at present, to undertake many things which are not undertaken by the Government at home—there are modes in which such encouragement may be offered in a perfectly legitimate manner; and this also I would say, that if ever there was a country in which it was of the highest importance that trade should flourish and spread, that manufactories should be established, and that new industries should be introduced, that country is India (*applause*); for I believe that there are very few things which would do more to benefit the great mass of the population of this vast peninsula—which is now mainly (I may almost say exclusively) dependent upon the land for its sustenance and support—than that there should be introduced in every part of India, other industries and other means of employment. (*Applause.*) I believe that the keen competition and the great pressure upon the land is one of the greatest difficulties with which the Government have to deal at the present time. Now, what can the Government do in this direction? This great Government is, as you all know, a very large consumer of goods, of many and varied descriptions. It makes vast purchases every year. Can those purchases be conducted in a manner more calculated in the future than they have been in the past to give legitimate encouragement to Indian industry? That was a subject which engaged the attention of the present Government of India at an early period, and when we came to look round and consider what was the source from which stores were derived, where they were purchased, and how they came into our hands, we were led to believe that sufficient efforts had not been made to procure in India itself many of those stores which, with some inquiry and with some trouble, might be purchased here as cheaply and in as good quality as they could be brought from Europe. (*Applause.*) Well, we thought that it was worth a good deal of trouble to ascertain what could be done in that direction, and we have for the last two years steadily devoted our attention to that subject. I dare say many gentlemen may have been sometimes amused

Calcutta Trades Association Dinner.

by the frequent resolutions which have appeared in the Government Gazette, very often with the signature of my excellent friend opposite, Mr. Barbour, pointing out what stores might with propriety be procured in this country; There were doubtless a lot of very small things, as it may appear, included in those lists; but yet I doubt whether, if there are any gentlemen here who are interested in the particular trades to which those lists were applicable, they object to have found that the Government had turned their attention even to those, as some persons may think, insignificant objects, and were paying real, earnest, and minute attention to discover how they might in this manner legitimately encourage all the different branches of trade and industry in the country. (*Loud applause.*) And, gentlemen, there has been in some quarters a good deal of misconception with respect to our views and intentions upon this matter. I was reading, a few weeks ago, an article in that very excellent newspaper the London *Economist*, in which the Government of India were taken to task because it was supposed that they were pursuing an unwise policy in endeavouring to purchase things in India, dearer in price and inferior in quality to those which might be procured from England or from Europe. Now that is an entire misrepresentation of the course which the Government have been pursuing. In that article the writer said, "There is no reason why the Government should carry its custom abroad if it can be served as well at home, and many reasons why it should not." That brief sentence accurately represents the course which the Government has pursued in this matter. (*Applause.*) We have never thought of purchasing things in this country which could be procured cheaper elsewhere, nor of purchasing articles of inferior quality to those which could otherwise have been obtained. We should not have been justified in doing so; we should have thus been casting an unneccessary burden upon the tax-payers of this country. What we have done, and what

Calcutta Trades Association Dinner.

we intend to continue to do, is this: We intend to search carefully in order that we may see what are the things that can be produced for our use here as cheap and as good as we can get them elsewhere; and if they are of that character, then we think it our duty and our right to give the preference to Indian productions. (*Loud applause.*) That course I hold, gentlemen, to be perfectly consistent with sound economic principles; it is one which the Government have entered upon deliberately, and which they intend to continue to pursue, and in the pursuit of which they are most anxious to spare themselves no trouble in order to make known their wants to those who can supply them, in order to ascertain, by every means open to them, whether there are traders or manufactures in the country who can meet the requirements of the Government with regard to goods of which they are the purchasers; and they are quite prepared, and most desirous, that all their arrangements with respect to the purchase of articles of this kind should be those which are most convenient to the persons engaged in the trade, and most calculated to afford the facilities to them for coming forward and offering those supplies in any department in which the Government may require them. (*Applause.*)

Then again, gentlemen, there is another direction in which the Government can do something to promote private trade and enterprise in this country,—at least, in which it can abstain from doing that which would be injurious to private trade and private enterprise,—and that is, the Government can do its best as far as possible to abstain from entering into any kind of competition with the private trader (*hear, hear, and applause*)—a competition which, with the vast resources and practically unlimited capital at the command of Government, must be ruinous to private trade. (*Hear, hear.*) We have taken some steps in this direction already, and one of them has been embodied in a resolution which was issued a short time ago with respect to jail manufactures. But, gentlemen, when I mention that topic,

Calcutta Trades Association Dinner.

I remember that it is one upon which considerable dfference of opinion exists; and under these circumstances, I will not dilate upon it now, because it would be altogether inconsistent with the courtesy and good feeling which ought to distinguish a meeting of this description, if I were to touch even for a moment upon any controversial question or to make allusion to any matter upon which difference of opinion exists, or which could in the smallest degree mar the harmony of this friendly gathering. (*Applause.*) I will therefore pass away from that question, merely repeating that it is the earnest desire of the Government of India to abstain in every way from interfering injuriously, by any of its acts, with the utmost possible developement of private enterprise and the most fruitful employment of private capital in this great country. (*Applause.*)

I will not, gentlemen, detain you longer. There is a long list of toasts before us, and there are many others whom you will desire to hear. It is sufficient for me, in conclusion, heartily to wish every possible success to the Calcutta Trades Association. (*Loud and continued applause.*) I attach great importance to associations of this description, to Chambers of Commerce, to Trades Associations, and to other bodies of a similar character. I believe that they are calculated to confer many benefits upon their members, upon the trades and industries which they represent, and also upon the Government. We have on more occasions than one derived great advantage from the representations made to us by the Calcutta Trades Association. I trust that there will always exist between that Association and the Government of India the utmost harmony and friendship. The existence of such relations will often enable the Government to explain the meaning of the measures which it may take, and to remove misapprehensions which may exist in the public mind; while on the other hand, by consulting associations such as this, and by freely listening to the opinions which they may express, this or any other

Distribution of Prizes, Sridhar-Bansidhar School.

Government will be saved from falling into many a mistake (*Hear, hear.*) Therefore, gentlemen, I look upon this Association and other similar bodies as highly useful institutions. I am rejoiced to have been able to be present on this occasion and I thank you again for the cordial welcome which you have given to me.

[His Excellency resumed his seat amid loud and prolonged applause. A number of other toasts were then proposed and replied to, and Lord Ripon left the Hall about 1 A.M.]

DISTRIBUTION OF PRIZES AT THE SRIDHAR-BANSIDHAR SCHOOL, NAWABGUNGE.

10th Feb. 1883. [ON Saturday afternoon, the 10th February, Lord Ripon distributed the prizes to the pupils of the Sridhar-Bansidhar School, Nawabgunge, situated about two miles from Barrackpore. The institution was founded in April 1880 by Babus Sridhar Mandal and Bansidhar Mandal (who contributed Rs. 18,000 for the erection of a building and Rs. 15,000 for the maintenance of the school), to meet the educational wants of the people of Nawabgunge and the adjacent neighbourhood, and who continue to take an active interest in its maintenance and progress. The number of scholars on the rolls during the year was 243, the average daily attendance being 166. The school consists of nine classes, of which the first five are Anglo-Sanscrit, the next three Anglo-Vernacular, and the last and lowest purely Vernacular. The pupils, from the 6th class downwards, are taught all subjects, except English, through the medium of the Vernacular. The school teaches up to the Entrance Examination of the Calcutta University. A number of ladies and gentlemen, European and Native, went down from Calcutta to witness the proceedings, special accommodation having been provided for their conveyance by rail and by road ; these, with a number of visitors from Barrackpore, formed a considerable assembly, and, by the time His Excellency arrived at the school, every portion of the large hall in which the ceremony was held was occupied. The approach to the school, for nearly half a mile, was decorated on both sides with flags and greenery, and overhung with banners bearing appropriate inscriptions, while a large triumphal arch was erected at the entrance. The school-room itself was tastefully decorated with evergreens, flags, mirrors, and pictures, and the band of the 4th N. I. played a selection of music during the afternoon. Lord Ripon, accompanied by

Distribution of Prizes, Sridhar-Bansidhar School.

Mr. H. W. Primrose and Captain Harbord, A. D. C., arrived shortly after 5 o'clock, the boys from an adjoining room chanting the National Anthem in Bengali as His Excellency took his seat on the dais at the head of the room. The Secretary, Mr. Audoeto Charan Mandal, having read the second annual report, a competition for a gold and two silver medals for recitation took place. The recitations were very good, and His Excellency found some difficulty in awarding the gold medal. The prizes were afterwards distributed, and the Viceroy addressed the assembly as follows :—]

Ladies and Gentlemen,—I must say that I rise on this occasion with an unusual amount of trepidation. I thought that I was coming to this school rather in the position of a country gentleman who visits a village school in his neighbourhood and distributes the prizes, than in that of a public character. When I entered this room, I found myself in the presence of a most formidable assembly. My eye first fell upon my honourable and learned friend the Legal Member of Council, and by his side I saw a yet more formidable individual, the President of the Education Commission, and then, which was more alarming still, I observed in a corner of the room the representatives of the Calcutta Press. (*Laughter.*) This, I must say, took me altogether aback, and instead of this being, as I expected, a quiet gathering in a country school, I find Members of Council, representatives of the Press, of the Foreign Office, and other public departments, assembled here to meet me ; and then, beyond that, I have been called upon to discharge one of the most difficult duties which can by any possibility fall to the charge of any man, namely, to pronounce upon the respective and relative merits of youths who, all of them, performed their part so well as those who have recited before us this afternoon. However, I must do my best. If I had known the audience I was about to address, I should, of course, have sat up last night and burnt a large number of candles in preparing an elaborate oration *(laughter)* ; but, if I am to speak the truth, I did nothing of the kind ; I went quietly to bed in perfect innocence of what was to come. (*Laughter.*)

Distribution of Prizes, Sridhar-Bansidhar School.

I have been speaking now for between thirty and forty years upon the subject of education, and I suspect my audiences are nearly as tired of hearing me on that subject as I am of speaking about it; and, therefore, I hope that on this occasion you will excuse me if I do not come up to your expectations. I can only say that I will do my best. I will not now trouble you with those—shall I say, commonplaces?—on the subject of education which we hear (happily, as I think) in these days throughout the length and breadth, not of Europe only, but also of India ; but it seems to me that there is a feature connected with this school which is one so interesting and so important that it will suffice for the few observations which I desire to address to you on this occasion. The circumstances under which this school has been founded afford me, I must say, the highest gratification. I find here two gentlemen, Babus Sridhar Mandal and Bansidhar Mandal, who have come forward to supply at their own cost the wants of this neighbourhood. It appears to have struck them that the people of Nawabgunge were in need of a school. What did they do? They did not go to the Government and beg for a large amount of funds out of the public money, with which that school might be erected; but they came forward with a generosity and public spirit which does them the highest honour. They said, " We will do this for our friends and neighbours; we will found this school, and establish it among them, that it may be for the lasting benefit of those among whom we ourselves have dwelt." (*Cheers.*) Now, I can truly say that I derive the very greatest possible pleasure from seeing two native gentlemen taking this course. I feel, as is well known, the deepest interest in the question of education, and I desire to see education in all its branches spread more widely throughout the land in India. But we all know that education cannot be supplied without funds, and no one who has attended to this subject at all can doubt that, if the education of the people of

Distribution of Prizes, Sridhar-Bansidhar School.

India were to be made complete and full, it would require an amount of money which it would alarm the boldest financier to contemplate. I find, ladies and gentlemen, that all people throughout the world have a great dislike to taxation. An English Statesman once spoke of the people of England as having what he called an ignorant impatience of taxation. (*Laughter.*) Well, I always thought that was the characteristic of my countrymen; but I must say that I do not know any people in the world who have a greater dislike of taxation than the people of India (*laughter*), and I am quite sure that if my honourable friend Major Baring were to propose to supply the educational wants of this country thoroughly and completely by the imposition of the taxation which would be required for that purpose, his popularity would very speedily disappear. Well, then, how is the thing to be done ? Our revenue is inelastic; the sources from which it is derived are few. How is this great work to be accomplished ? It can only be accomplished by private individuals coming forward and taking a share in it (*loud cheers*), and, therefore, it has been to me a source of great pleasure to have had this opportunity of coming here to-day, and of marking, in the clearest and most distinct manner in my power, my high appreciation of what has been done by these gentlemen in the establishment of this school. (*Cheers.*)

Ladies and Gentlemen,—I feel, and have felt ever since I first came to Barrackpore, a great interest in the other school which exists at Barrackpore. I am very fond of Barrackpore as a residence, and have always felt an interest in the school there, which has been supported by many successive Viceroys. I know that it may be said that the establishment of this school here at Nawabgunge may interfere with the attendance of the children at the Barrackpore school. Probably to some extent it has; but I am a friend to competition in education ; I believe that it is a great advantage that a school established and supported

Distribution of Prizes, Sridhar-Bansidhar School.

by the Government should have in its immediate neighbourhood another school established and founded by private liberality to enter into competition with it, and keep it up to the mark. (*Cheers.*) I am quite sure that when I say that, I do not speak only my individual opinion, but that that view of the subject will be endorsed by those distinguished gentlemen connected with the Education Department whom I see here on the present occasion. You all know the valuable effects of competition in a matter of this kind, and, although I think the day is far distant when, as my friend Mr. Croft said on the last occasion on which he visited this school, the time may come when the Education Department will be superfluous, nevertheless I think that it is a very good thing that Government schools in all parts of the country should have keen competition to encounter with schools established by private individuals. (*Cheers.*) Ladies and gentlemen, for these reasons I am very glad to have been able to come here to-day.

I find in the report just read, that it is the intention of the gentlemen who have founded this school to found also, in connection with it, a library and a scholarship with which they have done me the honour to connect my name; and when I say that they have done me the honour, I am not making use of an empty phrase. I *do* esteem it an honour to have my name connected with anything calculated to promote the spread of education in this great country, and I readily accept the proposals which these gentlemen have made. (*Cheers.*)

I have been asked also to become a patron of this institution: I shall very gladly do so, and I can truly say that it is my most sincere wish that this school, founded with so much generosity, may continue for many and many generations to confer large benefits on the children o this district, and to keep alive in the grateful memory o its inhabitants the names of the brothers Mandal. (*Loud and continued cheers.*)

UNVEILING OF LORD NAPIER OF MAGDALA'S STATUE.

[THE ceremony of unveiling the statue of Lord Napier of Magdala, 15th Feb. 1883. which has been erected on the Maidan, a short distance east of Prinsep's Ghat, was performed by the Viceroy on Thursday evening, the 15th February, in the presence of a large gathering, amongst whom were the Commander-in-Chief and his Staff, the Lieutenant-Governor and his Staff, the Members of Council, the Chief Justice, the Bishop of Calcutta, &c. The ground about the statue was ornamented for the occasion with venetian masts, entwined with leaves, and supporting lines of banners one from another. On the south side of the statue a dais, draped in red, was erected for the accommodation of His Excellency the Viceroy and others; and about the dais most of the general public present took up their places. A number of troops and volunteers lined the ground around the statue. The Viceroy arrived at 5-30 P.M., and was received with a royal salute. Behind the Viceroy's chair was a flag-staff for the royal standard, round which a detachment of the Warwickshire Regiment was formed up as a guard of honour. The standard was hoisted on His Excellency's arrival. Lord Ripon having taken his seat, the members of the Memorial Committee were presented to His Excellency by Sir Richard Garth, who opened the proceedings with the following address:—

"Your Excellency, Sir Rivers Thompson, my Lord Bishop, Ladies and Gentlemen,—It is a matter of regret to me that the honour of addressing you upon this occasion has not devolved upon one more worthy than myself.

"My only claim to that honour, if claim it may be called, consists in this,—that I and my friends here, whom I have just now had the pleasure of presenting to Your Excellency, are the only remaining members in Calcutta of a Committee which was formed so long ago as the year 1876 for the purpose of erecting this statue.

"On the 26th of March in that year, a public meeting was held in the Town Hall of this city, at which it was resolved, on the motion of Sir R. Temple, 'That the virtues and great public services of His Excellency Lord Napier of Magdala during a long and eminently distinguished career are worthy of being commemorated by a permanent memorial.' It was further resolved that this memorial should take the form of a statue, and we, the Committee, were appointed to carry out the necessary arrangements. It is now, Sir, no small gratification to us, who are left of that Committee, that under Your Excellency's

Unveiling of Lord Napier of Magdala's Statue.

kind auspices our duties are being brought this day to what I hope will be considered a successful conclusion.

"I can only say that if it be a success, the credit will be due, not to any exertions on our part, but mainly, I need hardly say, to the pains which have been bestowed, and I ought to add, the generosity which has been shown us, by the eminent sculptor Mr. Bœhm, who has been kind enough to undertake the work, as well as to the generous assistance and cordial co-operation which we have received from all quarters, both here and in England.

"We are greatly indebted, in the first place, to the Government of India for so kindly presenting us with the metal of which the statue is composed. We are extremely grateful to our friends in England (and amongst them, I hope I may be allowed to mention His Royal Highness the Prince of Wales) for the warm interest which they have shown and the trouble they have taken in making the arrangements there. I desire also to thank my honourable friend the Lieutenant-Governor for the kind and liberal aid which has been afforded us by the Government of Bengal; and last, but by no means least, I beg to thank our good friend Colonel Crookshank for the admirable manner in which he has performed that troublesome, and too often, I fear, thankless, office of Secretary to the Committee. (*Applause.*)

"And, Sir, I feel that I should be omitting a very important part of my duty on this occasion, if I failed to recognise in the most public manner a fact which I know will be a real gratification to Lord Napier himself, that amongst the numerous contributions to this statue, which have showered in upon us from all parts of India, a very large proportion has been received from the Native community and another large share from soldiers in the Army. (*Applause.*) Lord Napier, we all know, was pre-eminently the soldier's friend. He not only led him on to victory in the field, but he always endeavoured to promote his welfare in the camp and in the barrack. He devoted his energies not only to maintaining the efficiency but to promoting the health, the recreation, and the moral improvement of the Army, and I feel sure that it will be a real pleasure to him to learn how large a share the private soldier, both native and European, has had in erecting this tribute to his memory. (*Applause.*)

"Sir, I feel that in Your Excellency's presence, it is neither my place nor my privilege on this occasion to enlarge upon the virtues and achievements of the great and good man in whose honour we are here assembled; and I beleive I shall be consulting the wishes of all who hear me when, without further prelude, I ask Your Excellency, on behalf of the Committee, to be kind enough to unveil this statue. (*Applause.*)

Unveiling of Lord Napier of Magdala's Statue.

His Excellency the Viceroy then rose and said :—]

Sir Richard Garth, Mr. Rivers Thompson, Ladies and Gentlemen,—Before I proceed to discharge the duty to which I have just been invited by the Chief Justice, I will in accordance with the custom upon occasions of this description, ask your permission briefly to recall to your recollection some of the deeds which have marked the career of the eminent man in whose honour we are gathered together to-day; and yet it seems to me that it must be superfluous that I, or any man, should speak of Lord Napier's deeds and of his virtues to such a distinguished audience of the inhabitants of Calcutta; for there must be many here assembled to-day who have watched his honourable career, and who knew him well during the half century in which he devoted himself to the service of India; but still we are always glad to hear something of the actions of our friends, and therefore, I am sure that you will not think that I am needlessly occupying your time if, for a brief space, I mention some of the chief characteristics of Lord Napier's life.

It is now ladies and gentlemen, fifty-five years since Lord Napier entered the Bengal Engineers, and I believe that, not far short of the first twenty years of his career, he was engaged in the useful, though perhaps not brilliant, duties which attach to civil engineering employment in the lower ranks in this country; but we have plenty of evidence of the skill and the zeal with which he devoted himself to the discharge of those duties, and I am told that those who visit Darjeeling may yet see—in the excellent roads which, I understand, distinguish that station—the result of Lord Napier's labours. Somewhere about 1844 he was selected by the far-seeing eye of Lord Ellenborough to be sent on special duty to Umballa. While he was engaged in laying out the cantonments which now exist at that station, sounds of war reached his ears, and his martial spirit was roused by the tramp of troops advancing to the first Sikh war. He saw

Unveiling of Lord Napier of Magdala's Statue.

that his opportunity was come, and if a little bird that has spoken to me has not told me an untruth, and has only let out an open secret, I believe that on that occasion, without asking leave of anybody, Lord Napier jumped on his horse and galloped to the field of Moodkee. (*Applause.*) He came just in time to take a distinguished part in that bloody field and to bear his full share in the yet harder contest which followed at Ferozshah. He was present at the victory of Sobraon, which closed the first Sikh war; but, as you all know, that war did not bring our difficulties with the Sikh nation to an end, for a few years afterwards hostilities again broke out. In the siege of Mooltan Lord Napier took a highly distinguished part, and had a principal hand, as history tell us, in advising the plan of the attack which was made upon that fortress. When the battle of Goojerat ended that war, Lord Napier was called upon to take his share, as an officer of the Punjab Government, which was then constituted under Sir Henry Lawrence, and he was a fellow-labourer with Henry and John Lawrence in the great work of ruling the Sikh nation and of making them, as they now are, though the latest conquered, one of the most contented provinces of India. (*Applause.*) And he had no small part in that work, because he, by his labours as an Engineer, by that great Bari Doab Canal which he constructed, and by other works, did as much as any man among the great Punjab Administrators to confer large benefits upon the people of that province. (*Applause.*) There was another work in the Punjab which was a great one in its day—the Grand Trunk Road from Lahore to Peshawar, constructed under Lord Napier's superintendence. It is true that that work now may be regarded as insignificant by the side of the yet greater engineering triumphs which have made the railway to the fortress of Peshawar, and which have spanned the Indus by the great Attock bridge, but, in its day, that work was one of the highest utility to the defence and development of the Punjab. Time went

Unveiling of Lord Napier of Magdala's Statue.

on and the Government of India, watching the career of this distinguished Engineer, thought that they could not do better than call him down to Calcutta to take over a not unimportant position in the Engineering Department here. Hardly had he come, when the great and terrible conflict of the mutiny commenced; and when he was selected by Lord Canning to bear a great part in that contest. He served as Chief of the Staff to the gallant Outram at the relief of Lucknow, and he was associated with Sir Colin Campbell as his Chief Engineer; afterwards he was one among the foremost of those who led that wondrous chase, going on from day to day and week to week, which ended at last in the capture of the great rebel Tantia Topee; and foremost among the foremost was Robert Napier. (*Applause.*) When the mutiny was over, he was not allowed to rest, but was sent forth after a short interval to bear a great part in the China war, which broke out shortly after the mutiny was brought to a conclusion. Returning to India, I have heard it said, so modest was his own estimation of his great powers, that there was a moment when he contemplated retiring from the service; but the Government that he served knew him better, and they put him into the Council of the Governor-General as Military Member, where he discharged his duties with that zeal and energy and with that devotion to the interests of the army, which were his most marked characteristics.

From the Council of the Governor-General, he went to be Commander-in-Chief in Bombay, and in that capacity he was selected to lead forth the expedition which was sent to Abyssinia. He there to led our troops over successive ranges of lofty mountains, to the assault of a position believed by those who held it to be impregnable, and which fell, almost as the walls of Jericho fell before the Israelites at the very sight of Lord Napier's army. (*Applause.*) Then, covered with the honours that he had won in this long and distinguished career, he returned once more to

Unveiling of Lord Napier of Magdala's Statue.

India to fill the great office of Commander-in-Chief. While he held it, he was not called upon to take part in a great war, or to conduct any military operation; but he won for himself that title—to my mind more honourable than that of victor—to which Sir Richard Garth has alluded, for he was called the soldier's friend. (*Applause*) And I believe that none will contradict me when I say that, distinguished and eminent as were the men who filled the office of Commander-in-Chief in India before Lord Napier, none of them so truly fulfilled the character of the soldier's friend as he did,—that friend, mind you, of European and Native soldier alike (*applause*), for he knew the Native army well, and loved it; he knew the British soldier well, and cared for him; he cared alike for their welfare, for their health, and for their amusement, and he took care to provide for them in all these respects.

Such, then, ladies and gentlemen, was Lord Napier's career. The time came when he left the shores of the country that for nearly half a century he had served with so much zeal; and he still received further marks of his Sovereign's favour, for, as we all know, he has until the last few months been employed in the command of England's greatest fortress. (*Applause.*)

Now, ladies and gentlemen, such is a brief and very unworthy account of a noble life. What is the key to the deeds that have been accomplished and to the qualities that have been displayed? The Poet Laureate has said,—

Not once or twice in our rough island story
The path of duty was the way to glory.

(*Applause.*)

It seems to me that in those two lines, written with the pen of Genius, is described the chief characteristic of the British soldier.

The soldiers of other nations may be as brave as ours; they may have won for their respective countries victories

Unveiling of Lord Napier of Magdala's Statue.

as brilliant as any that are inscribed on British banners; but they seem to me, generally speaking, to have made the aim of their efforts the attainment of glory; to have "sought the bubble reputation at the cannon's mouth." With the soldiers of England it has been otherwise : for the end of their efforts has been to do their duty (*applause*); they have not even sought their country's glory, in the vulgar sense of the term ; they have sought to do their duty that England might be able to do hers *(applause)*; and in that, if I am not greatly mistaken, lies the true secret of the almost unvarying success which has attended the British arms. Now, ladies and gentlemen, surely if ever there was any man who laboured in that spirit in the discharge of his duties, that man was Robert Cornelius, Lord Napier. (*Applause.*) Brave among the bravest,—foremost in the hour of danger, —firm and enduring in the weary march and in the hot pursuit, he was in times of peace the gentlest among the gentle, and he has borne with a singular modesty the many honours and well-earned distinctions which have been showered upon him by his grateful Sovereign, and of which the last has made him the first Field Marshal who ever rose from the ranks of the Indian Army. (*Applause.*) He never regarded his soldiers as instruments to his own advancement. He cared for them and watched over them in times of peace with the same zeal and earnestness and vigour as those with which he led them to victory in war. He loved European and Native alike, and therefore by Native and European alike he was loved. (*Applause.*) Surely, then, it is right that we should do honour to such a man—that we should hold up his bright career for the imitation of all the members of his noble profession ; and it seems, therefore, to me to be eminently fitting that the statue of Lord Napier should take its place beside those of Hardinge, Lawrence, of Canning and Outram,—of the chiefs whom he served so well, and of the friends by whom he was so loved. (*Applause.*)

Distribution of Prizes, Barrackpore School.

[The cloth enveloping the statue was then removed by a squad of the Royal Warwickshire Regiment, and, as the statue stood revealed, the guns in the Fort boomed forth, the troops gave a general salute due to a Field Marshal—that is, the regimental colours were drooped, arms presented, and bands played a march. His Excellency the Viceroy, having examined the statue of Lord Napier, then drove off under the escort of the Body-Guard, the troops giving a royal salute. The proceedings having thus terminated, the troops were ordered back to quarters, and the large gathering gradually dispersed.]

DISTRIBUTION OF PRIZES TO THE PUPILS OF THE BARRACKPORE SCHOOL.

17th Feb. 1883. [ON Saturday afternoon, the 17th February, the Viceroy distributed the prizes to the Pupils of the Barrackpore School. The proceedings took place close to Government House, on the lawn, the boys being seated on two long rows of benches placed opposite each other. His Excellency was accompanied by the Marchioness of Ripon, Mr. H. W. Primrose, and Captain Harbord, A. D. C.

At the conclusion of the reading of the annual report by the Head Master, a recitation from Shakespeare was given by two of the boys. It showed a marked improvement on previous similar recitations, both as to manner of delivery and pronounciation, and the boys, much to their gratification, subsequently received a prize each from Their Excellencies for their efficiency. The distribution of prizes then took place, after which His Excellency addressed the boys as follows :—]

My Young Friends,—I am very glad to welcome you once more to this park, and to see you again assembled here. I heard with great pleasure the recitations which have just taken place, in which the boys who took part in them fully sustained the character which the representatives of this school attained in that respect last year. I have listened with great attention to the report which was read at the commencement of these proceedings ; and, though I regret to find that the students from this school have not been so successful on a late occasion at the Entrance Examination of the Calcutta University as

Distribution of Prizes, Barrackpore School.

they had been previously, yet I am quite ready to accept the explanation which has been offered by your head master for your failure at the present time, in the earnest hope that you will use every endeavour to retrieve the reputation of this school upon a future occasion. I can assure you that I shall watch the matter with very great attention for I feel a strong interest in this school, as all my predecessors in the office of Governor General of India have always done. I enjoy my visits to Barrackpore very much, and, from the first time I came here, I learned to feel a strong interest in the prosperity and advancement of this institution. The circumstances which have attended the Entrance Examination this year have led me to think that it is desirable that I should make some alteration in the character of the prizes which I have hitherto offered to the students of this institution. I think that, on the first occasion when I met you here, I said that I should very likely change the subjects for which these prizes were given from time to time, and what I propose to do now is this: Instead of the two books which have been offered for prizes in particular subjects this year and last year, I intend next year to offer a prize of Rs. 100 to the student who takes the best position in the Entrance Examination of the Calcutta University; and I earnestly trust that all of you, my young friends, who are sufficiently advanced to take part in that examination will do your utmost to win the prize.

In the report, allusion has been made to the school which has recently been established at Nawabgunge. I am not surprised to learn that the establishment of that school in this immediate neighbourhood has diminished the number of students attending at the Barrackpore school. That was natural, and to be expected. But I am very glad to find that your master is not inclined to view with undue jealousy the establishment of that institution, which is calculated undoubtedly to confer many benefits upon the

Distribution of Prizes, Barrackpore School.

people who dwell at Nawabgunge itself; and I trust that the friendly rivalry which will exist between that school and this school will ultimately tend to the mutual advantage of both. You should recollect, my young friends, that this Barrackpore School has a great advantage (at all events, in one respect) over the school at Nawabgunge,—in that it has been established many years, and that it has something of a history. This school has been in close connection with a long series of Viceroys and Governors General of India, and it behoves you, who belong to an institution which is comparatively old as an educational institution in this country, to do your utmost to uphold its reputation, and, by devoting yourselves zealously to your studies, to take care that it does not fall in the smallest degree into disrepute. (*Cheers.*)

Now, I do not know that I could employ any better means of inciting you to take the utmost advantage of the benefits which this institution is calculated to confer upon you if you make the best use of the instruction which is here offered to you, than by briefly alluding to the life of one who was, now many years ago, a student in the Barrackpore School. The student whose example I desire to set before you on this occasion is the late Dr. Bolanath Bose. His family lived in the neighbourhood of Barrackpore, but his father died when he was still very young, and left his mother with young children in a state of much distress. Young Bolanath had therefore only to rely upon his own abilities and his own energy; but he had one great advantage when he was about eight or ten years old—this Barrackpore School was established in the neighbourhood of the residence of his family, and he was at once sent there, and he made the best use in his power of the advantages of the institution. At an early period of his career as a scholar he attracted the attention of Lord Auckland, who was at that time Governor-General

Distribution of Prizes, Barrackpoore School.

of India; and that nobleman followed his career with very great interest for many years. When his time of schooling in the Barrackpore School came to an end, Lord Auckland testified the interest that he felt in him by taking measures to enable him to attend the Calcutta Medical College; and I understand that while he used to spend his weeks in Calcutta, he was in the habit of walking back to Barrackpore every Saturday to see his family, and of returning to Calcutta on foot the following Monday. Well, he made good use of his time at the Calcutta Medical College, and at last, by the generosity of the late Baboo Dwarkanath Tagore and other gentlemen, he and three companions, I think, were enabled to undertake what was then regarded as the perilous journey to England, in order that he might have the advantage of studying in the medical institutions there. In the course of that study he won many a prize, and, if I mistake not, he was the first native of India who took the degree of Doctor of Medicine in the University of London.

While in England he enjoyed still the favour of Lord Auckland and of other gentlemen who had felt an interest in him in his own country, and efforts were made to get him admitted to the regular Indian Medical Service; but unfortunately that Service was not then open, as it now is, to the natives of this country, and those efforts failed; but Dr. Bolanath Bose returned to India with a strong recommendation in his favour to the Government, from his friends in England. He was immediately employed in his profession by the Indian Government, and filled many important medical offices during his long career, both in time of peace and in time of war; for he was present in the second Sikh campaign, and received, I think, a medal for the battle of Chillianwala. A few years ago he retired from the service upon pension, and he died in the course of last year.

Now, my young friends, that is a short history of one who began life as a young boy in the Barrackpore School,

Distribution of Prizes, Barrackpore School.

—just as any of the younger boys I see before me should begin their tuition now—and you see to what a position he attained: you see what honours he won in the fair and open competition of the London University ; and you see what a career he made for himself. Well, I do not say that everybody in the Barrackpore School has the abilities which marked the career of Dr. Bolanath Bose ; but this I do say,—that if you will each of you set his example before you ; if you will each of you devote yourself to the studies in which you are now engaged, with the energy with which he attended to his studies when he was a schoolboy, although you may not attain to all the distinctions which he won for himself, nevertheless you have within your reach ample means in this institution for winning for yourselves a good position in life. Remember that he had no advantages of wealth—he was, as his story tells us, a very poor boy ; it was entirely by his own exertions and his own efforts that he attained to the positions which I have described to you ; and the best advice, my young friends, that I can give you, in the interests of this school and your own interests, is, go and do likewise. (*Cheers.*)

[The boys then adjourned to another portion of the grounds, where, provided by Their Excellencies, they found a sumptuous repast of Hindoo sweetmeats, served up in true orthodox style, awaiting them.]

BENGAL TENANCY BILL.

[IN the Legislative Council held on the 2nd March, the Hon. Mr. Ilbert introduced a Bill to amend and consolidate certain enactments relating to the Law of Landlord and Tenant within the territories under the administration of the Lieutenant-Governor of Bengal. Mr. Ilbert delivered an exhaustive statement on the subject of the Bill which occupied nearly three hours. He pointed out at great length the necessity for the measure, reviewed the whole history of past legislation on the subject, and explained in detail the principles of the Bill. At the conclusion of his speech, His Excellency made the following remarks :—]

2nd March 1883.

I believe it will be in accordance with the general understanding, and I think it will be the best course which I can suggest to my honourable colleague for the Council to pursue, that after the very able statement of my honourable and learned friend no discussion should take place upon this question at present; because it is obvious that in a matter of this magnitude members of Council would naturally desire to have time to consider that statement, and the Bill with which it is connected, and therefore what I would propose is this—that we should, when the motions now before the Council with regard to this measure have been passed, take the further consideration of it on Monday, the 12th, and, if it should be necessary to adjourn the debate, on Tuesday, the 13th of this month. The delay till Monday will give sufficient time, considering how fully the Bill has been discussed, and how long the matter has been before the public, to enable us to take the further discussion of this Bill on that day, it being clearly understood that no other steps will be taken upon it now, so that the public will have ample time—some eight months—to consider the whole question and make all representations to the Government before the Bill goes before a Select Committee.

The only other remark which I would desire to make is this. The Government propose to give to members of

Council, and to the public at once, all the papers connected with this case. As a rule, the Secretary of State objects to the publication in India of despatches to and from himself, but I have obtained Lord Kimberley's permission in this case, regarding it as one of exceptional importance, to publish at once, and without waiting for their being published in England, the despatches which have passed between the Government of India and the Secretary of State on this question ; so that the papers which will now be given to the public will be full and complete.

If my honourable colleagues accept the proposal which I have made, no further discussion will take place now. The Bill will be published, and we will take up the question again on Monday, the 12th of March.

DISTRIBUTION OF PRIZES TO THE CALCUTTA VOLUNTEERS.

3rd March 1883. [ON Saturday afternoon, the 3rd March, Her Excellency Lady Ripon distributed the prizes to the Calcutta Volunteers on the grounds of the Calcutta Cricket Club. The muster was a large one, numbering more then five hundred men, while the number of spectators present was unusually large. Their Excellencies arrived at half-past 5 o'clock, and after receiving and returning the salute of the Volunteers, the Viceroy walked down the line with Major Hutchison and inspected the corps. When the inspection was over, His Excellency returned to the centre of the line, and standing a little in advance of the audience, addressed the Volunteers as follows :—]

Major Hutchison, Officers, Non-Commissioned Officers, and Members of the Calcutta Volunteers,—I am very glad to have an opportunity of meeting you once more, and to be able on this, as on previous occasions—and even perhaps to a greater degree than on previous occasions—to offer to you my congratulations upon the position and progress of this corps. You have largely increased in numbers since we met twelve months ago, and two new companies

Distribution of Prizes to the Calcutta Volunteers.

have been added to your strength from the members of the Secretariat of the Bengal Government. I also rejoice to learn that the shooting of this year has shown a marked improvement upon that of the previous twelve months—good as that shooting was; and I am very glad to be able to congratulate Sergeant Spooner on having retained the pre-eminence which he won last year, and on having once more carried off the prize given by myself. I only hope that he does not mean always to monopolise the winning of that prize.

The Mounted Company has increased in a marked degree, not only in its numbers, which have doubled, but also in its efficiency, which is, I am informed, this year 50 per cent. better than it was last year; and I rejoice at this especially, because it shows that I was not wrong when I ventured to say twelve months ago that, although the task which the Mounted Company had undertaken was a more difficult task than that which fell to the lot of the infantry, neverthless, I was quite sure that by their exertions they would take care that the general standard and character of the corps did not suffer in their hands. That prophecy, I am pleased to think, has turned out to be correct. Major Hutchison, I owe the knowledge of these facts to your kindness, and to the information which you have placed in my hands. But I am able to appeal in regard to the efficiency of this corps to other testimony of a completely independent character; and I am very glad indeed to say that I have learned from General Hughes that he was greatly pleased at the improvement he observed in the corps at their inspection the other day, and with the hearty zeal and interest which was felt by officers and men alike in the duties to which they have devoted themselves. It is to me very gratifying to observe the strength in which this corps has mustered to-day, for I see in it a proof of the progress of its numbers, and of the devotion of its members to the duties which they have

Distribution of Prizes to the Calcutta Volunteers.

undertaken. I was somewhat sorry to find that, during the last twelve months, this corps was unable to avail itself of the means which were placed at their disposal by the Government with a view to their going for a few days into a camp of exercise. I can very well understand the difficulties that might come in the way of carrying out a project of that kind; at the same time I must say now, as I said last year, that I believe even a day or two in camp is a very excellent training for any volunteer corps, and that it gives them an amount of experience which cannot be otherwise obtained. But you have here in Calcutta a great advantage—an advantage which makes up to no inconsiderable extent for an occasional want of the benefits of a camp—in being able to drill from time to time with Her Majesty's regular troops. I am glad to hear that you have availed yourselves of that advantage largely, and I am quite sure that all of you will have found the benefits which are to be derived from taking your place side by side with Her Majesty's regular forces. They no doubt must be your model. We volunteers are not conceited enough to suppose that with the limited opportunities at our disposal we can attain to their efficiency or to their skill; but, at least, they are an example which every volunteer can set before him; they are the model on which volunteer corps should be formed; for, after all, they and you obey the same gracious Sovereign; they and you are equally engaged in her service and form part of her military forces.

One of the principal circumstances of the past year in connection with this corps has been the absence of your commanding officer, my friend Colonel Graham. When he went on leave, it became my duty to consider whom I should select to officiate in his absence, and, after turning the matter over very carefully, I came to the conclusion that the best choice I could make in the interests of the corps was to offer the post of commandant to Major Hutchison; and it is a great pleasure to me to know from

Distribution of Prizes to the Calcutta Volunteers.

subsequent circumstances that you yourselves appreciate the justice of that choice, and that you have found the benefits which have resulted from his command. I know this, because some months ago, when a new Regulation, issued by the Horse Guards at home, would have suddenly removed Major Hutchison from the command of this corps, you gave me to understand how much you felt that it was for your interest that he should remain with you, at all events for a time. I knew that the Regulation being a general one, there was little chance of any exception being made to it upon a general representation from the Government; but I took the course of making, as your Honorary Colonel, a personal appeal to the Commander-in-Chief at home, and His Royal Highness the Duke of Cambridge most gladly and willingly listened to that appeal and readily gave his consent to waive the Regulation in this case, so far as to allow Major Hutchison to remain with you until the termination of the present drill season. Well, we have seen in the results attained, and the good report which the General has just given of you, the fruits of Major Hutchison's labours, and it will be a pleasure to me to have the opportunity of assuring the Duke of Cambridge that his kindness in this matter has not been thrown away. But, alas! gentlemen, that kindness was only able to keep Major Hutchison with you until the conclusion of the present drill season. That period is close at hand; and as Colonel Graham will not return to you for another year, I again have the duty of selecting an officiating commandant. I can assure you that, in making that choice, I shall endeavour to find an officer well qualified for that important post, and worthy of this gallant corps. I shall take counsel with my friend Major Hutchison in the matter, and I have no doubt that in a short time I shall be able to select some one who will not be unworthy to succeed those who have hitherto filled the office of Commanding Officer.

Distribution of Prizes to the Calcutta Volunteers.

This is the third occasion upon which I have had the pleasure of meeting you since at your request I have worn this uniform. On the first occasion I impressed upon you the great importance of drill. Last year I urged you to devote yourselves with zeal to your duties, and to remember that they were real and substantial duties, and not matters of show and parade. This year I have no need to repeat that advice, because the progress which you have made during the last twelve months proves that no such advice is needed from me or from any man. You have shown that you are determined to go on from year to year, not merely maintaining, but advancing the character of this corps; and by so doing you maintain the place which you ought to hold among the honourable roll of the Queen's Volunteers, and you make the wearing of your uniform a proud distinction for any man.

Major Hutchison, I am confident that this excellent corps will, in the future as in the past, uphold the reputation which it has obtained, and that it will prove itself worthy of its position, by its dicipline, by its drill, by its success in shooting, and, above all, by its loyal devotion to our gracious Sovereign.

[The prizes were then distributed by the Marchioness of Ripon.]

VISIT TO HER MAJESTY'S SHIP "EURYALUS."

[On Wednesday afternoon, the 7th March, the Viceroy visited Her 7th March 1883.
Majesty's Ship *Euryalus*. His Excellency was received on board
by Rear-Admiral Sir William Hewett, Captain Hastings, and a large
number of ladies and gentlemen who had been invited for the occasion, amongst whom were His Excellency Sir Donald Stewart, Commander-in-Chief in India ; the Hon. Rivers Thompson, Lieutenant-
Governor of Bengal ; Mrs. and Miss Thompson ; His Excellency Sir
Frederick Roberts, Commander-in-Chief of Madras, and Mrs. Roberts ;
Lord and Lady Charles Beresford, Lady Elizabeth Clough Taylor,
Colonel Pretyman, and others. On His Excellency's arrival the yards
were manned, and a guard of honour of marines was drawn up on the
quarter-deck. The weather was very unfavourable, and heavy rain
fell during His Excellency's visit. After the crew had been put through
some broadside exercise on the gun deck and the Viceroy had inspected the ship, Sir William Hewett conducted His Excellency to the
poop, where the officers and men were assembled, and addressing His
Excellency spoke as follows :—

My Lord Marquis,—I have to thank Your Lordship for the honour
Your Lordship has paid the East Indies Squadron by coming on board
the *Euryalus* to-day, and in the name of the Captains, officers, and
crews of the ship, I beg leave to present Your Lordship with this gun
which Captain Hastings took at Chalouf with a party of seamen
and marines, and two companies of the Seaforth Highlanders. I
trust Your Lordship will accept it as a memento of the Egyptian
Campaign of 1882, in which British sailors and soldiers fought side
by side with the native troops of India for the honour of the Queen-
Empress.

His Excellency replied as follows :—]

Sir William Hewett,—I thank you very much for presenting me with this memorial of an action which, though
it was not one of great magnitude, afforded an opportunity
for the display of those qualities of courage, of firmness, and
of dash, which distinguish British soldiers and sailors, and
I shall always preserve this little gun as a memento of the
deeds which have been done in the late campaign ; but I
have not only to thank you, Sir, for this present which will
form a valuable portion of my family, and, as I trust, of my
hereditary, possessions, but still more for the most invaluable

Visit to Her Majesty's Ship "Euryalus."

and untiring assistance which you gave to the troops that were sent from India to take part in the late operations in Egypt. I can assure you that the Government of India will ever fell deeply grateful for the cordial aid which you rendered to them and to their officers, without which that Expedition could not have been so speedily and readily disembarked, and could not have won for itself those commendations which it has received from the hands of all who witnessed that disembarkation. And I must avail myself, with your permission, of this opportunity not only to thank you, Sir, the Admiral of this Squadron, but also your officers and seamen and marines, for the aid which they too gave to that Expedition. Even your zeal and energy, Sir, would not have been sufficient to have accomplished that which was done so speedily and effectively on that occasion, if you had not been heartily seconded by every officer and every man under your command. It is not, however, only on account of the help which was thus readily given to the Expedition from India, that I rejoice to have this opportunity of meeting for a few moments those whom I may take as the representatives of the Indian Squadron. I rejoice also because it enables me to recognise the other services which those seamen rendered upon that occasion to their Queen and country.

I recollect how speedily and skilfully they secured the safety of the canal; how they protected that great waterway of all nations from the danger of interruption throughout the military operations; and I recollect still more that smart and gallant operation by which you, Sir, seized the town of Suez in the face of an almost overwhelming force with that vigour and boldness which always distinguish British sailors. I shall always be proud to feel that I had some little hand in the success of that operation, because when you contemplated the sudden occupation of Suez, you asked me to aid you in obtaining permission from the

Visit to Her Majesty's Ship "Euryalus."

Government at home to undertake that operation. I was most happy to do so. I knew that it was a somewhat risky undertaking; I knew that you might be opposed by a large force the exact strength of which you did not know, but I had confidence in you that you would not undertake anything which you felt you could not accomplish; and I had confidence, too, that those under you would be able to accomplish anything which you undertook. Therefore it was to me a great pleasure to second your efforts so far as it was in my power to do so. But it was not only in these ways that valuable services were rendered by the men under your command in the late operations. They had another task to perform much more trying, and, to English sailors, much more disagreeable than that of facing any number of foes in battle. They had the hard and trying work of disembarking stores and of aiding in the landing of troops, of patrolling the canal through long weary weeks with no hope in the minds of most of them that any of them would have the advantage of going to the front and meeting their enemy face to face; and I think that services of that kind—trying in their nature and wearying to gallant men—require as much commendation as the most gallant performances under fire.

But, Sir, the British Navy, though not represented in great strength in the Egyptain operations, was represented there by one gallant man whose name will always be recorded when the story of Tel-el-Kebir is told; for, gentlemen, there are few instances of bravery and devotion more touching than that which is told us in the story of Lieutenant Rawson, who, when he had conducted the troops to the front of the enemy's position by the light of a star, and had fallen beneath the fire of the foe, turned to his General and with his dying voice said, " Did I not lead you straight ?"

Sir, I am glad to have had this opportunity of welcoming to Calcutta the representatives of the Indian Squadron.

Visit to Her Majesty's Ship "Euryalus."

The services that that Squadron renders in ordinary times may win for them little reputation and may be little seen by others, but I can assure you that they are highly appreciated by the Government of India.

We know that service on the Indian station is in many respects peculiarly trying—indeed, I believe it may be said to be one of the most trying stations of the British Navy; and we know, also, that should the hour of danger come and should we have to make a call on you, you would be ever ready to answer.

Sir William Hewett,—I rejoice to have had this opportunity of meeting you, your officers and your men, and I shall always cherish that gun as a memorial of the services of the Indian Squadron in the Egyptian War and of the pleasant visit paid to your ship this afternoon.

[His Excellency and party then returned on shore, under a salute of 31 guns from the *Euryalus.*

The following is the inscription on the gun presented to His Excellency:—

Captured on the 20th of August 1882 at Chalouf, on the west bank of the Suez Canal, twelve miles from Suez, by landing parties of seamen and marines from Her Majesty's Ships *Euryalus, Seagull,* and *Mosquito,* and two companies of the second battalion of the Seaforth Highlanders; and presented to His Excellency the most Honourable the Marquis of Ripon, K.G., G.M.S.I., C.I.E., Viceroy and Governor General of India, by Rear-Admiral Sir William N. W. Hewett, K.C.B., K.C.S.I., V.C., Commander-in Chief of Her Majesty's Naval Forces, East Indies, on behalf of the captors.—Egypt, 1882.

CRIMINAL PROCEDURE CODE AMENDMENT BILL.

[THE Criminal Procedure Bill was brought up again in the Legis- 9th March 1883. lative Council on Friday, the 9th March, when Mr. Ilbert moved that the Bill, so far as it relates to the exercise of jurisdiction over European British subjects, and Statement of Objects and Reasons be published in the *Gazette of India* and in the local official Gazettes in English and in such other languages as the Local Governments think fit. The Council sat till a quarter to 8 o'clock in the evening, nearly nine hours, all the members (with the exception of Messrs. Baring and Hope) taking part in the debate on the Bill. At the close of the discussion the Viceroy spoke as follows :—]

I am very sorry that I should feel it my duty to detain the members of this Council yet a while after the lengthened and able discussion to which we have listened for so many hours; but I feel bound to make some statement, before this discussion closes, of the grounds upon which the Government have proceeded in introducing this Bill, and to explain the reasons which led them to think that it was a right and a reasonable measure. The observations which I wish to make now will be, as far as possible, of a strictly practical character. I do not intend or desire to enter into needless controversy, for I wish to reserve to myself the freedom carefully to weigh and consider the arguments which have been adduced in the course of this debate on both sides of the question at issue. It has been to me a source of regret that I have not had an opportunity before to-day of explaining the course which the Government has pursued; but that I have not had an earlier opportunity of doing so has not been my fault. It was the intention of the Government to have taken a discussion upon this Bill upon the 23rd of February. We never had the least intention of hurrying this measure through the Council, or of proceeding with it further than the stage which I described when it was brought in as the second reading stage during the present Calcutta season; but we did propose, and it was necessary that we should propose

Criminal Procedure Code Amendment Bill.

as the rules stood when this Bill was brought in, that it should have been referred to a Select Committee before we left here, with a view to its being afterwards circulated and published as the rules required. But when my honourable friends Mr. Evans and Mr. Miller became acquainted with the intention of the Government to take a further stage of this Bill on the 23rd of February, they represented that they were somewhat taken by surprise by that proposal. Not that I understood them to make any complaint of want of good faith on the part of the Government; but they urged that they did not expect any such discussion to come on on that date. In consequence of those representations, I had an interview with my honourable and learned friend, Mr. Evans, on the 19th of February, and I then said to him that I was anxious that this discussion should take place, because I felt that it was only fair to the Government that they should have an early opportunity of explaining at greater length than had been explained by my honouarble and learned friend Mr. Ilbert, when he brought in this Bill, the objects of this measure, and the reasons which had induced them to submit it to this Council. I said to my honourable and learned friend Mr. Evans—" You may perhaps object to a discussion, in the nature of second reading, but it is possible for us under the present rules to take a formal discussion upon a reference of this Bill to Local Governments; that would afford a sufficient opportunity for the statement that I propose to make, and would not involve a discussion upon the principle of the Bill." My honourable and learned friend took time to consider whether he could agree to that proposal, or whether he must adhere to the objection previously urged on his own behalf and on that of Mr. Miller to the discussion on the date proposed, and on the next day he informed me that he could not waive that objection. I then had to choose between putting my honourable and learned friend and Mr. Miller at some disadvantage, and putting

Criminal Procedure Code Amendment Bill.

myself and the Government at some disadvantage. I chose the latter alternative. It has been one of the many accusations made against the Government, that they delayed a further explanation on this subject: those who have used that argument will now have an opportunity of judging of the justice of their charge. I may as well also say, as my honourable and learned friend is here and will bear me out, that, when I saw him on the 19th of February, I explained to him that the Government had no intention of passing the Bill during the present session; to that my honourable and learned friend assents. I was, therefore, somewhat surprised when I saw next day a statement in Reuter's telegram, that something had been said in the House of Commons, which appeared to imply that this measure was going to be pressed forward now; and I immediately explained to the Secretary of State that that statement was not correct. It was founded on an entire misapprehension of the intentions of the Government. It would have been totally inconsistent with the declared policy of the present Government of India, if they had thought of unduly pressing forward this measure, and of not affording the fullest opportunity to the public and those interested in the matter to consider it. My honourable friend Mr. Miller touched upon that point, and he seemed, I thought, somewhat to complain that the public had not been consulted in this case in the manner in which we professed to consult them in respect to our legislative measures. Now, that charge—if it was meant as a charge—is founded on a mistake. The Government never professed that they would submit their Bills to the public before being brought in. No Government ever did, or could do, such a thing. All that we said was that, when our measures were brought in and published, the public should have the fullest opportunity of considering them; and that we ourselves desire to consider any representations which might be made to us, upon any proposal for

Criminal Procedure Code Amendment Bill.

legislation which we might so submit. To that course we have strictly adhered in this case, and have acted in perfect and absolute accordance with all our professions in respect to giving the public full time to consider our legislative proposals.

I thought it necessary to make these observations in order to clear away some misapprehensions and misrepresentations which have surrounded this matter for some time.

And now I will proceed to state very briefly the history of this transaction. Something was said upon the occasion of the introduction of this Bill by Sir Jotíndra Mohan Tagore about an undertaking which had been given him last year to the effect that this subject would be considered by the Government of India. What took place on that occasion was this. When the Criminal Procedure Code was before the Council last year, one of my honourable colleagues—I cannot exactly remember which—who was a Member of the Select Committee on that Bill, came to me and said that Mahárájá Jotíndra Mohan Tagore had told the Select Committee that he intended to raise the question of the powers of Native Magistrates to exercise jurisdiction over European British subjects. That was at a time when the Bill had nearly reached its last stage, and my honourable colleague said, with perfect justice, that it would be entirely impossible to take up a question of such magnitude upon that stage of the Bill; and he said to me, "I think, if you were to speak to the Mahárájá and tell him that, if he did not bring this matter forward now, the question would be considered by the Government, he probably would not press his notice of amendment." I replied, " I will consult my colleagues;" and I did consult the Members of the Executive Government at that time, and it was with their full consent that I told Mahárájá Jotíndra Mohan Tagore that the subject in which he was interested should receive the full consideration of the

Criminal Procedure Code Amendment Bill.

Government. Of course, by so saying I gave no pledge whatever to the Mahárájá as to what would be the decision at which the Government would ultimately arrive. All that I did say was—and that promise I and my colleagues intended to keep—that we would consider this question after the new Criminal Procedure Code had passed. But, before we had taken any steps whatever to fulfil that pledge, we received from Sir Ashley Eden a letter which is contained in these papers, and that letter winds up as the summary of the opinion of Sir Ashley Eden with these words :—

" For these reasons Sir Ashley Eden is of opinion that the time has now arrived when all Native members of the Covenanted Civil Service should be relieved of such restrictions of their powers as are imposed on them by Chapter XXXIII of the new Code of Criminal Procedure, or when at least Native Covenanted Civilians who have attained the position of District Magistrate or Sessions Judge should have entrusted to them full powers over all classes, whether European or Native, within their jurisdictions."

That opinion was expressed to us by the Lieutenant-Governor of Bengal ; it was a clear and distinct opinion. There is not one word in Mr. Cockerell's letter from which I have quoted which indicated any probability that a proposal of that kind would be received,—I will not say with resentment, but even with disapproval—by any portion of the community. Now, it is not necessary that I should recall to the recollection of this Council who was the person who made that recommendation. You all know that Sir Ashley Eden had been for five years Lieutenant-Governor of Bengal ; you all know that he was a man of large experience, and that he was intimately acquainted with the feelings of the European population ; and certainly there was ample proof that he had their respect and confidence in the remarkable ovations which he received just before he left the country. Sir Ashley Eden did not accompany that letter by any other communications upon the subject, and therefore I had no doubt

Criminal Procedure Code Amendment Bill.

whatever that it contained his deliberate opinion and advice to the Government of India. My honourable and learned friend Mr. Evans says that Sir Ashley Eden only wanted to put his opinion on record ; and he did not at all mean that anything should be done about it now. He only desired to say what he should like to see done at some future opportunity. But, in the first place, he says distinctly, in the summing up of his letter, "the time has now arrived for the change ;" and, in the next place, it must be borne in mind that, if Sir Ashley Eden did not mean that the question should be taken up at an early date upon his proposal, he had a perfect opportunity of saying so ; because, by a singular coincidence marking the high respect entertained for that distinguished man by Her Majesty's Government, he went straight from the Government of Bengal to the Council of the Secretary of State at Home ; he was a member of that Council when our proposals were submitted to and sanctioned by the Secretary of State : and, therefore, if we had misinterpreted his views as my honourable and learned friend appears to think, or if we had acted hastily on his opinion, he would undoubtedly have said so : and I cannot for a moment think that my noble friend Lord Hartington would not have communicated the fact to me: he did not do so. I should like to say one other word about Sir Ashley Eden. In the earlier stages of this controversy, before a large number of persons took to using strong language, they used language of a milder kind, and they talked about this Bill as an ideal and sentimental measure. Now, I must say that, if ever I came across a man in my life who was not remarkable for the sentimental side to his character, that man was Sir Ashley Eden. I do not think that I ever knew a man less likely to be led away by vague sentiment or mere theory than Sir Ashley Eden. Then, what did Government do ? If they had been so very keen to carry out this proposal, if they had been so very ready to

Criminal Procedure Code Amendment Bill.

proceed rashly in this matter,—they would have had a very fair ground for acting at once, in the mere fact that a man so experienced as Sir Ashley Eden had recommended them to take that action. But they did nothing of the kind; they consulted the Local Governments on the subject, and the opinions of those Local Governments are before this Council. I have heard it said that those Local Governments felt themselves bound to give opinions which they thought would be agreeable to the Government of India. Well, really it is needless on behalf of the Local Government that we consulted—of men so eminent as those who fill the office of heads of those Governments—for me to reply to a charge of that description. The question was very carefully considered by those Governments, and their opinions are, with the single exception of the Local Government of Coorg, in favour of amending the present law. It is quite true that the Government of Madras were divided among themselves, and that the opinion given in favour of the Bill was only decided by the casting vote of the Governor of that Presidency. It is also true that another gentleman, Mr. Howell, has given an opinion which, if not absolutely clear, must on the whole be regarded as unfavourable to this proposal, but he reported as Commissioner of the Birárs to the Resident at Haidarábád, who advocated the principle of this Bill; and therefore I am strictly correct in saying that all Local Governments, with the exception of Coorg, were in favour of an alteration of the law. My honourable and learned friend Mr. Evans, said that the only Local Government that is really concerned with this question at all is the Government of Bengal. But it was the Government of Bengal which started the question. I do not observe, however that the European community in other parts of India appear nclined to admit that they have nothing to do with this subject; and I venture to think that all Local Governments have an interest in this matter, and are entitled to speak

Criminal Procedure Code Amendment Bill.

upon it. Can it be supposed that those distinguished men—many of them personal friends of my own—who are at the head of Local Governments, if they had anticipated—I will not say danger, but—serious inconvenience, would not have advised me privately that this was a measure that ought not to be pressed forward. There are, doubtless, in these papers differences of opinion between different Local Governments, as to the extent to which this measure should go, just as there have been differences among members of the Executive Council on the same subject. My honourable and gallant friend the Commander-in-Chief says that, though he supports the measure, he would confine it to District Magistrates and Sessions Judges. Sir Charles Aitchison, on the other hand, went further than any other head of a Local Government; and the measure as produced and brought forward by the Government of India is one which has struck a mean between these different proposals, and which, on the one hand, does not go so far as Sir Charles Aitchison recommended, and, on the other, goes somewhat further than the recommendations of some other Local Governments. Indeed, as a matter of fact, the measure was drawn up mainly in accordance with the amendments of the Code suggested in Sir Alfred Lyall's letter. Now, what was the next step taken with regard to this question? The next step taken was that the Government of India sent a despatch to the Secretary of State, Lord Hartington, last September, containing their proposals and forwarding the papers now before the Council. Lord Hartington must have received that letter late in September. It was upon the 7th of December that, in an answer to that letter, he stated that he had very carefully considered our proposals in Council, and that he gave them his sanction. My honourable and learned friend Mr. Evans alluded to the fact that this circular to Local Governments was not sent to the Government of Bengal. The course taken on the

Criminal Procedure Code Amendment Bill.

occasion was in accordance with the practice generally pursued; and it is a perfectly reasonable and intelligible practice followed by all the departments of the Government of India that, when one Local Government originates a proposal on which the Government desires to consult other Local Governments, the original proposal is sent round to those Governments, but not sent back to the Government from which it, in the first instance, emanated. The Bill was prepared and drafted in strict accordance with the proposals sanctioned by the Secretary of State. Leave was given to introduce it on the 2nd of February. It was brought in on the 9th of February; and the papers, containing the opinions of Local Governments, were circulated to members of Council and given to the public at the earliest possible oportunity. I believe I am right in saying that they were circulated to members of Council on the 12th February.

That is the history of this transaction up to the introduction of the Bill. And I turn now to consider what was the state of things in respect to the position of Natives of India in the Civil Service of the Crown, with which we had to deal. I am dealing now solely with the case of Covenanted Civil Servants. I leave aside the question of the non-regulation provinces, which is not material to the present argument. I say nothing of Cantonment Magistrates, because my honourable and gallant friend the Commander-in-Chief has explained that Cantonment Magistrates are almost invariably military officers, and that no Native gentlemen are likely to be appointed to positions of that kind. The question, therefore, we have to consider here relates to the Native members of the Covenanted Civil Service, because it must be borne in mind that, although, in departmental practice, it has been the custom to describe the members of the Covenanted Civil Service admitted under Lord Lytton's rules, as members serving under the statutory rules, they are under

Criminal Procedure Code Amendment Bill.

those rules themselves—rules approved by the Secretary of State, Lord Cranbrook, and laid before Parliament—admitted to employment in Her Majesty's Covenanted Civil Service. These are the words of the rule as sanctioned by the Secretary of State and by Parliament; and therefore, the persons with whom we have to deal are the members of the Covenanted Civil Service. Our proposal, I would just point out, is a very much narrower one than that which was made in the year 1857, and to which Mr. Evans alluded. In that year there were no Native members of the Covenanted Civil Service. The proposal of 1857 would have subjected European British subjects to the jurisdiction of all the Mufassal Courts of every grade. The present Bill does not go nearly so far. Well, what is the state of things with which we have to deal now? I have said that in 1857 there were no Native members of the Civil Service at all. They have come in since ;—first, by competition, having gone home and competed on equal terms with Englishmen, Irishmen and Scotchmen, and won their way in that competition into the Civil Service; and recently under the new system inaugurated in the time of Lord Lytton. The time has now arrived when some of these gentlemen have risen to high judicial positions. Mr. Tagore is one, and I have been informed that Mr. Dutt has also been raised to a similar office. Therefore, they are now beginning to reach these positions, and the number of those who fill such appointments must gradually and steadily increase. Mr. Miller asks in what have the times changed since 1872. They have changed in this respect, that some of these Native gentlemen have acquired these important positions, and others will go on rising to them in increasing numbers in coming years. But the great change which has taken place in regard to this question from an administrative point of view has been that which was made by Lord Lytton's Government in 1879. That change was made by the express order of the Government

Criminal Procedure Code Amendment Bill.

at home: indeed, after the reiterated orders of successive Secretaries of State. I am not about to express any opinion as to the mode in which these gentlemen are now admitted into the Covenanted Civil Service under the rules of 1879. It may be that these rules can be improved. Nothing is more probable than that experience may show that they are capable of amendment. But what we have to consider is, what is the position in which these rules place the gentlemen admitted under them, and what will be the effect of them as time goes on? These gentlemen will rise in the Covenanted Service year by year, and they will be entitled to hold higher and higher offices as they advance, until, ultimately, they will attain to the highest judicial offices below the High Court. Now, it has been contended that the Local Governments, when they spoke of Covenanted Civilians, only meant those who had got in by competition. I have no reason to suppose that that is the case with any of the opinions which have been expressed, because the words " Covenanted Civil Service " cover all the members of that service. The Honourable Mr. Evans quoted Mr. Elliott the Chief Commissioner of Assam, and he said that Mr. Elliott only proposed that these powers should be conferred upon persons who had got into the Covenanted Service by competition; Mr. Elliott no doubt drew a distinction between the two classes; but he said that he would extend the powers to the second class when they became District Magistrates or Sessions Judges. Now, it seems clear to me that, as these gentlemen in the Civil Service rise to the higher appointments, especially to the appointments of District Magistrates and Sessions Judges, increasing administrative inconvenience must ensue unless these additional powers are conferred on them. If they are to hold these offices it appears to me that inconvenience of a serious kind must arise as time goes on; indeed I shall have to show that it has arisen already. The Honourable Mr. Evans has said that

Criminal Procedure Code Amendment Bill.

what we ought to do is to give the best justice we can to every one in the country without giving rise to administrative inconvenience. I entirely concur in that opinion, and I say administrative inconvenience has already begun to be felt, and it will increase. That being the state of things with which we had to deal, some of these gentlemen being already in high administrative positions, and a still larger number coming on from below, we felt it our duty to see in what way we could best remove this administrative inconvenience, and, I must also say, the injustice to suitors which would be caused by dragging them long distances over the country.

I turn to consider what is the scope of the Bill. I have shown you that the extent of our Bill is very much less than that of the Bill of 1857. It is very much less than that of the Bill brought in by Lord Dalhousie's Government in 1849. We have confined it to the strict necessities of the case, and the result of it would be that, if it were passed to-day, it would at once confer jurisdiction over European British subjects upon only two persons in India; and the number who would rise to that position during the next few years might not exceed four or five. That statement supplies, as it seems to me, the strongest argument against the proposal of the Government. It is said, why do this now when it will only affect Mr. Tagore and Mr. Dutt? Why do this now, when, if there is administrative inconvenience, it is only in one or two places; and I admit that I am bound to meet that objection, and to explain why the Government think that this is a convenient opportunity for making the change.

But, before I do so, I must point out that, of course, that argument cuts both ways. If the scope of the Bill is so very small, then it seems not altogether reasonable that it should have been encountered by such violent opposition. In stating the reasons why it appears to me to be desirable to make this change now, rather than to postpone it until

Criminal Procedure Code Amendment Bill.

the appointment of a much larger number of these gentlemen to high judicial positions, I desire to deal with this question strictly from a practical point of view. I am not going upon this occasion to enter into any examination whatever of any claims which these Native gentlemen may have to exercise this jurisdiction; but, at the same time, I cannot but ask members of this Council to consider whether—I do not speak now of justice or generosity—it is politic, if there be not an overwhelming necessity, for us to impose on these gentlemen restrictions which sensitive men would naturally feel. These men, it must be admitted, are the pick and cream of our Native Civil Service; those who are now in this position, or are about to enter into it, have won their way through a keen competition at home, and secured their position through their own ability. Under Lord Lytton's system, by which for the future at least one-sixth of the whole Covenanted Service will in course of time consist of Natives, we shall have to rely more and more year by year on the devotion and loyalty of these gentlemen. I think the question of policy is not undeserving of the consideration of this Council; but I pass from it to the practical question. My honourable friend Mr. Gibbs has shown you to-night that the idea that administrative inconvenience may arise is not an imagination or a theory; he has pointed out to you what are the circumstances in regard to Mr. Tagore, the Sessions Judge of Karwar; and he has explained that, if certain railway works, which, he says, are likely to commence there, are opened, they will bring European British subjects in considerable numbers into that district. If these persons are not tried by the Sessions Judge, they will either have to be sent by sea to Bombay, or have to march 80 or a 100 miles through a district which at many times of the year is very injurious to health. This constitutes a real administrative inconvenience, and it implies, not only an inconvenience to the administration of justice, but also a

Criminal Procedure Code Amendment Bill.

considerable hardship to the suitors and witnesses concerned. And it is surely clear that, though there is not at the present moment an irresistible necessity for introducing this measure, as Lord Lytton's system develops, an irresistible necessity will arise. When you have one-sixth of the Civil Service composed of Natives, it will be impossible to maintain the present restriction. Therefore, what we had to consider was—is it better to wait until this necessity becomes overwhelming and irresistible, or is it better to introduce the system now? I confess it appears to me that it is far wiser, and far more in the true and substantial interest of those over whom this jurisdiction is exercised, that it should be introduced now, when the persons who would obtain the powers are very limited in number, when the circumstances under which they enter the Civil Service insures their ability and character, and when all their proceedings can be carefully watched. Being few in number, it will be easier now than afterwards for the attention of the Local Governments and the public to be directed to their proceedings; and, being the men they are, it seems to me that they would be likely to set a good example and give a good tone to those who come after them. I hold it, therefore, to be wiser to introduce the measure now gradually, cautiously, and tentatively, than to wait till the change is forced upon us by necessity, and the powers which are now to be given only to a few men have to be given suddenly to a very much larger number of Native Civil Servants. This is the ground upon which I thought that the time had come when this change could best be made. The truth is, that the opposition to this Bill is in reality not so much an opposition to this particular measure, as an opposition to the declared policy of Parliament about the admission of Natives to the Covenanted Civil Service. That policy has been a deliberate policy; it commenced many years ago, and has been enforced steadily from time to time. It is not a

Criminal Procedure Code Amendment Bill.

policy of my invention or of the invention of the present Government at home or here ; it is the policy of Parliament. What does Lord Cranbrook say upon that subject writing to Lord Lytton's Government on the 7th of November, 1878 ? He says— ;

"The broad policy was laid down by Parliament so long ago as 1833, that no Native shall, by reason of his religion, place of birth or colour, be disabled from holding any office ; and Her Majesty's gracious proclamation in 1858 announced her will that, as far as may be, 'our subjects of whatever race or creed be impartially admitted to offices in our service, the duties of which they may be qualified by their education, ability and integrity duly to discharge.'"

And he goes on to say :—

"Since that period several of my predecessors in office, and especially Lord Halifax, Sir Safford Northcote, the Duke of Argyll and Lord Salisbury, have pressed upon the attention of the Government of India that the policy of Parliament, enforced as it was by the Royal proclamation, was not to remain a dead-letter, and two Acts of Parliament were passed to give further effect to it. But, as Your Excellency justly observes, all endeavours hitherto to deal with this question on a satisfactory basis have proved unsuccessful. It is gratifying to observe that Your Lordship's elaborate treatment of the subject will enable a practical course to be taken, that will prove, it may be hoped, both beneficial to the State and satisfactory to the natural aspirations of the educated Natives of India."

That is said not by me but by Lord Cranbrook ; and I cannot doubt that, if that policy is now applied under the rules laid down by Lord Lytton's Government in 1879, and is carried out as he proposed, an alteration of the law in the direction in which this Bill goes is inevitable at no distant time. The Government of India have not the power, if they had the inclination, which certainly I have not, to withdraw from that policy ; and Lord Cranbrook very distinctly tells us that, in his judgment, Parliament will not withdraw from it. Lord Lytton's original proposal was that, when he established a separate Native Service, permission to Natives to compete for the Civil

Criminal Procedure Code Amendment Bill.

Service in England should be withdrawn. What Lord Cranbrook says on that subject is this—

"But your proposal of a close Native Service, with a limited class of high appointments attached to it, and your suggestions that the Covenanted Civil Service should no longer be open to Natives, involve an application to Parliament which would have no prospect of success, and which I certainly would not undertake. Your Lordship has yourself observed that no scheme could have a chance of sanction which included legislation for the purpose of repealing the clause in the Act of 1833 above quoted; and the obstacles which would be presented against any attempt to exclude Natives from public competition for the Civil Service would be little less formidable."

Therefore, it appears to me to be evident that the intention of Parliament has been to admit Natives, more and more largely, into the Covenanted Service; that steps were taken in 1879 after a considerable delay and frequent injunctions from the Secretary of State to carry out that intention more fully; and that the result has been, as I have stated, that we have now to deal with a state of things in which, before many years have elapsed, it will be, as I have said, simply impossible, on account of administrative inconvenience, to withhold powers of this description from the higher ranks of the Covenanted Native Service. The Honourable Mr. Evans has said that he could not admit the force of the argument that because Presidency Magistrates had power to try Europeans, therefore similar powers should be given to Native Magistrates in the Mufassal. I admit a considerable portion of the argument of my honourable friend, but he must allow me to say that the fact that Natives of India have been trying Europeans for a considerable number of years in Calcutta and Bombay is a conclusive argument against the theory that Englishmen have a constitutional right to be tried by Englishmen only. No one is more convinced than I am of the advantage of having a case argued before a Magistrate by trained lawyers; and I would not for a moment think of underrating its importance. Nevertheless

Criminal Procedure Code Amendment Bill.

I was rather struck with what I saw in a Bombay newspaper this morning. It certainly did seem rather curious, after all that has been said on this subject, to find that certain European gentlemen, composing what is called the Salvation Army, are being tried at this moment in Bombay by Mr. Dossabhoy Framjee. Their religious feelings are very intimately involved in the case which is being tried by that Native Magistrate. I did not intend to have said anything about the past history of this question, because, as I have mentioned before, my main object has been to explain the reasons which have induced the Government to bring in this Bill. But Mr. Evans has spoken with personal knowledge of what was called the compromise of 1872. On that point I would say this. There may have been a compromise between the members of the European community and the members of the Select Committee. Of that I know nothing, although I have not the least doubt that the Honourable Mr. Evans has stated exactly what occurred ; but it is perfectly obvious that that compromise cannot have been a compromise with the Government ; because, if it had been, then Lord Napier, Lord Napier of Magdala, Sir Richard Temple, Sir George Campbell, and Mr. Barrow Ellis could never for a moment have given their support to an amedment inconsistent with it. My honourable friend Mr. Ilbert, in the speech with which he commenced this discussion, pointed out that all the safeguards now possessed by Europeans and all the special privileges now enjoyed by them, were left standing by this Bill, except the single one of being exempted from the jurisdiction of Magistrates who are not European British subjects. This Bill does not touch the rest of these safeguards ; and the Government has not the least intention of submitting any proposal now or hereafter, certainly not as long as I am here, with the view of interfering with those privileges. But there is another matter which I look upon as in some respects a more

Criminal Procedure Code Amendment Bill.

important safeguard, and that is the power of supervision exercised by the High Court over all the courts below. What would be the result if a Native Magistrate trying an European acted towards him in an unjust manner? If the case came before the High Court, or if they even heard of it, they would be able to call for the proceedings, and the consequence would be to deprive that gentleman of the position which he might have so abused. That is the history of the measure, and of the grounds upon which it was introduced, and of the extent to which it goes. I know very well that a great deal has been said, as is always said when changes are introduced, about this being the thin end of the wedge. I can only say that, so far as this question is concerned, it is not the thin end of the wedge, and that this measure represents the final views of the present Government in respect to changes regarding this portion of the Criminal Procedure Code. Passing from the history of the course we have taken, and the motives which have actuated us, I may now state that we are perfectly ready to listen to reasonable remonstrances, to statements of fact, and to legitimate arguments. But neither this nor any other Government that will ever exist in India will, I hope, listen to violence, to exaggeration, to misrepresentation, and, least of all, to menace. It is perfectly natural that those whose interests are affected by this Bill, that those who would lose under it a privilege to which they evidently attach a great value, should bring their views on the subject before the Government, and should press them earnestly upon their attention. I should be the last man to complain of that being done, and I should be the last man not to give to such representations the fullest and most careful consideration; and those who are animated by the dread, which has been expressed in many quarters, of the results of this measure, **may rely upon it that a fair representation of the opinions, supported by good arguments, will be listened to with the greatest attention.** It

Criminal Procedure Code Amendment Bill.

is, of course, true that in this, as in every other question with which the Government of India has to deal, it is obliged to take a wider view than that confined exclusively to the interest of any single class of the community; but it is also true that any special class of the community, which is specially affected by any particular measure, has a right to bring its views before the Government, and to expect that those views will be fully and carefully examined. I will not allude on this occasion to the character of a great deal of the opposition which has sprung up to this Bill, or to the means by which that opposition has been to a great extent conducted; I will say nothing of the charges which have been made against myself, or of the systematic misrepresentation of my feelings and objects in regard to this and other measures. I pass that by, but I can truly say that it is a source of deep regret to me and all my colleagues to observe the difference which has in this matter sprung up between the Government and, I admit, a very large portion of the European community, especially on this side of India. I do not know whether anything that I can say will tend to mitigate the bitterness of the controversy or to induce calmness; but if the vehemence of feeling is due in any degree to a misapprehension as to the scope of the Bill or the course which the Government intended to pursue in regard to it, or to a fear that we have ulterior designs which we never have entertained, then it is possible that this discussion may have done good. It is only right that it should be remembered that the Government never had the smallest idea of hurrying this Bill through the Council. They proposed to deal with it deliberately, and to afford the amplest opportunity for the representation of opinion in regard to it. It will be observed that it was before any such representations had reached the Government, and therefore before it had been in their power to consider them, that the proceedings which have been adverted to were adopted. This Bill will now,

Criminal Procedure Code Amendment Bill.

in accordance with the usual practice, be sent to the various Local Governments, and they will have an opportunity of recording their views upon it. These views will be sent up in due course, after careful examination by the Local Governments into all the circumstances of the case, for the consideration of the Government of India; and we shall then give to the observations of the Local Governments, and of the public which may have reached us in the meantime, the fullest weight and the most deliberate consideration. I frankly say that with those who desire—if any such there be—to retain the distinction which this Bill proposes to remove, merely because it is a race distinction, I have no sympathy whatever. To arguments which are inconsistent with the declared policy of the Crown and of Parliament it would be contrary to my duty to listen; but to fair reasons, urged in a manner to which the Government can give heed, the ears of myself and my colleagues will always be open on this and every other question. I observe that the opponents of this Bill speak of appealing to the House of Commons. I am the last man in the world to object to such a course being taken. To the decision of the House of Commons both parties to this controversy must bow. I do not think I have anything more to add now by way of explanation of the views of the Government. I have kept myself clear of controversy, because I wish to hold myself perfectly open to consider the arguments adduced on both sides in this debate. If I had thrown myself into this controversy, it might fairly be objected that I had not reserved to myself real freedom to consider those arguments. I have shown that this measure was recommended to the Government by Sir Ashley Eden, the Lieutenant-Governor of Bengal; that its principle has been approved by all the other Local Governments in India, with the exception of that of Coorg; and that it has been very carefully considered by the late Secretary of State for India, Lord Hartington, in Council, and sanctioned

Criminal Procedure Code Amendment Bill.

by him. I have recalled to the recollection of the Council the circumstances in which we stand at this moment, and those in which we shall stand in no distant future, with respect to the position of the Native members of the Covenanted Civil Service. I have pointed out how very limited the immediate effect of the Bill will be, and have stated the reasons which induce me to think that it is wiser to make the proposed change now, when it can be brought into operation gradually and cautiously, than to wait until administrative necessities and justice to suitors compel the Government to introduce it suddenly and extensively. Lastly, I have expressed the perfect readiness of the Government to consider and to weigh any remonstrances which may be made against this Bill, provided they are supported by arguments which are consistent with the policy of Parliament. The Government do not propose to take any further steps in this matter now, and ample time will thus be afforded for the deliberate examination by Local Governments, by the Government of India, and by the Government at home of any representations which may be made to them in connection with this measure.

CENTRAL PROVINCES TENANCY BILL.

20th June 1883. [AT a meeting of the Legislative Council held at Peterhoff, Simla, on Wednesday, the 20th June 1883, the Hon'ble Mr. Ilbert, in moving that the reports of the Select Committee on the Bill to consolidate and amend the Law relating to Agricultural Tenancies in the Central Provinces be taken into consideration, fully explained the objects of the proposed legislation, and moved for certain minor amendments in the Bill. A debate ensued, during which certain amendments were accepted and negatived; but with respect to an amendment moved by Mr. Barkley in Section 11, His Excellency the Viceroy spoke as follows :—]

I should just like to ask one question as to the effect of this clause. The Hon'ble Member moves an amendment to section 29, but moves no amendment to section 30, and I am not quite clear whether, supposing an ordinary tenant of sír land were to make an improvement with the consent of his landlord, there would be any provision in the Bill which would secure him legal compensation for the improvement so made.

[Mr. Ilbert furnished the above-required information, and His Excellency said :—]

I agree with the Hon'ble Sir Steuart Bayley in thinking that it is very desirable to maintain the distinction between sír land and raiyatwárí land. The amendments introduced by the Hon'ble Mr. Ilbert all tended in that direction. I should, therefore, be personally prepared to accept Mr. Barkley's amendment of section 29, provided that it is made clear that, if the tenant of the sír land makes an improvement at his own expense with the consent of his landlord, he shall have a legal right to compensation. I am quite ready, in regard to sír land, to make the consent of the landlord a *sine quâ non ;* but I am not prepared to admit that, that consent having been obtained, the tenant shall be entitled to no compensation for improvements made at his own expense. That appears to me to be a highly unjust proceeding and one which ought to be guarded

Central Provinces Tenancy Bill.

against by the law; but if that can be done, I shall be prepared to accept Mr. Barkley's amendment.

The Motion was put and agreed to.

[In connection with another motion by Mr. Barkley for amending section 43, the Viceroy remarked :—]

The question is one not altogether free from difficulty, but the weight of legal opinion appears to me to be so decidedly in favour of the Bill and opposed to the amendment, that I shall vote against it.

The Motion was put and negatived.

[Mr. Barkley then proposed certain alterations in the wording of section 58; and, after opposition from Mr. Quinton and Sir Steuart Bayley, His Excellency the President spoke as follows :—]

I cannot accept this amendment. The question, as my friend Sir Steuart Bayley has said, has been extremely carefully considered by the Select Committee and the Government. The original proposal was to fix the rate at ten times the increase, but, in consequence of representations received from the Central Provinces, that figure was reduced to seven times the increase of rent—a very small amount to be demanded for compensation for disturbance, and very greatly less than that demanded under the Irish Land Act. This is making the experiment on a small scale. It appears to me to be sufficient for the circumstances of the Central Provinces, where population is thin and where farms are rather seeking for tenants than tenants for farms. It seems to me to be the least that could be proposed, and, therefore, I cannot accept the amendment proposed by my hon'ble friend.

The Motion was put and negatived.

[Another amendment proposed by Mr. Barkley in section 62 was opposed by Mr. Quinton and Sir Steuart Bayley, and the Viceroy spoke as follows :—]

I most strongly object to the substitution proposed by my hon'ble friend. When he speaks of section 62 as an encroachment on the rights of landlords, it is necessary that we should consider what are the rights of landlords at

Central Provinces Tenancy Bill.

the present moment in the Central Provinces. We are not talking of the abstract rights of landlords. That subject is a very large one. What we have to deal with, are the rights of landlords in the Central Provinces now, and those rights are subject to the provision of Act X of 1859, which confers on the tenant the power of obtaining occupancy-rights if he occupies the same land for a period of twelve years; therefore the rights of landlords in the Central Provinces at present are limited by the rights of tenants to acquire, by a certain process, an occupancy-right in their lands. The framers of the Bill in its present shape were led to believe that it would be desirable to put an end to the existing mode of obtaining occupancy-rights by the tenants, in consequence of the serious objections which may be urged against any system under which a tenant acquires occupancy-rights by a mere lapse of time. It seemed, therefore, desirable to get rid of that system in the Central Provinces before it had produced there those evils and those difficulties in the relations of landlord and tenant which have been found to spring from it in other parts of India. The question, then, the Committee had to consider was, what substitute they should give to tenants for this power of obtaining rights of occupancy by the lapse of time. My hon'ble friend Mr. Barkley says that Bill No. I as introduced by Mr. Grant did not contain this proposal. Doubtless not; but it did not propose to abolish the twelve-years' rule. Bill No. I retained the twelve-years' rule, and gave tenants that mode of acquiring rights which the present Bill seeks to supersede. It appears to me that one of the great advantages of the present proposal over the twelve-years' rule is that, whereas, practically speaking, the twelve-years' rule gives occupancy rights to tenants by accident, this proposal, on the contrary, gives the power of obtaining such rights to thrift and to frugality. Under the twelve-years' rule, it depends on an accident whether a landlord gives a tenant

Central Provinces Tenancy Bill.

notice to quit before the expiration of twelve years, and thus takes the measures necessary to prevent the accrual of the right; on the other hand, it is the thrifty tenants who will under the new proposal be able to purchase an occupancy-right. The right will depend not upon accident—not upon whether the landlord will allow the tenant to remain in possession for twelve years, but upon whether by frugality he is able to lay by sufficient to enable him to purchase an occupancy-right in the manner proposed by section 62. Now, my hon'ble friend Mr. Barkley says there is not much evidence to show that this proposal has been accepted by those best acquainted with the Central Provinces. I may say that, in the first place, it has been accepted by Sir J. H. Morris, than whom no one is better acquainted with the circumstances and requirements of those provinces. It has also been most carefully and closely considered by my hon'ble friend Mr. Crosthwaite, who had charge of the Bill originally. I have discussed it with him several times, and it is most unfortunate that we have not his presence here to-day. I felt bound to call him to higher functions during the absence of Mr. Bernard, but, had he been present here, he would have given us the weight of his great experience in the Central Provinces to meet the objections taken by Mr. Barkley. I must also point out that, if we were to adopt the amendment proposed by Mr. Barkley in this matter, we should actually put the raiyats in the Central Provinces in a worse position than they are now in. We should have abolished their power of acquiring the right of occupancy under the twelve-years' rule, and substituted for it nothing but a legal power to the landlord to sell them this right if he chose to do so. It is quite impossible that the Council can accept a proposal of that kind. For a considerable time this clause may be made little use of, but it will enable those tenants who have laid by a small amount of capital to acquire the greater security which occupancy-rights afford,

Central Provinces Tenancy Bill.

and without it the result of the Bill would be to shut the door to all hope of raiyats ever acquiring that security at all.

Under these circumstances, I cannot give my vote in favour of the amendment proposed by my hon'ble friend Mr. Barkley.

The motion was put and negatived.

[Mr. Ilbert next moved that the Bill as amended be passed ; and, after some remarks from Mr. Quinton and Mr. Hunter, His Excellency the President wound up the debate as follows :—]

I should like to make one or two observations on the remarks which have fallen from my hon'ble friend Mr. Hunter. I listened with feelings of alarm to a great portion of that speech, because I felt it was a very powerful argument against the provisions of this Bill, and I began to fear that the Bill might be open to the objections which he was urging against it. But I confess I was somewhat comforted by the last sentence of his speech, in which he said that this Bill made ample provision for the right of the cultivators so long as the population was sparse. That, however, is really all that the Bill professes to do. Certainly it was all I thought that the Bill would do. It appears to me that, in dealing with this very difficult question of the relations between landlord and tenant, what we have to do is to treat it with reference to the varying conditions of different parts of India as they come before us when we undertake legislation. I feel strongly that legislation which might be wise for one province with a thin population might be altogether inadequate to provide proper securities for the cultivators of the soil in the more thickly populated districts of India.

In preparing the Bill, the object of its framers has been to deal with the circumstances of the province at the present time. It is undesirable to interfere more than may be necessary in the relations between landlord and tenant, because such interference is always a delicate matter. I

Central Provinces Tenancy Bill.

am not, however, one of those who object to interference of that kind when necessary, but I think it wise in undertaking such interference to pay careful regard to the agricultural arrangements of each district, and I am not at all inclined to attempt to force one uniform system upon all parts of the country.

My friend Mr. Hunter spoke of the case of Ireland. He said that some of the proposals in this Bill were borrowed from Bills passed in respect of Ireland, and that they were even less extended in their scope than the proposals contained in the Irish Land Act of 1870, which have been proved to be inadequate. My answer to that objection is this. In Ireland you have a much more keen competition for land than at present exists in the Central Provinces. What may be inadequate in Ireland may not be inadequate in the present circumstances of the Central Provinces. It is very possible that this measure may not afford sufficient protection for the rights of ordinary tenants in the Central Provinces if their circumstances should change. But if they do change, it will be the duty of the Government of India to consider what legislative arrangements will be necessary to meet their altered condition. What we have endeavoured to do now is to provide for these circumstances as we find them, and to have recourse to the minimum of interference in the arrangements between landlord and tenant, which appear to us to be sufficient to give the cultivators of the soil in those provinces due protection against exorbitant enhancement of rent and arbitrary eviction. It is my hope that this measure will be effectual for that purpose; but this remains to be seen. Ten or twenty years hence it is possible that these arrangements may be found inadequate, and, should that be the case, it will be for the Government of that day to apply a remedy.

I confess, with respect to the twelve-years' rule, that I cannot speak of it with the amount of satisfaction with

Central Provinces Tenancy Bill.

which it has been spoken of by my hon'ble friend Mr. Hunter. I share strongly the opinion expressed in an able paper on the Bengal rent question by my friend Mr. Justice Cunningham, who brings forward there, very clearly and plainly, the objections which lie against any system which makes the acquirement of occupancy-rights dependent on the efflux of a fixed and determined period of time. All the evidence goes to show that that system is open to objection, and it is very undesirable that it should be allowed to grow up. My hon'ble friend Mr. Hunter argues that the evils resulting from it have not yet sprung up in the Central Provinces; but there is evidence to show that they are already appearing there as the population increases; and it seems to me that it was advisable to put a stop to them now, rather than to wait till we have to encounter hereafter those difficulties which now meet us in Bengal. I yield to no man in the desire to protect the just rights of tenants, and I hope and believe that this Bill will operate to strenghen the position of the cultivating tenants of the Central Provinces. The Bill is not intended, as has been justly remarked by the Hon'ble Mr. Quinton, as a precedent to be followed in other provinces the condition of which is very different, but it is a measure applicable to the circumstances of the day in the Central Provinces; and, if hereafter it should require amendment, I have no doubt that the Government of India will know how to deal with any fresh circumstances which may arise.

The Motion was then put and agreed to.

NORTH-WESTERN PROVINCES AND OUDH LOCAL BOARDS BILL.

[The Hon'ble Mr. Quinton at a meeting of the Legislative Council 12th Sept. 1883, held at Peterhoff, Simla, on Wednesday, the 12th September 1883, moved that the report of the Select Committee for the constitution of Local Boards in the North-Western Provinces and Oudh be taken into consideration, and entered into a lengthy explanation of some of the more important changes made in the Bill as originally introduced. He was followed by the Hon'ble Mr. Hunter, His Honor the Lieutenant-Governor of the Punjab, and the Hon'ble Sir S. Bayley, who discussed some of the provisions of the Bill requiring elucidation. The desired explanation having been furnished by Mr. Quinton, Mr. Ilbert spoke in support of the proposed measure, and made some remarks on the financial clauses of the Bill, when His Excellency the Viceroy concluded the debate as follows:—]

The remarks which have been made by the Hon'ble Members on this and previous occasions at the several stages of the Bill have so fully explained the objects and purposes of this and the sister measure which will be passed, I trust, in a few minutes, and I myself have had so many occasions of expressing my views on the question of local self-government in India, that I need not now occupy the time of the Council. But I cannot let those two Bills pass without expressing my hope that they will prove to be measures calculated to make a substantial advance in the development of local self-government; and it is a great satisfaction to me that these Bills should be passed by this Council during the time I have the honor to preside over it.

[The Bill, as amended, was then put and agreed to.]